W(alter) J(ames) TURNER was born on October 14, 1889, in Melbourne, Australia, but spent most of his life in England. He was Music Editor of *The New Statesman* from 1916 to 1940, and Literary Editor of *The Spectator* from 1942 until his death in 1946.

He is the author of *Music: a Short History* (1932) and several biographies: Beethoven (1927), Wagner (1933), and Berlioz (1934).
MOZART: THE MAN AND HIS WORKS was first published in 1938.

MOZART:

THE MAN AND HIS WORKS

by W. J. Turner

DOUBLEDAY
ANCHOR BOOKS

Doubleday & Company, Inc.
Garden City, New York
1954

ACKNOWLEDGMENTS   I wish to thank Dr. Alfred Einstein for permission to make use of his edition of Köchel's catalogue of Mozart's works, published by Messrs. Breitkopf and Härtel in 1937.

I only learned of Miss Emily Anderson's edition of the letters of the Mozart family after I had made my own translations; but I have to acknowledge her friendly courtesy in discussing several matters with me. Although, in her opinion, the letter from Mozart I have reproduced on page 307, addressed, supposedly, to Lorenzo da Ponte, is not genuine, I have included it because until there is actual proof to the contrary, I prefer to follow the tradition which has ascribed it to Mozart.

"*Mozart is the most inaccessible of the great masters.*"
—SCHNABEL

"*On the heights it is warmer than one thinks in the valleys.*"
—NIETZSCHE

Contents

Introduction

I have gone to the original sources for the material of this book, and all the translations from the German, French, Italian, and occasional Latin, are my own, so I must take the responsibility for their accuracy. In translating the letters of Leopold and Wolfgang I have tried to be accurate and to reflect the spirit of the originals rather than dress them in smooth or graceful English. I have also retained the Mozarts' erratic spelling of names.

My object has been to present a sufficiently full and accurate account of the man revealed as far as possible in his own words. This picture will be found to differ considerably from most of those current, especially in the English language.

Æsthetic criticism has also been an important part of my task, but I have not attempted any formal analysis of particular compositions as this is a matter for specialist study. It has been undertaken notably by T. de Wyzewa and G. de Saint-Foix whose first two volumes dealing with the period of 1756–77 were published in 1912. The third volume, prepared after the death of Wyzewa by M. de Saint-Foix, published in Paris in 1936, only brings this examination up to the year 1784, two years before the composition of *Figaro*.

W.J.T.

MOZART

1. Birth and Parentage

In a letter dated Salzburg, February 9, 1756, Leopold, the father of Mozart, writes to Jakob Lotter in Augsburg:

"On the evening of January 27, at 8 o'clock, my wife was happily delivered of a boy . . . the boy is named Joannes Chrysostomus Wolfgang Gottlieb."

In the baptismal entry *Theophilus* was written, not *Gottlieb*; but, finally, the Latin form, *Amadeus*, was used. Mozart at first used to sign himself: "J. G. Wolfgang," but after 1770 he always subscribed himself: "Wolfgang Amadeus," and "Wolfgang" was the name he was known by in his family. There is something peculiarly significant in Mozart's second name of "God-lover" (*Theophilus*,[1] *Gottlieb, Amadeus*), as will be made clear to the discerning who read this book. Mozart's father, Leopold, born on November 14, 1719, in Augsburg, was thirty-seven years old, and his wife, Anna Maria Bertel (or Pertl), born on December 25, 1720, at Schloss Huttenstein, was thirty-six years old at the birth of their son.

Mozart's father's family had been in Augsburg since the beginning of the seventeenth century, where they were all small craftsmen. His paternal great-grandfather and grandfather were bookbinders. His father, Leopold, had two brothers, who continued their father's trade as bookbinders; but Leopold himself, possibly through the influence of his godfather, Canon Johann Georg Grabher, became a choirboy in the Monastery of St. Ulrich, Augsburg. On the 13th of October 1777 he writes to Mozart, who is then in Augsburg, that he well remembers singing a cantata at St. Ulrich, when the Hofrat Ofele married "the beautiful Lepin, a merchant's daughter, who sang well, played the clavier, and had 30,000 florins." Leopold also played the organ, for Mozart, in a letter to his father, dated Munich, October 10–11, 1777, writes:

"Do you recall the name Freysinger . . . he says he knows you quite well and studied with you. He remembers Wessobrunn especially, where you (this was quite new to me)

---

[1] Strictly, "beloved of God"; but to be beloved of God and to love God are necessarily identical.

played the organ quite incomparably. He said: 'It was astounding how the hands and feet flew, crossing one another, but incomparable. He was an excellent man. My father thought highly of him. And how he mocked the priests when they wanted him to turn monk!' . . ."

The last remark must have slightly surprised Mozart, who knew his father only as a strict and devout Catholic; but Leopold, in a letter to his son, dated Salzburg, December 15, 1777, refers to his own youth when he writes:

"May I ask whether Wolfgang has not forgotten to confess. God comes before everything; from Him must we expect our earthly happiness and have care always for the Eternal: young people hear such things unwillingly—I know it, I was also young; but God be thanked I always came to myself again after all my youthful follies, flew from all danger to my soul, and kept always God and my honour and the dangerous consequences of sin before my eyes."

Leopold in 1737, at the age of eighteen, was entered as a student at Salzburg University. This may be accounted for by the fact that the Benedictine order, to which the Monastery of St. Ulrich, Augsburg, belonged, had founded and still partly maintained the University of Salzburg. There Leopold studied jurisprudence as well as music, and he won distinction in an examination in 1738. The University of Salzburg was specially noted for its support of music, and music must have been Leopold's principal study, for in 1740 he took a position with Count Johann Baptiste of Thurn, Balfassina and Taxis, the Dean of the Cathedral, in the double role, as was customary in those days, of valet and musician. The Count was a music-lover and to him Leopold dedicated, in the same year of 1740, his first engraved work, the *Sonate Sei per Chiesa e da Camera a tre (Due Violini e Basso)*. In 1743 Leopold became fourth violinist in the Archbishop Sigismund of Salzburg's court chapel; by 1758 he had risen to second violinist, and in 1763 he became vice-Kapellmeister to Joseph Franz Lolli, who succeeded, in that year, Johann Ernst Eberlin as Kapellmeister. In addition to the instrumental chapel, there was a vocal chapel, consisting of thirty solo and choir singers and fifteen choirboys, whose function it was to perform the church music. From 1744 Leopold taught these boys the violin, and from 1777, after the death of the Cathedral organist, Antoni Cajetan Adlgasser, the clavier as well.

Leopold Mozart was also a composer, and it was his duty to provide music for the services of the church when required. His pay, outside anything he might get from private lessons, was four hundred gulden a year until 1762, when it was raised to five hundred. According to Schurig, this would have been the equivalent of, say, three thousand German marks in 1913, or, say, seven hundred and fifty American pre-war dollars. As Schurig curtly says, Leopold, after his marriage, on November 21, 1747, found this salary "scanty." But it must be remembered by English or American readers that the small towns of Germany and Austria have always given better value for the same money than has ever been obtainable in any English or American town or city. Further, in the eighteenth century in Salzburg no part of a man's income went in dog-licences, radio sets and licences, movies, automobiles, or any other of the new pleasures of the twentieth century; nor was it then necessary to travel twenty or thirty miles from one's home in order to get air to breathe and find a little unspoiled nature.

As a composer Leopold was industrious and capable. Here is a letter to his friend and publisher, Lotter, in Augsburg, dated December 29, 1755:[2]

"Have you a good subject for an oratorio? If I had time I would compose another for Lent. Have you *Christus begraben*,[3] which I composed last year? We have to produce two *Oratoria* every Lent, and where are we to find subjects enough? It must not be *de passione Christi*, but it might be some penitential story. Last year, for instance, we produced one on Peter's Repentance, and another is now being composed on David in the Wilderness."

The famous teacher and theorist Marpurg (1718–95), of Berlin, in his *Historisch-Kritische Beiträge zur Aufnahme der Musik* (Vol. III, pp. 183–4, published Berlin, 1757), has

---

[2]These early letters to Lotter from Leopold are not included in Schiedermair's collected edition.

[3]"*Christus begraben*: Cantata for three voices: Magdalena, Nicodemus, Joseph von Arimathea. Chorus of disciples, and friends of our Lord. Words by S. A. W[ieland]. Music by J. G. L. Mozart." Printed in Salzburg in 1741; so he must have composed on this subject twice.

a section on Leopold Mozart—possibly written by Leopold or based on material supplied by him—which reads as follows:

"He has made himself known in all kinds of composition, though none has been printed, and only in 1740 he himself engraved six Sonatas à tre on copper, chiefly for practice in the art of engraving. In July 1756 he published his *Violin School*. Among the manuscript compositions of Herr Mozart which have become known are principally many contrapuntal and other church pieces; further, a great number of symphonies, some for four, some for all customary instruments; over thirty serenades, containing solos for various instruments. He has also composed many concertos, especially for the flute, oboe, bassoon, French horn, trumpet, etc.; innumerable trios and *divertimenti* for various instruments; twelve oratorios and a number of theatrical pieces, even pantomimes and occasional music, such as soldiers' music with trumpets, kettle-drums, drums, and fife, besides the usual instruments; Turkish music, music for a steel clavier; and, finally, a Sledge-Drive music with five harness-bells; not to speak of marches, so-called night-pieces and many hundreds of minuets, opera-dances, and such-like things."

It is worth quoting here a description of Leopold's musical *Sledge-Drive* given in a program printed by himself for a performance at the Collegium Musicum in Augsburg on December 29, 1755:

MUSICAL SLEDGE-DRIVE

Introduced by a prelude, consisting of a pleasing andante and a spirited allegro.
Then follows:
A prelude with trumpets and drums.
After this:
The Sledge-Drive, with the sledge-bells and all the other instruments.
After the Sledge-Drive:
The horses are heard rattling their harness.
And then:
The trumpets and drums alternate pleasantly with the oboes, French horns, and bassoons, the first representing the cavalcade, the second the march.
After this:
The trumpets and drums have another prelude, and:
The Sledge-Drive begins again, but stops suddenly, for all the party dismount and enter the ball-room.

Then comes an adagio, representing the ladies shivering with cold.
The ball is opened with a minuet and trio.
The company endeavour to warm themselves by country dances.
Then follows the departure, and, finally:
During a flourish of trumpets and drums the whole party mount
their sledges and drive homewards.

There were fanatical pedants in those days as well as in
these, so it is no wonder that after the performance of one
of these occasional pieces of Leopold's in Augsburg he received the following anonymous letter:

Monsieur et très cher ami!

May it please you to compose no more absurdities such as
Chinese and Turkish music, sledge-drives and peasant wed-
dings, for they reflect more shame and contempt on you than
honour, which is regretted by the individual who herewith
warns you and remains,

Your sincere Friend.

Datum in domo veræ amicitiæ.

This letter, as Leopold himself believed, was probably sent
by a rival musician.

Leopold did not cease composing in order to devote himself wholly to the training of his two gifted children, as was
once believed; nor are his compositions as worthless as early
biographers of Mozart have supposed. Mozart, in a letter to
his father from Vienna dated March 29, 1783, asks Leopold to send some of his church music, and repeats his request on April 12, 1783, saying:

"I beg you, when it is warmer, to search under the roof
and send us some of your church music; you have nothing to
be ashamed of—Baron van Suiten and Starzer know as well as
you and I that taste is always changing—and even—that the
change of taste unfortunately extends as far as church music;
which, however, should not be—whence it comes also that the
true church music is to be found under the roof—and even
worm-eaten. . . ."

Schubart, in his *Ästhetik der Tonkunst*, prefers Leopold's
church music to his chamber music, mentions him as the
man who had "placed music in Salzburg on its then excellent
footing," and declares that he "showed great knowledge of
counterpoint, but was somewhat old-fashioned." Otto Jahn
examined a Litany, *De Venerabili*, in D major, composed in

1762, and sent to Munich in 1774 by Leopold, together with a grand Litany by his son. Of this work Jahn writes:

"It is written for solos, chorus, and the usual small church orchestra of the day, and shows throughout the learning of a musician skilled in the use of traditional forms. The harmony is correct, the disposition of the parts skilful, and the contra-puntal forms are handled boldly; nor does the composer fail to introduce regular, well-worked-out fugues in the proper places; '*Cum Sancto Spiritu*' and '*Et vitam venturi sæculi*' in the Mass; '*Pignus futuræ Gloriæ*' in the Litany.

"But there is no originality or inventive power either in the composition as a whole or in isolated passages. Leopold Mozart's sacred music gives him a right to an honourable place among contemporary composers, but to no higher rank."

Apart from the music of Leopold's printed in his own life-time, a selection was made and published in the *Denkmäler der Tonkunst in Bayern*.[4] This "excavation," says Schurig, has only a historical interest and is a mere act of piety to the father of a great artist; but elsewhere Schurig, comment-ing on Mozart's letter to his father about his church music which I have already quoted, expresses his opinion that Mo-zart spoke with conviction when he praised his father's church music, and goes on to say that Leopold was "a super-pious Catholic, not from diplomacy but in a sort of fatalistic belief. In his church compositions rather than elsewhere is the expression of his inner life, also true art."

Everything depends on the point of view. My own opin-ion is that Leopold Mozart as a composer was as good as is the average well-known and accepted composer of the day—and I mean of any day. "In Leopold Mozart lived and stirred not a spark of genius," writes Schurig. Well, the same may with equal truth be written of the majority of artists—writers, painters, and musicians—who achieve a contemporary celeb-rity. But from another point of view there is, sometimes, in some of these men, a spark of talent, though not the burning fire of genius. I think this spark was in Leopold.[5]

---

[4] IX Jahrgang II Bd. (published by Breitkopf and Härtel, Leipzig, 1908).

[5] Wyzewa and G. de Saint-Foix are of the opinion that Leopold's compositions are "models of artistic probity and technically excel-lent," but without originality or life.

Herman Abert, who made a much more thorough study of the music of Leopold's contemporaries and predecessors than did Otto Jahn, has a more favourable opinion and says of Leopold:

"What distinguished him . . . chiefly from his contemporaries was that instead of dealing with the higher problems of nature, fable, and story, he, like his countryman Schubart, in his songs, plunged boldly into the daily life of the common people. Sturdy peasants, jolly hunters, soldiers with drums and fifes, postillions, a gay sledge-party—these were things after his own heart, and, above all, he did not overlook in them the harsh, comic sides, as his 'ladies shivering with cold' in the *Sledge-Drive* and the 'bewailing of the bridal wreath' in the *Peasants' Wedding* show. . . ."

Of Leopold's *divertimenti* and symphonies Abert remarks that they show an undoubted kinship with the work of his son, as regards both the "demoniacal" and the "cantabile" traits of his art:

"Only the son, from the beginning, heightened the light, social tone of the whole of this kind of music into something noble and spirited, while the father remained within the limits of the sturdy, common citizen. But also, in details, distinctly perceptible ties link both together here and there. For example, in rhythm Leopold inclines to syncopation as a means of excitement; in melody he has the tendency to a spicing with retards, chromatic appoggiaturas, etc., and often remarkably moving, tortuous figuration; in harmony, finally, besides the . . . characteristic use of the minor key, the predilection for whole series of sixths for the expression of quiet dreaming or passionate urge. All these are traits which, immensely heightened and spiritualized, repeat themselves in the son, and not, like the immediate similarities with the father, merely in the youthful works. . . ."

Abert, rightly, points out that it is hard to understand that anyone should have denied the influence on such a susceptible nature as Mozart's of the one musician nearest at hand—namely, the father. To conclude with this necessary account of Leopold's accomplishment as a composer, I shall just mention the three sonatas for clavier, composed (according to Seiffert) in the years 1762–3, which have survived print in Haffner's *Œuvres mêlées*, published in Würz-

burg. Faisst,[6] in his *"Beiträge zur Geschichte der Clavier-
sonate,"* printed in the periodical *Cäcilia*, 1846, says of these
sonatas that they might well be the work of Leopold's son, so
great is their likeness in form and spirit; and other critics
have found in them points of favourable comparison with
Domenico Scarlatti and Philipp Emanuel Bach.

I said that I believed there was a spark of true talent in
Leopold Mozart, though certainly not the burning fire of
genius, and here I will quote what might be considered as
suggesting such a musical spark—namely, the following bars
from the first movement of No. 3 of the six *divertimenti*
for two violins and violoncello, belonging, probably, to the
year 1760, which I have taken from Abert:

This is the place for a slight digression upon musical
standards. That there are many different elements in music
besides the three fundamentals of melody, harmony, and
rhythm—though these may be reduced to tone and time,
or simply to tone, since it is impossible to hear a tone without some time duration—is certain. Musical talent is not,
as one may at first be inclined to think, a simple, but is a
complex talent. The idea that a musician of genius is simply
a man with a peculiar and specialized gift for combining or
relating tones which are mere tones in the abstract without
relation to life or anything else is an illusion. That this faculty can exist in a man without reference to other qualities
or gifts is true, just as the mathematical faculty can; but such
an unrelated faculty does not, by itself, make a musician of
genius—it only makes a musician. The faculty itself varies
enormously in degree; that is a matter of common experience, and it explains why even among musicians of genius
some have this pure musical faculty to a greater degree than
others. Gluck, for example, had it less than Haydn. It is
even possible for a musician of no genius—say, a Sterndale

[6]Immanuel Gottlob Friedrich Faisst (b. 1823, d. 1894), organist,
composer, and theoretical writer.

Bennett, or even a Max Reger—to have this musical faculty more strongly developed than a composer whose work is, nevertheless, superior to theirs; superior, that is, by virtue of other qualities of which this faculty is the instrument.

In a great musician of genius every human quality must enter, and he will be great in so far as his musical faculty is at the service of and expresses his human nature and, therefore, according also to the depth and capacity of that nature. Music *is* the man. But not only is it the man, it is—in the case of the greatest artists—a universe, and that is what Schopenhauer really meant when he said that "music is the world over again." It was also what Goethe was alluding to when he makes Werther say, in a letter to his friend, that he is always being praised for his intelligence and his knowledge, whereas it is his heart—which nobody ever mentions —that is the really remarkable thing about him. During the past hundred years men have been apt to assume that they varied individually to a greater degree as regards intelligence or specific gifts than, say, in the qualities of the heart. A comic illustration of this is Charles Kingsley's well-known:

Be good, sweet maid, and let who will be clever.

These lines are always quoted as if it were more within individual control to be good than to be clever, whereas, in truth, one is born more or less "good," as one is born more or less "clever"; education and experience can only develop what natural powers in these directions exist already. The qualities of the heart are as many and as various as those of the head, and no great artistic genius is possible without possessing the qualities of both highly and richly developed. We shall come, in the course of this book, to realize that where Mozart surpassed his father—as, indeed, perhaps he surpasses all the great musicians of genius before or since— is not only in his possession of a greater degree of purely musical talent than has been possessed by any man, but also in the combination in him of such a variety of human qualities of head and heart in so high a degree of vitality that we may say of him that he had a truly Shakespearean nature.

In order that this problem of artistic genius may not have been made to appear too simple in the foregoing analysis, I must now add that there is a still unmentioned element of mystery in it. What this element is may best be suggested by indicating that in artistic genius there is a specific love in addition to, although linked with, our ordinary human loves. The prototype of human love is the love of God, and men's and women's capacity to love one another and nature depends on this primary love of God dwelling within them. But in the great artist of genius there is also another prototype, which, in the case of musicians, I may best define by calling it, not the love of God, but the love of the God of Music; and it is from this specific love that musical talent derives. "Do you think that I make music for my pleasure?" wrote Berlioz once bitterly, in a letter. This phrase suggests the difference I am trying to make clear between the enjoyment or pleasure in music and the love of it. True love is always a source of pain as well as of joy, and the passionate, concentrated love of music in a great musician of genius, such as Mozart, may be likened in its intensity to personal love, for which reason I describe it, not as the love of music, but of the God of Music.

And just as God loves those who love Him, so Music loves those who are its true lovers and showers its riches upon them. Finally—and most mysterious of all—there is some hidden connection in great creative musical genius between the love of God and this love of the God of Music. The one enriches the other as if there were a marriage between them.

The differences between the character and nature of Leopold and of his son will come out more clearly in the narrative of Mozart's life; but the reader will have already gathered that Mozart's father, Leopold, was no ordinary man. As a musician he was on a level with the majority of the best-reputed of his contemporaries, both as a composer and as an executant, and it remains now to say something of his work as a teacher.

In 1756, the year in which his great son was born, Leopold published his *Versuch einer gründlichen Violinschule*,[7] which very soon made him famous among all contemporary musicians and proved that he was not only a practical musician, but a fine theorist and teacher. His lengthy corre-

---

[7]*Essay at a Fundamental Method for the Violin*, first published by J. J. Lotter in Augsburg, 1756; further editions 1769–70, 1787, 1791, 1804; translated into French, 1770; into Dutch, 1766.

spondence with his publisher, Lotter, shows how exceptionally scrupulous in all matters of detail Leopold was. I shall quote a few sentences at random from this celebrated *Violin Method*, for the light they throw on Leopold and hence also on the sort of training his son was likely to get from him:

"Nothing can be more ridiculous than to seem afraid even to grasp the violin firmly; or merely to touch the strings with the bow—held perhaps with but two fingers—and to attempt so expressive an up-bow to the very bridge of the violin so that a note here and there is all that is heard in a whisper without any notion of what it means, as if in a dream. . . .

"It is dispiriting to go on playing at random without knowing what you are about. . . .

"To advance before the pupil is ready is the greatest error that either masters or pupils can fall into. The former often lack patience to wait for the right time or they let themselves be carried away by the pupil, who thinks he has done wonders when he can scrape out a minuet or two. . . ."

"These are the passages for practice. The more distasteful they are, the better I shall be pleased. I have striven to make them so."

Among many interesting remarks, apart from actual technical instruction, are his references to *tremolo* and *rubato*. He censures players who

". . . tremble upon every long note or cannot play a couple of bars simply without introducing senseless and ridiculous tricks and fancies . . . shake on every note as if afflicted with a fever . . . disdain to keep uniform time in the accompaniment of a concerted part and strive to follow the principal part . . . spoil the *tempo rubato* of an experienced artist by waiting to follow him. . . ."

He has a particular dislike to what he calls "virtuosos of the imagination." Such "virtuosos of the imagination" are still as plentiful today as they were in Leopold's time, and Leopold is bitingly sarcastic about them. A "virtuoso of the imagination," he says:

". . . often gives to a semiquaver in an *adagio cantabile* the time of half a bar before recovering from his paroxysm of feeling; and he cares nothing at all for the time; he plays in recitative."

Leopold was no enemy to true expression, for he recog-

nizes that the aim of the performer lies in what Philipp
Emanuel Bach described as "good execution"—namely, "the
power of expressing musical ideas to the ear correctly and
with full effect." As one of the means to this in violin-
playing, Leopold indicates the bowing as the "medium by
the judicious use of which it is possible to communicate the
pathos of the music to the audience." It is interesting to note
that Italian singers have not changed since Leopold Mozart's
day, for he refers to the fact that it is true that when playing
for some Italian singers:

". . . who learn everything by heart and never adhere to
time or measure, one has often to pass over the whole bars to
save them from open shame."

Everybody can remember occasions when conductors have
been adversely criticized for not giving singers time to
breathe, when all that they have been doing was to try to
make them sing more strictly in time, instead of dragging,
as all incompetent singers do habitually, just as they did in
Leopold's day.

Among contemporary criticisms of Leopold's *Violin
Method*, the following may be worth citing:

Marpurg, in his *Historisch-Kritische Beiträge*, compares
Leopold with Geminiani:[8]

"What Geminiani did for the English nation, Mozart has
accomplished for the German, and their works are worthy to
live side by side in universal approbation . . . a thorough and
gifted virtuoso, a sensible and methodical teacher, and a
learned musician. . . ."

Schubart, in his *Ästhetik der Tonkunst*, said:

"His *Method* . . . is written in good German and with
admirable judgment. The examples are chosen well and the
system of fingering is not in the least pedantic. The author inclines to the school of Tartini,[9] but he permits greater freedom
in the use of the bow."

It is also worth quoting the opinion of Goethe's musical

[8]Francesco Geminiani (b. Lucca, 1667; d. Dublin, 1762); famous
violinist and composer, author of *The Art of Playing the Violin*, published in English, London, 1731–4.

[9]Giuseppe Tartini (b. 1692; d. Padua, 1770); famous violinist and
composer and originator of improvements in the construction and
technique of the bow.

adviser, Zelter.[10] who has the following claims to our interest nowadays:

1. He told Goethe that Berlioz's *Huit Scènes de Faust*—which the young French composer had sent in admiration to the German poet—were horrible nonsense;

2. He criticized the poet's *Werther* to the effect that Werther should have shot Albrecht instead of himself;

3. He rewrote some of J. S. Bach's music with the notion that he was improving it; and

4. He was the teacher of Mendelssohn.

Zelter was enthusiastic over Leopold's *Violin Method*, adding to his praise: "It is well-written, too." This is worth remarking, because it is abundantly clear that Leopold Mozart was not only a man of superior culture, but a man of considerable general intellectual force. One has to bear this very clearly in mind when considering the character of his son. The nineteenth-century notion of the "childlike" Mozart, the pure, lovable, unconscious, naïve, innocent genius, is completely at variance with the facts. I doubt if in the history of men of genius there is another example of a father having so great and persistent an influence on his son as Leopold's, and the cool, calculating, sharp, sarcastic turn of mind of Leopold, his inclination to biting satire, his scepticism in all material affairs, his extreme man-of-the-worldness—all these qualities (except the last) are visible also in his son, as we shall see in due course from his letters. Mozart was as sharp and severe in his criticism of men and women and as realistically penetrating in his judgment as his father; he even shared his practical sagacity; but what he utterly lacked was his father's caution. This lack of caution was not due, however, to defect of judgment, to simple-mindedness —no man of genius was ever less simple-minded than Mozart —but to the possession of a positive quality to a quite inordinate degree—namely, sensibility. Some sensibility the hardheaded Leopold must, of course, have had or he would not have been an artist. He was even capable of enthusiasm, since he wrote a letter to the poet Gellert which moved Gellert to the following answer:

"I should be indeed insensible if the extraordinary kind-

[10]Carl Friedrich Zelter (b. Berlin, 1758; d. 1832); director of the Berlin Singakademie and founder of the German Liedertafeln.

ness with which you have honoured me had left me unmoved
. . . I accept your love and friendship, my dear sir, with the
same frankness with which they are offered. Do you, indeed,
read my works and encourage your friends to do the same?
Such approbation, I can truly say, was more than I could have
dared to hope for from such a quarter. Does my last poem,
Der Christ, meet with your approval? I venture to answer myself in the affirmative, since I am encouraged in this by the
subject of the poem, your own noble spirit—as unwittingly
you display it in your letter—and by my consciousness of
honest endeavour."

Leopold has been described by some writers as a pedant
and a bigot. It is quite clear from his own letters that he was
neither. He was a devout Catholic, being born in Catholic
South Germany, but also by conviction; yet, nevertheless,
he became a Freemason towards the end of his life. He was
not superstitious, and, speaking of a ghost-story, said: "It
must be only a hysterical illusion." He remonstrates with his
daughter when ill for risking endangering her health rather
than abstain from going to Mass; while writing, on one occasion, that he had "invariably found that begging sisterhoods
were the signs of much moral degradation concealed under
the cloak of hypocrisy." But one of his most characteristic
utterances was the following:

"Accept it as a universal truth that all men tell lies and
add to the truth, or take away from it, just as it suits their
purpose. Especially must we believe nothing which, if known,
would add to the reputation of the speaker or flatter his inter-
locutor, for that is sure to be false."

This saying, which is worthy of La Rochefoucauld and
undeniably true, was not of much assistance to his son. Mozart, as we shall learn, could see through men just as clearly
as his father; there was nothing wrong with his head. What
was wrong with him was his heart and his general sensibility,
which was, indeed, extreme. The old Biblical utterance that
the truly virtuous shall be light of heart, if applied to Mozart,
would make him out to be one of the most virtuous of men,
for his natural buoyancy and gaiety of heart were quite extraordinary. It was this sheer light-heartedness and vivacity
which made him do rash things and involve himself in difficulties and responsibilities which his more cautious father

would have avoided. After all, a man is not a man of genius for nothing. Men of such genius as Mozart's must be conscious of it. It must be an exhilarating element in their lives to a degree of which we can hardly conceive. It may amount, indeed, to what we might call an intoxication of the spirit to which lesser men can only aspire through being in love or in drink. Mozart was gay and, in a sense, reckless. That Mozart was aware of his genius is abundantly clear from his letters. In fact, he took it so for granted that when writing to his father from Vienna on August 17, 1782, when he was twenty-six years old, he mentions without any surprise or even comment, when talking about his prospects and whether he would have to leave Germany and go to France or England, how the Archduke Maximilian, speaking of him, said: "Such people only come into the world once in a hundred years."

As to his sensibility, we have a piece of astonishing contemporary evidence. J. A. Schachtner, who died in 1795, four years after Mozart, had been court trumpeter at Salzburg since 1754 and had known the family well since Mozart's childhood. Shortly after Mozart's death he wrote to Mozart's sister a letter answering questions which she had put to him. Her fourth question and his answer are as follows:

"Fourth Question: 'What particular qualities, maxims, rules of life, singularities, good or evil propensities had he?'

"Answer: He was full of fire; his inclinations were easily swayed; I believe that had he been without the advantage of the good education which he received he might have become a profligate scoundrel—he was so ready to yield to every attraction which offered."

When reading this, one cannot help being reminded of Keats's:

"Men of genius are great as certain ethereal chemicals operating on the mass of neutral intellect—but they have not any individuality, any determined character. . . ."[11]

Schachtner's letter is the source of so much of the authentic information about Mozart as a child that it must be quoted in full. I therefore give the rest of it here:

[11]Letter to Benjamin Bailey, November 22, 1817. See the rest of this letter; also, in his letter to George and Thomas Keats, December 21, 1817, the passage on "negative capability."

Salzburg, April 24, 1792

Honoured and gracious Madam,

Your very welcome letter reached me, not at Salzburg, but at Hammerau, where I was visiting my son. . . .

From my habitual obligingness towards everyone and especially towards the Mozart family, you may judge how sorry I was that I could not at once discharge your commission. To the point, then!

Your first question: "What favourite pastimes, outside his occupation with music, your late-lamented brother had as a child?" is not to be answered, since as soon as he began to give himself up to music his mind was as good as dead to other things[12] and even his childish games and toys to be interesting to him had to be accompanied with music. When we (he and I) carried his toys from one room into another, the one who went empty-handed had always to sing and fiddle a march. Before he began to study music he was so keenly alive to any bit of fun enlivened with a spice of mischief that he would forget about eating and drinking and everything else. As you know, he became so extremely fond of me (being devoted to him) that he would ask me ten times a day whether I loved him, and if I jokingly answered: "No," immediately bright tears came into his eyes, so tender and affectionate was his good little heart.

Second question: "How did he behave as a child with the great when they admired his talent and proficiency in music?" In truth he betrayed very little pride or veneration for rank,[13]

---

[12]It is noteworthy that Leopold writes to his son from Salzburg, February 16, 1778:

"My son! in all your affairs you are hot-headed and hasty. Your character now is wholly altered from what you were as a child and youth. As a boy and child you were serious rather than childish and when you were at the clavier or otherwise occupied with music nobody dared make the least joke. Your very countenance was so serious that many observant persons . . . prophesied your early death on account of your precocious and reflective expression. Now, it seems to me, you answer hastily in a joking tone on the slightest provocation."

[13]In a most interesting letter from Salzburg dated February 16, 1778, Leopold writes to his son:

"It is your good heart that causes you to give your complete trust and love to anyone who unreservedly praises you, esteems you, and lauds you to the skies: whereas as a boy your modesty was so ex-for he could have shown both by playing before the great who understood little or nothing of music, but he never wanted to play unless there were musical connoisseurs among his audience or unless he were deceived into thinking that there were.

Third question: "What studious occupation did he like best?" Answer: in this respect it was much the same to him what he was set to learn; he only wanted to learn and left the choice to his beloved father. It seemed as if he realized that he could find in the world no teacher or guide like his ever-memorable father.

Whatever he was given to learn, he gave himself so completely to that that everything else, even music, was laid aside. For example, when he was learning arithmetic tables, stools, walls, and even the floor were chalked over with figures.

Fourth question. . . .[14]

Let me add some remarkable and astonishing facts relating to his fourth and fifth years of whose truth I can guarantee. Once I went with his father to your home after the Thursday service and we found the four-year-old Wolfgangerl busy with the pen.

Father: "What are you doing?"

Wolfg.: "Writing a concerto for the clavier, the first part is almost done."

Father: "Let me see."

Wolfg.: "It's not quite finished."

Father: "Never mind, let me see it, it must be something very fine."

Your father took it from him and showed me a daub of notes for the most part written over dried ink-blots. (N.B. The little Wolfgangerl dipped his pen every time to the bottom of the inkwell so that a blot fell every time he touched the paper, but that did not disturb him, he rubbed it off with his hand and went on writing.) We laughed at first at this apparent nonsense, but then your father began to note the

---

treme that you began at once to weep when you were overpraised. The greatest art is to learn to know yourself and then, my dear son, do as I and study other people so as to know them well. You know it has ever been my study and it is indeed a fine, useful, even essential study."

[14]Already quoted, see p. 27.

theme, the notes, the composition; his study of the sheet became more intent until at last tears of wonder and delight fell from his eyes.

"Look, Herr Schachtner," he said, "how correct and orderly it is; only it is of no use because it is so very difficult that nobody could play it." Then Wolfgangerl struck in: "That is why it is a concerto, one must practice it until one can do it; look! this is how it goes." He played, but could only bring out enough to show us what he intended. He had then the notion that playing concertos and working miracles were the same thing.

Once more, gracious madam! You will doubtless remember that I had a very good violin which Wolfgangerl on account of its soft and full tone always called "butter-fiddle." One day, soon after you came back from Vienna (early in 1763) he played on it and could not praise it enough; a day or two after, I came to see him again and found him playing with his own violin; he said: "What is your butter-fiddle doing?" and went on playing to his fancy. At last he reflected a little and said: "Herr Schachtner, your violin is half a quarter of a tone lower than mine; that is, if it is tuned as it was when I last played on it." I laughed at this, but your father, who knew the extraordinary ear and memory of the child, begged me to get my violin and see whether he was right. I did and right he was.[15]

Some time before this, the day after your return from Vienna, Wolfgang having brought with him a small violin which he got as a present from Vienna, then came in our then excellent violinist Herr Wenzl, who was a beginner at composition.

He brought six Trios with him which he had prepared in the absence of your father, to have his opinion on them. We played these Trios, your father taking the bass part on the viola, Wenzl the first violin, and I the second. Wolfgangerl begged to be allowed to play the second violin, but your father reproved him for his silly request since he had not had the

---

[15]It must be said for the benefit of non-musicians that such accuracy of ear and retentiveness of memory, although, of course, exceptional, are not quite so rare as might be supposed. Many musicians totally lacking in genius—to say nothing of genius of Mozart's order —have possessed this faculty. See my remarks on pp. 20-21.

slightest instruction on the violin and your father thought he was not in the least prepared for playing.

Wolfgang said: "One does not need to have learned to play the second violin," and when your father told him to go away and not disturb us further, Wolfgang began to cry bitterly and toddled off with his little violin. I interceded for him to be allowed to play with me and at last his father said: "Play with Herr Schachtner, but so softly that you are not heard or you must go away at once." Wolfgang played with me. Soon I perceived with astonishment that I was quite superfluous; I put my violin quietly down and looked at your father, down whose cheeks tears of wonder and delight were rolling, and so he played all six Trios. When we had finished, Wolfgang grew so bold with our applause that he declared he could play first violin. We let him try as a joke and we almost died of laughter to hear him play, with incorrect and uncertain execution certainly, but without breaking down.

In conclusion: "Of the delicacy and fineness of his ear."

Almost up to his tenth year he had an insurmountable dread of the trumpet when it was played alone without other instruments; if one merely held out a trumpet towards him it was as if one had pointed a loaded pistol at his heart. His father wanted to rid him of this childish fear and asked me once in spite of his objections to blow towards him, but, my God! I had to desist. Wolfgang no sooner heard the clanging sound than he turned pale, began to totter, and would have fallen into convulsions had I not stopped.

This is all I can say, I think, in answer to your questions. Pardon my scrawl, I am too cast down to do better.

I am, honoured madam,

With the greatest esteem and regard,

Your most obedient servant,

Andreas Schachtner,

Court Trumpeter.

Mozart's mother, Anna Maria Pertl[16] (written also as Bertl or Bertel), was the daughter of Wolfgang Nikolaus Pertl, steward of the Convent of St. Gilgen by St. Wolfgang-See, and Rosina Altmann. Her letters—all of which

---

[16]Born December 25, 1720, at Huttenstein, near St. Gilgen, in the Salzkammergut; married Leopold Mozart November 21, 1747; died Paris, July 3, 1778.

I have carefully read—confirm her reputation of being a
cheerful, happy-natured woman, perhaps less intellectual
than her husband, though more tolerant and humorous, but
nevertheless with a real love of music[17] and a lively interest
in politics.[18] It is not to be imagined that so exacting a man
as Leopold, who did not marry until he was twenty-eight,
would have married a stupid woman, and from her portrait
now in the Mozarteum at Salzburg one can see that she was
a woman of character and capacity. In my opinion Mozart
owed more of his character to his mother than to his father.
From all the evidence she seems to have been gay and lovable
and although a capable, industrious, and unselfish wife and
mother—in short, a true, sound-natured woman—not at
all authoritative and domineering, but lively and accommodating. She seems to have had the Salzburg bias to the
droll and comical.[19] Schubart in his *Ästhetik der Tonkunst*
writes:

"The Salzburg mind is addicted to low comedy. Their
popular songs are so drolly burlesque that one cannot listen to
them without dying of laughter. The clownish spirit shines
through them all, though the melodies are often fine and beautiful."

Who can fail to see this characteristic in the operas of Mozart?[20] This side of his genius he certainly got from his
mother and the well-known Salzburg proverb: "He who
comes to Salzburg becomes in the first year stupid, in the
second year idiotic (*ein fex*), and in the third a true Salzburger," might have been written by Mozart himself in one
of his letters, it is so exactly in his spirit.

Leopold and Anna Maria had seven children, of whom
only two survived: a daughter, Maria Anna (called Nannerl

[17]She writes to Leopold from Mannheim on January 3, 1778:
"Here, on account of the death of the Elector, all is in deepest
mourning, no Opera (which is a great grief to me), comedy, play,
concerts, sledge-drives, music; everything has been suspended."

[18]Her letters to her husband from Mannheim and Paris are full of
references to politics.

[19]The buffoon (Hanswurst) on the Viennese stage, the creation of
Stranitzky, was given the Salzburg dialect.

[20]Another feature inherited from his mother by Mozart was his
long and prominent nose. Mozart's father and mother were considered the best-looking bridal couple of their time in Salzburg.

or Marianne in the family), born on July 30, 1751,[21] and the
son, Wolfgang, born on January 27, 1756. Nannerl, who
was thus five years older than Wolfgang, showed very
early a decided talent for music, and Leopold taught her
the clavier. The teaching of his sister made a great impression on Wolfgang; when he was only three years old he used
to seat himself at the clavier and amuse himself striking
thirds with great delight.

When Wolfgang was four years old his father began to
teach him minuets and other pieces on the clavier, and soon
he could play them with perfect correctness and in the
proper time. In his fifth year he began to compose little
pieces which he played to his father and which he then
wrote down."[22]

In addition to the memoir sent by Mozart's sister in December 1799 to Messrs. Breitkopf, another source of reliable
information about Wolfgang's earliest studies is the music-
book provided by her father for Marianne's exercises which
was presented by the Grand Duchess Helene in 1864 to the
Salzburg Mozarteum. It contains minuets and other little
pieces, also longer ones such as a theme with twelve variations, and passages from the composers Agrell, Fischer, and
Wagenseil written in the hand of Leopold and his musical
friends. The book has the title: *"Pour le Clavecin. Ce livre
appartient a Marie Anna Mozart, 1759,"* but unfortunately
there are a number of pages missing. However, to the eighth
minuet there is a note by Leopold:

"The preceding minuet was learned by Wolfgangerl in his
fourth year."

There are other similar observations—for example:

"This minuet and trio Wolfgangerl learned in half an hour
at half past nine o'clock on January 26, 1761, one day before
his fifth birthday."[23]

[21]Nannerl survived her brother. She married in 1784 Baron von
Berchtold zu Sonnenberg, Hofrath of Salzburg and Warden of St.
Gilgen. On his death, in 1801, she returned to Salzburg and taught
music. She became blind in 1820 and died on October 29, 1829.

[22]Schlichtegroll's *Nekrolog*, an annual obituary of eminent persons
compiled for the year of Mozart's death, 1791, by Professor Schlichte-
groll, which appeared in 1793 and 1794—described as containing "an
authentic biography of my brother" by Marianne Mozart.

[23]Otto Jahn says: "They are simple, easy pieces in two parts, but

A second book, intended for Wolfgang, is complete.[24] Some details of it were given in the *Mitteilungen für die Berliner Mozartgemeinde,* published in Berlin in March 1908, and Abert gives a thorough analysis of it. On the back of the first page is written:

"To my dear son Wolfgang Amadée on his sixth birthday from his father Leopold Mozart. Salzburg, October 31, 1762."

One of the first[25] compositions of Mozart's that we possess is a minuet transcribed into Marianne's book by Leopold with the note that it was composed by his son in January 1762. Here it is:

Minuet in F (K.2)

requiring an independence of the hands not possible without a degree of musical comprehension surprising in so young a child."

[24]It was in the possession of Dr. L. König in Kiel.

[25]Abert and others consider the Minuet in G (K.1) to be Mozart's first. This is on the authority of his sister Marianne, who has written on the MS. (now in the Municipal Museum at Salzburg) that it was composed by her brother and "written by his own hand in his fifth year."

Wolfgang's music-book, given to him in 1762 by his father, has been painstakingly examined by Abert. It consists of 135 pages and includes examples of songs and dance music from popular collections; also pieces by Philipp Emanuel Bach, Telemann, Kirchhoff, Schmidt, Hasse, and others. Not only the old dances—allemandes, courantes, and so on—are included, but what were then the new dance forms of minuet and polonaise. "The book shows," says Abert, "how much stronger on Mozart's early development was the influence of the North German school than was formerly suspected."

11. *The Prodigy Children*

1762–1766

Leopold decided to show his two wonder-children to the world. In January 1762 he took Nannerl (aged eleven) and Wolfgang (aged six) on their first experimental journey to Munich. They stayed three weeks and played before the Elector. In September of the same year they set out for Vienna, breaking the journey at Passau, where the Bishop wanted to hear the prodigies and then rewarded them with— one ducat! They also stayed at Linz, giving a concert under the patronage of Count Schlick. A Count Herberstein[1] and a Count Pfalz also heard them there and promised to spread the news about them in Vienna. The information about these tours comes chiefly from Leopold's letters to Lorenz Hagenauer, a Salzburg business man in whose house the Mozarts lodged. Hagenauer was a good friend of the family and lent Leopold most of the money for his various tours. His house, in

---

[1] In 1785 this Count Herberstein, then Bishop of Passau, told Mozart how he remembered his extreme concern as a child on seeing a beggar fall into the water.

which Mozart was born, still stands in the Getreidegasse, and
the floor occupied by the Mozarts has been turned into a
museum where the portraits and many other interesting Mozartiana are now exhibited. Extracts from Leopold's letters to
Hagenauer will give the best account of this second tour, the
first one to Vienna:

Linz, October 3, 1762

. . . This delay [in Passau], for which His Grace's favour
is responsible, is also responsible for costing me the eighty
gulden I had made in Linz. . . . Wolfgang had the honour
to perform before His Grace, but not the girl, and for this he
received a whole ducat, that is four gulden and ten kreutzer.

. . . On the 26th we left Passau with Count Herberstein
in the morning and arrived at 5 o'clock in the evening at
Linz. . . .

The children are happy and just as if they were at home.
The boy[2] is as intimate with everybody, especially with the
officers, as if he had known them all his life.

Vienna, October 16, 1762

On the feast of St. Francis in the afternoon at 4.30 we left
Linz by the so-called "water-ordinary"[3] and arrived the same
night by dark at Mauthausen. The following Tuesday at midday we reached Ibbs, where our Wolferl[4] . . . played so well
on the organ that the Franciscan fathers . . . with a guest
. . . left their eating and ran to hear open-mouthed with
astonishment. By night we were at Stein and Wednesday the
6th at 3 o'clock in Vienna. We had much rain and wind on
the journey. Wolfgang had already a cold in Linz, but in spite
of all discomfort, early rising, unusual food and drink, and the
wind and rain, remained, thank God! well.

I must mention that we got through the customs quickly
and without payment, owing to Wolferl, who made friends
with the officer, showed him his clavier . . . and played him
a minuet on his little fiddle. . . .

The Countess von Zinzendorf is busy on our account and
all the ladies have lost their hearts to the children. When I

[2]Leopold always uses the South German expression *Der Bub* for the
five-year-old Wolfgang.

[3]No doubt the boat service on the Danube between Linz and
Vienna.

[4]Wolfgangerl.

was alone in the Opera on the 10th I heard the Archduke Leopold[5] saying from his box that there was a boy in Vienna who played the clavier wonderfully, etc. The very same evening about eleven I received a command to go to Schönbrunn. . . .

I had the firm intention to let you know as soon as we came from Schönbrunn but we had to go direct from Schönbrunn to the Prince von Hildburghausen . . . now there is only time to tell you that we were so graciously received that as I tell it it will be reckoned a fairy-tale. Let it suffice that Wolferl sprang on the lap of the Empress,[6] put his arms around her neck, and vigorously kissed her. We were with her from three till six. . . .

Vienna, October 19, 1762

. . . The treasurer paid me one hundred ducats with the statement that Her Majesty will soon send for us again. . . .

Would you like to know what Wolferl's dress looks like? It is of the finest cloth, lilac-coloured; the vest of silk of the same colour, the coat and waistcoat embroidered with broad gold braid. It was made for the Archduke Maximilian. Nannerl has the Court dress of a Princess of white embroidered and hand-trimmed taffeta.[7]

Wolfgang fell ill with scarlet fever, and the Viennese nobility sent their doctors and much attention was paid to Leopold and his children,[8] but Leopold complains to Hagenauer (November 24, 1762) that through this illness they lost four weeks, which have cost them one ducat a day. After making a journey to Pressburg in Hungary on December 11, Leopold and his two children returned from Vienna to Salzburg early in January. There was now a slight change in his position, for the Kapellmeister at Salzburg, Ernst Eberlin, died in 1762 and Joseph Lolli became Kapellmeister in his

[5] Later, the Emperor Leopold II of Austria.

[6] Maria Theresa.

[7] Leopold had the two children's portraits painted in these gala clothes, which were presented to them by the Empress.

[8] Wolfgang became very fond of the Archduchess Marie Antoinette and once when she had picked him up after a fall he said: "You are very good, I will marry you." "Why?" asked the Empress, who was standing by. "From gratitude," he answered; "she was good to me but her sister stood by and did nothing."

place, Leopold Mozart being now appointed vice-Kapell-meister.

The success of this tour decided Leopold to make a more ambitious one. As their possible public was almost exclusively the nobility, they left Salzburg again on June 9, 1763, to pay a round of visits to the German courts and principal cities, with Paris as the ultimate goal. Again I shall extract from Leopold's letters to Hagenauer the most interesting details of this tour:

Wasserburg, June 11, 1763

. . . Two hours from Wasserburg one of the back wheels broke in pieces . . . to amuse ourselves we went to look at the organ and I explained the use of the pedal to Wolferl, whereupon he began to try it—pushing away the stool and standing, he preluded, using the pedal as if he had practised it for months. Everybody was astonished and what many achieve after much labour comes to him as a new gift of God.

From Wasserburg they proceeded to Munich, where they played before the Elector of Bavaria and the Archduke Clemens. Wolfgang played a concerto on the violin and extemporized two cadenzas. Leopold received one hundred gulden from the Elector and seventy-five from the Archduke. They then left for Augsburg. They remained there fifteen days and gave three concerts, at which the audience was "almost entirely composed of Lutherans." From Augsburg they went to Ludwigsburg, which was the summer residence of the Duke of Württemberg, whose capital was Stuttgart. The Italian Jomelli[9] was Kapellmeister to the Duke and had raised the standard of music in Stuttgart to a high level. Leopold mentions to Hagenauer his salary of four thousand gulden yearly and appointments and says: "What do you think of that for a Kapellmeister!" He did not succeed in getting the Duke to hear his children, for which he blamed Jomelli, declaring that he used his influence all for Italian music and musicians and did not believe a German musician could have real talent; but this seems to have been only imagination on Leopold's part, for there is much evidence that Jomelli was an amiable man and not biased against Germans. In Ludwigsburg

[9]Niccolo Jomelli (b. Naples, 1714; d. Naples, 1774), celebrated composer of the Neapolitan school.

Leopold heard Nardini[10] play the violin and wrote enthusiastically to Hagenauer:

"Tell Herr Wenzel that I have heard a certain Nardini play and that for beauty, cleanness, and evenness of tone and for expressive cantabile nothing finer is to be heard."

From Ludwigsburg they went to Schwetzingen, the summer residence of the Elector Palatine, Karl Theodor, to whom they had introductions from Prince von Zweibrücken and Prince Clemens of Bavaria. The court assembled to hear them on July 18 from five till nine o'clock and they made a great impression. Here Leopold heard for the first time the famous Mannheim orchestra; he writes:

Schwetzingen, July 19, 1763

. . . I had the pleasure to hear besides good singers a remarkable flautist, Herr Wendling. The orchestra is without question the best in Germany—respectable young men, well behaved, neither tipplers, gamblers, nor boors, as praiseworthy for their behaviour as for their playing. . . .

Mainz, August 3, 1763

. . . We took a trip from Schwetzingen to Heidelberg to see the castle. . . . In the Church of the Holy Spirit Wolfgang played the organ to such effect that the Dean as a remembrance ordered his name to be inscribed upon it.

They did not appear at court in Mayence, owing to the illness of the Elector, Joseph Emmerich von Breitbach, but gave two concerts and made two hundred florins and then proceeded to Frankfurt.

Frankfurt, August 20, 1763

Our concert was on the 18th. It was good. All were astounded. On the 22nd, 25th, and 26th we gave others. Wolfgang is quite extraordinarily lively, but also naughty. Nannerl is no longer suffering in comparison; all speak of her and admire her skill.

I have bought a pleasing clavier from Herr Stein in Augsburg that has been of great service for practice on the journey.

Once since we have been travelling—I think it was in Augsburg—Wolfgang when he awoke in the morning began

[10]Pietro Nardini (1722–93), famous violinist and composer, pupil of Tartini. Solo violinist and leader of the Stuttgart court orchestra, 1753–67.

to weep. I asked him why and he replied that it was because he never saw Herr Hagenauer, Wenzel, Spitzeder, Deibel, Leitgeb, Vogt, Nazerl, and other friends.[11]

The effect made in Frankfurt by the children may be gathered from the following newspaper notice which appeared on August 30, 1763:

"The general astonishment awakened in all hearers by the never before seen or heard-of ability of the two children of Herr Leopold Mozart, Kapellmeister at the court of Salzburg, has necessitated the threefold repetition of the single concert originally intended. . . .

"The little girl who is in her twelfth and the boy who is in his seventh year will not only play concertos on the clavecin or harpsichord and concertos by the greatest masters, but the boy will also play a violin concerto, will accompany symphonies on the clavier—the manual or keyboard being covered with a cloth—with as much facility as if he could see the keys; further, he will name exactly all tones singly or in chords given on the clavier or on any other instrument, bells, glasses, clocks, etc. Finally, he will improvise from his head on the harpsichord or organ in the most difficult keys as requested for as long as desired in order to show that he understands how to play the organ as thoroughly as the harpsichord though it is quite a different matter."

It is noteworthy that Goethe, then fourteen years old, a native of Frankfurt, heard Mozart at one of these concerts, as he relates to Eckermann many years later:

"I saw him as a seven-year-old boy when he gave a concert. . . . I was about fourteen years old and I remember still quite distinctly the little fellow with his powdered wig and sword."

From Frankfurt they travelled to Coblenz, Bonn, Cologne, and Aachen, where the Princess Amalie, a sister of Frederick the Great, tried to persuade Leopold to take his children to Berlin. He writes to Hagenauer from Brussels on October 17, 1763:

"If the kisses which she bestowed on my children, especially on Master Wolfgang, had been louis d'or all would have been well, but neither the hotel nor the post-horses can be paid

[11]Salzburg friends of the Mozart family. This charming touch reminds one of what one keeps forgetting—that Mozart on this tour was a child of seven.

with kisses. . . . Prince Karl [von Lothringen] has promised to hear my children but has not yet done so. He does nothing but hunt, eat, and drink and so has no money. . . .

"If you have been astonished in Salzburg at my children you will be absolutely astounded when, if God wills, we return. . . ."

From Brussels they travelled by post-horses, arriving on November 18, 1763 at Paris, where they lodged with the Bavarian Ambassador, Count von Eyck, whose wife was a daughter of Count Arco, the Chamberlain at Salzburg. They were introduced to the court at Versailles, where the most important person was Madame de Pompadour.[12] Leopold writes to the wife of Hagenauer at Salzburg as follows:

Paris, February 1, 1764

One must not always write to men but also remember the beautiful and devout sex. Whether the Paris ladies are beautiful I cannot surely say for they are contrary to nature, like the Berchtesgadner dolls, so painted that to the eyes of an honest German even a naturally beautiful person becomes insufferable through this detestable ornamentation.[13] . . . It is to be noted that here it is not the custom to show homage to the King or to any member of the royal family by bending the knee or head, but one remains standing upright without the slightest movement . . . you can imagine what a sensation it must have caused the French when the King's daughter not only in her apartment but also in public on seeing my children let them kiss her hands and returned their kisses. . . .[14]

No doubt you would like to know what Madame the Marquise de Pompadour looks like? She must have been very beautiful, for she still looks well. She is tall and stately, stout but well-proportioned, blonde, and has some likeness to the Kaiserin about the eyes. She is very proud and has a remark-

[12]Madame de Pompadour, mistress of Louis XV (1710–74). The Seven Years' War, in which France lost India and Canada to England, had just finished (1763), Rousseau (1712–78) had published *La Nouvelle Héloïse* (1760), *Émile*, and *Le Contrat social* (1762).

[13]The "honest" German has returned to life in the Third Reich (1932–1945). I find his bigotry more detestable than the very ancient and, to me, charming fashion for women of painting the face.

[14]An oil-painting, by G. M. B. Ollivier, of Mozart at the clavier in the salon of Prince Conti, is in the Louvre at Paris.

able mind. Her rooms in Versailles are like a paradise . . .
and in Paris in the Faubourg St. Honoré she has a wonderful
house newly built. The room where the clavier stood, which
was completely gilt and elaborately lacquered and painted,
contains a life-size portrait of her and of the King.

What else! There is a permanent conflict between Italian
and French music. All French music is worthless, but they
are beginning to alter it thoroughly . . . and in ten or fifteen
years I hope to see the present French taste extinguished.[15]
The Germans take the lead in having their work published.
Among them Schobert,[16] Eckard,[17] and Honnauer for clavier
and Hochbrucker and Mayr for harp are very popular. Le
Grand, a French clavier-player, has quite given up his style,
and his sonatas are now according to our taste. Schobert,
Eckard, Le Grand, and Hochbrucker have brought their
printed sonatas to us and made a present of them to my children. Four sonatas by Monsieur Wolfgang Mozart are now at
the engravers.

Imagine the sensation these sonatas will make in the world
when one sees on the title page that it is the work of a seven-
year-old child and how when a proof is wanted of this incredible capacity, as has already happened, he will put a bass
immediately to any minuet without touching the clavier and
also, if wished, a second-violin part! You will be able to hear
how good these sonatas are. There is one andante of quite exceptional merit and I can assure you, Frau Hagenauer, that
God daily performs new miracles with this child. . . . He
accompanies and transposes at sight and reads any piece,
French or Italian, that is put before him.[18]

[15]It is worth remembering that Rameau (1683–1764) died in Paris
in the September of this year in which Leopold is writing.

[16]Johann Schobert (b. c. 1720; d. 1767), eminent pianist and composer.

[17]Johann Gottfried Eckard (b. Augsburg, 1735; d. Paris, 1809), famous pianist and composer, also a celebrated miniature-painter.

[18]Lest this be thought paternal exaggeration, the following notice
by Suard (*Mélanges de littérature*, II, 337) may be quoted:

"He was from six to seven years old. I heard him play on the
clavier at the *Concert Spirituel* and in private houses. He astonished
all music-lovers by the facility and precision with which he executed
the most difficult pieces. He accompanied at sight. He improvised on
his instrument and produced the happiest melodies and already
showed a profound feeling for harmony."

My girl plays the most difficult pieces of Schobert and Eckard . . . with incredible clarity. . . .

These four sonatas, the first printed works of Mozart, were entitled:

Sonatas[19] pour le Clavecin qui peuvent se jouer avec l'accompagnement de Violon, dédiées à Mme. Victoire de France par J. G. Wolfgang Mozart de Salzburg âgé de sept ans. Œuvre première, à Paris aux addresses ordinaires.

Another set of sonatas[20] were published with a dedication to the Comtesse de Tessé, lady-in-waiting to the Dauphinesse. This dedication was by Grimm,[21] author of Correspondence littéraire, a German settled in Paris. He was for a time secretary to the Duke of Orléans and had become an influential personage and rendered Leopold Mozart valuable assistance. Of this dedication Leopold writes to Hagenauer:

Paris, April 1, 1764

. . . In several days the sonatas which Wolfgang has dedicated to Mme. la Comtesse de Tessé will be ready. They would have been ready sooner but the dedication by our best friend, Herr Grimm, was not acceptable to the Comtesse and had to be altered. It is a pity . . . the Comtesse and my boy were very vividly described in it but the fact is she will not have herself praised. . . .

In this same letter he announces with satisfaction to Hagenauer that he will shortly receive from the bankers Turton and Baur two hundred louis d'or; also that he has had permission to give two public concerts in the Théâtre de M. Félix, rue Saint-Honoré, which is reserved by the King for the opera, plays, and the Concerts Spirituels. He also mentions that a Baron von Bose, whom Leopold describes as being "all that a truly noble man should be in this world," has presented Wolfgang with Gellert's Geistliche Oden und Lieder, in which he has inscribed:

Take, little seven-year-old Orpheus, this book from the hand of your admirer and friend. Read it often and know its divine songs; lend them in blessed hours of grace your irresist-

---

[19]K. 6 and 7. Wyzewa and Saint-Foix give a careful analysis of these and the following sonatas.

[20]K. 8 and 9.

[21]Friedrich Melchior Grimm, Baron von (1723–1807), not to be confused with the brothers Grimm, collectors of fairy-tales, etc.

ible harmonies so that the senseless scorners of religion may mark and perceive so that they hear and fall down and worship God.

Friedrich Karl
Baron von Bose

Finally, he mentions the services of Grimm:

"Herr Grimm alone, to whom I had a letter from a Frankfurt merchant's wife, has done everything. He has fixed up the court; he has looked after the first concert. He himself has paid me eighty louis d'or for three hundred and twenty tickets he has disposed of and also defrayed the cost of the wax candles—there were more than sixty table candles. This Grimm has obtained the permission for the concert and will now look after the second, for which one hundred tickets are distributed. See what a man can do who has sense and a good heart! He is from Regensburg. . . .

"Monsieur de Mechel, a copper-engraver, is working day and night to engrave our portraits, which Herr von Carmontelle, an admirer, has painted extremely well.[22] Wolfgang plays the clavier. I stand behind and play the violin and Nannerl has one arm on the clavier and with the other holds the music as she sings."

On April 10, 1764 Leopold and his wife and two children left Paris for London. At Calais they saw the sea for the first time and crossed not in the usual packet-boat, which was full, but in a boat he chartered, arriving in London on April 23.

London, May 28, 1764

. . . On April 27 we were from six to nine o'clock with the King and Queen[23] in . . . St. James's Palace. . . . The present was only twenty-four guineas but the favour which His Majesty and the Queen showed us is not to be described; one would never, in short, think that these friendly people were King and Queen of England—the way we have been received here surpasses everything. Eight days later we were walking in St. James's Park. The King and Queen drove past and although we were in other clothes they recognized us. . . .

[22]This charming picture of Carmontelle is now in the Musée de Chantilly.

[23]King George III and Queen Charlotte of Mecklenburg-Strelitz. The King was a great admirer of Handel's music, and the Queen played and sang.

The King opened the window, nodded, and smilingly greeted us, especially Master Wolfgang.

. . . On May 19 we were brought to court and were from six to ten o'clock with the King and Queen. . . . The King put before Wolfgang not only pieces by Wagenseil but also by [Christian] Bach, Abel, and Handel. He has played them all at sight. He played on the King's organ in such a way that they preferred it even to his clavier-playing; he accompanied the Queen in a song and a flautist in a solo; finally he took the bass of a Handel aria and improvised a most beautiful melody on it to the astonishment of all. In a word, what he knew when we started from Salzburg is a mere shadow of what he knows now. It surpasses all imagination.

The Mozarts gave a concert on June 5 in a hall at Spring Gardens, near St. James's Park, at the hour of twelve o'clock, out of which Leopold made a large profit, being able to send Hagenauer at Salzburg one hundred guineas on June 28. He allowed Wolfgang to play at a charity concert in aid of the Lying-in Hospital on the Surrey side of Westminster, whose foundation stone was laid in the following year (1765), but soon after this Leopold caught a severe chill and was ill for some time, retiring to Chelsea, whence he writes:

Chelsea, August 9, 1764

. . . It is one of the loveliest prospects in the world. Wherever I look I see nothing but gardens and beyond the most beautiful houses. . . .

During his father's illness Wolfgang began composing symphonies,[24] and his sister relates that he said to her once as she was sitting near while he worked: "Remind me to give something really good to the horn."

They returned to town in October and lodged in Frith Street, Soho. They were invited to court again and on January 18, 1765 were published:

Six Sonatas pour le clavecin qui peuvent se jouer avec l'accompagnement de Violon ou Flaute traversière tres humblement

---

[24]Mozart composed three symphonies during his stay in England:

B Flat,	K.17	.	Chelsea, July–September 1764;
E Flat,	K.18	.	London, December–January 1764–5;
D	K.19	.	London, January–April 1765.

The symphony in E Flat (K.18) is, according to Wyzewa and Saint-Foix, a copy of an overture by Abel.

dédiées à Sa Majesté Charlotte Reine de la Grande Bretagne, composées par J. G. Wolfgang Mozart âgé de huit ans Œuvre III London. Printed for the Author and Sold at his Lodgings at Mr. Williamson in Thrift [Frith] Street, Soho.

From the Queen, who had accepted the dedication, Leopold received fifty guineas, but the novelty of the child prodigies was wearing off. A concert was postponed to make room for Dr. Arne's oratorio *Judith* and finally took place on February 21 at six o'clock in the small Haymarket Theatre and Leopold informs Hagenauer that he has only made a profit of one hundred guineas,[25] being less than he expected. For a final concert on May 13, announced as their last appearance before leaving London, Leopold was obliged to reduce the price for seats from half a guinea to four shillings. On this occasion Wolfgang played on a two-manual harpsichord which Tschudi[26] had made for the King of Prussia. The Italian opera under Giardini was then flourishing in London, and one of the favourite singers of the time, Manzuoli,[27] became a friend of the Mozarts and gave Wolfgang singing-lessons. But the most important musical acquaintance made by the Mozarts was that of Johann Christian Bach,[28] the youngest son of J. S. Bach, whose opera seria *Adriano in Siria* was first produced in London at the King's Theatre on January 26, 1765 and was no doubt heard by Wolfgang, to whom he showed great kindness. Christian Bach was music-master to the Queen and it is related that he used to take Wolfgang on his knee and go through a sonata with him, playing each a bar in turn so precisely that one would not have suspected two performers. Also he began a fugue which Wolfgang completed.

A scientific examination of Wolfgang's powers was made by the Honourable Daines Barrington and the circumstantial

[25]Let the young and inexperienced reader not be disturbed by this constant preoccupation of Leopold with money. The money was needed; his was miserable pay at Salzburg, with no hope of more, but only the prospect of an indigent old age.

[26]Burkat Tschudi (b., Switzerland, 1702; d., London, 1773), celebrated harpsichord-maker and founder of the house of Broadwood. He was the younger son of a noble Swiss family and came to England in 1718 as an ordinary journeyman joiner.

[27]Giovanni Manzuoli (b., Florence, 1725), a successor of the famous Farinelli.

[28]Johann Christian Bach (b., Leipzig, 1735; d., London, 1782).

report was published in *Philosophical Transactions*, 1770, Volume XL, and reprinted in Barrington's *Miscellanies* (1781).[29] I take the following extracts from the latter:

". . . At seven years of age his father carried him to Paris where he so distinguished himself by his compositions that an engraving was made of him.[30] The father and sister who are introduced are exceedingly like their portraits; so is also little Mozart, who is styled: '*Compositeur et Maître de Musique âgé de sept ans*.' After the name of the engraver follows the date which is in 1764; Mozart was therefore at this time in the eighth year of his age.

"Upon leaving Paris, he came to England where he continued more than a year. As during this time I was witness of his most extraordinary abilities as a musician, both at some public concerts and likewise having been alone with him for a considerable time at his father's house, I send you the following account, amazing and incredible almost as it may appear.

"I carried to him a manuscript duet, which was composed by an English gentleman to some favourite words in Metastasio's opera of *Demofoonte*. The whole score was in five parts —viz., accompanyments for a first and second violin, the two vocal parts and a bass. I shall here likewise mention that the parts for the first and second voice were written in the countertenor cleff; the reason for taking notice of which particular will appear hereafter.

"My intention in carrying with me this manuscript composition was to hear an irrefragable proof of his abilities as a player at sight, it being absolutely impossible that he could ever have seen the music before.

"The score was no sooner put upon his desk than he began to play the symphony in a most masterly manner, as well as in the time and stile which corresponded with the intention of the composer. I mention this circumstance because the greatest masters often fail in these particulars on the first trial. The symphony ended he took the upper part, leaving the under one to his father.

[29] It was published by J. Nichols and fronting the account of Mozart is a charming engraving of the seven-year-old child by T. Cook, with verses from Homer's *Hymn on Mercury*.

[30] This must be the engraving of Carmontelle's picture and it is interesting to have an eyewitness's testimony to its likeness.

"His voice, in the tone of it, was thin and infantine but nothing could exceed the masterly manner in which he sung.

"His father, who performed the under part in this duet, was once or twice out, though the passages were not more difficult than those in the upper one; on which occasions the son looked back with some anger, pointing out to him some mistakes and setting him right.

"He not only, however, did complete justice to the duet by singing his own part in the truest taste and with the greatest precision: he also threw in the accompanyments of the two violins, wherever they were most necessary and produced the best effects. It is wellknown that none but the most capital musicians are capable of accompanying in this superior stile.

". . . When he had finished the duet he expressed himself highly in its approbation, asking with some eagerness whether I had brought any more such music.

"Having been informed, however, that he was often visited with musical ideas, to which, even in the middle of the night, he would give utterance on his harpsichord; I told his father that I should be glad to hear some of his extemporary flights.

"The father shook his head at this, saying that it depended entirely upon his being as it were musically inspired, but that I might ask him whether he was in humour for such a composition.

"Happening to know that little Mozart was much taken notice of by Manzuoli, the famous singer who came over to England in 1764, I said to the boy that I should be glad to hear an extemporary *Love Song*, such as his friend Manzuoli might choose in an opera.

"The boy on this (who continued to sit at his harpsichord) looked back with much archness,[31] and immediately began five or six lines of a jargon recitative proper to introduce a love song.

"He then played a symphony which might correspond with an air composed to the single *affetto*.

"It had a first and second part, which, together with the symphonies was of the length that opera songs generally last: if this extemporary composition was not amazingly capital, yet

[31]Connoisseurs will never understand the amusements of genius but it does not matter so long as they are sincere.

it was really above mediocrity, and showed most extraordinary readiness of invention.

"Finding that he was in humour, and as it were inspired, I then desired him to compose a *Song of Rage* such as might be proper for the opera stage.

"The boy again looked back with much archness and began five or six lines of a jargon recitative proper to precede a *Song of Anger*.[32] This lasted also about the same time with the *Song of Love*; and in the middle of it he had worked himself up to such a pitch that he beat his harpsichord like a person possessed, rising sometimes in his chair.[33] The word he pitched upon for this second extemporary composition was, *Perfido*.

"After this he played a difficult lesson, which he had finished a day or two before; his execution was amazing considering that his little fingers could scarcely reach a sixth on the harpsichord.

"His astonishing readiness, however, did not arise merely from great practice; he had a thorough knowledge of the fundamental principles of composition as, upon producing a treble he immediately wrote a bass under it which when tried had a very good effect.

"He was also a great master of modulation and his transitions from one key to another were excessively natural and judicious. . . .

"The facts which I have been mentioning I was myself an eye-witness of. . . . Witness as I was myself . . . I must own that I could not help suspecting his father imposed with regard to the real age of the boy, though he had only a most childish appearance, but likewise had all the actions of that stage of life.[34]

"For example, whilst he was playing to me a favourite cat

[32]This worthy intellectual, Barrington, is a model of the intellectuals or "highbrows" of all time; but he is a good model, one which contemporaries of his kind should look up to if this attitude were within their capacity.

[33]Here we have the most illuminating piece of information. It is precisely in this passion that the *prodigy* Mozart showed his chief difference from other prodigies who have never fulfilled their early promise.

[34]Barrington made inquiries and obtained proof of Mozart's having been born in 1756 from the register in Salzburg. This examination was made in June 1765.

came in, upon which he immediately left his harpsichord, nor could we bring him back for a considerable time.

"He would also sometimes run about the room with a stick between his legs by way of horse. . . ."

It must be repeated here that musical precocity is no indubitable sign of genius but only of a certain musical talent. Samuel Wesley, William Crotch, and the father of the Duke of Wellington[35] were all musical prodigies almost as remarkable in their way as Mozart. It is a part of the materialistic philosophy of a certain type of mind common in every age among the educated (who of course display in this the fact that they are semi-educated, or what the Germans call *halbgebildete Leute*) to be always asking for a sign. These signs are to be supplied only on the lower planes, never on the higher ones. That is the reason why the true superiority of musicians such as Mozart, Schubert, Berlioz, and Beethoven is even to this day invisible to a great many musicians and connoisseurs. The prowess of child prodigies has its proper uses and among them may be mentioned the fact that the seven-year-old Mozart's musical capacity was accepted in Vienna during the heyday of Jewish proselytization to Christianity as evidence that at the age of seven the circumcized had acquired the capacity of deciding to become baptized.[36]

Before leaving London, Leopold presented to the British Museum a manuscript composition by Wolfgang for four voices, entitled *God is Our Refuge*, which was acknowledged as follows:

Sir,

I am ordered by the Standing Committee of the Trustees of the British Museum to signify to you, that they have received the present of the Musical performances of your very ingenious son, which you were pleased lately to make Them, and to return you their thanks for the same.

M. *Maty*,
Secretary

---

[35]Garrett Colley Wellesley, Earl of Mornington (b. 1735; d. 1781), composer of glees and madrigals.

[36]Hanslick: *Geschichte des Concertwesens in Wien* (Vienna, 1869). This has reference only to the age at which a child may be considered to be rational. There was no Jewish blood in Mozart so far as is known.

British Museum, July 19th, 1765

The Mozart family left London on July 24, 1765 for Canterbury, where they stayed with Sir Horace Mann, and finally left England on August 1 for The Hague at the pressing solicitation of the Dutch Ambassador, speaking for Princess Caroline of Nassau-Weilburg, sister of the Prince of Orange. They went from Calais to Lille when Wolfgang was ill with a severe cold. On the way to The Hague Wolfgang played the organ of the Church of St. Bernard in Ghent and also in Antwerp Cathedral. No sooner had they got to The Hague than Marianne and then Wolfgang fell ill. Leopold writes to Hagenauer:

Hague, November 5, 1765

. . . My poor daughter if not quite lost is in the last extremity . . . she caught cold the second day after our arrival; namely, September 12. At first it seemed slight . . . but on the 26th . . . she seemed to have fever in the throat . . . the doctor himself lost hope . . . on October 21 she . . . received the Last Sacrament. She was so weak she could hardly speak. Had anyone been able to hear the conversation which we three, my wife, I, and my daughter, had together many evenings . . . he could hardly have refrained from tears. During them Wolfgang occupied himself in another room with his music.

On October 21 the Princess of Weilburg sent to me the noble old Professor Schwencke, who soon showed that he understood his craft better . . . the whole time my daughter was delirious and in her sleep talked English, French, German in such a way that in spite of our trouble we often had to laugh. That had the effect of relieving Wolfgang a little of his sadness on account of his sister. . . .

Hague, December 12, 1765

. . . My daughter was hardly a week out of bed when [Wolfgang] fell ill and in four weeks was scarcely recognizable, being reduced to nothing but bone and skin . . . on the 30th he was in danger, but on December 1 better. After this he slept for about eight days and never spoke till at last his strength returned. Then he spoke day and night, but quite unintelligibly. . . .

In Holland Wolfgang composed six sonatas[37] for piano and
violin for the Princess of Nassau-Weilburg, which were engraved; also variations on the song *Wilhelmus von Nassau*[38]
and other trifles which were also published.[39] Wolfgang played
in concerts at The Hague and Amsterdam and Leopold's
Violin Method was translated into Dutch and published with
a dedication to the Prince of Orange. From Holland they
returned to Paris, arriving on May 10, and the two children,
Marianne and Wolfgang, again played several times at Versailles. Wolfgang also composed on June 12 a *Kyrie*[40] for four
voices with stringed accompaniment. Leaving Paris on July 9
with six post-horses, they went to Dijon, staying there fourteen
days at the request of the Prince of Condé on the occasion of
the assembly of the Estates of Burgundy; then on to Lyons,
where they stayed a month, arriving at Geneva in the midst
of the civil war.

In a letter to Hagenauer Leopold remarks:

Munich, November 10, 1766
. . . You perhaps know that quite near Geneva the celebrated Voltaire[41] has a place called Fernay where he lives . . .
from Lausanne we went to Berne and then to Zurich.[42] We
stayed only eight days at the former and fourteen at the latter.
In both places we had an opportunity to make the acquaintance of the intelligentsia;[43] at the latter the two learned Herr
Gessners[44] made our stay very pleasant and our departure sad.

[37]K.26–31.

[38]K.25.

[39]*Galimathias Musicum in F* (K.32).

[40]K.33.

[41]B. 1694; d. 1778.

[42]The Mozarts gave a concert at Zurich, as they did in most of the
larger towns where they made a prolonged stay.

[43]Leopold's word is *Gelehrten*.

[44]The physicist Johannes Gessner and the poet Salomon Gessner.
The latter presented Leopold and his wife with a copy of his works
inscribed:
"Accept this gift, dear friends, in the same friendly spirit in which
I offer it. May it preserve my memory fresh among you. May you,
venerable parents, long enjoy the sight of the happiness of your children, wherein consists the most precious fruit of their education; may
they be as happy as their merit is extraordinary! In the tenderest

. . . Thence via Winterthur to Schaffhausen. Here also our two weeks' stay was very pleasant.

In Donauschingen His Highness [Prince Joseph Wenzel von Fürstenberg] received us with extraordinary kindness . . . we were there twelve days; for nine days we had music from five to nine every night. . . . The Prince gave me twenty-four louis d'or and to each of my children a diamond ring. The tears streamed from his eyes as we took our leave of him. In short we all wept together at parting and he asked me to write often to him.

Then we went hell-for-leather via Messkirch, Ulm, Günzburg to Dillingen . . . after a day in Augsburg we arrived the night before last in Munich. . . .

PS. We beg you or rather your wife to find us a good maid-servant. . . .

God (the for me, unworthy man, all too good God) has given to my children such talents as incite me—apart from the obligations of a father—to devote everything to their good education. Every moment that I lose is lost for ever and if ever I have realized how invaluable time is for the young it is now. You know that my children are accustomed to work. Should they become used to idleness my whole edifice is overthrown. Habit is an iron shirt and you yourself know how much my children, especially Wolfgang, have to learn. Who knows what our return to Salzburg brings. Perhaps we shall be received in such a way that we shall gladly take up our pack and set off again. At any rate I bring the children back to their Fatherland. If they are not wanted I am not to blame. . . .

On the way to Munich, at Biberach, at the request of Count Fugger von Babenhausen, Wolfgang competed on the organ with Sixtus Bachmann, who was two years his senior, and this competition aroused great interest. In Munich Wolfgang was again taken ill, and on his recovery the family returned to Salzburg at the end of November 1766, after an absence of more than three years.[45]

---

youth they are an honour to their country and the admiration of the world. Happy parents! happy children! . . .

"SALOMON GESSNER

"Zurich
    "August 3, 1766"

[45]They had left Salzburg on June 9, 1763.

III. Mozart's Development as a Child

1763–1766   AGE 7–10

Mozart left Salzburg on his great European tour as a child prodigy at the age of seven and returned to Salzburg at the age of ten. During this period, as we have seen, he visited most of the principal towns of South Germany, of France, of Belgium, and of Holland besides staying over a year in England. Apart from his public concerts he was frequently playing at courts and in private houses. He also met most of the eminent musicians and composers in every city and was everywhere taken by his father to the opera and to the principal churches where there was music worth hearing. In addition he composed a quantity of music, which comprises, in the old Köchel catalogue, numbers from K.6 to K.33; in addition to which we must add, according to Wyzewa and Saint-Foix, the twenty-five *Petites Pièces de musique* (K. *anhang* 109[b]), of which the autograph is in Berlin, composed at Chelsea between April and December 1764, and the *Trois Sonatas pour clavecin de Jean-Chrétien Bach*, in D, G, and E flat (K.107), arranged as concertos with accompaniment of two violins and a figured bass.

It is worth briefly reviewing the chief musical contacts which he made during this three-year tour, some of which I have already mentioned in the previous chapter. At Stuttgart he heard the famous violinist Nardini and the orchestra under Jomelli. At Schwetzingen he heard the Mannheim orchestra, reputed the best in Germany, the creation of J. W. A. Stamitz.[1] At Brussels he was introduced to the sonatas of J. G. Eckard,[2] who had settled in Paris in 1758. Eckard was a pupil of Philipp Emanuel Bach, who took from

[1] Johann Wenzl Anton Stamitz (1717–57), a Bohemian violinist and composer; his brother, Anton Thaddeus, was a 'cellist in the Mannheim band.

[2] Johann Gottfried Eckard or Eckardt (b., Augsburg, 1735; d., Paris, 1809), a famous pianist and composer, considered by Burney and Grimm to be superior as a pianist to his rival Schobert. He was also a brilliant miniature-painter.

his master the newly conceived sonata form and contributed to its evolution: namely, to its principle of thematic development and to its three-movement construction. Eckard made much use of the Alberti[3] bass, which enters largely into Wolfgang's sonatas composed in Paris and London. The sonata was a musical product of mixed Italian-German origin, and in the eighteenth century music was as international as it is now, the influence of any inventive or originating mind spreading quickly among all the musicians throughout Europe. More gifted as a composer than Eckard was Schobert,[4] who had settled in Paris in 1760 and had many of his compositions printed there. It was a musical period in which the pianoforte was about to be substituted for the harpsichord, the sonata had already taken the place of the suite, and homophony was encroaching upon counterpoint. Here are a few bars from the first allegro of the Sonata in C (K.6), composed by Wolfgang at Brussels on October 14, 1763.

Here we find the Alberti bass, and the sonata as a whole, according to Wyzewa and Saint-Foix, shows distinct traces of the style of Eckard, whose *Six Sonatas for the Harpsichord*

[3]Domenico Alberti (b., Venice, 1710; d., Rome, 1740) probably did not invent the Alberti bass, but he made such persistent use of it that it bears his name. It consists of breaking the notes of a chord conveniently for the left hand on the keyboard. It is the popular tum-ti tum-ti bass.

[4]Johann Schobert (b. c. 1720; d. 1767), educated at Strassburg, sometime organist at Versailles. According to Burney he was one of the few composers of his time not influenced by Philipp Emanuel Bach.

were printed at Paris in May 1763 and were among the sonatas
played in public by Wolfgang, so Leopold informs us.

Another composition of the seven-year-old Wolfgang, written between June and October 1763, and probably also at
Brussels, must be quoted, as it shows more than precocious
skill. The manuscript, written in Wolfgang's own hand, is in
the Mozarteum at Salzburg.

Andante (incomplete) in B flat for Harpsichord (K.9b)

We know from Leopold's letters that Wolfgang met Eckard and Schobert in Paris and played their sonatas. Schobert was harpsichordist in the service of the Prince de Conti, and possibly Schobert himself is among the figures in the salon of the Prince shown in the painting by Olliver.[5] The French harpsichord-players such as Le Grand and Charpentier were at this time all publishing sonatas in the German style, just as their theatrical music was under the influence of Italy. Schobert is claimed as a French composer by Wyzewa and Saint-Foix although his name suggests a Germanic origin[6] and he was educated at Strassburg. However, his music was influenced by the French tradition and had a grace and sensitiveness which made it more attractive to Wolfgang than the more learned and scholastic work of Eckard. According to Wyzewa and Saint-Foix, Schobert was the first composer to write sonatas for harpsichord with a violin part and is thus the creator of the modern sonata for pianoforte and violin. One of the signs of his influence on Wolfgang is that after his visit to Paris Wolfgang only published sonatas *"pouvant se jouer avec l'accompagnement du violon."* It was from Schobert, according

---

[5]Original in the Louvre.

[6]Grimm says: *"Schobert était Silésien."*

to the same authority, that Mozart got the practice of often using the minuet form for the finale of his sonatas.

But it was not so much the form of Schobert that influenced Wolfgang as the spirit, for the most striking characteristic of Schobert was his sensibility, with an inclination to the minor keys and to strongly pathetic and emotional expression and *tempo rubato*. Wyzewa finds in the first Sonata in D of Op. III of Schobert, published in Paris in 1764, hints of the Schubert of the *Erl-King* and *The Wanderer*. This access of sensibility in music was something rather new and here we may, as we like, either find the influence of Rousseau[7] or consider that it was just part of the general development of the romantic spirit, the urge to a more natural and free expression, of which Rousseau was only one of the manifestations. Musical historians and critics are apt to forget—if they ever knew—that Goethe's *Sorrows of Werther* was published in 1774, when Mozart was only eighteen years old, and that, so far from belonging to a formal and so-called classical age or to the stiffest period of eighteenth-century routine or its final decadence in rococo triviality, Mozart was born in the *Sturm und Drang* period and belongs as completely and characteristically to the European romantic revival as William Blake, who was born in 1757, the year after Mozart's birth. It was Mozart's father, Leopold, who belonged to the pre-Revolutionary epoch; whereas Mozart was twenty-four years younger than Beaumarchais,[8] and the French Revolutionary spirit was in full flood during his lifetime. Nearly all Lessing's[9] finest literary work, for example, was published during Mozart's childhood, and the German writers of this new age—Klopstock, Wieland, Herder, and so on—were all Mozart's seniors.

The fact is that the picture some musical writers have been

[7] Jean Jacques Rousseau (b., Geneva, 1712; d., near Paris, 1778), author of the celebrated *Confessions*, *Émile*, and *Le Contrat social* (1762). Rousseau was also a composer and writer on music; his best-known composition was *Le Devin du village*, produced at the Paris Opéra on March 1, 1753 and often repeated until 1829, when some wag (supposed to be Berlioz, who, however, denied it) gave it its death-blow by throwing an immense powdered perruque on the stage.

[8] Pierre Augustin Caron de Beaumarchais (1732–99), author of the famous satire on the old regime, *The Marriage of Figaro* (1778).

[9] Gotthold Ephraim Lessing (1729–81), perhaps the greatest German writer between Luther and Goethe.

pleased to draw of Mozart as a highly refined and sophisti-
cated product of aristocratic eighteenth-century dilettantism,
the last and over-delicate flower of salon culture, is historically
as well as psychologically false. This, certainly, was the environment in which he was born, but the seeds of revolution had
already been sown. Voltaire had long ago done his great work
and was looked upon by Mozart's father as very little better
than the devil, while Rousseau's *Le Contrat social* was published when Mozart was six years old. Mozart's whole social
outlook was entirely different from his father's and the difference in temperament is strikingly shown even when as an
eight-year-old child in Paris in 1764 he was attracted to the
music of Schobert by an affinity of nature, whereas his father,
Leopold, did not approve of Schobert, describing him as "low
and not at all what he should be."

Mozart is hardly likely to have come into contact with
Rameau, whose *Castor et Pollux* was the piece with which the
Paris Opéra reopened on January 23, 1764, for Rameau was
an old man of eighty-one; his music was already out of fashion
and Italian opera had become the vogue; the operas performed
in Paris during the winter of 1763–4, while the Mozarts were
there, which were more to the taste of the public were by
Duni,[10] Philidor,[11] and Monsigny.[12] It is worth noting that
Philidor's famous *Le Sorcier*, just performed at the Comédie-
Italienne on January 2, 1764 with enormous success, was influenced to some extent by Gluck's *Orphée*, which had
appeared in Vienna in 1762, but was not to be heard in Paris
in the revised form until 1774. Monsigny had been inspired
to the composition of comic opera by Pergolesi's[13] *La Serva
Padrona*, which was first produced in Paris in 1746, but met
with its real success on its revival there in 1752. The capricious-
ness of fame is shown in the fact that such an eminent musi-

[10]Egidio Romoaldo Duni (b., Naples, 1709; d., Paris, 1775).

[11]François André Danican Philidor (b., Dreux, 1726; d., London,
1795) is considered by some authorities to surpass his contemporaries
Monsigny and Grétry as an operatic composer. He was a chess
prodigy and at the age of eighteen was equal to the best masters and
earned his living at the game. He wrote a well-known treatise, *Analyse
du jeu des échecs*, which was translated into English.

[12]Pierre Alexandre Monsigny (1729–1817), one of the best of
French comic-opera composers.

[13]B. 1710; d. 1736.

cologist as Professor Edward J. Dent considers Pergolesi to be inferior in comic opera to his contemporaries Leo and Logroscino, composers whose work is now known only to scholars and historians. But the idea that the best works are those which are most frequently performed one or more hundred years after they were written is as naïvely untrue as the idea that the best works are those which are most popular during their author's lifetime. The truth is contrary to both these superstitions and it is this—that there is always a general tendency for the best works to disappear from public sight or hearing and to be replaced by inferior ones; it is by dint of a constant effort made by the few that the best survives from generation to generation. Duni is said to have remarked to Pergolesi after the performance of his *L'Olimpiade*: "Your opera is far too good to succeed," and whether true or not of this particular work, this remark expresses an everlasting truth. Even today Mozart's *Die Entführung aus dem Serail* is more popular than the finer *Così fan Tutte*, for example.

In England the Mozarts must have heard a great deal of the music of Handel, who had died only five years before their arrival in London. We know that Wolfgang heard the overture to *Esther* and that during his visit Handel's *Messiah*, *Judas Maccabæus*, *Alexander's Feast*, *Israel in Egypt*, and *Sampson* were performed at Covent Garden, while Handel was the favourite composer at the court of George III. But perhaps the chief influence on the child was that of Johann Christian Bach, with whom Wolfgang was brought into close personal contact. Of all the sons of Johann Sebastian, this, the youngest and so-called "English" Bach, was the most Italianate; so that the Italian influence which was prevailing in opera in Paris was reinforced in London, especially as the opera in London was wholly Italian, there being no English opera whatsoever.

Another composer he made contact with was Abel,[14] a pupil at the Thomasschule of J. S. Bach. Wolfgang actually transcribed in his own hand a symphony by Abel. This work in E flat (K.18) was for long considered as an original work by Mozart but was discovered by Wyzewa and Saint-Foix to be a transcription, without the change of a single note, of the

[14]Karl Friedrich Abel (b., Cöthen, 1725; d., London, 1787), a famous viola da gamba player and composer.

last of the six overtures published by Abel as his Op. VII. An interesting fact is that in Mozart's transcript there are parts for two clarinets which in Abel's published score are written for oboes; but Wyzewa and Saint-Foix believe that this alteration was made later by Abel, owing to the rarity in those days of the clarinet, whereas it is known that there were two clarinet-players at the opera in London in 1763, used in J. C. Bach's *Orione*. Abel and J. C. Bach were close friends and collaborators and their influence is to be seen in Wolfgang's sonatas and symphonies composed in London. Of the symphonies composed by Wolfgang in London I shall quote only the first few bars of the Symphony in D (K.19), which was written in the spring of 1765 for two violins, alto, bass, two oboes, and two horns. The horns are only used for doubling, but the oboes have a definitely characterized part. This is the opening rhythmic subject:

It is worth remarking that in these London symphonies—the first he composed—Mozart makes much use of alternations of *forte* and *piano* and occasionally of *mezzo forte*, *forte piano*, and *sempre piano* marks, gives a certain independence to the alto, and distinguishes the 'cello from the double-bass. From the careful analysis made by Wyzewa and Saint-Foix of these early compositions of Mozart, Abert drew the conclusion that Mozart arrived in London in 1764 a child of genius of nine years of age and left it in 1765, aged ten, an accomplished master of the contemporary craft of composition equal to any living composer of the time. The extraordinary impressionability of Mozart, which is one of his outstanding characteristics, is shown by the way in which he was always being affected by and absorbing the music he met with and reflecting it in his own work. It is the opinion of Wyzewa and Saint-Foix that in Holland, after his departure from London, Wolfgang first came across the early clavier sonatas of Joseph Haydn, which were first published by Breitkopf in 1766. It is certain that Haydn, who in this year was thirty-four years of age, was already well known as a composer outside his own country, and symphonies and quartets of his were to be had in print in Amsterdam, Paris, and London. The official gazette, *Wiener Diarium*, speaks of Haydn in 1766 as *der Liebling unserer Nation* (the darling of our nation) and compares him with Gellert, at that time not only Leopold Mozart's but the nation's most esteemed poet.[15]

It is worth mentioning here some observations made by Hermann Abert, based more or less on Wyzewa and Saint-Foix's exhaustive studies of Mozart's early music, but which even a cursory examination of Mozart's music and personality would support. "The young Mozart," he says, "is not to be placed wholly in either of the two main groups into which most great composers fall; neither in form nor in expression does he appear as a conscious innovator, but he is also just as free from having a fixed goal in the light of tradition. He is, indeed, the most impressionable of all the great composers. There was not a single musical influence of his age which he did not feel, and in his youth, like the young Goethe, he gave himself up to them without reservation or plan, like a butterfly flitting from flower to flower."

But this sensibility, as Abert properly takes care to add, was no sign of chaos or of lack of individuality. It was rather the discovery of himself in others and a sign of his quite extraordinarily catholic and universal nature. Mozart was never a mere imitator, but he was so exceedingly many-sided that he found himself everywhere in the world of music that surrounded him.

---

[15]The habit of bracketing Haydn and Mozart together as if they were contemporaries overlooks this great discrepancy in their ages; actually Haydn belonged to the generation of Mozart's father, Leopold.

iv. Salzburg and Vienna

Let us consider for a moment this prodigy of nature, Wolfgang Mozart, now returned to his home in Salzburg, a child of ten who is already not only an accomplished musician but a master musician. We may compare the portrait of him in his Viennese gala clothes, aged six, in 1762, or the delightful one by Zoffany painted in London in 1764, described as "Mozart with the bird's nest," with the one by Thaddeus Helbling on his return to Salzburg in 1776–7, seated at his clavier. The difference is notable. About his eleventh birthday Mozart is visibly leaving childhood behind him. The expression is serious and reflective although still immature; but quickly comes the thought: how unlike all the pictures of Mozart must be to his living appearance! For Mozart, perhaps even more than most great men, must have showed his genius in his expression and his eyes.

We know nothing of what literary or general instruction Wolfgang received in Salzburg on his return, but his musical instruction continued and he was soon kept busy with composition. On the exercises his father set him his lively fancy made him give names to parts such as *il Signor d'Alto*, *il Marchese Tenore*, *il Duca Basso*, and this same fancy constructed on his return journey homewards an imaginary kingdom, named by him *Rücken*, inhabitated by children, of which he was King. What he imagined was so real to him that he got the servant, who happened to be a good draughtsman, to make a map of it, which he furnished with names of places.

Wolfgang's study of counterpoint, directed by Leopold, was based on Fux's[1] *Gradus ad Parnassum* and his exercise book of eighty-two pages, now in the Mozarteum, consists

[1]Johann Joseph Fux (b., Styria, 1660; d., Vienna, 1741), composer and theorist with a marvellous knowledge of counterpoint. His *Gradus* was published first in Latin in 1725, in German 1742, Italian 1761, French 1773, English 1791.

chiefly of examples of two- and three-part counterpoint. His musical activity during the year 1767 in Salzburg may be judged from the fact that within this period he composed— at the command of the Archbishop Sigismund and on commission from other residents—one part of the oratorio *Die Schuldigkeit des ersten Gebotes*,[2] a Latin cantata, a German cantata for Lent, an offertory, a *Licenza* or festival music for the anniversary of the Archbishop's consecration, a symphony, a serenade, and a cassation (instrumental music for the open air). In addition to these works the catalogue made by his father in 1768 mentions the following compositions now lost: namely, six *Divertimenti* in four parts for various instruments; six trios for two violins and violoncello, and a number of minuets, marches, and fanfares for trumpets and kettle-drums.

It is not my intention to analyse these works or give detailed particulars of them although I shall mention that the Latin cantata was a sort of academic comedy presented at the Salzburg University on May 13, 1767, entitled *Apollo et Hyacinthus seu Hyacinthi Metamorphosis*,[3] which consisted of long, detached airs and duets, recitatives, choruses, and overture, with a Latin text. Mozart's Latin at eleven years old may be judged from the following letter he wrote to an unknown friend two years later, which shows he was still studying it:

Dear Friend,

I beg your forgiveness for taking the liberty of troubling you with these few lines; but since you said yesterday that you understood everything and that I might write Latin to you as much as I liked, I cannot refrain from sending you at once some Latin lines; when you have read them, please send the answer back by one of your servants, for ours cannot wait. But you must send me the answer in a letter.

[2] *The Obligation of the First Commandment* (K.35), printed in Salzburg 1767. First part, music by Herr Wolfgang Mozart, aged ten years, second part by Herr Johann Michael Heiden (Haydn), Court Concertmeister, third part by Herr Anton Cajetan Adlgasser, Court Composer and Organist. The autograph of this score in Mozart's boyish writing was found by C. F. Pohl in the Royal Library at Windsor (A.M.Z., 1865, p. 225).

[3] K.38. Manuscript autograph at Berlin, composed for two sopranos, two altos, one tenor, and choruses, with accompaniment of two violins, two altos, two oboes, two horns, and bass.

Cuperem scire, de qua causa, aquam plurimis adolescenti-bus ottium usque adeo aestimatur, ut ipsi se nec verbis nec verberibus, ab hoc sinant abduci.

Wolfgang Mozart

A quotation from the cantata entitled *Grab-Musik*, 1767 (K.42), a dialogue between the Soul and an Angel, may be given as an example of what Mozart was composing at the age of eleven; the autograph is in Berlin:

On September 11, 1767 Leopold and his whole family set out on a visit to Vienna, where the approaching marriage of the Archduchess Maria Josepha to King Ferdinand of Naples gave hope of festivities at which opportunities for making known the talents of Wolfgang might be plentiful. The letters from Leopold to Hagenauer provide the particulars of this journey. On September 22 he writes from Vienna: "Of our doings here I have nothing to report yet. Every day there is an opera seria or buffa or a comedy." On the 29th he writes: "Hasse's[4] opera *Partenope* is good but the singers are nothing special, particularly for such a festival . . . the dancing, however, is superb, the principal being the Frenchman Vestris."[5]

Unfortunately an attack of smallpox broke out in Vienna and the Archduchess Josepha caught it. This held up all their expectations. "Do not be surprised," Leopold writes from Vienna on October 14, "if we take out four hundred or even five hundred gulden. *Aut Cæsar aut nihil!* A day will perhaps come that will alone pay for everything. We have not yet played anywhere because we have not yet played at court." His next news, on October 17, was that the Archduchess had become "a heavenly bride!" Leopold had been advised when in Paris to follow the example of the Duke of Orléans and have his children vaccinated, but he wrote on February 22, 1764: "I prefer to leave it all in God's hands; let Him in His divine mercy dispose as He will of the life of this wonder of nature."

Now, however, he and his family fled, but too late, from Vienna to Olmütz, from whence he writes on November 10, 1767:

"*Te Deum laudamus!* Wolfgangerl has happily recovered from the smallpox. And where? In Olmütz. And where? In the house of His Excellency Count Leopold Anton von Podstatsky. . . . We reached Olmütz on Monday, the 26th. To our disgust we had to put up with a bad, damp room in the Schwarzen Adler, since all the others were taken. We were obliged to have a fire and, more vexation, the stove smoked so that we were almost blinded. At ten o'clock Wolfgang complained about his eyes. I noticed that his head was hot, also his cheeks, which were very red, while on the contrary his hands were icy cold. His pulse was also not normal. We gave him some *Schwarzpulver* and put him to sleep. He was rather restless all night and still more hot and dry in the morning.

---

[4]Johann Adolph Hasse (b., Hamburg, 1699; d., Venice, 1783), the most popular German opera-composer of the first half of the eighteenth century, a pupil of Porpora and A. Scarlatti.

[5]Marie Françoise Thérèse Vestris (b., Florence, 1731; d., Paris, 1808), a member of the famous family of dancers and singers.

We got two better rooms and wrapped Wolfgang in furs. . . .
His temperature increased. We gave him *Mark-grafenpulver*
and *Schwarzpulver*. Towards evening he became delirious and
remained so the whole of October 28.

"After church I went to Count von Podstatsky, who received me most graciously, and told him that my little one was
ill and I feared he might have smallpox, whereupon he said he
would take us in as he was not afraid at all of it. He called his
housekeeper, instructed him to get two rooms ready, and sent
for a doctor. . . .

"In the afternoon at four o'clock we wrapped Wolfgang in
shawls and furs, put him in the carriage, and took him to the
Count's. On the 29th he had small red pock-marks, but we
doubted he had smallpox as he seemed less ill. He took
nothing but a powder every six hours and always *Skabiosentee*.

"On the 30th and 31st on my birthday the smallpox came
fully out and as soon as this happened all distemper was gone.
And, thank God, he felt better. He was astonishingly swollen
and had a thick nose. When at last he saw himself in the
mirror he said: 'Now I look like Mayrl!' by which he meant
the musician Mayr.

". . . I cannot describe the kindness and goodness with
which we have been treated. I will only ask how often it has
happened that a whole family and child in such circumstances
have been taken in and cared for out of pure humanity.
This act will do no little honour to Count von Podstatsky
in the biography of our little one that I intend to publish
some day, for I consider that a new epoch in his life begins
now. . . ."

No sooner had Wolfgang recovered from smallpox than
his sister Marianne caught it; when she recovered they returned to Vienna. Wolfgang had to be careful of his eyes for
some time—he had been blind for many days—and relieved
his convalescence by learning to play cards and fencing. He
was at all times very fond of bodily activity; as soon as he
could compose again, he wrote a little aria for the daughter
of his physician, Wolf.[6]

They arrived back in Vienna on January 10, 1768 and were

---

[6]Leopold refers to this in a letter to his son ten years later, dated
May 28, 1778, when he writes: "From Ollmütz came Dr. Wolf, for
whose daughter Wolfgang composed an aria. . . ."

received at court by the Empress Maria Theresa. "His Majesty
the Emperor," writes Leopold to Hagenauer from Vienna on
January 23, 1768:
"came into the antechamber where we were waiting until they
had had their coffee and himself led us in. There were present
only Prince Albert of Sachsen-Teschen and the Archduchesses
. . . you cannot imagine with what kindness the Empress spoke
with my wife about the children's illness and our great tour,
pressing her hand and stroking her cheeks compassionately
while the Emperor spoke with me and Wolfgang about musical and other matters and made Nannerl blush very often. You
must not conclude from this affability that we shall get an
exceptional present."

Leopold's realistic clear-headedness was not deceived; in
spite of her geniality the Empress presented them with no
more than a fine but valueless medal. Since the death of her
husband the Empress had ceased to visit the opera or to give
musical parties, and musical commissions depended now upon
her son, the Emperor Joseph, who was notoriously parsimonious. The Mozarts, however, had many friends at court
—namely, Count von Dietrichstein, the Master of the Horse,
Fräulein Josepha Guttenburg, "the Empress's right hand,"
the court physician, L'Augier, a talented and accomplished
music-lover whose house was the meeting-place of learned and
cultured society, and, especially important, the Duke Johann
Carl of Braganza, a man of spirit and character who had distinguished himself in the Lisbon earthquake and in the Austrian army and to whom Gluck[7] dedicated later, in 1770, his
opera *Paride ed Elena*. It was now the carnival season and
nothing was thought of but balls, masquerades, and dances,
which it was the habit—according to Leopold—of the court to
farm out, sharing the profits with the contractors. Quite apart
from this seasonal form of legitimate gaiety the Mozarts had
other obstacles to contend with. One of them was the general
low level of taste of the majority of the nobility and wealthy
classes.

The pictures that some writers have drawn, looking back
upon the eighteenth century from the depressing standpoints
of their contemporary scenes in the nineteenth and twentieth

[7]Christoph Willibald Ritter von Gluck (b. 1714; d., Vienna,
1787).

centuries, are much too rose-coloured. The majority, as at all times and everywhere in the past (and as it will be in that Utopian future so dear to the young and enthusiastic), is always the same in this respect—that its *niveau*, its habitual level, is lower than that of the truly superior minority. There is only one change which time and occasion bring with varying intensity, and that is the degree and extent of the majority's education. There are ages of widespread or lesser-spread culture; there are countries and towns more illiterate than others. The spread of education and literacy may add rather more opportunities to the many, but it chiefly adds a new and even more potent barrier to the activity of the few; because for every new and better-equipped appreciator of music, poetry, or any other form of art, it produces one hundred additional "highbrows," intellectuals, connoisseurs, dilettantes—call them what you will—who are mere egoists, devoid of either understanding, respect, or love, and who are the bitterest enemies of art and of artists although their talk is of nothing else. They have knowledge—the knowledge of dates, of periods, of æsthetic theories—and they have seen and heard everything, but experienced nothing.[8] Of all audiences, this is the worst for the genuine artist, but it comprises ninety per cent of what is described as the cultured audiences everywhere. The real tastes of such people are shown in their enthusiasms; they are never enthusiastic about art; they know too much and their only pleasure is in airing their knowledge; but when it comes to their real pleasures on lower levels, then they are not critical at all, but extravagantly enthusiastic. In the twentieth century the real pleasures of such cultured people—"highbrows," intellectuals, etc.—remain what they have always been. Let Leopold Mozart himself describe them. He writes to Hagenauer:

Vienna, February 3, 1768

The Viennese—to speak generally—are not eager for anything serious and sensible and have little or no understanding of it; that they care for nothing but utter trash, burlesques, harlequinades, ghost tricks, farces, and devil's antics, is well known and their theatres furnish proof of it daily. You may

---

[8]"What is a connoisseur?" asked Oscar Wilde rhetorically, and replied with profound truth: "A man who knows the price of everything and the value of nothing." One might add "date" to "price."

see a fine gentleman, even with an order on his breast, laughing till the tears run down his face and applauding with all his might some senseless buffoonery or simple joke, while in a most affecting scene where the situation and action are irresistibly fine and stirring and where the dialogue is of the highest order he will chatter so loud with a lady that his better-disposed neighbours cannot hear a word. . . .

This, Leopold tells Hagenauer, is the chief cause of their difficulties; another is the character of the court, with its parsimonious Emperor. He also describes amusingly the fear of smallpox, which prevented Prince Kaunitz, a well-known musical connoisseur, from doing anything for them, as he ran from all who showed a trace of it, and Wolfgang, adds Leopold, "has still many red spots, small, it is true, but clearly visible in the cold weather." In this same letter of February 3, 1768 Leopold continues:

"As I now reflected over these matters and thought on how much money I had spent and that to return home now without further waiting would be great cowardice, there was a new development. I found that all the clavier-players and composers in Vienna were opposed to us with the single exception of Wagenseil,[9] who, being ill, however, could be of little use to us. The tactics these people used were to avoid carefully any opportunity of seeing us and of learning the extent of Wolfgang's capacity. And for what reason? In order that, when asked whether they had heard the boy and what they thought of him, they might be able to reply that they had not heard him and that what was said of him could not be true, but must be an imposture of humbug and that what he was given to play was prepared and it was ridiculous to suppose he could compose. You see that is why they avoid us, for if they saw and heard him, then they could not talk thus without endangering their honour.

"But I set a trap for one of these gentry. I persuaded someone to give us private notice of when he would be present and

[9]Georg Christoph Wagenseil (b., Vienna, 1715; d. 1777), famous clavier-player and composer, music-master to the Empress Maria Theresa. When Wolfgang, aged six, in Vienna on his first visit, was playing before the court, he inquired: "Is not Herr Wagenseil here? He knows all about it," and when Wagenseil came forward, said to him: "I am playing one of your concertos, you must turn over for me."

to induce him to bring an exceptionally difficult concerto which should be put before Wolfgang. We arrived and he had the opportunity of hearing his concerto played by Wolfgang as if he knew it by heart. The astonishment of this clavier-player and composer, his expression, and his exclamations in his amazement made us all realize the truth of what I have already told you. In the end he said: 'As an honest man I can only say that this boy is the greatest musician living in our time in the world. I could not have believed it.'

"And so to convince the public of what it has before it I determined on something quite exceptional: to wit, that Wolfgang should compose an opera. Can you imagine the outcry that arose among the composers? 'What! shall we hear Gluck[10] today, and tomorrow see a boy of twelve years of age sit at the harpsichord and conduct his own opera?' Yes, and in spite of all braying idiots! I have even brought Gluck over to our side, at least so far that even if he is not whole-hearted he can't let it be noticed, since our protectors are also his. And in order to secure the actors, who habitually cause most vexation to the composer, I have spoken with them myself and one of them will keep me informed. The first idea to let Wolfgang write an opera came to me in truth from the Emperor himself, since he twice asked Wolfgang whether he would like to compose an opera and conduct it himself. Wolfgang replied eagerly: 'Yes. . . .' But it will not be an opera seria, for no more are being given and they are not popular, but an opera buffa. Not a short one, but one lasting two and a half to three hours. For opera seria there are no singers. Even Gluck's tragic opera *Alceste* has been performed by opera-buffa singers. Now Gluck is writing an opera buffa. The opera-buffa singers are excellent.[11] . . . What do you think of this? Is not the renown of having written an opera for Vienna the best way to win credit not only in Germany but also in Italy?"

A few words on opera seria, opera buffa, and singspiel are needed here, as these terms will often recur. At this stage, however, I shall only say briefly what is necessary. Opera seria means, roughly, serious opera, which in the early eighteenth century had a rather stereotyped form, consisting of recita-

[10]Gluck's *Alceste* had been produced in Vienna on December 16, 1767—only about a month before the time of Leopold's writing.

[11]Leopold names eight singers, all Italian.

tives and arias with the leading roles taken by *castrati* (artificial male sopranos); opera buffa was a more popular form,
derived from the lighter intermezzi, with which opera seria
was interspersed; its structure was also made up of recitatives
and arias, but bass voices were introduced and given important
roles. The difference between opera buffa and singspiel is that
the latter is a German form in which the music plays a less
important dramatic and a more lyrical part; also in singspiel
there is usually, though not always, spoken dialogue in the
place of the recitative *secco*[12] or *stromentato*[13] of opera buffa.
All these forms were in full development in Italy, Germany,
and France in Mozart's childhood.

The novelty of *Alceste*, which Leopold and Wolfgang had
heard in Vienna during this visit, consisted chiefly in the
genius of Gluck. In principle he was only composing an opera
seria in accordance with the ideas of Benedetto Marcello, who
in his *Teatro alla Modo* (1720) appealed for dramatic propriety in opera. Marcello was a poet as well as a composer, and
his ideals in opera have been those of every great operatic
composer at all times. They can be simply summed up in one
sentence from Gluck's celebrated preface to *Alceste*, which
runs as follows:

"I endeavoured to reduce music to its proper function, that
of seconding poetry by enforcing the expression of the sentiment and the interest of the situation without interrupting the
action or weakening it by superfluous ornament."

I have elsewhere[14] remarked that there is only one word
wrong in this famous sentence of Gluck's and that is the
word *reduce*, which should be changed to *heighten* or *raise*.
For music can have no higher goal than expression; when it
becomes mere abstract pattern or "ornament" it sinks to the
level of the decorative, which in all the arts is on a lower plane
than the expressive.

But Gluck's use of the word *reduce* is an unwitting sign of
the limitation of his musical genius—which is a matter I shall
have cause to speak about when I am dealing with the great

---

[12]*Secco*—dry or bare; i.e., in free verbal rhythm spaced with accompanying chords.

[13]*Stromentato*—instrumental; i.e., with a more musical rhythmic
accompanying pattern.

[14]*Berlioz, the Man and His Works* (Dent, 1934).

operas of Mozart's maturity.[15] It suffices to say here that in dramatic truthfulness and power of expression Gluck's *Alceste*, when first produced in Vienna on December 16, 1767, was far superior to all other contemporary operas. Yet it did not escape the fate of most great works on their first appearance, as we learn from Sonnenfels, in his *Gesammelte Schriften*, who mimics the gossip of the nobility in the boxes of the Vienna opera-house as follows:

"What! this is meant to be pathetic? Well, perhaps we shall shed a few tears presently—from ennui.

"Come, this is throwing money away! It is too absurd, a fool of a woman dying for her husband!"

This is typical of the stuff talked by the "snobs" throughout the ages.

Through the recommendation of the Emperor and the influence of his court friends Leopold was able to get a contract from Affligio,[16] the entrepreneur who held the lease of the theatre, for Wolfgang to compose an opera to a text by Marco Coltellini, who had been "theatrical poet" in Vienna since 1758 and had written librettos for Gassmann,[17] Hasse, and Salieri.[18] Coltellini delivered the text, and Wolfgang set to work on his first opera, *La Finta Semplice* (K.51), to try to get it completed by Easter 1768, and in due course finished his score of three acts, containing twenty-five numbers, written on five hundred and fifty-eight pages.

Even before the opera was finished the usual intrigues inseparable from theatrical enterprise began. Affligio put them off from Easter to Whitsuntide, and as soon as one difficulty was disposed of, another arose. At length Affligio declared that he would put on Wolfgang's opera if Leopold insisted, but would take care to have it hissed off the stage. In the

[15]See note p. 319.

[16]One of the tribe of impresarios so necessary to the theatre; an adventurer who obtained a commission in the army by swindling and ended his life in the galleys for forgery. He had a good run on other people's money and was probably superior to most of his critics.

[17]Florian Leopold Gassmann (b., Bohemia, 1729; d., Vienna, 1774), composer and in 1772 appointed court Kapellmeister by the Emperor Joseph II.

[18]Antonio Salieri (b., Legnano, 1750; d., Vienna, 1825), a pupil of Gassmann, composer and court Kapellmeister after Gassmann's successor, Bonno.

meantime Leopold's long absence from Salzburg was endangering his position as first violin and assistant Kapellmeister; he was told he might stay away as long as he liked, but that he would no longer be paid during his absence. He writes to Hagenauer:

Vienna, July 30, 1768

. . . Nothing but our honour keeps us here; otherwise we should long since have been in Salzburg. Would you like the whole of Vienna to be saying that Wolfgang was not able to finish the opera or that it had turned out so badly that it could not be produced or that his father, not he, had written it? Would you care to have such lies spread in all countries? . . .

What does His Majesty the Emperor say to it all? On this point I can only touch briefly . . . the theatre is leased or, rather, given over to Affligio, who must pay annually one thousand gulden, which the court otherwise would have to pay. The Emperor and his whole family have the right of free entry. Consequently the court cannot say a word to this Affligio, as he takes all the risks. . . .

The singers, who in any case scarcely know their notes . . . and must learn by ear, now began to say they could not sing their arias (which they had already heard in our room, approved of, and applauded) as they were not suitable, the orchestra that it would not be conducted by a boy, etc., etc.

Meanwhile others declared the music was not worth a groat . . . because the boy did not sufficiently understand Italian. When I heard this I let it be known in important quarters that Hasse and the great Metastasio[19] had declared that these calumniators might come to them and hear from their own lips that thirty operas had been produced in Vienna which in no single number reached the level of this boy's, which they both admired extremely.

As to the idea that the father, not the boy, had composed

[19]Metastasio (b., Rome, 1698; d., Vienna, 1782), Italian poet and the most famous of all opera-librettists. Burney describes him at the age of seventy-four (in 1772) thus: "For that time of life he is the handsomest man I ever beheld. There are painted on his countenance all the genius, goodness, propriety, benevolence and rectitude which constantly characterize his writings. I could not keep my eyes off his face, it was so pleasing and worthy of contemplation."

it . . . I took the opportunity to open a volume of Metastasio and put the first aria I came to before Wolfgang. He took his pen and wrote, without reflection, in the presence of the onlookers, music to it, with many instruments, at an astounding pace. He did this in the presence of the Kapellmeister Bonno, the Abbé Metastasio, Hasse, the Duke of Braganza, and Prince Kaunitz. . . .

Had it been an opera seria . . . I should have departed and presented it to His Grace [the Archbishop of Salzburg], but as it is an opera buffa and one that requires special buffa character I must save our honour here, cost what it will. . . .

I am responsible to Almighty God in this affair, otherwise I should be the most ungrateful creature. And if ever I were responsible for convincing the world of this miracle it is just now when one ridicules all that is wonderful and denies all miracles. They must be convinced. Was it not a great joy and a great victory for me to hear a Voltairean[20] say to me in amazement: "Now I have for once in my life seen a miracle. And it is the first." Just because this marvel is so visible and undeniable they would suppress it. They will not allow God to have the glory of it. They think to themselves that in a few years it will pass into the category of the normal and cease to be a miracle of God. . . .

You may well wonder why Prince Kaunitz and others, even the Emperor himself, do not order the opera to be produced . . . actually Prince Kaunitz against the wishes of the Emperor had induced Affligio to bring the French comedians here, which cost him over seventy thousand gulden . . . for which Affligio puts the blame on Prince Kaunitz, who, however, hoped . . . to get the Emperor to make good the loss, with the result that His Majesty has not been inside a theatre for many weeks. . . .

On September 21 Leopold lodged a formal complaint against Affligio's non-fulfilment of his contract to the Emperor through the Court Director of Music, Count Johann Wenzel Spork, but it was fruitless. It has been estimated[21] that Leopold brought back to Salzburg about seven thou-

[20]Grimm, in Paris, speaking of Wolfgang in 1764, when he was eight years old.

[21]By Schurig.

sand gulden from his three years' tour through Europe, to say nothing of the costly presents, most of which the sensible Leopold sold although some remained in the family, notably the two rings—given to Wolfgang respectively by the Empress Maria Theresa at Schönbrunn and by the Prince Archbishop at Augsburg—which are now in the Mozarteum. Although the year of 1768 spent in Vienna must have been expensive, it is thought that enough remained of the gains of the prodigy children's tour to finance the later visits to Italy made by Leopold and Wolfgang, for which he was already preparing in Vienna.

In the meantime Wolfgang received a commission which must have partly compensated for the non-performance of his opera buffa *La Finta Semplice*. This came from a Dr. Anton Mesmer,[22] who had built a little theatre in his garden and some time in the late summer of 1768 had the commissioned work *Bastien und Bastienne* (K.50) performed there. In addition to these two operas Wolfgang composed three symphonies between the departure from Salzburg and his return there from Vienna; namely:

Symphony in F (K.43) for two violins, two altos, 'cello, bass, two oboes (or flutes), and two horns;

Symphony in D[23] (K.45) for two violins, alto, 'cello, bass, two oboes, two horns, trumpets, and kettle-drums, dated Vienna, January 16, 1768;

Symphony in D (K.48) for seven violins, alto, bass, two oboes, two horns, trumpets, and kettle-drums, dated Vienna, December 13, 1768.

Another commission came Wolfgang's way. It was for a Mass from an acquaintance of the Mozarts, the famous Jesuit, Father Ignaz Parhammer, who had been zealous in purifying the country after the emigration of Protestants from Salzburg in 1733. He was director of the Orphan Asy-

---

[22]This was the celebrated Friedrich Anton Mesmer (1733–1815), promulgator of the theory of animal magnetism, who added the word "mesmerism" to our language and is one of the long line of distinguished Austrian physicians who, culminating in our time in Sigmund Freud, have added to the gaiety of the world.

[23]This Symphony in D was later transformed into the Overture to *La Finta Semplice*. In this work Wyzewa and Saint-Foix see the disappearance of Paris and London influences, to give place to German and Viennese ones.

lum, where the musical education of the orphans was only secondary to their religious instruction; so much so, in fact, that they were occasionally employed in the opera. For Father Parhammer, on the occasion of dedicating a new chapel, Wolfgang composed a Solemn Mass with four trumpets which was performed in the presence of the Emperor, as the following extract from the *Wiener Diarium*, 1768, 10 Christmon, No. 99, records:

"On Wednesday 7th His Imperial Majesty with the Archdukes Ferdinand and Maximilian and the Archduchesses Maria Elizabeth and Maria Amelia visited the Orphan Asylum in the Rennweg to be present at the festival service and dedication of the newly erected Chapel. . . .[24]

"The entire music, sung by the choir of orphans, was newly composed for the occasion by Wolfgang Mozart, the twelve-year-old son of the Salzburg Kapellmeister Herr Leopold Mozart, well known for his extraordinary talent; it was conducted by the composer himself with the utmost correctness and received with general applause and admiration."

The music of this Mass is lost, so that Mozart's earliest extant Mass is the *Missa Brevis* in G for four voices, quartet, and organ (K.49), composed afterwards in the month of December 1768.

Shortly after this the Mozarts left Vienna and returned to Salzburg.

v. *First Operas and Other Compositions*

Salzburg, 1769 AGE 13

Sigismund, Count of Schrattenbach, Archbishop of Salzburg, was a very different man from his successor, the Archbishop Hieronymus, who was to play such an unpleasant part later in Mozart's life. He was proud of his Salzburg prodigy and

[24]The notice goes on to say that the royal party was received by His Eminence the Cardinal Archbishop and attendant clergy "amid the liveliest fanfares of trumpets and drums and the firing of guns and cannon." The world has sadly deteriorated since the days when orphan asylums were opened in this manner.

gave orders for Wolfgang's opera to be performed in the palace. The program, which Köchel discovered, was as follows:

La Finta Semplice Dramma Giocoso per Musica
Da rappresentarsi in corte per ordine di S. A. Reverendissima
Monsignor
Sigismondo Arcivescovo
e Prencipe
di Salisburgo
Prencipe del S.R.L.
Legato Nato della S.S.A.
Primate della Germania e dell antichissima famiglia
del Conti di SCHRATTENBACH, etc., etc.
Salisburgo Nella Stamperia di Corte 1769
Personaggi:

Fracasso, Capitano Ungarese .	Il Sigr. Gius Meisner
Rosina, Baronessa, Sorella di Fracasso la quale si finge semplice	La Sgra. M. M. Haydn
Giacinta, sorella di Don Cassandro e Don Polidoro . .	La Sgra. Mar. An. Braunhofer
Ninetta, Cameriera	La Sgra. Mar. An. Tesemair
Don Polidoro, Gentiluomo sciocco, fratello di Don Cassandro	Il Sgr. Francesco Ant. Spitzeder
Don Cassandro, Gentiluomo sciocco et avaro, fratello di Polidoro	Il Sgr. Hornung
Simone, Tenente del Capitano .	Il Sgr. Felice Winter

Tutti in actual servizio di S. A. Reverendissima.
La Musica è del Signor Wolfgango Mozart in età di anni 12.

Of the libretto of Mozart's first opera I shall give no details. Most of these contemporary books for Italian operas were, as Wyzewa and Saint-Foix put it, "veritable *tours de force* from the point of view of futile complication." *La Finta Semplice* (K.51) is a masterpiece from this point of view, which "Mozart himself [age twelve!] had some difficulty in understanding." As for the music, which Wolfgang composed in four months (April to July 1768), it consists of twenty-one airs, three finales, one duet, and one chorus. The manuscript is in Berlin. The libretto was not one to stir the interest of Wolfgang (two out of the four male characters are described as "stupid") and it is worth remarking that Wyzewa and Saint-Foix consider that, although Mozart put poetry and charm into some of the lover's airs, what he expressed with most justness and "remarkable musical beauty" are the comic sentiments, the cowardice and drunkenness of the old Cassandro, the droll spleen of the valet Simone, and the remarks of the soubrette Ninetta, to whose music he gives the light and lively form of *petites chansons*. It may be worth quoting a few bars from one beautiful air given to Rosine, No. 15, in which strings and bassoons are combined with delightful effect:

After the performance of *La Finta Semplice* the Archbishop appointed Wolfgang to be Concertmeister and this was entered in the Court Calendar of 1770.

The singspiel *Bastien und Bastienne* was a one-act opera of the new kind of which Rousseau's *Le Devin du village*[1] was the prototype, influencing Philador's *Le Sorcier* and Monsigny's *Rose et Colas*, which had been produced with great success in Paris during the Mozarts' visit there. A German variety of this new form of simple, natural, and less conventionalized opera—which had developed in Italy out of the popular intermezzi played between the acts of the more exalted and ambitious opera seria as a sort of sop to the groundlings—had been introduced to Vienna by J. A. Hiller.[2] These were Wolfgang's models when he composed *Bastien und Bastienne* in 1768, but whether before or after

[1] See p. 58.
[2] Johann Adam Hiller (b., Prussia, 1728; d. 1804), originator of the Leipzig Gewandhaus concerts, formerly *Concerts Spirituels*, founded the German singspiel based on the simple lied (song) as the French operettas were based on the French chanson. Successor to Doles as Cantor and Director of Bach's Thomasschule in Leipzig.

La Finta Semplice is not quite certain. The likeliest is that it was composed partly before and partly afterwards.

The text of Wolfgang's singspiel was based on a parody of Rousseau's *Le Devin du village*,[3] which had been performed first in 1752 before King Louis XIV at Fontainebleau and then before the Académie Royale de Musique in Paris on March 1, 1753, with enormous success. Everybody from the King downwards was soon singing "*J'ai perdu mon serviteur*," and even twenty years later, in 1774, Rousseau's singspiel rivalled Gluck's *Orpheus* in success with the Paris public.

The parody of Rousseau's work appeared at the Théâtre des Italiens on September 26, 1753, with the title *Les Amours de Bastien et Bastienne*. Rousseau had aimed at natural feeling and unity of tone, expressed in flowing melodies and intelligible recitatives with a certain general character of Arcadian idealism. Rousseau's plot is as follows:

Colette, a village maiden, inconsolable for her faithless swain, goes to a soothsayer, who tells her that Colin has been seduced by the lady of the manor but still loves Colette and will return to her. She must punish him and inflame his desire by assumed indifference. The soothsayer informs Colin that Colette loves another, whereupon he begs for help and the soothsayer undertakes to summon Colette by magic. Colette appears and plays the prude, whereupon Colin rushes off in despair but she recalls him and scenes of reconciliation follow in which the soothsayer is rewarded and the villagers share in the joy of the lovers.

The parody was written by Harny in collaboration with the gifted singer and actress Madame Favart and as a parody it carried Rousseau's naturalism still further and made the characters real peasants. Madame Favart appeared (and was the first to do so on the stage) in linen peasant clothes, with bare arms and wooden sabots, and made a sensational hit. The character of the parody may be judged from the first air of Colette, which in Rousseau's original has the words: "*J'ai perdu tout mon bonheur*," whereas Bastienne sings: "*J'ai perdu mon ami*," to the tune of a popular song, "*J'ai perdu mon âne*." In 1764 a German translation was

---

[3]The origin of this piece is described by Rousseau himself in the eighth book of his *Confessions*.

made by Weiskern and this was the text used by Mozart,
with certain alterations made by Schachtner. Compared
with its predecessors and contemporaries in German singspiel Mozart's has a more pastoral and less burlesque character. It was composed with an orchestral part for two violins, alto, two oboes, horns, and bass and consists of eleven
arias, two duets (the duets are confined to the singing of the
melody in thirds when the two characters sing together),
and a trio which is of a more developed type. The recitatives
were composed later (1769) in Salzburg. *Bastien und Bastienne* is a charming work and may still be heard with pleasure. I have heard it performed by an Italian marionette opera
company with excellent effect.

Instead of quoting any of the music of *Bastien und Bastienne* I shall give the principal theme of the opening allegro
of the Symphony in D (K.48), composed in Vienna at the
end of 1768 just before returning to Salzburg.

Wyzewa and Saint-Foix remark that here we may find a
trait characteristic of Mozart at this period,—that of giving
to the violins sudden and frequent leaps upwards or downwards. The andante is a true German lied, but with a varia-
tion section treated contrapuntally; the minuet, according
to the same authorities, shows the influence of Joseph
Haydn; the trio is bizarre in rhythm; the finale has a multi-
plicity of ideas; and the whole work "is new, deeply original, with a breadth of inspiration that we shall not find again
during the succeeding period even in the instrumental works
of Mozart's first sojourn in Italy."

Apart from his musical compositions practically nothing
is known of how Wolfgang was occupied during his thir-
teenth year (1769) spent in Salzburg. Among the works
of this period is a *Missa Brevis* in D minor (K.65) composed
in January 1769, and a Mass in C (K.66) composed in October of the same year for his friend Dominicus Hagenauer,

who had become a priest and was the son of Leopold's
Lorenz Hagenauer. This latter Mass was the first which
broke to some extent with the older style of ecclesiastical
music and showed the influence of the developments which
had taken place in operatic and symphonic music. It may be
interesting to see a few bars from the *Missa Brevis* in D minor
written for four voices, two violins, bass, and organ. Here
is the opening of the *Kyrie* and of the *Dona nobis*:

In addition to these Wolfgang composed the Cassation[4]
in G (K.63) for two violins, two altos, bass, two oboes (or
flutes), and two horns; he also wrote many others which
have not survived. Cassations and serenades were a Salzburg
specialty and his fellow-citizens frequently called upon Wolf-

[4]There is considerable doubt about the derivation of this word, but
in the eighteenth century it was used for a piece of instrumental
music played in the open air, and some derive it from the German
Gasse—a street. Perhaps it implies a farewell. This work is also described as *Divertimento* (*Final-Musik*).

gang to compose this sort of charming and delightful music for their festival occasions. As early as 1684 in a travel book published in Nuremberg a Dr. Browne remarks on the fact that in Vienna "not a night passed without one hearing a *Nachtmusik* under our windows."

Towards the end of the year 1769 Leopold was preparing to take his son to Italy, and on December 13, 1769, Leopold and Wolfgang, now aged thirteen and eleven months, left Salzburg on their first Italian tour.[5]

vi. *The First Italian Tour*

December 13, 1769–March 28, 1771 AGE 13–15

This first Italian tour, unlike the grand European tour, was undertaken by Leopold and Wolfgang alone, leaving Wolfgang's mother and sister at home in Salzburg. Wolfgang is approaching his fourteenth birthday and now we shall have his own letters home as well as his father's to quote from.

In the eighteenth century musicians from all parts of Europe went to Italy as the head-spring and fountain of musical life just as in the nineteenth century they went from all parts of the world to Germany. Owing to the number and independence of large and important cities with their rival princely and episcopal courts, there existed throughout Italy a magnificent and widespread organization for the production of music. Music had become the national art, and the taste for it was more generally diffused among the population than in any other country. Music, as known in Europe since the Dark Ages following on the collapse of the Roman Empire, originated in Italy—notation and all—and was an entirely new art. The richly endowed monasteries and churches rivalled the court theatres in their sup-

[5]In the Salzburg Court Calendar of November 27, 1769 appeared the following announcement:

"*Hodie D. Wolfgangus Mozart iuvenis 14 annorum cum facultate abeundi Italian litteram decretalem accepit quod sit imposterum Concert Maister cum permissione quod post reditum ex Italia iam sit competentem huic officio pensum percepturus.*"

port of music and, indeed, the musical instruction of the
young was largely given in religious institutions. In Venice
alone there were four special foundations in which boys
and girls received musical tuition preparatory to their service in the Church: namely, the Ospidale della Pietà, intended
for foundlings; the Ospedaletto, of which Sacchini[1] was at
this time Kapellmeister; Gli Mendicanti; and Gl'Incurabili,
of which Galuppi[2] was head. Similar institutions in Naples
were De Poveri di Gesù-Christo; Della Pietà de Turchini;
S. Onofrio; Loretto. Such institutions, mostly dating from
the sixteenth century, were true conservatoires of music,
giving excellent and thorough instruction in singing, instrumental music, and composition. In addition to these ecclesiastical establishments there were a number of aristocratic
academies, the fruit of the Renaissance, such as Degli Arcadi
in Rome, Della Crusca and Degli Elevati in Florence, and—
particularly valuable regarding music—the two famous
academies of Bologna: Dei Filomusi (founded by Banchieri
in 1615) and Dei Filarmonici (founded in 1666 by Carratis).
The last had the greatest reputation of all at the time of the
Mozarts' Italian tour and to belong to it was perhaps the
highest honour a musician could obtain.

Mozart was the last great German musician to study in
Italy. Among his predecessors on this journey in their youth
to the Mecca of music were Schütz[3] (in 1609 and again in
1629), Handel, Hasse, Gluck, and J. C. Bach. Haydn was
the first great exception to this Italian training and it is notable that Haydn does not count as an opera-composer.

Leopold had furnished himself with a letter of introduction[4] from the composer Hasse to the Abbé Ortes in Bologna,
from which I take the following:

[1]Antonio Maria Sacchini (b., near Naples, 1734; d., Paris, 1786),
famous opera and church composer, son of a fisherman, studied at
San Onofrio, Naples, through the influence of Durante, whose pupil
he became for composition at the same time as Jomelli and Piccini.

[2]Baldassare Galuppi (b., near Venice, 1706; d. 1785), famous
opera-composer, collaborated with Goldoni.

[3]Heinrich Schütz (b. 1585; d. 1672), perhaps the most notable of
all German composers before J. S. Bach.

[4]Published by H. Kretschmar in the original Italian in the Zeit-
schrift der Internationalen Musikgesellschaft (Leipzig: Breitkopf and
Härtel; 1899–1914), Vol. III, p. 263.

I have made the acquaintance of a certain Herr Mozart, Kapellmeister to the Bishop of Salzburg, a gifted and cultured man of the world who, as I believe, understands not only music but other matters. He has a daughter and a son. The former plays the clavier extremely well and the latter, who cannot be more than twelve or thirteen, is already at this age both a composer and Kapellmeister. I have seen his compositions; they are certainly good and I have noticed nothing in them of a twelve-year-old boy. I have no reason to doubt that they are his own. I have tested him in various ways and he has done things which for such an age are somewhat incomprehensible and would be remarkable in a grown-up man.

"As the father now wants to bring him to Italy . . . and has asked me for a letter of recommendation I take the liberty to give him one to you [here follows the request to Ortes to help with advice and introductions]. Herr Mozart is a highly cultivated and polished man, his children are well brought up. The boy is, in addition, beautiful, lively, charming, and behaves in such a way that one absolutely cannot help loving him. One thing is certain: if his development keeps pace with his age something wonderful will come of him. Only the father must not over-indulge him or spoil his nature with the incense of excessive praise. That is the only danger I fear. I have written you a long letter, receive it in goodwill. . . ."

This letter, first published by H. Kretschmar, is of exceptional interest for several reasons. In the first place it was written by Hasse, then about sixty-nine years old, the most famous of living German composers and a man of exceptional musical gifts, some of whose operatic melodies have great beauty.[5] Secondly it is written in the deliberately cool tone of a professional musician giving an expert opinion. The gush which is pronounced by music-lovers and dilettantes of all sorts upon musical performances and musical compositions is quite worthless as a criterion, since such people are not really equipped to give a reliable judgment in such matters—no matter how genuine their emotions may be. Here we have a greatly talented musician of vast experience who thoroughly understands his art and who at his

[5] Two of his airs from the opera *Artaserse*—"*Pallido è il sole*" and "*Per questo dolce amplesso*"—were sung every night to Philip V of Spain for ten years by Farinelli, the greatest *castrato* singer of all time.

time of life must have already met with such numbers of
prodigies and musically gifted people as to be able to dis-
count ninety per cent of what the laity think is talent and
discern whether there showed in this boy signs of something
truly unusual on the highest plane. With true understanding Hasse puts his finger on the deciding point: "If his development keeps pace with his age something wonderful
will come of him." Hasse did not quite live to see the
wonders that came, for he died in Venice, an old man of
eighty-four, in 1783, three years before the production of
Figaro.

Armed with this and other letters, the Mozarts arrived
at Innsbruck, where, on December 16 Wolfgang played at
sight at the house of Count Künigl a concerto put before
him as a test and received twelve ducats, to which feat the
Innsbrucker Zeitung gave due notice. They travelled over
Steinach, Brixen, and Bozen to Rovereto, where Leopold
found an old acquaintance, an official named Cristani, who
had studied the violin with him in Salzburg. Leopold writes
to his wife from Verona on January 7, 1770 that this Cristani, whom she will remember, said as soon as they entered
that Wolfgang resembled his mother, whose face he had not
forgotten.[6] In Rovereto Wolfgang played at the house of
Baron Todeschi; also he played on the organ at the principal
church, and the rumour of his prowess, which had spread
through the town, brought such a crowd that a way had to
be made for them to get into the choir.

And now I shall print the first letter of Wolfgang's which
has survived—excepting that already quoted, and of uncertain date, about his Latin to Frau Hagenauer. It is an
enclosure to his father's letter from Wörgl dated December
13th, 1769:

Dearest Mother,

My heart is completely ravished from sheer joy because
this journey is so jolly because it is so warm in the coach and
our coachman is a splendid man who when the road permits
goes like the wind. Papa will have written the description of
our journey, the reason I have written, Mamma, is to show

---

[6]A fact worth noting, especially in view of my contention that
Mozart's temperament came rather from his mother than his father.

that I know my duty and that I am with the deepest respect
your faithful son,

Wolfgang Mozart

Carissima sorella mia
Siamo arivati a wirgel.[7]

One of the most extraordinary of the many unusual traits
of Mozart is his docility, filial obedience, and respect for
his parents. This he maintained throughout his life and
the reader will often be astonished at his letters to his father
written long after he was a fully grown-up and independent
man. It is an absolutely genuine and integral part of his
nature and in no way a formality; nor does he ever abate
one jot of his individual independence, but acts as he himself thinks right, however much his father is in opposition;
but we shall see how he will take great pains to explain
patiently to his father what he does and why he does it. I
lay particular stress on this since this characteristic has far-
reaching consequences in his creative work with which I
shall deal when the time comes. In the meantime I would
point out to people of this age who gape at and swallow
whole post-Freudian psychoanalyses pushed to absurdity,
just as their forefathers did with their post-Mesmer hyp-
notic fancies, that Mozart had neither a father- nor a mother-
complex but a merely natural love for each of his parents,
neither excessive nor deficient. This perfect poise is no
doubt rare, rarer even than "normal" eyesight, but it cannot be called unnatural. Its significance in Mozart is cardinal, for Mozart's amiability and docility were not negative
—that is, not due to a lack of vitality—but were the result
of an extraordinary balance and harmony of opposites in
his nature which, as we shall see, plays a decisive role in his
creative genius.

Leopold writes twice from Innsbruck and once from
Bozen. In his letter of December 17, 1769, from Bozen,
we meet with the simple code which the Mozarts used
in their correspondence when they thought discretion was
advisable. This was certainly due to Leopold—whom Hasse
did not call a man of the world for nothing. It is quite clear

[7]Written thus in Italian in the original (i.e., "Dearest Sister, We
have arrived at Wirgel").

that Leopold was well versed in the intriguing duplicity of
the world and quite a match for all the politicians he met
with among musicians, officials, and other hangers-on to
courts and institutions. Sometimes what Leopold thinks
worthy of coding seems laughable to us, as in this letter,
where he uses it merely to tell his wife that the usual fee
they get is twelve ducats. From the inn of the Due Torri at
Verona Leopold writes:

Verona, January 7, 1770

. . . In Verona it was seven days before the nobility could
arrange a concert . . . because there was opera daily. These
gentlemen to whom we were recommended are Il Marchese
Carlotti, Il Conte Carlo Emili, Il Marchese Spolverini, Marchese Dionisio, Conte Giusti del Giardino, Conte Allegri. We
had a permanent invitation from Carlotti, also from Locatelli.[8] We have dined twice with Carlotti, with Emili, and
with Giusti, who has a beautiful garden and picture-gallery.
You will find it perhaps in Kaysler's Travels. Yesterday we
dined with Locatelli. . . .

The Receiver-General for Venice, Sgr. Luggiati, requested
the gentlemen to ask me to allow Wolfgang's portrait to be
painted.[9] . . . Yesterday it was started and today after church
he must sit again for it. . . . Later we went to the church San
Tomaso to play on its two organs, and although this decision
was only taken while at table and was made known by a couple
of notes to the Marchese Carlotti and Count Pedemont, yet
on our arrival there was such a crowd that we had scarcely
room to get out of the coach . . . when it was over the uproar was still greater because everyone wanted to see the little
organist. As soon as we were in the coach I ordered it home;
locked our room and began to write this letter, otherwise we
should have had no peace. . . .

Tomorrow we are going with Locatelli to see the Amphi-
theatre and other sights. . . . Was it fine and not cold in Salz-

[8]Pietro Locatelli (b., Bergamo, 1693). Whether this famous violinist and composer, a pupil of Corelli, is the Locatelli mentioned
would seem likely if it were not that some authorities give the date of
his death as 1764. As very little is known of his life, this date may be
a mistake.

[9]This is the portrait of Mozart at the clavier, in 1770, painted by
Cignaroli. Luggiati called Wolfgang, in a letter to his mother about
the portrait, a *"raro e portentoso giovane."*

burg during the Christmas holidays? We have had it very cold
for eight days and imagine! everywhere we eat there is neither
a stove nor heating in the dining-room. One's hands get blue
with cold. I would rather eat in a cellar;[10] more of this subject, which is our greatest trial another time. . . .

Leaving Verona, they arrived at Mantua on January 10,
1770. Wolfgang made a serious impression on more than
one of the ladies of Mantua. A Signora Bettinelli wept at his
departure and a Signora Sartoretti sent him a pomade for his
hands, which had suffered from the cold, and a vase with a
beautiful bouquet and tied in its red ribbon a poem written by
herself and (with an eye on Leopold, no doubt) four ducats.

At Mantua, in the Philharmonic Society's hall, a concert
was given with Wolfgang as the principal performer. Leopold writes to his wife:

Milan, January 26, 1770

On the 16th in Mantua there was the usual weekly concert. . . . I wish you could have seen the little theatre (*tea-
trino*) . . . I have never in my life seen anything more beautiful. It is not a theatre but a hall built like an opera-house with
boxes. Where the stage should be is a platform for music and
behind the music again a gallery for listeners built like a box.
The crowd, the calls, the applause, uproar, and bravos, in short
the general admiration is not to be described. . . .

I must tell you that neither for this concert nor the one
in Verona was there payment. Entry is free; in Verona only
for the nobility, since they are supported by them alone; in
Mantua, however, nobility, military, and reputable bourgeoisie
are admitted, as it has a grant from the Empress. From this
you will realize that we shall not become rich in Italy, but you
know it is enough if we pay our travelling expenses. This I have
managed so far. In the six weeks since we left Salzburg we
have paid out seventy ducats, for even though one lives *a pasto*
and mostly does not eat at home, still the food at night, the
firewood and room cost so much that one never comes out of
an inn under six ducats for a stay of nine or eleven days. I

---

[10]Everywhere in Austria and in Germany the cosiest place to have
meals is in the famous cellars of the town halls, hotels, etc. Our English word "cellar" has unfortunately damp and depressing associa-
tions utterly alien to the gay and delightful German *Keller*, which
perhaps ought to be translated by the word "tavern."

thank God I left you at home. Firstly you would not have
stood the cold, secondly it would have cost a terrible lot, for
we should not have had the choice of lodging we now have;
for example, in the Augustine monastery of San Marcho,
where, although we pay, we are better off, more comfortable,
and near to His Excellency Count Firmian.[11] Every night our
beds are warmed so that Wolfgang at bedtime is always happy.
We have a Brother Alfonso to wait on us.

As an example of the sort of concert given by Wolfgang
in Italy on this tour the program of the concert at Mantua
may be worth quoting in its original Italian:

Serie delle composizioni musicale da eseguirsi nell' accademia
pubblica filarmonica di Mantova la sera del di 16 del corrente,
Gennajo, 1770.

In occasione della venuta del espertissimo giovanetto Sign. Amadeo
Mozart.

(1) Sinfonia di composizione del Sign. Amadeo.

(2) Concerto di Gravecembalo esibitogli e da lui eseguito all'
improvviso.

(3) Aria d'un Professore.

(4) Sonata di Cembalo all' improvviso eseguita dal giovane con
variazioni analoghe d'invenzione sua e replicata poi in tuono diverso
da quello in cui è scritta.

(5) Concerto di Violino d'un Professore.

(6) Aria composta e cantata nell' atto stesso dal Sign. Amadeo
all' improviso, co' debiti accompagnamenti eseguiti sul Cembalo,
sopra parole fatte espressamente; ma da lui non vedute in prima.

(7) Altra sonata di Cembalo, composta insieme ed eseguita del
medesimo sopra un motive musicale propostogli improvvisamente dal
primo Violino.

(8) Aria d'un Professore.

(9) Concerto d'Oboè d'un Professore.

(10) Fuga musicale, composta ed eseguita dal Sign. Amadeo sul
Cembalo; e condotta a compiuto termine secondo le leggi del contrappunto, sopra un semplice tema per la medesima presentatogli all'
improvviso.

(11) Sinfonia dal medesimo, concertata con tutte le parte sul
Cembalo sopra una sola parte di Violino postagli dinanzi improvvisamente.

(12) Duetto di Professori.

(13) Trio in cui il Sign. Amadeo ne suonerà col Violino una parte
all' improvviso.

(14) Sinfonia ultima di composizione del Suddetto.

[11]Count Karl Joseph von Firmian (b. 1716), Governor-General of
Lombardy, described by Winckelmann as "one of the greatest, wisest,
most humane, and learned men of his time and country."

It is worth remarking on the amount of improvising that Wolfgang was always set to do. His capacity in this respect was clearly phenomenal and it is not surprising that a savant in Verona wrote of him as a "wonder-work of nature." I shall now transcribe for the benefit of those, like myself, who are curious to see the unbowdlerized, unimproved original matter as it came from the writer's hands a letter— the first written to his sister which we possess—in which Wolfgang's queerly spelt (even for an Austrian!) German is to be seen mixed with Italian as it came fresh from his hand, not as it was originally printed by Nissen in 1828. The matter of this letter is not important, so I do not translate it; what is important is the evidence it gives of Wolfgang's extraordinary vivacity. The mixture of languages —German, Italian, French, and even, but rarely, English— is a characteristic of a great many of his letters.

Verona, al sette di Jannuarro [1770]

Allerliebste Schwester,

Einen spang langen habe ich gehabt, weil ich so lang auf eine Antwort vergebens gewartet habe; ich hatte auch ursache weil ich deinen brief noch nicht emfangen habe. jetzt hört der teutsche tölpel auf und fängt das wälsche tölperl an.[12] Lei è piu franco nella lingua italiana di quel che mi hò imaginato. lei mi dica la cagione, perchè lei non fu nella comedia che anno giocato, i cavalieri? Adesso sentiamo sempre opere: una è titolata: il Ruggiero.[13] Oronte, il padre di Bradamanta, è un prencipe (fà il sign. afferi[14]) un bravo cantante, un paritono,[15] mà gezwungen, wen er in Falset hinauf, aber doch nicht so sehr, wie der Tibaldi zu Wien. Bradamante, figlia d'orionte, inamorata di Ruggiero mà (si soll den Leone heyrahten, sie will ihm aber nicht), fà una povera Baronessa che ha avuto una gran disgrazia, mà non so che? Recita (unter einem fremden Nam, ich weiss aber den Namen nicht) ha uno voce passabile, e la statura non sarebbe male, ma distona come il diavolo. Ruggiero un ricco principe, innamorata di Brada-

---

[12]"Now the German blockhead stops and the foreign blockhead starts"—an early and rather simple example of the habit of playing with words which was almost a mania of Mozart's.

[13]An opera by P. Guglielmi.

[14]Name of a singer.   [15]Baritone.

mante, un Musico, canta un poco Manzolisch[16] ed à una
bellissima voce ed è gia vecchio ha cinquante cinque anni ed
à una leuffige gurgel. Leone, soll die Bradamente heyrathen,
reichissima est; ob er aber asser dem Theatro reich ist, das
weis ich nicht, fà una donna, la moglie di Afferi . . . à una
bellissima voce, ma è tanto sussuro nell theatro che non si
sente niente[17] Irene fà una sorella di Lolli dell gran Violinisto,
che abbiamo sentito a Vienna. à una schnosselte voce, e canta
sempre um ein viertil zu tardi, ò troppo a buon ora. ganno
fà, un signor che non so come egli si chiama, è la prima volta
che lui Recita. Zwischen einen jeden act is ein Balet: es ist
ein braver Tanzer da, der sich nenet: Monsieur Ruesler. er
ist ein teutscher, und tanzt recht brav, als wir das letzte Mahl
(aber nicht gar das letzte mal) in der opera waren, haben wir
den Mr. Ruesler in unseren balco heraufkomen lassen, (dan wir
haben den balco des Marquis Carlotti frey, dan wir haben den
schlössel darzu) und mit ihm geredet: apropos: Alles in der
Mascara iezt, und was das comote ist, wen man seine Larve auf
den Hut hat, und het has privilegium den hut nicht abzu-
ziehen, wen einer mich grüsst, und nimer beym namen nen-
nen, sondern allzeit, servitore umilissimo giora Mascara. Co-
speto di Baco, das spritzt: was aber das rareste ist, ist dieses:
das wir um 7ben uhr gegen halber 8 urh schon zu bette gehen.
Se Lei indovinasse questo, io dirò certamente, che Lei sia la
Madre di tutti indovini. küsse anstatt meiner der mama die
Hand, und dich küsse ich zu tausend mahl, und versichere
Dich, das ich werde bleiben immer

dein aufrichtiger Bruder
Wolfgang Mozart

Portez vious bien et aimez moi toujours.

In this letter, written just before his fourteenth birthday,
we may notice how critical Mozart is of the singers he hears
and how concisely he expresses himself.

In Mantua they heard Hasse's opera *Demetrio* and Wolfgang writes to his sister from Milan on January 26, 1770:

"The *prima donna* sings well but lifelessly . . . the *seconda*

---

[16]A reference to Manzuoli which shows that Wolfgang had not
forgotten this singer, whom he heard in London at the age of nine.

[17]"But there is such a noise in the theatre one can hear nothing."
This is an interesting observation showing how little Italian audiences
have changed.

donna looks like a grenadier and also has a powerful voice and really does not sing badly. . . . The principal man sings well but his voice is uneven, he is called Casselli, the second man is already old and I didn't like him. . . . A tenor named Otini sings not badly but with a very heavy voice, like all Italian tenors. He is a good friend of ours; I don't know the other's name, he is still young but nothing out of the way. *Primo ballerino* good, *Prima Ballerina* good and it is said she is by no means a fright but I have not seen her close to, the rest, however, are much as usual. In Cremona . . . the orchestra good[18] and the first violinist is called Spagnoletto. *Prima donna*, not bad, already old I think, looks a fright, doesn't sing as well as she acts and is the wife of a violinist who plays in the opera . . . the opera is *La Clemenza di Tito*.[19] *Seconda donna* on the stage no fright, young, but nothing special. *Prima uomo* . . . a pretty voice and a beautiful cantabile. The two other *castrati* young and passable. . . . *Ballerino primo* good, *Ballerina prima* good and a real horror. . . . In Milan . . . we have not yet been to the opera. . . ."

For the two young *castrati* Wolfgang composed in Milan two Latin motets to which probably belong the *Quære superna* (K.143) and the *Offertorium* (K.117). Count Firmian, who had presented Wolfgang with the works of the poet Metastasio,[20] gave a *soirée* at his palace, inviting the Duke of Modena and his daughter and the Cardinal Archbishop of Milan. In order to show his capacity to write an opera—Piccini was at that moment in Milan from Paris, preparing for the performance of his new opera *Cesare e Cleopatra* (*Cesare in Egitto*)—Wolfgang composed the great recitative and aria in E flat (K.77) *Misero me et Misero pargoletto*[21] for soprano, two violins, two altos, two oboes, two bassoons, two horns, and contrabass. Of his astonishing production Wyzewa and Saint-Foix remark:

"In truth this piece is one on the greatest scale that he has

[18]Wolfgang writes very curtly, omitting most verbs. I have tried to retain his style everywhere when translating, even at the cost of writing uncouth English.

[19]By Hasse, text by Metastasio. This text was later set also by Mozart.

[20]Turin edition in nine volumes.

[21]From Metastasio's *Demofoonte*.

produced in this style and one of those in which the precocity of his genius appears most astonishing. The recitative
and the air are made one by means of brief repeats in the air
of the rhythm in the accompaniment to the recitative; and
already this latter gradually becomes more melodic and takes
a more definite form to lead into the magnificent burst of
music in the air."

Wolfgang tells his sister in his letter of January 26 that he
had just finished this aria before writing to her.

The success of this and other arias composed by Wolfgang had the desired result of obtaining for him a commission to compose a new opera for the next season for
which the best singers were to be engaged and he was to
get about one hundred ducats and free quarters during its
production in Milan.[22] The libretto was to be sent on to
him, the recitatives had to be forwarded to Milan in October, and at the beginning of November the composer
himself was to be there to complete the opera and prepare for its production at Christmas. These conditions were
most convenient, for they enabled the Mozarts to continue
their tour.

Wolfgang's mother must have shown some concern about
his health, for Leopold writes:

Milan, February 17, 1770

We are, thank God, both well. That the winter, as you
say, is not so dangerous in Italy as the summer I can well
believe. But if one does not ruin one's health through dis-
orderly and superfluous eating and drinking and also has no
inner organic weakness, then there is nothing to worry about.
We are everywhere in God's keeping. Wolfgang will not be
injured either by eating or drinking. You know how moderate
he is and I can assure you that I have never seen him more
careful of his health than in this country. He avoids everything that he doesn't think good for him, has very little to
eat many days and yet is fat and healthy and the whole day
long is lively and gay.

With this same letter of his father's Wolfgang encloses
a note to his sister:

[22]One of the musicians to test Wolfgang's quality in Milan was the
famous Giovanni Battista Sammartini (b. 1700; d. 1775).

Milan, February 17, 1770

. . . Mariandel I am so glad you have been so terrifically jolly. . . . *Addio* . . . farewell, I kiss Mamma's hand a thousand times and to you I send a hundred loving smacks or pats on your wonderful horse-face. To make an end, I am thine. . . .

"Wolfgang in Germany, Amadeo in Italy"—as he writes in another letter.

On the way from Milan to Parma, at Lodi on March 15, dated seven o'clock in the evening, Wolfgang composed his first String Quartet (K.80). Of this work in G major Wyzewa and Saint-Foix write:

"Though one must not suppose that the child had composed the whole of this quartet in a single evening (at the inn at Lodi): this time, as usual, he has sat down to write a work only when he already had it, almost entirely completed, in his head; at most he will have improvised the minuet because, unlike the other movements, there are so many erasures that his father has been obliged to copy out again the whole of the trio."

This quartet consists of three movements only, in the Italian style, as follows: *Adagio, Allegro, Menuetto e trio*. Wolfgang added a finale (*Rondo*) in 1773. And the same authorities say that although Wolfgang must already have been familiar with the first quartets of Joseph Haydn, Starzer, Stamitz, Hoffmann, and Michael Haydn—superior in form if not in content to the quartets of Boccherini and Sammartini—yet this first quartet of his is entirely Italian in character.

They arrived at Bologna on March 24 and on that day both Leopold and Wolfgang wrote home about the celebrated singer in Parma, Lucrezia Agujari, known as *La Bastardella*, who invited them to supper and sang three arias for them. Leopold writes:

"That she could sing the C in *altissimo* I could not have believed if I had not heard it with my own ears. The passages Wolfgang has written down were in her aria and she sang these somewhat softer than the deeper notes but as clearly as an octave pipe in an organ. Short trills and all were note for note as Wolfgang has written out. Also she has good alto notes down to G. She is not pretty but not ugly, has at times a wild look in her eyes like people who are subject to fits, and limps with one leg. Otherwise she has a good presence, also a good character and reputation. . . ."

Wolfgang's letter to his sister is as follows:

[*Bologna*], *March 24, 1770*

O you Industrious One!

As I had been lazy so long I thought there'd be no harm if I again became industrious for a bit. Always on days when the German post comes the food and drink tastes better to me. I beg of you to tell me who sings in the oratorio, also what its title is. Write also how the Haydnish minuets please you and if they are better than the first. I am glad from the bottom of my heart to hear that Herr von Aman is well again; tell him, I beg you, that he must be careful; he must take things quietly, tell him that, I beg of you, and also say that I often think of how we played[23] . . . and tell him also that I often recall how many times he has said to me: "Shall we divide?" and how I always replied: "As before." Next time I shall send you a Minuet which Mr. Pick danced in the theatre and which is danced by everybody at the *feste di ballo* in Milan, just to show you how slowly they dance. The Minuet is in itself very good. It comes, naturally, from Vienna, also is certainly by Teller or Starzer. It has a lot of notes. Why? because it is a theatre minuet which goes slowly. The minuets of Milan and most Italian ones have many notes, go slowly and with many bars, e.g. the first section has sixteen, the second has twenty and even twenty-four bars.

At Parma we met a singer, the celebrated Bastardella, and heard her splendidly in her own home. She has (1) a fine voice, (2) a luscious larynx, (3) an unbelievable range. I heard her sing the following:

[23]Here follows a reference to some game of their own devising. Leopold writes a postscript to his wife in his letter from Milan on Carnival Tuesday: "The misfortune of Basily [von Aman] upset us very much, especially Wolfgang, who shed many tears, you know how sensitive he is."

In Bologna on March 26, 1770 Field-Marshal Count Pal-
lavicia arranged a brilliant concert, attended by one hundred
and fifty persons, in order to introduce Wolfgang to the nobility, including the Cardinal Legate Antonio Colonna Branci-
forte and the greatest Italian musician of the time, Padre
Martini.[25] Leopold writes to his wife the next day:

Bologna, March 27, 1770

. . . I wish you might know Count Pallavicini. He and
Count Firmian are a pair of noblemen who possess similar
tastes, modes of thought, and are equally amiable, courteous,
and generous. . . .

What pleases me especially is that Wolfgang is more admired here than in any of the other Italian towns since this is
the seat and residence of so many masters, artists, and scholars.

[24]This is written by Mozart in the old Soprano clef—i.e., two tones
lower than the treble clef.

[25]Giambattista Martini, commonly called Padre Martini (b.,
Bologna, 1706; d. 1784), composer, scholar, and mathematician, one
of the most learned musicians of history. Burney estimated his library
at Bologna to consist of 17,000 volumes. Author of *Storia della
Musica*, three volumes (1757–81) and *Exemplare Ossia Saggio . . .
di Contrappunto*, two volumes (1774–5).

He is also most in request here and this increases his fame throughout Italy since Father Martini is the god of the Italians and he speaks of Wolfgang with such admiration and has personally tested him. Twice we have visited Father Martini and each time Wolfgang has composed a fugue of which P. Martini has only supplied him with the *ducem* or *guida* in a few notes. We have visited the Cavaliere Broschi, better known as Signor Farinelli,[26] at his estate outside the town. We have seen Spagnoletta[27] . . . Manfredini.[28]

. . . Farewell, I kiss you and Nannerl a thousand times, remember me to all Salzburg. I am your true and sleepy husband,   MZT

[March 28]: It was not a bad idea to send us the Ball-Minuet to Bologna to be arranged for clavier because there is nobody in Salzburg who could do it. It has given Wolfgang the greatest pleasure. . . . He will himself write next time; I wrote yesterday as he was already in bed . . . he is now asleep and the post is going.

From Bologna they went to Florence, arriving on March 30 and presenting a letter from Count Firmian to Count Rosenberg, the Austrian Ambassador at the Tuscan court, on April 1. A concert was arranged for the next day. Leopold writes to his wife:

Florence, April 3, 1770

. . . We stayed until ten o'clock. It went as usual and the admiration was all the greater since the musical director, the Marquis Ligniville,[29] is one of the first contrapuntalists in Italy and put before Wolfgang the most difficult fugues and gave him the hardest subjects, which Wolfgang developed and played as one eats a piece of bread. Nardini accompanied. Today we see Manzuoli. The *castrato* Niccolini is also here. I am very troubled that we must depart next Friday to go to Rome. I wish you could see Florence and its surroundings. You would say that here one should live and die. . . .

In Florence Wolfgang met and became very friendly with

---

[26]See p. 93.   [27]Giusseppe Useda from Milan.

[28]A famous singer (*castrato*).

[29]Ligniville was an expert in canon-writing and Wolfgang copied out a number of his canons and experimented himself (see K. *anhang* 238) in composing them.

an English boy of his own age (fourteen) named Thomas Linley who was a pupil of the violinist Nardini. Linley's promising career was cut short by his accidental death by drowning in 1778.

The Mozarts arrived in Rome on April 11, the Wednesday of Holy Week, and Leopold writes to his wife:

Rome, April 14, 1770

. . . In Rome they say that they have had rain for four months and we truly had an experience of it for on Wednesday and Thursday we went in fine weather to hear the *Miserere* in the Sistine Chapel at St. Peter's and were . . . overtaken by such rain that our cloaks have never been so soaked. Of the horrible journey here I shall say little. Imagine a mostly unbuilt country and horrible inns . . . filth and nothing to eat except, with luck, here and there some eggs and cabbage. . . .

You will perhaps have heard of the celebrated *Miserere* in Rome, which is so highly treasured that the musicians are forbidden under threat of excommunication to let a single part of it be taken out of the Chapel or to copy it or give it to anyone. *We alone have it.* Wolfgang has written it down . . . we shall bring it home with us and as it is one of the secrets of Rome we will not let it pass into other hands so as not to incur directly or indirectly the displeasure of the Church. . . .

This celebrated feat of Wolfgang's refers to the *Miserere* of Gregorio Allegri (1582–1652). He wrote it out from memory on returning to their inn after a single hearing on the Wednesday, and when the performance was repeated on the Good Friday he took the manuscript with him and, hiding it in his hat, made some corrections. This feat became known and made a great sensation and he was called upon to produce his copy in the presence of the papal singer Cristofori, who was amazed at its correctness. Leopold's news, however, excited consternation in Salzburg, Wolfgang's mother and sister believing that he had sinned in transcribing the *Miserere*, and Leopold writes, in reply to their misgivings, from Naples on May 19, 1770:

". . . When we read your ideas about the *Miserere* we both had to have a good laugh. There is nothing in the least to be worried about. It is taken in quite another way here. All Rome knows of it. The Pope himself knows that Wolfgang has written down the *Miserere*. There is nothing to be afraid of; it has brought him great honour. . . . You must not fail to show this letter everywhere and let His Grace the Archbishop know of it. . . ."

In Rome they presented their letters of introduction and were welcomed by the Chigi, Barberini, Bracciano, Altemps, and other important families, on whom Wolfgang's playing and improvising made a great impression since, as Leopold writes:

Rome, April 21, 1770

. . . the deeper we penetrate into Italy the greater grows the astonishment. Wolfgang does not stand still but develops so from day to day that the greatest connoisseurs and masters cannot find words to express their admiration. . . .

We have met an incredible number of English here, among others Mr. Beckford,[30] who met us at Lady Effingham's in London, with whom early today we went walking, in company with other English people, in the gardens of the Villa Medici, belonging to the Grand Duke of Florence.

We have changed our first lodging and Herr Marcobruni has brought us to the house of the Papal Courier Uslenghi in the Piazza del Clementino. Here we are very comfortable, both mother and daughter cannot do enough for us. The master is in Portugal and they look on us as the heads of the house; we eat together, have a large room, which is very healthy as it gets the morning sun. When friends visit us we can use all the other rooms and as the daughter is a beginner learning to play we are not without a harpsichord. . . .

Yesterday we were at Prince Chigi's, where among others was the so-called King of England or Pretender and the secretary of state, Cardinal Pallavicini. . . .

In Rome Wolfgang composed two arias: "*Se ardir e speranza*" (K.82) and "*Se tutti i mali miei*" (K.83) to words taken from Metastasio's *Demofoonte*, both for soprano voice with orchestra. He also composed a Symphony in D (K.81), which appears in Breitkopf's catalogue in 1775 as by his father; but Wyzewa and Saint-Foix declare it to be Wolf-

[30] Author of *Vathek*, or, more probably, his cousin Peter Beckford?

gang's work on internal evidence: "There is not a note of this symphony which could have emanated from the heavy and banal invention of Leopold Mozart," and explain the confusion as due to a misunderstanding of Wolfgang's possible reference to a symphony by his father in his letter to his sister dated April 23, 1770, which must refer to another work. He also composed a Contredanse in B flat for two violins, bass, two oboes, and two horns (K.123). It is interesting to read the particulars written by Leopold in sending this dance to Salzburg on April 14:

"Wolfgang is well and sends a Contredanse. He would like Herr Hofman [dance-master at the Salzburg court] to devise the steps to it and in such a way that only two persons dance when the two violins play as a prelude and then let the whole company dance together each time the whole orchestra plays. What would be most beautiful would be for five different couples to dance in turn the solos, as there are five solos and five *tuttis*."

This is an early example of the interest Mozart took in dancing, of which he was passionately fond all his life. Arithmetic was another of his pleasures, as the following letter indicates:

Rome, April 21, 1770

Cara sorella mia,

I beg you to find the Art of Reckoning which you wrote out for me and which I have lost. So will you please copy it with examples and send it to me . . . I am just working on the aria *Se ardir e speranza.*

Nonsense rhymes and drawings of places and people appear frequently in Wolfgang's letters, which also occasionally contain expressions of such grossness that the reader at first can hardly believe his eyes. These latter, one comes to realize, are invariably a sign of his being in extraordinarily high spirits, so much so that his pen flies to absurdity, extravagance, and coarseness of phrase out of the sheer animal vitality of the writer. This quality in Mozart is not to be mistaken. It appears in these earliest letters of the boy of fourteen and indeed in his father's letters one is constantly coming across the remark: "Wolfgang is indescribably lively."

Of these boyish epistles, written from Rome, there are a

number which are mere postscripts to his father's letters,
such as:

Rome, April 14, 1770

I am, God be praised and thanked, apart from my miserable
pen, well and kiss Mamma and Nanerl a thousand times. I
only wish that my sister were in Rome, for this city would
surely please her well since the Peter's Church is the real
thing[31] and so are many things in Rome. The finest flowers are
now of the past—this very moment Papa has said it. . . .
Now I have just drawn St. Peter with the keys, St. Paul with
the sword, and St. Luke together with my sister. I have had
the honour of the kissing of St. Peter's foot at St. Peter's and
as I have the misfortune to be so little they lifted me, your
old W. M. up.

Rome, April 28, 1770

I kiss my sister's face and my mother's hand. I have as yet
seen neither scorpions nor spiders,[32] one talks and hears nothing of them. . . .

Rome, May 2, 1770

I am, God be thanked and praised, well and kiss my
mother's hand and my sister's face, nose, mouth, throat, my
bad pen and backside if it is clean.

Sometimes he signs his letters:

Wolfgango in Germania
Amadeo Mozart in Italia
hinten wie vorn und in der Mitte doppelt.[33]

From Rome they travelled to Naples in company with
some Augustine monks, as the road was by no means safe,
owing to bandits, and arrived in Naples on May 14. They
gave a concert on May 28 and made many friends in Naples,
among them the English Ambassador, Sir William Hamilton,
and his wife, who played the clavier "with great feeling and
trembled when she had to play before Wolfgang"—as Leopold tells his wife in a letter dated May 19. In Naples they
heard opera buffa at the Teatro Nuovo, which was then dom-

---

[31]*Regulair*, Wolfgang writes. His German is strewn with French
or pseudo-French words.

[32]*Spinen* (?).

[33]"Behind as in front and doubled in the centre." He used this
expression to describe the year 1771.

inated by Piccinni and Paisiello, and at the San Carlo they heard Jomelli's opera *Armida Abbandonata* at its first performance, on May 30. The impresario Amadori, introduced by Jomelli, offered Wolfgang a libretto, which he was obliged to refuse owing to his contract to write an opera for Milan.

Naples and its beautiful surroundings were a joy to them. Leopold writes to his wife:

Naples, May 26, 1770

This is the third letter I have written to you from Naples. The situation of this town daily pleases me better and the town itself on the whole is not bad if the people were not so godless and some of them so stupid . . . and the superstition!![34]

Naples, May 29, 1770

. . . Until now we have had to endure no heat because there has been so much rain; yesterday there was a terrible wind and rain and it is something rare for Naples that the heat is not greater by now. Nevertheless we shall return home rather dark because of the air and also when the sun shines one realizes forthwith that one is in Naples. You know that Wolfgang has always wanted to be brown. . . .

Wolfgang can hardly wait for the post-days, he begs you now and then to write twice a week, especially when there is anything new; it is only in Salzburg that news is quickly written. . . .

Naples, June 5, 1770

. . . It is still always very cold in the mornings and at night and on June 2 we had fearful rain. . . . Our concert was very successful. . . . The Princess of Francavilla has made us a good present and we still have a few stray small expectations. You will be vexed that I do not let you know our receipts in detail. I don't give them because in Salzburg they consider only what we get and don't think of the expenses, for very few know what travelling costs. It is enough if I tell you that, God be praised, we lack nothing for our journeys to be made in decent comfort. . . .

[34]Wolfgang's playing at the *Conservatoire della Pietà* so astonished the gentry that they thought there was magic in the ring he wore and when he took it off and played without it they redoubled their applause.

Naples, June 9, 1770

. . . The situation of this place, its fruitfulness, liveliness, curiosities, and a hundred beauties make my departure from Naples very sad; the filthiness, the swarms of beggars, the detestable, yes godless people, the bad upbringing of the children, the unbelievable wantonness even in the churches, however, has the effect of lessening one's regrets. . . .

Rome, June 27, 1770

Yesterday at eight o'clock in the evening we arrived in Rome. We made this journey, which took four and a half days with the Vetturino, by the post in twenty-seven hours, but we have decidedly flown. . . . As we only slept for two hours during the twenty-seven and only had four baked cold *Hendl* and a piece of bread to eat you can imagine how hungry, thirsty, and sleepy we were. Our good Frau Uslenghi gave us an excellent gently cooked rice and we took nothing besides but a couple of soft-boiled eggs each and as soon as we entered our room Wolfgang sat down on a chair and fell so fast asleep that I completely undressed him and put him in his bed without his making the slightest sign of waking . . . when he awoke after nine o'clock in the morning he did not know where he was and the whole night through he lay without stirring from where I had put him.

From Wolfgang's letters from Naples, which are usually much briefer than his father's, I select the following:

[TO HIS SISTER]³⁵   *Naples, May 19, 1770*

. . . Write and tell me how is Herr Canary. Does he still sing? Does he still pipe? Do you know why I think of the canary? Because in our lobby there is one that makes a noise just like ours. . . . Yesterday we put on our new clothes; we looked as beautiful as angels. . . . Naples is beautiful and as populous as Vienna and Paris; in the impudence of its people I am not sure that Naples does not surpass London; for here the beggars have their own leaders or heads, who receive twenty-five ducats in silver monthly from the King to keep them in order.

Amicis sings at the opera. We have been with her. Caffaro

---

³⁵This letter, like many others, begins in Italian and continues in German. Some of his letters to his sister are entirely in Italian. Leopold's letters are all in German.

composes the second opera, Majo the third, but nobody knows yet the composer of the fourth. Go regularly to the Litany at the Mirabell and hear the *Regina cœli* or the *Salve Regina*, sleep soundly and have no bad dreams. Give H. von Schiden-hofen my most horrible greeting *tralaliera, tralaliera*. And tell him he must learn to play the Repetiter-Minuet on the clavier so that he does not forget to *do* it. Let him *do* it so that it *does* me good when I *do* accompany him. *Do* give my respects to all good friends and *do* be fit and *do* not die so that you *do* not fail to write and I *do* write again to you and let us always so *do* until we *do* all and still I *do* remain he who will *do* until there is no more to *do*.

[TO HIS MOTHER AND SISTER]   *Naples, May 22, 1770*

I am, God be praised and thanked, well and kiss Mamma's hand and both of you I kiss a thousand times.

[TO HIS SISTER]   *Naples, May 29, 1770*

The day before yesterday we were at the rehearsal of Signor Jommelli's opera, which is well written and truly pleased me. Signor Jommelli spoke to us and was very civil. We also went to a church to hear music by Signor Ciccio di Majo the music was beautiful. He also spoke to us and was very amiable. Signora De Amicis sings marvellously. Thank God we are well, I especially when a letter comes from Salzburg. I beg you to write to me every post, even if you have nothing to write I would like to have it just so as to have a letter every post-day. It would not be a bad thing if you wrote me some-times a letter in Italian.

[TO HIS SISTER]   *Naples, June 5, 1770*

. . . Now I begin to describe my daily life:

At nine o'clock, sometimes at ten o'clock I wake and then we go out and have breakfast at a restaurant (*trattore*), after eating we write and then go out and then lunch but on what? On meat-days, half a chicken or a small piece of roast meat, on fast-days a little fish, and afterwards we go to sleep.[36] *Est-ce-que vous avez compris*? Let's talk Salzburg, that's more sensible. We are, thank God, well, Papa and I. I hope you and Mamma are also well. Naples and Rome are two sleep-cities. Wonderful handwriting! Isn't it? Write to me and don't be

[36]This letter starts in German, continues in Italian, and then goes into Salzburg dialect.

so lazy. Otherwise you will have a beating from me. *Quel plaisir! Je te casserai la tête.* I am delighted with the portraits. . . . The opera here is by Jommelli; it is good but too clever and old-fashioned for the theatre. De Amicis sings incomparably as does Aprile also, who has sung in Milan. The dances are miserably pretentious. The King[37] is a raw Neopolitan product and at the opera stands always on a footstool so as to seem taller than the Queen. The Queen is beautiful and courteous and has greeted me in the most friendly way six times on the Molo (that is the place where one goes walking). I kiss Mamma's hand.

[TO HIS MOTHER AND SISTER]   *Naples, June 16, 1770*

I am still lively and perpetually jolly as usual and like traveling; now I have been on the Mediterranean Sea. I kiss Mamma's hand and Nannerl a thousand times and am the son Stefferl and the brother Hansl.

[TO HIS SISTER]   *Rome, July 7, 1770*

I have been astonished that you can compose so well. In a word the song is excellent. Try to compose more. Send me soon the other minuets by Haydn. *Mlle. j'ai l'honneur d'être votre très humble serviteur et frère Chevalier de Mozart—* Addio.

On July 8 the Pope conferred on Wolfgang the Order of the Golden Spur, which Gluck had received in recognition of his opera *Antigono* produced in Rome in 1756, the year of Wolfgang's birth, when Gluck was forty-two. This order brought with it the title of *Ritter* or *Chevalier*, which Gluck always used. Wolfgang used it for a few years at the instigation of his father, who wrote to his wife:

Rome, July 7, 1770

What I last wrote to you about the order was correct. It is the same that Gluck has . . . he must wear a fine golden cross that he has received and you can imagine how I laugh when I hear people address him as: *Signor Cavaliere.* We are to have an audience for this with the Pope tomorrow.

Leopold made Wolfgang sign his compositions *Del Sign. Cavaliere W. A. Mozart* and later advised him to wear his order in Paris; but Mozart let it drop completely when he grew

[37]Ferdinand IV of Naples (1751–1825). "What the King is," writes Leopold to his wife from Rome on June 30, "is better told than written."

up and it is never heard of again. The pedagogic Otto Jahn comments on this fact: "Mozart was too simple-natured and too essentially a musician to set any store by outward distinctions," which is as inept a remark as possible. Mozart was *not* simple; on the contrary, he was much too clever and realistic not to understand that a title only makes an artist look ridiculous in the eyes of the politicians and powers that be who confer it and who take care never to confer any but low-grade distinctions on artists—whom they correctly despise for taking them. Has it ever been heard that a poet or a composer was made a prince or a duke in recognition of his genius? No, it has never been and it never should be heard of. As for the rank and file it is certainly fitting that decent men of talent should have social recognition, but *Ritter* Mozart makes as ludicrous a combination as would *Sir* William Shakespeare.

Wolfgang had arrived at the age of puberty. His father writes from Rome on July 4 to his mother: "Wolfgang has visibly grown in Naples," and again on July 21 from Bologna: "If Wolfgang keeps on growing he will return home rather big." On August 25 Leopold tells his wife that Wolfgang's clothes are all too small for him but he must have patience until they go to Milan, when fresh ones can be made:

". . . He has now no singing voice, it has completely gone; it has neither high nor low notes and not five pure tones. This vexes him very much for he cannot sing his own things, which often he would like to sing to himself. . . ."

They had left Rome on July 10, travelling via Civita Castellana, Loretto, and Sinegaglia to Bologna where they arrived on July 20 and were invited to pass the hot season at the country house of Count Pallavicini. Wolfgang made friends with the son of the Count, who was his own age, and whom Leopold describes as very intelligent, playing the clavier and speaking three languages. In Bologna they met Mysliweczek (1737–81), who was to compose an opera for Milan, after Wolfgang. Here Wolfgang received the libretto for his opera, which was by a Turin poet named Cigna-Santi and was entitled *Mitridate, Rè di Ponto*.

During this summer at Bologna Wolfgang wrote a number of compositions, but it was his almost daily intellectual intercourse with Padre Martini, with whom he made a number of studies in counterpoint, that was most profitable to him. One

of the fruits of this association was the *Miserere* (K.85) for
alto, tenor, and bass with figured continuo, showing trace of
the influence of Allegri's Roman *Miserere*. The last three sections of this work, *Quoniam, Benigne,* and *Tunc acceptabis,*
are not by Mozart, but possibly are by Martini.

The Mozarts attended a festival of the famous Bologna
Philharmonic Society on August 30 at which Burney was
present and he writes in his *Travels:*

"I must not neglect to inform my musical readers that I
recognized in Herr Mozart's son the little German whose precocious and supernatural talent amazed us all in London some
years ago when he was a mere child. Since his arrival in Italy
he has been much admired in Rome and Naples."

The Bologna Philharmonic Society, founded in 1666, had
been given a position of unique authority in church music by
a bull of Pope Benedict XIV in 1749 and only its members
could be Kapellmeisters in Bologna churches, while for the
rest of the Papal domains its membership dispensed with any
examination. Members had to be twenty years of age, to have
been admitted into the first class of composers, and to have
been one year in the second class of *cantori* and *suonatori.* The
society elected Wolfgang a member, although he was only
fourteen years old, on his accomplishment of a prescribed
task, which was to write on a cantus firmus from the Gregorian
Antiphony a contrapuntal elaboration in duple time for four,
five, or eight voices *a capella* strictly according to rule, adher-
ing to the old church modes. Leopold describes the event in
the following letter to his wife:

Milan, October 20, 1770

On the evening of the 18th at five o'clock we arrived, God
be praised, safe and sound in Milan. We had to wait a whole
day in Parma because the rivers were so swollen on account of
the astonishingly heavy rain that it was impossible to cross
them. . . . For three weeks I have had severe rheumatism in
my right arm and I took this with me on the journey. Instead
of getting worse it got better although it has not quite gone.
I used nothing and have used nothing. It will go as it came.
The movement of the carriage did me no good but I kept
thinking: one must drive away evil with evil. . . .

We were delayed a couple of days in Bologna because the

Accademia Philharmonica elected Wolfgang unanimously.
. . . He had to appear in the Academy Hall on October 9 at
four o'clock in the afternoon. Then the *Princeps accademiæ*
and the two *Censores* (who are old Kapellmeisters) in the
presence of members gave him an antiphon from the Antiph-
onary which he had to set in four parts in a neighbouring
room into which he was locked. When it was ready it was
examined by the Censors and all the Kapellmeisters and composers, who voted on it by means of white and black balls. As
all the balls were white he was called in and everyone clapped
and wished him well as he entered and he was proclaimed a
member by the *Princeps*. He returned thanks and the ceremony ended. . . . I was on the other side of the hall in the
library all the time. Everyone was astonished that he was
ready so soon, for many have taken three hours on an antiphon
of three lines. You must know that this kind of composition
is by no means easy as many things are excluded. . . . He
finished it in exactly half an hour.

Mozart's test-piece is still in the archives of the Bologna
Philharmonic Society, where it was found by Gaspari in a
volume of various test-pieces, chiefly by Martini's pupils. The
cantus firmus *Cibavit eos ex adipe* (K.44) is another exercise
made by Mozart under Martini, and the piece published as
Wolfgang's own test-piece (K.86) is one of two workings-out
of the same test in this volume written out in Mozart's hand.

One or two letters written home by Wolfgang about this
period deserve quoting:

[TO HIS MOTHER] *Bologna, July 21, 1770*

I congratulate Mamma on her birthday and wish that she
may live many hundred years still and always remain in good
health, for which I am always asking God and pray every day
and will always pray every day for both of you. . . . I kiss
Mamma's hand a thousand times and remain until death,

Your true son

[TO HIS SISTER]

. . . May you live hundreds of years still and die when you
are a thousand. . . . I have not time to write more. The pen
is not worth a fig, like him who guides it. The title of the
opera I have to compose at Milan is not yet known. I have got

the *Thousand and One Nights* in Italian as a present from
our hostess in Rome; it is most amusing to read.[38]

[TO LORENZ HAGENAUER]   *Bologna, July 28, 1770*

I follow in the trail of the other congratulators and confirm
all that my dear father most sincerely has wished for you and
present my compliments to you and to dear Frau Hagenauer.

Your most obedient servant
                        Wolfgango Amadeo Mozart

[TO HIS SISTER]   *Bologna, August 4, 1770*

I regret sincerely from my heart that Miss Martha is so ill
and I pray every day for her that she may get well; tell her
from me she should not take too much exercise or eat very salt
things. Apropos! have you given Robinig[39] my letter? You
say nothing about it; I beg you, when you see him, to tell him
not to forget all about me. I can't write any better, for this pen
is a note-pen[40] and not a letter-pen. My violin now has new
strings and I play every day; but I only put this in because
Mamma asked once if I still played the violin. I have been
more than six times alone to churches and functions. I have
already composed four Italian symphonies besides arias, of
which I have written certainly five or six, also a motet.[41]

Does Herr Deibl[42] come often and honour you with his
amusing talk? And noble Herr Karl v. Vogt,[43] does he still
deign to listen to your insufferable voice? Herr von Schiden-
hofen must busy himself helping you in writing minuets or
he shall get no more sweets. . . .

Addio, farewell: my only diversion at present is walking
and Capriol and *spaccat-machen*. Italy is a land of sleep, one
is always sleeping. . . .

[TO HIS MOTHER AND SISTER]   *Bologna, August 21, 1770*

I am still active and in truth very gay. Today the whim

---

[38]This is one of the very rare occasions when Mozart mentions a
book. Leopold, on the contrary, makes many references to books and
was a very well-read man.

[39]Sigismund von Rubinig (1760–1823), son of a rich merchant.

[40]i.e., for writing musical notation.

[41]These symphonies are K.95, 97, 81, and 84. The arias are K.143,
88, 78, 79, 77, 82, 83. The motet is K.117.

[42]Franz Deibl, oboeist and violinist in Salzburg.

[43]Karl Vogt, violinist of the Salzburg Court Chapel.

took me to ride on a donkey; for it is the custom in Italy, so I thought I must also try it. We have the honour of the acquaintance of a Dominican friar who is considered holy. I don't quite believe it for he often takes a cup of chocolate at breakfast, then a good glass of strong Spanish wine; and I myself have had the honour to eat with this holy one, who after he had drunk a whole glassful of strong wine at table on top of plain wine had two good slices of melon, peaches, pears, five cups of coffee, a whole plateful of cloves, two full plates of milk and lemons. With industry he might do all this, but I don't believe it because it would be too much, besides all this he takes a great deal for tea[44] in the afternoon.

[TO HIS SISTER]   *Bologna, September 8, 1770*

So as not to fail in my duty I shall also write a few words. . . .

I am just reading *Telemachus*[45] and am already in Part Two, meanwhile farewell. I kiss Mamma's hand.

Bologna, September 22, 1770

. . . The six Minuets of Haydn[46] please me better than the previous twelve, we have often had to play them to the Countess[47] and we wish we could introduce into Italy the taste for German minuets since their own last almost as long as a whole symphony. Excuse my bad writing, I could do better but I am in a hurry. . . . I kiss Mamma's hand.

[TO HIS MOTHER]   *Bologna, September 29, 1770*

In order to make the letter longer I shall add a few words. I am sorry from my heart that poor Miss Martha has to suffer and bear patiently so long an illness, I hope that with God's help she will soon be better; if not one must not let oneself be too cast down, for the will of God is always for the best and God will know best whether it is better to be in this world or another,[48] but she must console herself meanwhile that now

[44]*Jausen*, Austrian dialect for afternoon meal.

[45]The *Télémaque* by Fénelon.   [46]Michael Haydn.

[47]Countess Pallavicini.

[48]The reader must not make the mistake of thinking these are conventional expressions of Mozart's. This attitude, which he had from childhood, he never lost, for it was completely personal and had nothing to do either with his being a Catholic or, later on, a Freemason.

she is coming from the rain into the fine weather. I kiss
Mamma's hand, farewell, *addio.*

Wolfgang Mozart

[TO HIS SISTER]   *Bologna, October 6,* 1770
    . . . It gladdens my heart that you have been so merry. I
wish I had been with you. I hope Miss Martha is better. Today I played the organ for the Dominicans. Give for me my
best wishes to Frau Hagenauer and Miss Theresia. . . . *Addio,*
farewell, a hand-kiss to Mamma. . . .

[TO HIS MOTHER]   *Milan, October 20,* 1770
    My dear Mamma.—I cannot write much as my finger hurts
through writing so many recitatives; I beg you to pray for me
that my opera goes well and that we can then be once more
happy together. I kiss Mamma's hand a thousand times and to
my sister I had a lot to say, but what? That only God and I
know, if it be God's will, then I shall soon say it to her by
word of mouth, meanwhile I kiss her a thousand times. My
compliments to all good friends. We have lost the good
Martha, yet we shall with God's help find her in a blessed
state. . . .[49]

Two days before this last letter was written—namely, on
October 18—they arrived in Milan from Bologna. Wolfgang
had to work on the libretto of his opera *Mitridate, Rè di
Ponto,* a version by Signa-Santi of Racine's tragedy. The
usual intrigues inseparable from the theatre set in, in addition
to all sorts of difficulties with the singers, which, however,
Leopold's tact and Wolfgang's infinite adaptability overcame.
Leopold writes to his wife:

Milan, October 27, 1770

    . . . Our lodging here is not far from the theatre and con-
sists of a large room with a balcony and three windows. There
is a stove in the room. The bedroom is the same size, with two
large windows but no stove. Thus, if we don't freeze we are
sure not to have stinking air. The bed is as broad as nine
good-sized men. . . .

We wish you both good health and especially cheaper
times as you are always giving me the depressing news that

---

[49]Leopold in this same letter writes to his wife: "I shall not reopen
the wound by writing a letter of condolence to Herr and Frau
Hagenauer. What cannot be altered one must leave in God's keeping,
what else is there to do?"

everything gets dearer. What will finally happen to Salzburg if nobody thinks out some means of introducing a sounder policy? For with such small incomes we shall become no better than beggars. The poor court officials have scarcely the wherewithal to still their hunger, and as their children learn nothing because they lack the means, so they grow up idlers and in twenty years the town will be full of a crowd of useless people living in want who will be a burden to the court and to the public. In a few years, even from year to year, it will be seen that I am speaking the truth. If one wants people to marry and the town to be populated one must first of all know how to give these people work and means to live. To people the place with beggars is easy.[50] One must be able to give them work and profit; then it is good to increase the population. And that does not seem to me impossible, although Salzburg is very small and is shut in right and left. . . .

We kiss your hand a billion times and I am your old

Mozart

Milan, November 3, 1770

Wolfgang thanks you for your good wishes for his birthday and hopes, if the good God allows us to see another happy one, to make return to you in perfect joy and happiness all you have wished him.

I have nothing further to write than that we are, thank God, both well and wish it were already the New Year or at least Christmas; for until then there is much to ponder and do. . . . Patience! . . . we shall, with God's help, happily bite our way through the unavoidable vexations which every Kapellmeister has to endure from the *virtuoso canaille*, just as Hanswurst gnawed through the Dreckberg.

Milan, November 10, 1770

. . . If our good friends from time to time can supply a joke in your letter it will be welcome, for Wolfgang is now so occupied with serious matters[51] and consequently very serious; I am delighted if something amusing comes his way. . . .

[50] A hit at the Church's policy. The notion spread by many of Mozart's biographers that his father was a narrow-minded bigot is absolutely false. The rest of this letter applies to all Europe and England today. Politicians everywhere continue to neglect realities for abstract principles and party strife.

[51] The composition of the opera *Mitridate*.

We have, thank God, won the first battle and beaten one
enemy who . . . tried to persuade the prima donna to sing
none of Wolfgang's arias . . . but there is another storm in
the theatrical heaven which we see far off brewing. . . . You
must not be at all surprised, these are unavoidable troubles
which the greatest masters meet with . . . one must not take
them too much to heart. . . .

Milan, November 17, 1770

. . . In the afternoons we usually take a walk, for I do not
wish Wolfgang to write immediately after eating unless under
the greatest necessity. . . .

Milan, December 1, 1770

I received safely your letter of the 16th. On the 16th I
wrote in haste and so forgot to tell you that your letter of the
9th filled with your and Nannerl's good wishes arrived safely.
It made Wolfgang melancholy when he read it and he said:
"Mamma and Nannerl pity me thoroughly because Papa has
written in the previous letter such comic catchwords." . . .
You believe the opera is already written. You are quite wrong.
If it depended on our son, then two operas would be ready,
but in Italy everything goes on in the most idiotic way. You
will hear all in good time, it would be too tedious to write
it. . . .

Yesterday as we were returning home we heard something
which seemed unbelievable and which I could not have believed to be possible to hear in Italy—namely, two beggars, a
man and a woman, in the street singing an entire song in
fifths without missing a note. I have never heard such a thing
in Germany. . . . I thought at once of Herr Wenzel; if these
two poor people sang across his grave, he would certainly rise
from the dead.

Milan, December 8, 1770

Today . . . is the second recitative rehearsal. The first went
so well that one only had to take the pen in hand occasionally
to make some literal corrections and alter *della* into *dalla*.
This is greatly to the credit of the copyist. . . .

As far as I can judge without fatherly partiality I find the
opera good and written with much spirit.

Milan, December 15, 1770

On the 12th was the first rehearsal with instruments, but

only sixteen, in order to see if everything was correctly written. On the 17th is the first rehearsal with full orchestra, consisting of fourteen first and the same number of second violins, two claviers, six contrabasses, two violoncellos, two bassoons, six violas, two oboes, two flutes, which, if there are no small flutes, play together with four oboes, four French horns, and two trumpets, amounting to sixty persons.[52]

Before the first rehearsal . . . there were not wanting people who with satiric tongues condemned the music beforehand as youthful and poor and prophesied, as it were, declaring it impossible that such a young boy, and above all a German, could write an Italian opera; they acknowledged him to be a great performer but denied that he could understand and achieve the *chiaro oscuro* needed for the theatre. Since the first rehearsal all these people are dumbfounded and have not a syllable to say. The copyist is delighted, which in Italy is a good omen since, if the music pleases, the copyist often gets more money by distributing and selling the arias than the Kapellmeister for composing them. The singers are delighted. . . . *Basta!* Now it comes before the caprice of the public. For us, except for the little empty honour, it is not of much importance. We have already attempted much in this strange world and God has always stood by us. Now we are on the edge of a no small—under the circumstances—achievement and God will be with us also this time.

Milan, December 22, 1770

. . . The greatest and most eminent composers of this town, Fioroni and Sammartini, are our true friends as also are Lampugnani, Piazza, Colombo, etc. . . . At least I hope that we do not have the bad fate of Herr Jommelli, whose second opera has just failed in Naples. . . .

Milan, December 29, 1770

God be praised, the first performance of the opera was generally acclaimed on the 26th. . . .

Never in living memory was there such a desire to see the first opera of the season in Milan as on this occasion. Patronage cannot help the success of an opera since everybody who

---

[52]The idea that Mozart's music should be played on small orchestras is one of those bogus antiquarian notions so dear to half-informed dilettantes.

goes in will talk, cry out, and judge for himself what he gets for his money. Patronage serves only and necessarily to prevent the composition of the work being hindered and to protect the composer at the rehearsals from any malice on the part of the orchestra. . . . I write this in haste as the third performance is today. You know that everything in Italy gets another name: Hasse is called Sassone, Galuppi is called Buranello, and our son is known as Il Sgr. Cavaliere Filarmonico. . . .

Milan, January 5, 1771

I can scarcely find time to write to you for we go daily to the opera and consequently only get to bed at half past one or even two o'clock, as we want something to eat afterwards; in the morning, therefore, we are up late and the already short day is thus made shorter. . . .

Our son's opera continues its success and as the Italians say is *alle stelle!* Since the third performance we go in the pit, the boxes, etc. . . . for the *maestro* is only obliged to conduct the opera three evenings. Lampugnani accompanied on the second clavier and now that Wolfgang doesn't play he takes the first and Maestro Melchoir Chiesa plays the second. If anyone had told me fifteen or eighteen years ago when I heard so much of the opera songs and symphonies of Lampugnani in England and Melchoir Chiesa in Italy that these two men would perform the music of your son and when he left the clavier take his place to accompany his music, I should probably have directed such a person to the madhouse. We see by this how the power of God works in us men when we do not bury the talents He has graciously imparted to us.

Wolfgang's opera *Mitridate, Rè di Ponto*, was given twenty times with unfailing success. Father and son then took a short trip to Turin, saw a good opera there, and returned to Milan on January 31, proceeding soon afterwards, for the Carnival season, to Venice, where Wolfgang gave a successful concert and enjoyed the usual festivities of a Venetian Carnival. A few brief notes from Wolfgang, written in Milan to his sister, refer to his fingers aching from writing and from Venice he writes that Venice pleases him very much.

On March 12 they left Venice and stayed at Padua, where Wolfgang received a commission to write an oratorio. They were in Vicenza on March 14, Verona on March 18, in Innsbruck on March 25, arriving home in Salzburg on March 28 with a commission to write an opera for Milan for the Carnival of 1773 with an increased fee of one hundred and thirty *gigliati*. They had been away from Salzburg from December 13, 1769 until March 28, 1771, a little less than two years. Wolfgang had spent his fourteenth and fifteenth birthdays in Italy and had now definitely left his childhood and all its triumphs behind him.

Of the opera *Mitridate, Rè di Ponto* (K.87),[53] not much needs to be said. It was an opera seria in three acts for four sopranos, one contralto, two tenors, with accompaniment of two violins, alto, two flutes, two oboes, four horns, two trombones, two bassoons, and bass. The book, as may be imagined, since it is an adaptation of Racine's tragedy, is an unusually good one; so much so, indeed, that Wyzewa and Saint-Foix express a regret that Mozart did not have such a libretto to compose in his maturity instead of a *Clemenza di Tito* or even *Idomeneo*. The opera consists of twenty-four numbers, exclusive of the overture; they are all solo arias with the exception of one duet and a concluding quintet. Wolfgang conformed to the rather strict rules of the Italian opera seria of the time, which were directed towards giving the principal singers opportunities to display their vocal talent and powers of expression in elaborate arias of a rather grave and formal beauty. In fact the music of such operas had much the same function as the verse in French tragedies. It was the beauty of Racine's verse in its superb and rhetorical justness and inventiveness that supplied the artistic element to these dramas and it was just this element that the composer had to supply *in music* instead of poetry when using the same plots.

That Wolfgang before his fifteenth birthday had succeeded in *Mitridate* in composing an opera at least as good as those of the majority of contemporary mature Italian masters is abundantly clear from the unquestionable success of the work with the public; but in many details of purity and refinement it also shows his real superiority as a natural musician without disclosing, however, the genius of his maturity.

But on the whole Wolfgang reached a higher level in the faultless declamatory recitatives of this opera than in the arias.

[53]Only fragments of the original manuscript score survive.

We may conveniently pause here and consider for a few moments the beautiful portrait of Wolfgang painted at Verona by Cignaroli in January 1770, the month of Wolfgang's fourteenth birthday (January 27). It is true that in this picture he looks older than his age and there is not much sign—except perhaps in the fine curves of the well-cut mouth —of his bubbling spirits and exceptional sense of humour. But the fullness above the eyes, the fine development of the forehead around the eyebrows, with a hint of voluptuousness in the mouth and chin (which is even more noticeable in the engraving from this portrait made by L. Sichling and now in the Salzburg Mozarteum) have an unmistakable reality which makes this in some ways one of the best portraits of Mozart we possess.

Most of the biographers of Mozart amuse themselves in psychological speculation for which they show themselves quite unfitted. This is true even of the good ones like Jahn, Schurig, etc., who, once they leave the secure ground of facts, occasionally utter the most preposterous nonsense, proving that they have little conception of the real nature of Mozart's genius but owe most of their appreciation to the renown of his name or the enjoyment of his music on its lower levels. It must be a matter for everlasting regret that no great painter —a Rembrandt or even an Ingres, a Cézanne, or a Seurat—had the opportunity to portray with fidelity to nature and to art what must have been one of the most remarkable of all human heads. Instead of a portrait of the real man we have only a number of superficial semi-likenesses against all of which the observer must be to some extent warned. The subtlety and complexity of Mozart's personality were unquestionably mirrored in his face. His was no physiognomical façade of plain, inherited features on which the average painter may be let loose without going astray. Rather did his features call for an extraordinary blend of sensuous and intellectual perception in the artist who observed them, for it is an extraordinary and ever-disregarded truth that he who looks sees only what exists in himself, and what is not within him, if only in germ, he cannot behold though it be staring him in the face.

Hence it is that every critic and every performer of Mozart's music gives us an image not of Mozart but of himself. That it is not ludicrously apparent how minified or contracted this image is in nine thousand out of nine thousand and one cases is only due to the restraining influences on mediocrities of the great men who have seen Mozart as he really was. "Ah! we shall never be able to do anything like that," remarked Beethoven once to Cramer at an Augarten concert in Vienna after hearing a performance of Mozart's Concerto in C minor (K. 491). I once quoted this remark to a hero-worshipper of Beethoven, a very clever man, and he said: "Beethoven must have been speaking ironically." To such ridiculous lengths does blind and stupid partisanship take those who are clever but have no instinct! If Beethoven had not been able to make that remark with complete and passionate seriousness he would not have been Beethoven. For no element of rivalry enters into the work of the greatest masters since it is the distinctive mark of a great master that nobody else can do what he does. It does not diminish Mozart one jot to say that he could not have written Beethoven's G major Pianoforte Concerto. And it is also true—and Beethoven knew it—that even he, Beethoven, was incapable of composing the C minor Concerto of Mozart. Such works are not only unsurpassable—they are unique.

So Jahn tells us that Wolfgang returned to Salzburg at the end of March 1771, aged fifteen and two months, with his nature as "simple, modest, and childlike as when he had set out." Two things that seem to be the same may be vastly different and let me say that the word *simple* as applied to Mozart is not only profoundly true but is also so utterly different from *simple* as generally understood that it is highly misleading to all but those few who can truly understand it. "*Consider the lilies how they grow: they toil not, neither do they spin.*" That is a simple, a Mozartian remark; but it is profounder than all the wisdom of Solomon, the aphorisms of Lord Bacon, and the wisecracks of a *simple* American. Modest! Yes, Mozart was—with the possible exception of Shakespeare —the most modest of all the great artists of history. But what was this modesty? It was the natural expression of the certainty of what he was, a God-given genius. An artist of Mozart's rank cannot be proud; he may show pride in certain unfavourable circumstances which put an unbearable strain upon some elements in his nature, and this is the root of the pride which Beethoven and Berlioz occasionally showed. But they were not proud or vain men, they simply failed occasionally in compassion. It is one of the most remarkable facts about Mozart that one may truthfully say that he never failed in compassion. This unfailing, universal sympathy—in whose possession he resembles such a Russian character as Tchekov—was combined with an astounding vitality, so that in Mozart we may find that rarest of all human beings, a saint who is not a bore; a nature so sound, sweet, and passionate that I, personally, have for many years felt that among all the great artists of history Mozart and Shakespeare were the only ones whose moral superiority strikes to the core of one's being.

As for the third of Jahn's epithets, "childlike," which is used by Mozart's own sister and nearly all who knew him personally, it is quite clear to any perceptive and adult person what that means. It means the possession of an eternal freshness of heart. "Suffer the little children to come unto me, for of such is the kingdom of heaven" was the remark of someone who knew the roots of life. Every great creative artist must possess this freshness and purity of heart, for without it there can be no creation, only impotent cerebration.

So we can imagine Wolfgang settling down again in the little town of Salzburg quite as unspoiled by his Italian successes as he was by his earlier triumphant career as a child prodigy. Through Count Firmian he received a commission in the name of the Empress Maria Theresa to compose a theatrical cantata for the celebration at Milan in October 1771 of the marriage of the Archduke Ferdinand with Princess Maria, daughter of Prince Ercole of Modena. In the meantime at Salzburg during the next five months he composed the Italian oratorio commissioned in Padua, *La Betulia Liberata* (K.118),[1] a *Litany* (K.109), a *Regina Cœli* (K.108), several

---

[1] *La Betulia Liberata* is an oratorio on the subject of Judith, in two parts, for four sopranos, one contralto, one tenor, one bass, and chorus, with accompaniment of two violins, alto, two oboes, two bassoons, four horns, two trumpets, and bass. In 1786 Mozart,

symphonies, perhaps also the remarkable Psalm *De Profundis* (K.93), of which the manuscript is in the British Museum, and a beautiful *Offertorium* (K.72) founded on the famous chorale of St. John the Baptist which Wagner borrowed for *Die Meistersinger*.

On August 13, 1771 Leopold and Wolfgang again left Salzburg, arriving in Milan on August 21. At the beginning of September he received the libretto for the commissioned theatrical cantata or serenata and immediately began composing the music. At Milan they were in the midst of famous musicians, including the great soprano Catarina Gabrielli,[2] the tenor Manzuoli, and the composer Hasse, who was busy working at an opera on a text by Metastasio entitled *Ruggiero* which had been commissioned for the same festival occasion. Wolfgang's libretto was by a well-known Milanese poet, the Abbé Parini, who held the chair of Rhetoric in the University. It was an allegorical pastoral play in two acts with choruses and dances (these by Favier).

The marriage was to take place in Milan Cathedral on October 15; on the 16th a public banquet was to be given to more than four hundred bridal couples to whom the Empress had given dowries; in the evening Hasse's opera *Ruggiero* was to have its first performance in the newly decorated theatre, with two ballets in the entr'acte by Pick and Favier, and on the next day, the 17th after a magnificent procession on the Corso, Wolfgang's *Ascanio in Alba* was to be produced. Wolfgang, therefore, had very little more than a month in which to compose the work. Some idea of the conditions of opera-composing is given by Hasse's statement that six months were needed for a good opera, while Naumann[3] declared that

---

hoping to get it performed in Vienna, added a chorus and a quintet, but unfortunately these two pieces are lost. This is a remarkable composition worth reviving on account of its superb choruses. See Wyzewa and Saint-Foix, Vol. 1, pp. 362–6.

[2] Of Gabrielli, Mozart writes to his father from Mannheim on February 19, 1778, with reference to the young Aloysia Weber: "It is all true what they have written about the Weberin except one thing, that she sings like Gabrielli; for that would not please me at all. . . . Whoever has heard Gabrielli can only say that she is nothing but a passage and roulade machine."

[3] J. G. Naumann (1741–1801), a renowned operatic and church composer.

in Venice it was expected that an opera should be written, learned, and produced all within a month. From Leopold's and Wolfgang's letters written home during this trip I take the following:

[FROM LEOPOLD]   *Verona, August 18, 1771*
    . . . The first day of our journey was a pleasant medley. In Kalterl we ate standing . . . while the postilion gave our horses a little hay and drank . . . a quart of quite good March beer. In Waidring we had soup and drank a not at all bad Johanserbier. At St. Johann we stayed and dined, and on the 14th we ate at the Post at Kundl and stayed the night at Innsbruck. On the 15th at midday in Steinach, the night in Brixen, midday on the 16th in Botzen, the night in Trent. On the 17th we arrived in Rovereto . . . and today left at about seven for Verona, where at 12.30 we got out at Sgr. Luggiati's and went at one o'clock to lunch. Now, after eating, everyone has gone to sleep and I have taken the opportunity with a bad pen in a by no means middling heat to scrawl this letter. Wolfgang, very tired, has also gone to sleep. . . .

    Now I must tell you that in my haste I forgot to bring several clavier sonatas and a trio for a good friend in Milan who has done much for us . . . Nannerl can also get out the two trios, one by Joseph Haydn in F with violin and 'cello and one in C by Wagenseil with variations. . . .

[POSTSCRIPT BY WOLFGANG]
Dearest Sister,
    I have not slept more than half an hour for I don't enjoy sleeping after eating. You can hope, believe, suppose, be of the opinion, have confidence, find it certain, imagine, conceive, and live in assurance that we are well but I can also let you know it. I must hurry, farewell. My compliments to all good friends. Ask Herr von Hefner . . . if he has seen the Anna girl.[4] *Addio* . . . my hand-kiss to Mamma. Lovely writing!
                                                                Wolfgang

[FROM LEOPOLD]   *Milan, August 24, 1771*
    . . . I must tell you that the poetry[5] is not yet come. It is ardently awaited since without it they cannot get on with the preparation of dresses, etc. . . . On October 15 the Arch-

---

[4]An affair of the heart? See also the following letter.
[5]The book of the cantata had to be sent to Vienna for approval.

duke enters Milan and arrives at the Cathedral and they are married straightway, then there is the kissing of hands, afterwards a great supper-party and then good-night! The next day festivities begin . . . meanwhile I have seen twenty thousand wax candles which are ready for the lighting of the Cathedral, the court, etc.

[POSTSCRIPT BY WOLFGANG]

My dearest Sister!

We have had to endure great heat on the journey and the dust has parched us with such faithful impertinence that we should have suffocated and perished had we not been cleverer. Here it has not rained for a month. . . .

What you have promised (you know well what . . . O my dear one!) don't forget. I shall be most grateful. . . .[6]

Above us there is a violinist, beneath us another, close by a singing-master is giving a lesson, in the room opposite is an oboist. That is fine for composing!

Now I melt with heat! Now I have got rid of my vest. *Addio.* My hand-kiss to Mamma.

Wolfgang

Milan, August 31, 1771

My dearest Sister,

We are well, God be praised and thanked. I have eaten for you many good pears, peaches, and melons. My only amusement is to use the deaf and dumb language for I can do it to perfection. Herr Hasse[7] came here yesterday; today we visit him. The book of the serenata arrived last Thursday. I don't know what to write.

About that quite other matter of which there can be no more, you understand me. . . .[8]

[6]Again a reference to some affair of the heart; perhaps the daughter of Dr. Barisani. See p. 133.

[7]It is interesting to note that Hasse wrote on March 23, 1771 to the Abbé Ortes: "The young Mozart is certainly a marvel for his age and truly I love him boundlessly. The father, as far as I can see, is eternally discontented with everything . . . he idolizes his son a little too much and so does all he can to spoil him, but I have such a high opinion of the natural sense of the boy that in spite of his father's flattery I expect him not to let himself be spoiled but to grow into a proper man."

[8]A quite obscure reference in the German, probably to his love-affair.

[FROM LEOPOLD]   *Milan, September 13, 1771*

The serenata, which actually is more like a play in two parts, will be finished by Wolfgang, with God's help, in twelve days. The recitatives with and without instrumentation are all ready, as well as the choruses, of which there are eight, five of which have dancing. We saw the dance rehearsal today and were astonished at the industry of the two ballet-masters Pick and Favier. . . .

[PS. FROM WOLFGANG]

I write only . . . in order to write, it is not at all to my mind as I have a bad cold. . . .

[FROM LEOPOLD]   *Milan, September 21, 1771*

. . . By Monday or Tuesday at latest Wolfgang will have seen everything finished. Sgr. Manzuoli often comes to us; we have been over to him. Sgr. Tibaldi [tenor] comes almost daily about eleven and remains . . . till about one o'clock while Wolfgang is composing. Everyone is uncommonly polite and has the greatest regard for Wolfgang; yes, we have not had the slightest trouble, because they are all good and famous singers and sensible people. This serenata is actually a small opera, and the opera [of Hasse] is itself no longer, apart from the two big ballets after the first and second acts, each of which lasts three-quarters of an hour.[9]

. . . All Milan is in upheaval . . . everyone is working, partly for the reception . . . for the lodgings and rooms . . . for the preparation and lighting of the Cathedral . . . for costumes, liveries of the retainers . . . carriages . . . horses . . . balls . . . renovation and decoration of the whole theatre . . . in short, for hundreds of things which don't just occur to me . . . everything, everything is astir! . . . In some previous letter you mentioned that many persons had become crazy and now you write that many are dying of dysentery. That is very bad. If people go wrong both at the top and bottom they are indeed in a bad way.

[PS. FROM WOLFGANG TO HIS SISTER]

Thank God I am well. I cannot write much; firstly, because I know nothing; secondly, my finger is so sore from writing. Farewell, my hand-kiss to Mamma. I pipe on my pipe

[9]Abert in his edition of Jahn does not seem to have understood this reference and thinks it refers to ballets by Mozart.

and nobody answers. Only two arias are now needed for the serenata, then I am finished. My compliments to all good friends . . . I have no more desire to be in Salzburg. I fear I also might become crazy.

[FROM LEOPOLD]   *Milan, October 5, 1771*

Herr Caplan tells me . . . that you and Nannerl would have liked to take this trip with us. If you were really serious about this you ought to have told me so frankly, although the extra cost merely to travel here and back would have been at least sixty ducats. Do not have too many regrets about it. You would have had to endure incredible heat, and although many things are happening here, yet they are partly things such as you have already seen—and finer even—or things which on account of the crowds one sees in great discomfort, even in danger of one's life if one is bent on seeing every blessed thing. . . .

[PS. FROM WOLFGANG TO HIS SISTER]

I am, God be praised and thanked, well but always sleepy. . . .

[FROM LEOPOLD]   *Milan, October 19, 1771*

Marcobruni presents his compliments, he is with me at this moment and we are now going to the theatre, for on the 16th was the opera and on the 17th the serenata, which pleased so greatly that it is to be repeated today. The Archduke has ordered two copies; all cavaliers and other people come up and speak to us in the street to congratulate Wolfgang. In short, I am sorry that Wolfgang's serenata has so eclipsed Hasse's opera. I shall answer your last letter and Nannerl's postscript when I write next. You will be able to see Italy with much more enjoyment than at present in the midst of this uproar. Farewell, we both kiss you ten thousand times, your old   MZT

[FROM LEOPOLD]   *Milan, October 26, 1771*

. . . Perhaps news will reach Salzburg of the great success of Wolfgang's serenata since the young Herr Kerschbaumer, who was here some days, was an eye- and ear-witness the day before yesterday, the 24th, how the Archduke and Archduchess not only clapped and had two arias repeated but . . . both bowed from their balcony to Wolfgang and showed him their pleasure by calling: *"Bravissimo, Maestro!"* . . .

On the 24th there was a terrible mishap . . . a stand collapsed and fifty people were not only severely hurt but many lost an arm, leg, hand, or foot . . . while two women were killed . . . luckily we were late . . . and went on to the court stand, but had we been earlier we should have been on the same stand that collapsed. Let us thank God; we go on no more stands. You see that it is true what I wrote in my previous letter and you may believe that on such occasions there is little to be seen without running risks. . . .

. . . The Archduke and his wife are well and very happy, which has greatly pleased Her Majesty the Empress because one was apprehensive lest he might be little pleased with his bride since she is not beautiful; but she is very amiable, pleasing, and virtuous and is consequently liked by everybody and has greatly charmed the Archduke. . . .

[PS. FROM WOLFGANG]

Dearest Sister,

I am, God be praised and thanked, well; now my work is finished I have time to write, only I don't know what, for Papa has already said everything. I know of nothing new, except that numbers 35, 59, 60, 61, and 62 have been drawn in the lottery and if we had had these numbers we should have won, but since we have not entered we have neither lost nor won but have the laugh on others. The two arias encored in the serenata were sung by Manzuoli and Girelli.

I hope you will enjoy yourself in Triebenbach with shooting and if the weather permits with walking . . . my hand-kiss to Mamma! Farewell. I am always your faithful brother,

Wolfgang

Forgive the wild writing, but I am in a hurry.

[PS. FROM WOLFGANG TO HIS
  MOTHER AND SISTER]   *Milan, November 2, 1771*

. . . Herr Kerschbaumer . . . certainly can give a better account of his journey than others of our friends, one of whom said he could not see Paris because the houses were too high. Today is Hasse's opera, but as Papa does not go out I cannot go. Luckily I know all the arias thoroughly by heart and so can see and hear it in my mind at home.[10]

[10]This is truly a remarkable statement because it means that Mozart could have written Hasse's entire score down from memory as he did Allegri's *Miserere*.

[PS. FROM WOLFGANG TO HIS MOTHER AND SISTER]

Milan, November 30, 1771

So that you shall not think I am ill I write these two lines. Farewell. My hand-kiss to Mamma, my regards to all good friends. I have seen on the Domplatz here four fellows swing. They swing here *wie zu lion*.[11]

A few words are necessary about the pastoral serenade *Ascanio in Alba* (K.111). It is described as a *Festa teatrale* in two parts and is written for four sopranos, one tenor, and choruses, with accompaniment of two violins, alto, two oboes, two bassoons, two flutes, two horns, two serpents, bass, two trombones, and kettle-drums. The original score, which is now in Berlin, has four hundred and eighty pages in two volumes. The serenata has thirty-three numbers, consisting of recitatives, arias, and choruses, and one Trio (No. 31). The choruses are divided into two kinds, those with and those without dancing. Wyzewa and Saint-Foix state that the choral part "seems to have been written by Mozart with much more pleasure and participation than the dramatic part" and they praise very highly the series of small choruses for shepherds and shepherdesses, accompanied often only by wind instruments, as being full of grace, beauty, and rhythmic variety.

It is possible that the long sketch for a ballet entitled *Le Gelosie del Seraglio* (K. anhang 109),[12] which is of the same date, was intended for performance between the two acts of *Ascanio in Alba*, especially as it bears the names of some of the dancers—for example, Pick, Binetti, etc. The plot of *Ascanio in Alba* is as follows:

Venus descends from Heaven with her grandson, Ascanio, promising to give him for wife the beautiful Sylvia, descended from Hercules. Sylvia relates to the priest, Aceste, that in a dream she has seen a beautiful young man destined to be her husband. Ascanio disguises himself on the instruction of Venus to test Sylvia, who hesitates to recognize in him her destined hero. After certain trials, reconciliation takes place

[11]I take *wie zu lion* to mean: "as at Lyons."

[12]Dr. Einstein, in his 1937 edition of Köchel, is of the opinion that *Le Gelosie del Seraglio* is the first of three ballets composed by Mozart for the later opera in Milan *Lucio Silla*.

and Venus pronounces to the lovers the duties of their future life.[13]

Leopold and Wolfgang returned to Salzburg from Milan on December 15, 1771. On December 16 the Archbishop Sigismund died and his successor was elected on March 14, 1772. The new Archbishop, Hieronymous Joseph Franz von Paula, Count of Colloredo, Bishop of Gurk, was extremely unpopular and was elected, according to Koch-Sternfeld, "to the general surprise and grief of the populace."

Wolfgang was commissioned to write an opera for the installation of the new Archbishop, and the subject chosen was also of the classical, allegorical variety: *Il Sogno di Scipione* (Scipio's Dream) by Metastasio. But before he set to work on this he had a severe illness during January 1772. We know this from a letter written after his death by his sister to Sonnleithner, dated July 2, 1819, about a portrait of Mozart's, an unsigned water-colour dated 1771–2, now in the Mozarteum in Salzburg,[14] of which she says:

"It was painted when he had returned from the Italian tour, at sixteen years of age; but as he was just recovering from a severe illness, the picture is sickly and yellow."

Previous to this, on December 30, Wolfgang had composed a Symphony in A (K.114) for two violins, alto, two flutes (two oboes in the andante), two horns, violoncello, and bass, consisting of an allegro moderato, andante (in D), minuet and trio (in A minor), and allegro molto. But this was only the first of a long series of compositions which were composed during the first part of this year—namely, between February 1772 and October 24, 1772, when father and son left Salzburg again to go to Milan for the production of the new opera which had been commissioned. I shall merely enumerate the works which are known to have been composed during this period, without much comment:

Mass in C minor (K.139).
Symphony in G (K.124).
Sonata for four hands in D for Clavier (K.381).

[13]*Ascanio in Alba* is worth the attention of musical directors. A delightful choral ballet might be made of it.

[14]Schurig puts this illness back to the autumn of 1769 on the ground that Sonnleithner was corresponding about the Cignaroli picture, which, however, was in oils.

Sonata d'église in D for two violins, bass, and organ (K.144).

Sonata d'église in F for two violins, bass, and organ (K. 145).

Litaniæ de Venerabile Altaris Sacramento in B flat (K.125).

Divertimento in D for two violins, alto, and bass (K.136).

Divertimento in B flat for two violins, alto, and bass (K.137).

Divertimento in F for two violins, alto, and bass (K.138).

Six Dance Minuets with trios for two violins, two oboes, one flute, two trumpets (or horns), and bass (K.164).

Symphony in C for two violins, alto, two oboes, two horns, and bass (K.128).

Symphony in G for two violins, alto, two oboes, two horns, and bass (K.129).

Regina cœli in B flat for four voices, two violins, alto, two oboes (or flutes), two horns, bass, and organ (K.127).

Symphony in F[15] for two violins, two altos, bass, two flutes, two horns in F, and two horns in C (K.130).

Divertimento in D[16] for two violins, two altos, flute, oboe, bassoon, four horns in D, and bass (K.131).

Symphony in E flat for two violins, two altos, two oboes, four horns, violoncello, and bass (K.132).

Symphony in D[17] for two violins, alto, two oboes, two horns, two trumpets, violoncello, and bass (K.133).

Symphony in A[18] for two violins, alto, two flutes, two horns, violoncello, and bass (K.134).

Tantum ergo in D for four voices, two violins, alto, two trumpets, bass, and organ (K.197).

Two German songs on the poems of J. C. Gunther (K.149 and 150).

Song for soprano in F. *Die Zufriedenheit* (K.151).

In addition to this considerable quantity of work there was the one-act opera, composed for inauguration of the new Archbishop of Salzburg, entitled *Il Sogno di Scipione* (K.126),[19] composed for two sopranos, three tenors, choruses, with accompaniment of two violins, alto, two flutes, two

[15]This symphony marks a great progress; it is dated May 1772 and shows the influence of Joseph Haydn.

[16]This *divertimento* in six movements is a wonderful piece testifying to the maturing genius of Mozart at sixteen. It is often performed in the concert-hall today.

[17]One of the finest of Mozart's early symphonies.

[18]Another remarkable work, in which J. Haydn's influence is less strong.

[19]The plot, based on Cicero's *Somnium Scipionis*, is simple: The young Scipio, asleep in the palace of Massinissa, is visited in dream by the Goddess of Fortune and the Goddess of Constancy, who call on him to decide between them as his guide through life. Then his ancestors come, among them Scipio Africanus and Æmilius Paulus, and warn him. Finally Scipio chooses Constancy.

oboes, two trombones, kettle-drums, and bass. This work consists of ten arias, two choruses, overture, and recitative. It was performed at Salzburg during April 1772.

It is worth noting that just during this period when Wolfgang was developing so fast a correspondent of Burney[20] visited Salzburg in the summer of 1772 and heard Wolfgang and his sister play duets together; he informs Burney that although Wolfgang is an undoubted master of his instrument, yet he appears to have reached his climax and, judging from his orchestral music, "he affords another example that premature fruits are more rare than excellent." One wonders if this visitor could possibly have heard the Divertimento in D (K.131), composed in June of that year, with its wealth of melodic beauty and wonderful skill in the varied use of the wind instruments, or either of the two Symphonies (K.133 or K.134)? It seems hardly possible that after hearing such works —so far beyond the capacity of any living composer except perhaps Joseph Haydn—anyone could have come to any other conclusion than that the young Wolfgang was at sixteen a more wonderful phenomenon than ever.

Leopold and Wolfgang left Salzburg for Milan on October 24 without Wolfgang having written any part of his commissioned opera other than a few recitatives, which he had to scrap as he found on his arrival that the poet's text had been revised by Metastasio. The best account of this third Italian journey is to be got from the letters of Leopold and Wolfgang, from which I take the following brief extracts:

[FROM LEOPOLD]   *Botzen, October 28, 1772*

Have we not travelled astonishingly fast to be in Botzen? . . . One always forgets something. I bought and brought along a new calendar, but we have left this year's somewhere, so I must buy a new one, which is a joke. That I should have left my little seal at home is, however, no joke and annoys me excessively.

My health this time, praise God, has been brought, as it seems, into good order by disorder. If travelling is necessary for my health I shall seek a courier's job or to become the conductor of a mail-coach. Wolfgang is well; he kills time by writing a Quartet. . . .[21]

[20]Burney's *Travels*, III, p. 263.
[21]Quartet in D (K.155).

[PS. TO HIS SISTER BY WOLFGANG]

Now we are already at Botzen. Already? Only! I am hungry, thirsty, sleepy, I am lazy but well. At Hall we saw the convent and played on the organ. . . . I hope you have kept your word and gone last Sunday to D.N. Farewell, write to me the news! Botzen deep Swinepool!

A poem by one who was devilish ferocious and furious over Botzen:

> I'd rather stick my groats in
> My guts than go to Botzen.

[FROM WOLFGANG TO HIS MOTHER][22]

Milan, November 7, 1772

Do not be frightened at seeing my writing instead of Papa's; the reason is (1) that we are with Herr von Aste and Baron Cristani and they have so much to discuss that it is impossible for him to find time to write and (2) he is too—lazy. We arrived here safely on the 4th at midday and are well. . . . All the talk in Germany about the Italian war and the fortification of castles is untrue. Forgive my bad writing. When you write, write direct to us, for it is not the custom here as in Germany to carry the letters round, one must fetch them from the post. . . . There is no news here, we await news from Salzburg. We hope you will have had our letter from Botzen. I have nothing more to say, so I shall stop. We kiss Mamma 100,000 (I haven't brought any more noughts) times. I kiss Mamma's hand and my dear sister I embrace *in persona* as in imagination.

[FROM LEOPOLD] *Milan, November 21, 1772*

Thank God we are well and active like fish in water, for it has rained incessantly for eight days. Today is the anniversary of our wedding. It is, I think, twenty-five years since we had the good idea to get married. We had this idea in truth many years before. Good things take time! The *primo uomo*, Sgr. Rauzzini, has now arrived, so there will be more to do and it will be livelier. There will also be no lack of the usual little comedies customary in the theatre. But these are trivialities. The figs which Wolfgang brought with him from Salzburg

---

[22]Note the imaginative care Wolfgang shows for his mother in beginning this letter.

were as miraculous as the loaves and fishes in the Gospel; they have lasted till now. . . .

[PS. FROM WOLFGANG TO HIS SISTER]

I thank you, you know what for—I cannot possibly write to Hrn. von Heffner. When you see him let him read this. I beg him meanwhile to be satisfied. . . .

[FROM LEOPOLD]   *November 28, 1772*

You ask me to write at length but what shall I write? That we both, thank God, are well is the most important and best news; there is nothing new here, most people are still in the country. . . . As regards my headaches, these come only occasionally, at night . . . otherwise my appeite is good and when I can eat I am the healthiest of men. However, we eat only once a day, at about two o'clock. At night we have an apple, a piece of bread, and a glass of wine. . . . Wolfgang has written nothing more for the *primo uomo* as yet than the first aria; it is, however, incomparable and he sings it like an angel. . . .

[PS. TO HIS SISTER FROM WOLFGANG]

We both congratulate Herr von Aman and tell him from me that I am vexed that he made a secret of it when I have spoken to him of his bride. I took him to be more candid . . . tell him that if he is minded to have a regular wedding he should wait till our return so that what he promised me may come true—namely, that I should dance at his wedding. Farewell! I kiss Mamma's hand. . . .

[FROM LEOPOLD]   *Milan, December 5, 1772*

We are, thank God, well although I am writing with a bad pen; for at Mm. D'Aste—who sends her compliments—the pens are always bad . . . as the *prima donna* only arrived yesterday and the tenor is not yet known it is easy to guess that the main and most important part of the opera is not yet composed. . . .

[PS. TO HIS SISTER FROM WOLFGANG]

I have still fourteen pieces to do, then I shall be ready, for one can reckon the terzet and duet as four pieces. I cannot write much for I know nothing and secondly I don't know what I write while my thoughts are always on my opera and there is a danger that instead of words I shall write you a whole aria. . . .

I have learned here in Milan a new game called: *Mercante in fiera*; as soon as I come home we shall play it. I have also learned a new language from Fr. von Taste, it is easy to talk, troublesome but useful to write, though it is a little . . . childish, but good for Salzburg. (*Addio, farewell!*) My compliments to all good friends, my regards to our lovely Nandl and to the Canary bird for these two and you are the most innocent in our house. Fischietti[23] will soon begin on an opera buffa (in German) and start working on his idiotic opera. *Addio*, my hand-kiss to Mamma.

[FROM LEOPOLD]   *Milan, December 12, 1772*

. . . The tenor from Turin is out of the Royal Chapel and is expected on the 14th or 15th. Then, first of all, four arias must be composed for him. Sgra. de Amicis sends her regards to both of you; she is extremely well contented with the three arias she has till now. Wolfgang has written her principal aria with passages which are novel and quite especially and astoundingly difficult; she sings these astonishingly and we are the best and most trusted friends. I write with a bad pen and ink. Wolfgang has the good ink, he is writing at another table. . . .

We have had rain here for some time, but the last three days have been fine and not cold. We have not yet had a fire lit. It was wrong of Wolfgang not to give Frl. Waberl[24] the Minuet, but she will forgive him when she reflects that he is a fickle fellow who readily forgets. Why he thought of Frl. Barisani,[25] however, is natural enough and needs no explanation. . . .

How is Mlle. Zezi, is she learning? Is Nannerl industrious with her? My love to Nannerl and tell her to practise assiduously and teach patiently the little Zezi. I know it is to her own advantage if she accustoms herself to teach another patiently and thoroughly. I don't write this aimlessly.

[FROM LEOPOLD]   *Milan, December 18, 1772*

Today three recitatives were rehearsed. Last night the tenor arrived and today Wolfgang wrote two arias for him and

[23]Domenico Fischietti, a Neapolitan opera-composer made Church Kapellmeister at Salzburg in 1772.

[24]Daughter of Eberlin.

[25]Daughter of the Archbishop's physician, Dr. Sylvester von Barisani, whom Wolfgang then admired.

still has two to do. Sunday, the 20th, is the second rehearsal,
Tuesday, the 22nd, the third rehearsal. Wednesday, the 23rd,
the dress rehearsal. Thursday and Friday nothing and on Saturday the 26th, the first performance of the opera. . . . I write
this at eleven o'clock at night just as Wolfgang has finished
the second aria. . . .

[PS. FROM WOLFGANG TO HIS SISTER]

I hope you are well, my dear sister. When you get this
letter, my dear sister, that very evening, my dear sister, my
opera is staged. Think of me, my dear sister, and imagine
vividly, my dear sister, that you, my dear sister, are seeing and
hearing it also. . . .

. . . My dear sister, tomorrow we dine with H. V. Mayer
and why, do you think? Guess! Because we are invited. The
next rehearsal is in the theatre. The impresario, Sig. Casti-
glioni, has implored me to tell nobody, otherwise everybody
will rush there and that we don't want, so, my child, I beg you
to tell it to nobody, otherwise too many people will rush there,
my child. *Approposito* do you know the story that is going
about here? Now I shall tell it to you. We left Count Firmian
to go home and when we came to our street we opened our
door and what do you think then happened? We entered.
Farewell, my *lungel*. I kiss you my liver and remain my stomach always your unworthy

frater Wolfgang
bruder

Please please my dear sister something bites me, scratch
me.[26]

[FROM LEOPOLD]   *Milan, December 26, 1772*

Since lunch we have remained at Mme. D'Aste's, where I
am now writing . . . in about two or three hours the opera
will begin.[27] God favour us. The dress rehearsal went so well

[26]Every other line of this letter is written by Wolfgang upside
down, which was a favourite trick of his. The whole letter is utterly
characteristic.

[27]It was the custom to begin an hour after *Ave Maria.* At 5.30 P.M.
the theatre was full. The Archduke had retired before *Ave Maria* to
dispatch five New Year messages to Vienna, which caused a delay
until the arrival of the court at about eight o'clock. The singers were
then irritable and nervous and the first performance finished at two
o'clock and did not go well. The next performance was good and
twenty performances to crowded houses followed.

the day before yesterday that we hope for a good success. The music alone without ballets lasts four hours. We received your letter and all its news. Joseph Hagenauer's misfortune has gone to our hearts. Today we both earnestly prayed to God in the church for his recovery. The ghost-story of the Barisani household is nothing but a hysterical delusion . . . on the 21st, 22nd, and 23rd there was every evening a great gathering of the whole nobility in Count Firmian's house; there was continuous music from five o'clock until eleven. We were invited and Wolfgang played. . . . On these three evenings the best houses of the town were lit with great torches; near Count Firmian's house in the church towers were peals of bells like the carillons in the Netherlands, and in the street there was music with trumpets and kettle-drums. . . .

[FROM LEOPOLD]   *Milan, January 16, 1773*
. . . We are, praise God, well and my head remains better.[28] . . . Wolfgang's opera has now been played seventeen times and will be given twenty times in all. The second opera was to have been begun on the 23rd but as it goes so well the second will not be staged until the 30th. . . .

[PS. FROM WOLFGANG TO HIS SISTER]
I am busy writing a motet[29] for the *primo uomo*[30] which must be ready by tomorrow. Farewell. . . .

Leopold was hopeful of obtaining for Wolfgang a post with the Grand Duke Leopold of Tuscany. He had the powerful support of Count Firmian and at first the prospects seemed favourable. It was for this reason that he stayed on in Milan, giving as an excuse—for he was no doubt fearful of the new Archbishop of Salzburg and of exceeding his leave of absence—that he was confined to his bed with an attack of rheumatism. On January 30 he writes a long letter to his wife describing his illness and his inability to travel, to which he adds in cipher the following postscript:

[28]Leopold complains often of dizziness and remarks that he suffers from giddiness and overheating of the head after playing, just as in Salzburg every night after music.

[29]*Exultate* (K.165). I heard this beautiful work, of which only the "Alleluia" is generally known, performed at the Salzburg Festival in 1937 at the St. Peter's Church under Dr. Paumgartner. The andante aria *"Tu virginum corona"* is extraordinarily fine.

[30]Venanzio Rauzzini.

"From Florence no answer has come yet from the Grand Duke. What I have written about my illness is all untrue. I was in bed a few days but am well and am going today to the opera. You can destroy this slip so that it gets into nobody's hands"

Unfortunately, Wolfgang was not to have the good luck of Beethoven or of Haydn, both of whom found permanent patrons who provided for their livelihood until they died. The negotiations with the Grand Duke came to nothing; as they had done in 1771 with the Archduke Ferdinand of Austria, who actually contemplated taking Wolfgang into his service and wrote to his mother, the Empress Maria Theresa, on the subject, who, however, replied on December 12, 1771:

"You ask me about taking into your service the young Salzburger. I don't think so, for I do not believe you have any need of a composer or of useless persons. If, however, it would please you I don't want to prevent you. What I say is not to burden yourself with useless people. . . ."

The failure of his negotiations with the Grand Duke of Tuscany led to Leopold's and Wolfgang's return to Salzburg at the beginning of March. Leopold now falls back upon the idea of another great European tour, for which, however, money must be saved: "I grudge," he writes to his wife, "every kreutzer spent in Salzburg." They arrived in Salzburg on March 13 in order to be present at the anniversary of the Archbishop's election, March 14.

Something must now be said about the opera seria *Lucio Silla* (K.135), produced in Milan in January 1773. The text was by Giovanni de Gammera, partly revised by Metastasio.[31] It is a rather stiff and dry libretto, making a *Dramma per musica* in three acts composed by Wolfgang for four sopranos, two tenors, with choruses, and two violins, alto, two oboes, two flutes, two bassoons, two horns, two trombones, kettledrums, and bass. It consists of an Overture and the following:—

[31]The plot is as follows: Silla (the Roman Sulla) loves Giunia, promised bride of the Senator Cecilio, and determines to kill Cecilio after vainly having represented him as dead in order to win over Giunia. The lovers decide to die together. Silla then pardons them and gives his sister Celia in marriage to Cecilio's friend, Cinna, renounces the dictatorship, and gives Rome back her freedom.

This opera, written in November and December 1772, about one month before Wolfgang's seventeenth birthday (January 27, 1773), ought to have been a masterpiece, because at this age Mozart was capable of such, as his instrumental and church compositions during that year—not to speak of his earlier opera *Mitridate* and other dramatic works —abundantly show. *Lucio Silla* is decidedly a remarkable opera seria with some marvellous things in it, but the reason that it is not more than this is best explained, I think, by Wyzewa and Saint-Foix in the following words:

"Never, perhaps, during his whole career was he further from the ideal state of mind for a composer of Italian opera than at this moment with a whole world of personal emotions in his heart[32] and in his head a world of new ideas not one of

[32]Wolfgang had this year fallen in love—for the first time—with the daughter of Barisani.

which belonged to the kind of music he had now to deal with. Nevertheless, with his native suppleness perhaps he could have freed himself from these preoccupations and given himself entirely to his opera had he had this time, as before, a good libretto such as the tragedy of Racine; but it so happened that the new libretto was quite incapable of interesting him, containing neither moving situations nor sentiments human and profound enough to cause him to feel them reawaken in his soul. The fact is that one could not imagine more mediocre material than that of *Lucio Silla* as a subject for the dramatic genius of a musician so serious and reflective as Mozart."

Nevertheless, quite apart from one magnificent scene, which I shall mention presently, some of the arias in this opera would be well worth hearing if we possessed singers capable of singing them. And by "capable" I don't mean singers who can merely sing the notes and think it wonderful to have done so; but singers to whom the difficulties would be a delight since they would transcend them with audacious and breath-taking (in more senses than one) ease. The aria of Giunia (No. 11) is in Wyzewa's and Saint-Foix's opinion "the most brilliant and most difficult Mozart ever wrote." This was sung by the Anna de Amicis often mentioned in the Mozart letters. As I shall have occasion to say again, later, the art of singing as it existed at its perfection during the latter part of the eighteenth century is scarcely imaginable today. Firstly, we have lost the *castrati*—apparently for ever, although I, personally, should not be surprised if centuries hence they returned—and, secondly, there is no demand, opportunity, or suitable environment for the development of the art of singing nowadays to any high degree of perfection. What passes for singing at our concerts and—with very rare exceptions—in our operahouses in either Europe or America today is relatively the merest amateurish, undeveloped note-scraping and, quite apart from the toneless barking in Wagnerian operas (where singing anyhow is unimaginable), has about as much resemblance to real singing as has yodelling. Therefore such an opera as *Lucio Silla* must remain at present a sealed book since it depends primarily upon that highly developed singer's art which has vanished. Should, however, a good and capable soprano—such as Toti dal Monte was at her best —read this book I recommend to her the Recitative and Aria No. 22, in C minor, of Giunia: "*Sposo mia vita*" and "*Fra i pensier.*"

The instrumentation of *Lucio Silla* is richer than any previous known in Italian opera and here for the first time in operatic history, as Wyzewa and Saint-Foix point out, "the vocal and the instrumental parts are treated symphonically like two members of one body, united for the same life."

But the gem of *Lucio Silla* is the scene of the encounter of Cecilio and Giunia in a gallery of tombs where Giunia, accompanied by a choir of attendants, has come to invoke the spirit of her father. This scene was apparently written by the librettist in imitation of the invocation scene in Gluck's *Orfeo*. When the day comes that civilized countries possess properly equipped and endowed schools of music it will be a delight to an enlightened conservatoire director to have his students produce this scene from *Lucio Silla* in the same program as the scene from *Orfeo* to show the students and connoisseurs the difference in musical character between Gluck and Mozart. Of this scene, which comprises Nos. 6 and 7, Wyzewa and Saint-Foix write: "It is one of the grandest and most poetic ensembles he has ever composed," and Hermann Abert says: "In this scene of *Lucio Silla* appears for the first time not only the dramatic Mozart but also the great master of the demoniacal."

In addition to this opera Wolfgang composed before his return to Salzburg the following:

Quartet in D (K.155), October 1772.
Quartet in G (K.156), November–December 1772.
Finale in D (K.163) for two violins, alto, two flutes, two oboes, two horns, trumpets, kettle-drums, and bass; a symphonic version of the overture to *Sogno di Scipione*.
Motet[33] in F (K.165) for soprano, *Exultate, jubilate*.
Symphony in C (K.96) for two violins, alto, two oboes, two horns, trumpet, and kettle-drums.
Quartet in C (K.157).
Quartet in F (K.158).
Sonata in F (K.55) for violin and clavier.
Sonata in C minor (K.59) for violin and clavier.
Sonata in F (K.57) for violin and clavier.
Quartet in B flat (K.159).

[33]See p. 135.

Sonata[34] in E minor (K.60) for violin and clavier.
Sonata[35] in E flat (K.58) for violin and clavier.
Adagio in E minor for string quartet, written to replace the adagio
in the Quartet in G (K.156).
Divertimento in B flat (K.186)[36] for two oboes, two clarinets, two
cors anglais, two horns, and two bassoons.

Thus concluded the last visit Mozart was destined to make
to Italy. The compositions which he wrote during this third
sojourn in Italy have a character entirely their own and his
return to the less joyous environment of Salzburg affected
him profoundly. Even his father wrote to his wife from Milan
on February 27, 1773:

"It is very hard for me to leave Italy."

Wolfgang is now seventeen years of age and from this
time on we shall find developing in him an ever-increasing
dislike of Salzburg and its conditions.

VIII. Four Years at Home

1773–1777   AGE 17–21

The conditions in Salzburg on the return of Wolfgang and
Leopold were not too favourable. Leopold, though vice-
Kapellmeister, had two Kapellmeisters over him, Lolli and
Fischietti, and he was not destined ever to improve his own
position in Salzburg with the new Archbishop, for Leopold
was not an easy servant. He was, in both character and general culture, much too superior and although, as Hasse remarked, he was an experienced man of the world, it seems
likely that the extraordinary genius of his son was clearer

[34]In this remarkable work, supposedly composed in Milan in February 1773, Wyzewa and Saint-Foix see the same wave of romanticism
which gave rise to the publication of Goethe's *Werther* the following
year (1774). Dr. Einstein, however, finds all six sonatas (K.55–60)
of doubtful authenticity and suggests they are the work of Schuster,
whose compositions made a great impression on Mozart in 1777.

[35]Another exquisite work but of a more tranquil character. These
beautiful Italian sonatas have been undeservedly neglected. Their
Italian character makes it unlikely that Dr. Einstein's suggestion that
they were composed not by Mozart but by Schuster is correct.

[36]A work of unique grace and serenity, a poetic masterpiece.

to him than to any other person and it was natural that he
should be more anxiously concerned about Wolfgang's future
than about anything else.

The four years from Wolfgang's seventeenth to twenty-
first birthdays were spent by Wolfgang at Salzburg, broken
by two short visits, one to Vienna in the summer and autumn
of 1773 and one to Munich for the Carnival season of
1774-5. We know less of this period of Mozart's life than
of any other since, all the family being most of the time at
home—with the exception of the two journeys mentioned
—there are few letters, so that the chief and most reliable
source of all biographical information is temporarily dried
up. But we have the record of Wolfgang's musical compositions during these four years as a guide to his development
and before mentioning the chief of these I shall say something about the general direction which his musical activity
took during this period.

It was during these four years that the influence of the
German school of musicians—especially those of Austria—
on Wolfgang became predominant, and Wyzewa and Saint-
Foix (to whom everyone must turn for an exhaustive study
of the early works of Mozart) divide this period into six
sections, which they classify as follows:

1. The influence of Vienna and the decisive return to the
German spirit (1773).

2. The great creative effort (1773-4).

3. The transition from the grand style to the polite style
(Galanterie).

4. The triumph of La Galanterie.

5. The twentieth year.

6. A period of religious music.

As Wyzewa and Saint-Foix devote the whole of one very
large volume to the consideration of the compositions of
these four years, as classified above, it is obvious that they
must be dealt with very briefly here. I shall not attempt an
analysis of the works; I shall merely give an idea of the influences acting on Mozart during this period.

The first influence was that of the Viennese musicians.
The Archbishop Hieronymus visited Vienna in July 1773,
and Leopold took the opportunity of following him there
with Wolfgang and received permission to stay in Vienna

until the end of September, as the Archbishop was going into the mountains and to Gmünd.

[FROM LEOPOLD]   *Vienna, July 21, 1773*

When we arrived in Vienna old Frau Fischer was at her evening meal for they have it at six o'clock: her daughter and son-in-law were at Badnerbade and only arrived home on Monday, 19th. They knew nothing of our coming, since the letter addressed to the daughter lay unopened as there had been no opportunity to send it on. The old lady was overjoyed to see us and only regretted you were not with us, too . . . we have splendid rooms and all we need at the Fischers'. . . .

On Sunday we ate at young Messmer's with Herr von Heufeld. Nobody recognized Wolfgang . . . Herr von Messmer, with whom we are, on Monday played to us on the harmonica or glass instrument of Miss Davis, and very well! It cost him fifty ducats, for it is beautifully made. The garden is incomparable, with views, statues, theatre, aviary, dovecots and up above a Belvedere looking on the Prater. We dined there on Sunday, also on Monday evening. . . .

This afternoon we were most cordially received at Herr von Mayer's. . . .

[FROM LEOPOLD]   *Vienna, August 12, 1773*

. . . Her Majesty the Empress was very amiable to us. . . . At the Feast of St. Cajetan the Theatin monks invited us to the service and a banquet and as the organ was not in use Wolfgang took a violin from Herr Teiber and played a concerto . . . the Jesuits at court performed a Mass of Wolfgang's, namely, the *P. Dominicus Mass*.[1] I conducted and the Mass pleased enormously. . . .

[FROM LEOPOLD]   *Vienna, August 14, 1773*

. . . When are we returning? Not yet, for His Highness [the Archbishop] has kindly given us leave to stay here awhile. . . .

[PS. FROM WOLFGANG TO HIS SISTER]

My Queen, I hope you are enjoying the best possible health and yet now and then or rather at times or, better, sometimes or still better *qualche volta*, as the Italians say, out of your weighty and urgent thoughts (which at all times spring from

[1] *P. Dominicus Mass* (K.66), composed in 1769.

the finest and soundest sense) that you, in possession of your beauty—although of such tender years and not required as a lady to have any of the aforesaid sense—that you, O Queen, are possessed of such virtue as to offer some to this man-person so as quite to abash the old fellow. Farewell.

[FROM LEOPOLD]   *Vienna, August 21, 1773*

A good friend of Herr Fischer's has invited all of us to Baden and as we have never seen the Badnerland we are eating today with Herr Fischer and set out after lunch to Baden, and tomorrow, Sunday, evening we return. We have two carriages; in one are Herr Fischer, his wife, and we two; in the other Herr Taiber and his family. . . .

Herr von Messmer is building two new rooms below to live in in the winter because above they burn an astonishing quantity of wood and yet the rooms are never warm. . . .

If we had any expectations or were earning any money I should certainly have written to you to come. There are many things one cannot write. . . . We don't know when we shall leave. . . . It depends on things I cannot mention. By the end of September we are certain to be, God willing, at home. Things must and will alter. Take courage! God will help us!

[PS. FROM WOLFGANG TO HIS SISTER]

When one considers the favours of the weather and does not forget the considerations of the sun, so it is certain that I am, God be praised and thanked, well. The second part is, however, quite different; instead of sun we should put moon and instead of weather, art,[2] then anyone gifted with a little natural sense will conclude that I am a fool because you are my sister. How is Miss Bimbes?[3] Deliver to her everything imaginable from me. My compliments to all good friends from Herr and Frau von Messmer. . . .

                              oidda. gnagflow Trazom[4]

[FROM LEOPOLD]   *Vienna, August 25, 1773*

. . . My purse is getting very empty, as my body gets fatter so my purse gets thinner. . . . Wolfgang is now playing the clavier so I cannot write. . . .

---

[2]Much of Wolfgang's play on words is scarcely translatable; here, for example, his *gunst* (favour) and *kunst* (art) cannot be given English equivalents.

[3]Their dog Bimberl.   [4]*Addio*, Wolfgang Mozart.

[FROM LEOPOLD]   *Vienna, September 4, 1773*

Now it is all over with the poor Jesuits.[5] I call them poor only because they were at the top of the tree, for the rabbis and the whole *corpus religionis* might be called rich. The individual members, however, had nothing. On the 16th of this month all Jesuit monasteries must be turned over to the court. Their church treasuries, the wine-cellars and wine—in short, all their possessions—are already sealed; the order is suppressed, they may dress like secular priests and, it is said, every one will get three hundred florins annually. That is not so bad! If one adds Masses to that, a young fellow may provide himself with a nice room and a dainty housekeeper; for he won't have much else to do, as preaching and confessing will not be allowed. . . .

Many good Catholics . . . are of the opinion that . . . the Jesuits would have been left in peace had they been as poor as the poor Capuchins. . . .

Herr Gassmann[6] was ill but is now better. I do not know what this has to do with our stay in Vienna. But fools are fools all the world over! Wolfgang has no time to add anything as we may lose the post.

[FROM LEOPOLD]   *Vienna, September 8, 1773*

. . . I am much obliged to the Salzburgers that they are looking forward so to my return. That means that I shall enter Salzburg with more pleasure and will take a walk all night through the illuminated or lighted streets so that the lights do not burn in vain. . . .[7]

I shall, God willing, leave at the end of next week. But as I have . . . never been to Mariazell it may be that I shall return via Mariazell and St. Wolfgang in order to take Wolfgang over the way of his name saint, where he has never been,

[5]The Society of Jesus, founded by Ignatius Loyola in 1534, was suppressed by a Bull, dated July 21, 1773, of Pope Clement XIV. It was, however, re-established on August 7, 1814, by Pope Pius VII. It was still forbidden in 1936 in Germany, Switzerland, Portugal, etc.

[6]Leopold Gassmann, the court Kapellmeister at Vienna. It was thought that Leopold was seeking this position for Wolfgang in the event of Gassmann's death. He died in 1774 and was succeeded by Joseph Bono.

[7]A good example of Leopold's sarcasm, which made him feared and unpopular.

and to show him the celebrated birthplace of his mother, St. Gilgen. . . .

That the money I had with me is now all gone to the D— you can well imagine and Herr Hagenauer will soon have news that I have drawn a trifle of twenty ducats from Herr Peiffer. That means nothing except that I need money but no doctor. . . .

Wolfgangerl has nothing to write as he has nothing to do, so is going round the room like a dog with fleas. . . .

[FROM LEOPOLD] *Vienna, September 11, 1773*

I hope that the departure of Dr. Niderl prepared you for a sad event so that the news of his death will not be so painful. . . . On Thursday the 7th between ten and eleven in the morning he was operated on . . . and in one and a half minutes or less it was done and I had the stone in my hands, which was larger than a large walnut. I left him the same afternoon as well as such a patient could be and there was no anxiety then. On Friday the 10th we went between ten and eleven in the morning . . . after midnight there had been a complete change. . . . *Requiescat in pace!* I am quite overcome. For the two nights I have had only a little restless sleep for I woke on Thursday at four o'clock as if I had myself to undergo the operation that morning. . . .

I have reason with the whole of Salzburg to be sad at the second loss of our Salzburg doctor; the newcomer is bound to send many to eternity before he learns the nature of our climate and people. . . .

[PS. FROM WOLFGANG TO HIS SISTER]

We are well, God be praised and thanked; this time we are writing to you in spite of being very busy. We hope you, also, are well. The death of Dr. Niderl has grieved us greatly, we assure you we have wept and mourned much. . . .

Vienna at our Residence,
September 15, 1773,
Wolfgang

[FROM LEOPOLD] *September 18, 1773*

. . . Write by the first post to Augsburg to Jacob Lottner, printer and music-publisher, that your husband asked you to write and tell him that . . . on his return from Vienna he

expects the account of the copies of the *Violin School* in
hand. . . .

Wolfgang is very engrossed composing something. . . .

By the end of September Leopold and Wolfgang were
back in Salzburg. Leopold says nothing in his letter of the
musical life in Vienna during this visit, which took place in
the off-season; but the Bourgtheater was still open and Wolfgang may have heard there the following buffa operas:
the *Puntiglioso Amoroso* of Galuppi and the *Metilde Ritro-
vata* of Anfossi, both of which were performed during his
stay; in the houses of his friends where Mozart played he
probably met with the sonatas and quartets of the contemporary masters such as Hoffmann, Vanhall, Ditters, Joseph
Haydn, Gassmann, and others.

According to Burney, as well as from the information
available from other sources, Vienna in 1773 was the most
musical—both in quantity and quality—of all German cities.
The Viennese composers of the day were learned musicians
with a strong contrapuntal bias. Gassmann, for example, had
just completed six quartets, each with two fugues, and Joseph
Haydn was writing quartets with fugal movements. The influence of this Viennese school was, in the opinion of Wyzewa
and Saint-Foix, the prevailing influence on Mozart until, at
the end of 1777, he visited Mannheim on the way to Paris.
While in Vienna Wolfgang composed the following:

Serenade in D (K.185) for two violins, alto, two oboes (two flutes
in the andante), two horns, two trombones, and bass.
Little Concerto for Violin in F.
March in D (K.189).
Quartet in F (K.168).[8]
Quartet in A (K.169).
Quartet in C (K.170).
Quartet in E flat (K.171).
Quartet in B flat (K.172).
Quartet in D minor (K.173).[9]
Symphony in G (K.199) (date uncertain).
Divertimento in D (K.205).

[8]This work especially shows the new German influence.

[9]Written, according to Wyzewa and Saint-Foix, under the influence
of the Quartets Op. 20 of Joseph Haydn; this quartet consists of four
movements, of which the last is a fugue. It is a particularly interesting
work for the study of Mozart's development.

March in D (K.290) (written probably for the Divertimento K.205).
Six variations in G for piano on the air *"Mio caro Adone"* from
Salieri's opera *La Fiera di Venezia* (K.180).[10]

Not only was the influence of Joseph Haydn a direct
one through those works of his which Mozart had the opportunity of meeting with in Vienna but it also operated
through Haydn's younger brother, Michael (a musician
not so very much less gifted as a composer than his more
famous brother), who since 1762 was official composer at
the Salzburg court. Although Michael Haydn[11] had been
at Salzburg since 1762, it is probable that Wolfgang had not
been much influenced by him until these four years at home
in Salzburg from 1773 to 1777. This would partly be due
to Wolfgang's frequent and long absences from home and
partly to the rather unfriendly relations existing between
the families of the two Salzburg musicians. The strict Leopold did not approve of the conduct of the more Bohemian
Haydn. He writes to Wolfgang on December 29, 1777:

"Who do you think is appointed organist at the Holy
Trinity? Herr Haydn! Everyone laughs. He is an expensive
organist; after every litany he drinks a quartern of wine and to
the extra services he sends Lipp, who drinks too. . . ."

On June 29, 1778 he writes:

"This afternoon Haydn played the organ for the litany,
and the *Te Deum* (at which the Archbishop was present), but
so badly that we were all horrified. . . . Haydn will drink himself to death soon; or, at least, being lazy enough already, he
will become still lazier the older he gets. . . ."

However, Michael Haydn outlived Leopold Mozart and
became more industrious as he grew older. Leopold, in
spite of the jealousy which he may have felt for a fellow-
musician who was not personally sympathetic to him, preserved his usual solid and objective judgment on musical

[10]On this work Wyzewa and Saint-Foix make some interesting remarks on the difference between Haydn's and Mozart's treatment of
variations. They find that Beethoven's Diabelli variations are more in
Mozart's character of using the form with freedom and fantasy rather
than with the ingenuity which sticks closer to the original material.

[11]Michael Haydn (b. 1737; d. 1806), director of the Salzburg orchestra, composer of opera and of much fine church music. Weber
and Reicha were pupils of his.

matters. He thought that Michael Haydn's opera *Andromeda e Perseo*, composed in 1776, showed that he had no dramatic talent and that the principal arias might have been written for a choirboy; but in 1777 he writes to Wolfgang praising Haydn's entr'acte music for *Zaire*, telling him that at table the Archbishop had said to him that he could not have believed Haydn capable of composing such music and that he should henceforth drink nothing but Burgundy instead of beer. He also wrote to Wolfgang on September 24, 1778: "Herr Haydn is a man whose musical merits you will not deny."

Wolfgang copied out in his own handwriting many of Michael Haydn's scores.[12] Wyzewa and Saint-Foix consider that it is doubtful whether Mozart ever encountered during his whole life a composer whose genius was so akin to his own as Michael Haydn's or one whose work exercised so great an influence on him, an influence which they perceive even in the *Ave Verum* and *Die Zauberflöte*. What, then, was the quality in Michael Haydn which made him so influential? It was—according to Wyzewa and Saint-Foix —that, like Mozart, he had, essentially, "the nature of a poet." He also, they write:

". . . conceived things under the sole aspect of pure beauty. Even in his most careless compositions the melodic line reveals at his hands a grace and delicious sweetness which is found again in his treatment and lends, for example, to his quartets and quintets the singular appearance of works of Mozart from which only the soul of Mozart is absent. Just as in the elder brother of Michael Haydn exactness of expression was always superior to invention of melody, rhythm, and modulation of striking beauty, so in the younger brother it seems as if poetic beauty always flowed effortlessly, a beauty often a little monotonous, shut within narrow limits, but as adorably fresh, limpid, and '*galante*' as could be imagined."

It is impossible to give any idea of Wolfgang's musical activity during the period at Salzburg from October 1773 to December 1774 without mentioning the remarkable works he produced then. As we know practically nothing of his life during this year, I shall set these down here with a few comments:

[12]And a great number of Eberlin's as well.

Symphony in C (K.200).

Concerto in D (K.175), for piano and orchestra.

Revision of Quintet for strings (K.174).

Two Choruses for four voices and five Entr'actes for a heroic German drama by Gebler entitled *Thamos, King of Egypt* (K.345).[13]

Sixteen Dance Minuets (K.176).

Symphony in G minor (K.183).

Symphony in A (K.201).

Rondo Finale in G added to his first quartet in G (K.80).

Symphony in D (K.202).

Sonata in B flat for clavier, four hands (K.358).

Litaniæ Lauretaniæ in D for four voices, orchestra, and organ (K.195) (Kyrie, Sancta Maria, Salus Informorum, Regina Angelorum, Agnus Dei).

Concerto in B flat for bassoon and orchestra (K.191).[14]

Missa Brevis in F for four voices, two violins, bass, and organ (K.192) (Kyrie, Gloria, Credo, Sanctus, Benedictus, Agnus Dei).

Dixit et Magnificat in C for four voices, two violins, two trumpets, kettle-drums, bass, and organ (K.193).

Missa Brevis in D for four voices, two violins, bass, and organ (K.194).

Serenade in D for two violins, alto, two oboes (or flutes), two bassoons, two horns, two trumpets, and bass (K.203).[15]

Little Concerto for Violin in B flat (interpolated in the preceding Serenade) (K.203).

March in D for the preceding Serenade (K.237).

Sonata in C for clavier (K.279).[16]

Twelve Variations in C for clavier on a minuet of Fischer (K.179).

Sonata in F for clavier (K.280).

Sonata in B flat for clavier (K.281).

Sonata in G for clavier (K.283).

Allegro in G minor for clavier (K.312).

Sonata in E flat for clavier (K.282).

[13]This score was revised by Mozart in 1779. This work was a forerunner of *Die Zauberflöte*; see pp. 248-9.

[14]This fine work, which is well known in the concert-halls of today, was succeeded by two other Concertos for Bassoon composed a few months later (spring 1775) for a rich amateur, Baron Durnitz, which are, unfortunately, lost.

[15]Wyzewa and Saint-Foix remark that the Andante of this Serenade compensates in its poetic inspiration (henceforward more and more marked in Mozart's music) for the abandonment of the beautiful learned and elaborated style of his preceding period. In short, this work is one showing the transition from the grand style to *galanterie* (see page 164). The bassoon concerto (K.191) is a good example of the former style.

[16]This is one of the first sonatas conceived for clavier without violin accompaniment. From this separation was born the later combination of sonata for violin and pianoforte.

These sonatas for the clavier were probably directly inspired by a collection of clavier sonatas published by Joseph Haydn in 1774, and like most of Mozart's compositions for this instrument were chiefly composed for performance by himself. The church music in the above list was officially composed for the church services in Salzburg. The Archbishop maintained a school of fifteen choristers who passed into the Court Chapel choir, or if they showed special talent were sent to finish their training in Italy. Archbishop Sigismund allowed the male sopranos (*castrati*) to die out and in their place had women sopranos; for example, he sent the daughter of the Cathedral organist, Maria Magdalena Lipp, to be trained in Italy; and when she returned she married Michael Haydn. Perhaps it was this tendency of women sopranos to marry that caused Archbishop Hieronymus, in 1778, to take another male soprano, Antonio Ceccarelli, into his service.

The Cathedral organist at this time was Cajetan Adlgasser, a pupil of Eberlin; the assistant organist was Franz Lipp, the father-in-law of Michael Haydn, who was Concertmeister and director of the orchestra. As vice-Kapellmeister Leopold Mozart had plenty of opportunities of performing Wolfgang's instrumental compositions because there was a constant succession of festivals and fête-days on which symphonies and cantatas, etc., were performed by the court orchestra. Leopold also had charge of the music at the metropolitan church, and a letter from Wolfgang to Padre Martini in Bologna, dated September 4, 1776, may be quoted here for the information it gives about the conditions under which Mozart produced practically all his church music, Masses, etc.:

Much Revered Father and Master,[17]

The veneration, esteem, and respect that I bear towards

[17]This letter is written in Italian. A portrait of Mozart sent to Padre Martini, now in the possession of the Liceo Musicale in Bologna, is reproduced as frontispiece. This portrait was sent by Leopold Mozart with his letter to Martini dated Salzburg, December 22, 1777. Martini had asked for the portrait and Leopold says they had delayed in the hope of coming across a good painter but had decided to get it painted in Salzburg before Wolfgang's departure. He says of it: "It has not much value as a work of art but the resemblance, which I attest is extreme, gives it value as it is."

your revered person stimulates me to importunate you with the present letter and to send you herewith a feeble example of my music,[18] submitting it to your sovereign judgment. Last year I wrote for the Carnival at Munich in Bavaria an opera buffa (*La Finta Giardiniera*). A few days before leaving there His Highness the Elector desired to hear some of my contrapuntal music; hence I was obliged to write this motet in great haste so as to allow time to copy this score for His Highness and to transcribe the parts so as to be able to perform it the following Sunday in the offertory of the full Mass.

Dearest and most esteemed master, I beg you sincerely to tell me frankly and unreservedly your opinion of it. We live in this world to compel ourselves industriously to enlighten one another by means of reasoning and to apply ourselves always to carrying forward the sciences and the arts. How many times, oh, how many times I have wished to live nearer you in order to be able to discuss things with you, my reverend father! I live in a country where music meets with little good fortune although, not to speak of those who have left us, we still possess excellent artists and particularly composers of great science, depth, and taste.

For the theatre we are ill situated through lack of singers. We have no *castrati* and will not find them easily since these folk wish to be well paid and liberality is not a vice of ours. For my part I write chamber and church music. There are two other contrapuntists here; namely, Haydn and Adlgasser. My father is Kapellmeister at the Cathedral, which gives me opportunity to write for the Church as much as I like. However, my father, having been already thirty-six years in the service of this court and knowing that this Archbishop does not like to see people of advanced years about him, does not take much part in musical services but devotes himself to the literature of his art, always his favourite study.

Our church music is very different from that of Italy and the more so as a Mass including Kyrie, Gloria, Credo, the Sonata to the epistle, the Offertory or Motet, Sanctus and Agnus Dei even on the most solemn occasions when the Prince in person officiates must not last longer than three-quarters of an hour.

[18]The motet *Misericordias Domini* in D minor (K.222), composed in 1775, at Munich.

This sort of composition requires a special study all the more since, notwithstanding, it must be a full Mass with all instruments—including military trumpets and kettle-drums!

Oh, how many things I should have to say to you were you not so far off, dearest master! I salute devotedly all the members of the Philharmonic Society and commend myself always to their good graces. I do not cease to deplore that I have to live so far from the person in the world I most love, reverence, and esteem and whose most devoted and humble servant I remain.

Wolfgang Amadeo Mozart

Salisburgo, 4 Settembre, 1776

Before commenting on this letter I may mention that we have a description of the contemporary arrangements for musical services in the Salzburg Cathedral which reads as follows:[19]

"The Cathedral contains a large organ at the back by the entrance, four side organs in front of the choir, and a little choir organ below the choir where the choristers sit. The large organ is only used on grand occasions and for preludes; during the performance one of the four side organs is played, generally that next to the altar or on the right side, where the solo-singers and basses are. Opposite, by the left-side organ, are the violinists, etc., and on the two other sides are two bands of trumpets and drums. The lower choir organ and double-bass join in when required."

The Archbishop Hieronymus was a worldly man who seems to have liked the more superficial of musical qualities, but it would be too much to impute solely to him the tendency of Mozart during the year 1775—a year before he wrote the above letter to Martini—to write a more facile church music than he wrote earlier. This is the period aptly described by Wyzewa and Saint-Foix as *"le triomphe de la galanterie"* and it includes a number of compositions which I shall not enumerate here but which are listed in an appendix.[20] There are, however, two works among them about which I shall have a little more to say presently, after dealing with the significance of Mozart's letter to Padre Martini.

[19]Marpurg: *Historisch-Kritische Beiträge zur Aufnahme der Musik*, Vol. III, p. 195.

[20]See Appendix II.

It would appear from the tone of this letter and from the change in character of the music Mozart wrote towards the latter half of 1776 that something like a psychological crisis occurred in Wolfgang about his twentieth year. This is interestingly and ingeniously argued by Wyzewa and Saint-Foix and their analysis of his compositions from the years 1773 to 1777 seems to bear it out. After a period of, at times, a slightly superficial fluency, he seems to have turned away dissatisfied and it was here probably that he crossed the artist's Rubicon—inevitable to him, given his creative nature —and instead of pursuing the path of the successful professional purveyor of accomplished music passed into the solitary track of his own genius.

Mozart's nature was so optimistic, owing to his prodigious vitality and to the well-balanced harmony of his many-sidedness, and his musical gifts also were so extraordinary that it is not to be wondered at that he should have thought he could do anything. Worldly failure was inconceivable to him, as a young man, and for this reason we find him behaving in a way that seemed reckless to his cautious and more disillusioned father. Consequently there were several periods in his adult career—like the period (1774–6) described by Wyzewa and Saint-Foix as *"Le triomphe de la galanterie"*—when Mozart appears to have been hopeful of worldly success and all the financial benefits which would flow from it. Nobody ever set out better equipped with natural gifts for opening the world's oyster and extracting its pearl. When from our present point of observation and with our present knowledge we look back upon these incessant tours of father and son in search of El Dorado (or simply *Gold*), beginning when Wolfgang was six years old, and see how every intention was frustrated, how not one single position at any court in Europe was ever obtained in spite of the utmost persistence and the most adroit strategy of Leopold, we cannot avoid a strong conviction of fatality.

This constant pruning of Mozart's worldly hopes seems as if absolutely intended by a higher power in order to bring to light a finer bloom and more perfect fruit. It is impossible, I maintain, for any perceptive person to read through this sober and truthful account of Mozart's life, which I

am here setting down with a deliberate fullness and with
as much accuracy as I can command, not to have the feeling
as he reads it of witnessing the action of something like a
Greek tragedy, the working out of an inescapable destiny,
the destiny of Mozart's genius.

Did Mozart himself ever realize this sacrificial nature of his
destiny? I am certain he did; but it seems as if it came only
in occasional flashes of insight. His extraordinary ebullience,
what one might almost describe as the ferocity of his high
spirits (the source of that demoniacal quality in his music
which Abert and other writers have noticed), prevented him
from a fuller realization of his destiny for a long time; but
we shall see it slowly penetrating his consciousness and re-
issuing forth in those strange and enigmatic compositions of
his maturity until at last this awareness of his destiny and of
himself floods his mind completely and results in the astounding works of the crowning and most bitter years at the end
of his life.

The tours of Leopold and Wolfgang in search of a haven
for the genius of the young Wolfgang put in my mind the
travels of Don Quixote and Sancho Panza. Nothing turned
out to be what they first thought it was. Don Quixote is
Wolfgang and Sancho Panza is his father and at the end of
this story we shall find Wolfgang returning like Don Quixote to his own mind, in which alone all the riches of this
journey have lain. The giants were windmills, the armies
were sheep, the princes were lackeys, the Dulcinea was a
commonplace wench, and the Flying Horse was merely his
musical science. What gave the colour, life, virtue, and existence to all these things was his own creative soul, his un-
alienable and indestructible genius.

One of these early flashes of insight was at work in this
letter to Padre Martini, in spite of any more immediate cause.
An immediate cause then was, namely, his father's desire
that he should set forth again to seek a remuneration and
stable position worthy of his talents. In this search a certifi-
cate of his ability from the celebrated and well-respected
Martini would be useful—so Leopold may have thought;
but whether or not this was the immediate motive of writing the letter, its heartfelt and spontaneous expression of

Wolfgang's musical solitude has its unmistakable origin in his purely artistic ambition.

From Martini's reply I shall quote the following passage about the motet:

"I have found in it everything which distinguishes modern music; that is to say, good harmony, rich modulations, excellent flowing violin parts, a natural use of the voices, and a remarkable elaboration. . . ."

Only in Martini's phrase "remarkable elaboration" may we read any expression of surprised admiration; but this elaboration is even more surprising nowadays to ears unaccustomed to such musical science. The church music of Mozart is one part of his work which has not as yet had the full recognition in praise and in performance which it deserves; it still awaits the more careful and thorough attention of first-class choral societies and singers. The very great demands it makes, however, on their vocal and musical capacities, though they ought to be a stimulus, are likely to keep it unknown until a more favourable age for singing. I shall have more to say on this subject when I come to his last (C minor) Mass.[21]

We now return to the one event about which we have some biographical information during this period of 1773-7: namely, the excursion from Salzburg to Munich made by Wolfgang. He received a commission (which he refers to in his letter to Martini) to write an opera buffa for the Carnival season of 1775 at Munich. As this came from the Elector of Bavaria, Maximilian III, the Archbishop of Salzburg was unable to refuse leave of absence, so Leopold and Wolfgang set out for what was to be their last journey together on December 6, 1774. Leopold writes:

Munich, December 9, 1774

. . . Our lodging is indeed small but comfortable enough and H. von Pernat shows us, indeed, more politeness and honour than we merit and I am certain that he sacrifices his comfort in many respects to us. About the opera I have nothing to write yet. Today we met our colleagues, who were all very amiable and especially His Excellency Count Seau. . . .[22]

[22]Count Seau was the Intendant or director of the music and opera in Munich.

[FROM LEOPOLD]   *Munich, December 14, 1774*

. . . As for Nannerl I have as yet no suitable lodging for her as in this respect great care is necessary here in Munich. There is another thing. Here as in Salzburg an opera to which one pays to go cannot be given more than twice running, otherwise there would be few people in the theatre, so in two or three weeks another opera has to be produced and then the former revived as is done with the comedies and the ballets. . . . The opera of Wolfgang's will . . . I believe, be first performed on the 29th. It can so happen that Nannerl will not see it. Once the Carnival has properly begun, there will only be light little operettas played in a small theatre that is prepared in the Redoutensaal, where there is a crowd of masqueraders and many gaming-tables and nothing but noise, talking, etc. . . .

[FROM LEOPOLD]   *Munich, December 16, 1774*

Now I have a lodging for Nannerl and where do you think? At Madam or rather the widowed Frau von Durst's . . . Nannerl will have her own bedroom. True, it is rather dark but the rest of the time she will use Frau von Durst's room, which looks on the Market Square and in which a harpsichord will be put. . . . Nannerl must practise, especially the sonatas of Paradies and Bach and the concerto of Lucchesi. . . .

[PS. FROM WOLFGANG TO HIS SISTER]

I have toothache.

Johannes Chrisostomus Wolfgangus Amadeus Sigismundus Mozartus Maria annæ Mozartæ matri et sorori, ac amicis omnibus, præsertimque pulchris virginibus, ac frellibus, gratiosique frellibus.[23] *S.P.D.*

[FROM LEOPOLD]   *Munich, December 21, 1774*

. . . Nannerl must have a *Mausbelz* [mole fur?] on the journey, otherwise she will not be able to endure it in a half-covered chaise [coach]. She must take care to keep her head warm and her feet must be looked after apart from the *filzschuehen*, which in the long run do not help much. So she must put on the fur boots which are in the chest under the

---

[23]"Johann Chrisostom Wolfgang Amadeus Sigismund Mozart to Maria Anna, mother and sister, and to all friends, especially beautiful virgins, and easy-going and pleasing ones." I have taken the liberty of assuming that by *frellibus* Mozart intended *facilibus*.

room and H. Geschwendner will be good enough to put a little hay on the floor of the chaise.

You know that we were well provided for; just think what we had to cover us. I had fur boots over the shoes and then we had foot-muffs and yet even so we could not have held out if at the third post-stage at Febertsheim I had not obtained a large bundle of hay and had it put in the chaise and covered our foot-muffs completely with it. . . .

Besides the Bach[24] and Paradies sonatas Nannerl can also bring Wolfgang's Sonatas and Variations and other sonatas, whatever she likes, for sonatas don't take up much room. But not many concertos! Wolfgang's Concerto we already have here[25] and if she brings another couple it is enough. . . .

[FROM LEOPOLD]   *Munich, December 28, 1774*
. . . the first rehearsal of Wolfgang's opera has pleased so much that it is postponed until January 5, 1775, so that the singers may know it better. . . . Wolfgang has been kept indoors for six days with a swollen face. The cheek was swollen inside and out, also his right eye, and for two days he could only take soup. So one must well protect the face and ears for in a half-open chaise the snow flies constantly in one's face. . . . Nannerl must take some money with her in case of need. Now Nannerl must know where to go. The following must be written out on a slip and given to Hr. Geschwendner or kept by her [here follow precise instructions as to the address in Munich].

[PS. FROM WOLFGANG]
My dear Sister,

I beg of you not to forget before you leave to have your talk; that is, to make the visit you know of—for I have my reasons. I beg you to give my greetings—but most expressive and tenderly—and—oh—I need not be so concerned about it, I know my sister, tenderness is so natural to her I am certain she will do her very best to give me pleasure . . . we will bicker about it all in Munich. Farewell.

[FROM LEOPOLD]   *Munich, December 30, 1774*
When you get this, Nannerl will have already packed but . . . nevertheless I want her to bring five or six copies of our

[24]Johann Christian Bach.   [25]Concerto in D (K.175).

Paris engravings.[26] Herr von Pernat insists on having one. . . .
I also forgot to say that Nannerl should bring a masquerade
costume even if it is only a Salzburg one. . . . Nannerl will
arrive on Wednesday, and on Thursday it will be performed.
If Herr von Mölk[27] comes with her he will also see it but if he
comes later he will not see it before Easter. . . .

You must know that Maestro Tozzi, who this year is writing the opera seria, wrote this time last year an opera buffa and
exerted himself so as to surpass the opera seria of Sales; he
succeeded in quite eclipsing Maestro Sales's opera.[28] Now it so
turns out that Wolfgang's opera is ready before Tozzi's and all
those who have heard the first rehearsal are now saying that
Tozzi is paid back in his own coin since Wolfgang's opera will
put his quite in the shade. I do not like this sort of thing and
do all I can to stop such talk and protest endlessly but the
whole orchestra and all who have heard the rehearsal say they
have never heard more beautiful music, in which every aria is
fine . . . *Basta!* God will put everything right. Farewell. . . .

[PS. FROM WOLFGANG TO HIS SISTER]

Please give my regards to Roxelana. . . . To Miss Mizerl
say everything imaginable, she is not to doubt my love, she is
constantly before my eyes in her bewitching negligee; I have
seen many pretty girls here but none to compare with her. My
sister is not to forget to bring the Variations on the *Minuet
d'exaude* of Ecart and my Variations on the minuet of Fischer.
. . .

Keep very warm on the journey, I beg of you, otherwise you
may have to sit in the house for fourteen days sweating by
the stove and who will look after you? I'll not get hot, now I
talk rot. I am ever

Thy Munich
brother 1774 30 *Anno Decembre.*

[26]The picture by Carmontelle.

[27]Herr von Mölk came and embarrassed Wolfgang and his father
by his excessive enthusiasm. "Anyone could see," writes Wolfgang on
January 11, "that he had never in his life been farther than Salzburg
or Innsbruck."

[28]The respective operas were *Orfeo ed Euridice,* opera seria by Antonio Tozzi, *Kapellmeister* at the Munich Court (1775), and *Achille
in Sciro* by P. Sales. I do not know the title of the opera buffa by
Tozzi which eclipsed Sales' opera seria.

Wolfgang's sister arrived in Munich on January 4th, 1775.[29] The first performance of Wolfgang's opera *La Finta Giardiniera* took place on January 13 with brilliant success as described by Wolfgang in a letter to his mother dated January 14:

"God be praised! my opera was produced yesterday and succeeded so well that I cannot possibly describe to Mamma the reception. Firstly the theatre was so full that many were turned away. After every aria there was a terrific uproar with clapping and cries of *viva Maestro*. . . .

"Afterwards Papa and I went into a room where the Elector and Electress[30] and the whole court were and kissed their hands and they were very agreeable . . . and congratulated me that the opera had so exceptionally pleased everybody. As for our return it will not be so soon. . . . One good reason is that next Friday the opera will be given again and it is essential that I should be at the performance, otherwise one would not recognize it—that is very strange here."[31]

We have two interesting contemporary notices of the performance of *La Finta Giardiniera* in Munich. One is by the Secretary of the Legation, Unger, who writes in his journal of January 15, 1775, as follows:

"Friday L.A.R.E. assisted at the first representation of the opera buffa *La Finta Giardiniera*; the music was much applauded; it is by the young Mozart of Salzburg, who is at the moment here. This is the same Mozart who was in England and elsewhere at the age of eight to play the clavier, which he does surpassingly well."

Schubart in his *Teutsche Chronik* (1775, p. 267) wrote:

"I also heard an opera buffa by the amazing genius Mozart;

[29]According to a letter from Leopold to his wife dated Munich, January 5, 1775. In Vol. I of Schiedermair's edition of Mozart's letters there are two letters dated Munich, January 11th and 14th respectively, printed as addressed by Wolfgang to his sister, which cannot be correct as she was then in Munich. Both letters are obviously addressed to his mother.

[30]No doubt the Elector's sister, Maria Antonia Walpurga of Saxony; both were good amateur musicians.

[31]In Leopold's letter of February 21 to his wife he remarks: "Wolfgang's opera has been performed again, but, owing to the singer who was ill, had to be cut. . . ." This refers to the second woman singer, who in any case was, so Leopold writes, "miserable." The principal role of Sandrina was written for an excellent singer, Rosa Manservisi.

it is called *La Finta Giardiniera*. Sparks of genius flash here and there; but it is not yet the calm fire from the altar rising to heaven in clouds of incense—a perfume for the gods. If Mozart is not a forced hothouse plant, then he must become one of the greatest composers that have ever lived."[32]

In addition to the opera, Wolfgang's Litany in B flat major (K.125) and his two small Masses, *Missa Brevis* in F (K.192) and *Missa Brevis* in D (K.194), were performed in the Court Chapel, conducted by Leopold, on successive Sundays.[33] It was at this time, also, that he composed for the Elector the *Misericordias Domini* (K.222) which he sent to Padre Martini.[34] Wolfgang and his sister Nannerl played in public and there is an interesting account by Schubart of Wolfgang's pianoforte-playing. He writes in his *Teutsche Chronik* (1776, p. 276):

"Last winter in Munich I heard two of the greatest clavier-players, Herr Mozart and H. von Beecke.[35] My host, Herr Albert, has an excellent pianoforte in his house. There I heard these two giants compete. Mozart plays the most difficult things and whatever is laid before him at sight. But nevertheless Beecke far surpasses him—winged speed grace, melting sweetness and a marvellous taste are weapons which none can wrest from the hands of this Hercules."[36]

In spite of these successes Wolfgang did not receive any appointment from the Elector of Bavaria nor the commission for the opera seria for the following year. A few words are now necessary on Wolfgang's opera.

La Finta Giardiniera (K.196),[37] opera buffa in three acts

[32]Even if we heard *La Finta Giardiniera* for the first time today, after all the musical developments since Beethoven and Wagner, it would strike any perceptive musician as a work of genius.

[33]A Litany by Leopold was also performed.

[34]See page 151.

[35]Ignaz von Beecke (1733–1803), a famous pianist who, with Schobert, inaugurated the modern technique; composer of numerous songs, operas, etc.

[36]An experienced and perceptive connoisseur of pianoforte-playing will understand readily from these epithets why Schubart preferred what I have no doubt was the inferior but more superficially striking playing of Beecke. It is always the same story.

[37]The original manuscript of the second and third acts, in two volumes, containing three hundred and forty-four pages, is preserved in

for three sopranos, one *castrato*, two tenors, and one bass, with orchestra, on a libretto written in Rome in 1774 for an opera buffa by Pasquale Anfossi, consisting of an overture and twenty-eight numbers, all but seven of which are arias.

This opera is thoroughly delightful in performance and, speaking as one who has seen it on the stage, I demur to the remarks of certain critics who point out that the music is not so appropriate to the text as Anfossi's, being far too elaborate and intense. Wyzewa and Saint-Foix, though they also make this comparison, in the course of so doing give such a just and perceptive description of the character of this most entrancing lyrical work that I shall quote it here. After saying that his music is often more powerful and passionate than the situations demand and that his comic arias are too subtle, elaborate, ingenious, and clever for the words, they go on to say that it is still worse when the situation or words permit the musician to express tender or melancholy sentiment. Then, they add, Mozart entirely abandons the conventions of opera buffa:

"The least trace of sadness or love inflames the imagination of the young artist . . . so that he treats the arias like the ariosos or cavatinas of opera seria, with a continued use of minor keys and an intensity of lyrical passion which would touch us more profoundly if we could forget that our concern was with carnival weathercocks quite incapable of experiencing the profound emotions which the musician of genius lends them. Thus, to give one example, the ensemble which makes up with their recitatives the two arias of Sandrina, Nos. 21 and 22, will have its counterpart, altogether similar, in one of Mozart's most tragic scenes, a scene from the opera *Andromeda* composed in 1777 for Mme. Duschek; and perhaps even this scene does not express grief as profound and pathetic as the two arias in *La Finta Giardiniera* sung by a young girl whom we have just seen and are about to see again humming trifles—to say nothing of the fact that this access of grief arises out of an imbroglio only invented to make us laugh and which, in addition, is so stupid as to be almost incomprehensible."

Berlin. The opera was revised with an excellent German text in 1779-80 and was also performed in German at Frankfurt in 1789. The complete score is in the Dresden Landesbibliothek. See Wyzewa and Saint-Foix for a detailed analysis of the changes.

Though from the purely artistic point of view such divergences between text and music are a defect in a work of art, yet in a work such as *La Finta Giardiniera* we may be free to let ourselves enjoy the entrancing music without reserve; for it has an inimitable charm and gaiety, tenderness and fertility of invention, allied to such musical science that I personally prefer it even to the later *Die Entführung aus dem Serail*. Unfortunately the *secco* recitatives of the first act are lost and mere spoken dialogue can never replace them. Nevertheless *La Finta Giardiniera* will always deserve performance on account of the superior quality, so pure and exquisite, of the music. This question of quailty is one to which insufficient attention is paid by scholars and historians, and it is this lack of proportion that blinds critics to the fact that an imperfect work of Mozart's, such as *La Finta Giardiniera*, may be superior to the most perfect of the works of a Wagner or a Richard Strauss.

Leopold, Wolfgang, and Nannerl returned to Salzburg on March 7, 1775. In April the Archduke Maximilian, youngest son of Maria Theresa and afterwards Archbishop of Cologne, paid a visit to Salzburg. He had been paying a visit to his sister, Marie Antoinette, in Paris and in his honour the usual musical festivities were arranged in Salzburg. On April 22 a serenata by Fischietti was performed and on the following day a festival opera hurriedly composed by Mozart, *Rè Pastore*, was given. We have a brief account by one of the suite of the Archduke Maximilian, written on April 24, which reads as follows:

"Music was the entertainment provided as on the preceding days; at its close the famous young Mozart was heard on the piano; he played various pieces from his head with equal skill and grace."

Only a few words are necessary on this festival opera of Wolfgang's:

Il Rè Pastore (K.208),[38] *dramma per musica* in two acts, for three sopranos and two tenors, with orchestra of first and second violins, alto, two flutes, two oboes, two bassoons, two cors anglais, four horns, and bass. The text is by Metastasio and this work is rather a pastoral serenade than an opera, thus resembling *Ascanio in Alba*, but without the dances and

[38]The original score in two volumes of two hundred and eighty-four pages is preserved in Berlin.

choruses. It consists of an overture and fourteen numbers, all of which are recitatives and arias except No. 7, a recitative and duet, and No. 14, a finale ensemble.

This work is a good example of Mozart's exquisite craftsmanship at this period, without having any greater significance. The character of the opera is well summed up by Wyzewa and Saint-Foix, who point out that all the arias are very well written for the voice and that the instrumentation is clear, easy, and evidently improvised, but always rich and exquisite. They add:

"There is little counterpoint and none of those great dramatic ventures that are to be found in *Lucio Silla*; but an extreme purity of melodic line, a very free and happy use of wind instruments, and invariably a poetic colour ravishing in its simplicity."

During the period after the production of *Il Rè Pastore* (April 1775) up to the date of Wolfgang's departure from Salzburg on September 23, 1777, Wolfgang passed his twentieth year. Within these two years and five months he composed more than thirty works, the list of which will be found in the Appendix. It includes violin concertos, pianoforte concertos, and a quantity of ecclesiastical music,[39] to say nothing of many sonatas and numerous instrumental works, such as the famous Haffner Serenade in D (K.250) and March (K.249) written for the marriage of Elise Haffner, the daughter of a wealthy Salzburg merchant and *Bürgermeister*, in July 1776; the delightful Serenata Notturna in D (K.239) for two small orchestras placed apart; the superb Divertimento or Notturno in F (K.247) composed for Countess Lodron in June 1776;[40] and the fascinating Divertimento in D (K.251) written for his sister's twenty-fifth birthday, July 30, 1776.

It must be added that during the last two years of this stay in his home town Wolfgang became intimately acquainted with the members of the higher nobility such as Countess Lodron, for whom he composed much music. This change of

[39]Two remarkable pieces must be mentioned here, the beautiful *Sancta Maria* for four voices, two violins, alto, bass, and organ (K.273) and the marvellous *Litaniæ de Venerabili Altaris Sacramento* (K.243), a large-scale work in eight sections, which is a masterpiece of the highest quality.

[40]This work may be taken as one of the finest examples of the flowering of the genius of Mozart in his twentieth year.

milieu is reflected in the character of many of his compositions of the period in which elegance, taste, and brilliance are chiefly aimed at. It is what Wyzewa and Saint-Foix describe as the style of *"la galanterie."*

IX. *Father and Son*

1777   AGE 21

On September 23, 1777 Wolfgang left Salzburg with his mother on a tour which was to keep him away from home until January 1779 and take him for the last time to Paris, where he was to bury his mother. The reasons for his departure are as follows:

The Mozart family were not popular with their lord and master, the Archbishop Hieronymus, whose tyrannical disposition[1] was combined with a sufficiently acute intelligence for him to see the stark independence underlying the formal correctness and subservience of Leopold. When the old Kapellmeister Lolli retired, in 1772, the post instead of being given to Leopold, who had a well-founded claim to it, was given to Fischietti, so that Leopold never advanced further than his vice-Kapellmeistership. Also, as we know from Wolfgang's letter to Martini, the Archbishop did not like to see elderly people about him and Leopold was in 1777 fifty-eight years old. This is not old, but Leopold was not the sort of pliant, accommodating nature to please a despot. Biographers of his son have often taken a superficial view of him and have tried to make out that he was as servile as Wolfgang was independent. This is quite false. Leopold had an iron nature and in recognizing a hard necessity he protected himself and his family by a punctilious observance of all the formalities cus-

[1] One of the favourites of Hieronymus, the singer Meissner, when suffering from a severe cold was told that he must sing and attend to the service or he would be dismissed. The character of Hieronymus was well known. On the day of his induction, according to Koch-Sternfeld, a dead silence reigned as the procession went by. "It was a fair day. An urchin in the midst of the gazing throng gave a 'Huzza!' and received a box on the ears from a merchant standing by, with the words: 'Boy, dost thou shout when all the people weep?'"

tomary between an eighteenth-century servant and the man who was not only his employer but also the ruler of his country and the local head of his Church.

It would be superficial not to realize that these obsequious forms—so alien to our present-day taste—admit, by their very nature, of a larger degree of independence than is often obtainable under the looser and supposedly more equalitarian relationships between the powerful and the weak of our present day. The weapons of and the defences against tyranny change from age to age. Nowadays tyranny takes an anonymous form and hides itself behind a bureaucratic machine. The oppressed can never get face to face with his oppressor. It would be a satisfaction to many a harassed individual today if he were able to confront his oppresser (who is a deaf, dumb, and blind machine or a system or an institution run by ungetatable committees or councils) as Leopold was able to confront Archbishop Hieronymus and, looking him full in the eye, make him the prescribed obsequious bow and address him, stating his grievances in the most Chinese of adulatory language.

As every English writer knows from his practice, under the present law of libel it is possible to get in some very hard and unpalatable truths in perfect good taste and under the guise even of flattery. Hieronymus was too intelligent a man not to be aware of the sarcastic and superior nature of Leopold, who, it must always be remembered, was a much-travelled man and had mixed with the best society in all the principal European courts. I advise the reader to study carefully the portrait of Leopold Mozart[2] now in the Mozarteum at Salzburg and he will see there, as he will perceive from his letters, the proud, stern character of the man conscious of his own strength acquired by enduring self-discipline and the strictest devotion to every duty as a servant, a musician, a husband, and a father. Leopold Mozart was built on a Miltonic scale and as is the case with all men who are truly strong he was capable of the utmost tenderness, as his relationship with his wife and children abundantly reveals. We may well understand, once we have become closely familiar with Leopold Mozart, the often-quoted saying of Wolfgang as a child:

"After God, Papa."

It may have sometimes occurred to reflective minds that life is very little worth living for a man if he does not possess genius. The answer to this implicit inquiry is a man like Leopold Mozart. Leopold had every virtue (in the Roman sense) a man can have, but he was denied genius in his own chosen and beloved art. It must have been a bitter pill for such an ambitious man—a man, too, of quite exceptional intellectual power—to see in the course of his life many men inferior to himself in character and even in musical science more successful and even gifted with more natural talent. Well, that hard, tough Spartan had his reward. God, as he fully recognized in his own heart, gave him Wolfgang. He in return protected, guided, and aided Wolfgang to achieve, what he might otherwise never have achieved, the *adequate* expression in a mass of completed marvellous musical works of what was probably the greatest natural musical genius that has ever been born into this world.

The Archbishop Hieronymus was one of those intelligent men of mean nature who have no instinct whatsoever but are impressed always by externals. Jahn, on information from Koch-Sternfeld, says:

"Mozart [Wolfgang] with his slender figure and boyish countenance made a poor personal impression on Hieronymus, who was singularly apt to be imposed upon by men of commanding height and appearance.

"He refused any recognition of Wolfgang's musical accomplishments and was unsparing in his criticism of them,[3] telling him—as Leopold wrote to Padre Martini [December 22, 1777]—that he knew nothing of his art and should go and study at the Naples Conservatoire that he might learn something; a sufficiently unreasonable proposal to an academician of Bologna and Verona—to a young man who had traversed Italy in triumph as a composer and virtuoso. True, Mozart had no great respect for the Archbishop's critical judgment,[4]

[3]"I did not venture to contradict," writes Wolfgang to his father (February 19, 1778), "because I had come straight from Salzburg, where one gets out of the habit of contradicting."

[4]Wolfgang writes ironically to his father from Mannheim on November 4, 1777: "I played my concerto . . . and although it was known to be mine it pleased very much. Nobody said it was not well arranged . . . they should ask the Archbishop—he could set them right at once."

but in the mouth of his Prince such an expression of opinion was of very unpleasant significance; for in point of fact Hieronymus was well aware of Mozart's genius[5] and never failed to honour[6] him with commissions when any new composition was required, for which he never paid him a penny. . . . He imagined that contemptuous expressions of opinion . . . would be the most effectual means of preventing the younger Concertmeister from preferring his claim to a higher salary than a hundred and fifty gulden a year."

Leopold early recognized the hopelessness of Wolfgang's future in Salzburg and spared no effort, as we have already seen, to get him a position at some other court. But all these efforts had been in vain and all Wolfgang's successes in Italy, Vienna, and finally Munich had led to nothing. No secure position had been offered to him, and if he were to live and compose, some security had to be found. The only thing left was to try another great tour on which Wolfgang could exhibit his prowess as an executant and his powers as a composer in the hope of their acquiring him the offer of some good position. He had not left Salzburg since the visit to Munich in 1775; he was now twenty-one and something had to be done without delay. Accordingly Leopold and Wolfgang made the necessary preparations for a tour and then applied to the Archbishop for leave of absence and permission to travel. This, as well as a petition for an increase in salary, was refused, the Archbishop giving as his reason that he would not have his subjects "going on begging expeditions." There was nothing then but for Wolfgang to resign his miserable post and proceed alone.

On August 1, 1777 he made a written application to Archbishop Hieronymus referring to his father's applications of March 14 and of June, both of which had been refused by the Archbishop:

"Your Grace observed that, at most, I (who moreover was only half in service) could travel alone. Our need is urgent: my father took the decision that I must go alone. But even then your gracious Excellency made some most gracious ob-

[5]This is more than questionable. Jahn merely means that he could not fail to be aware of his exceptional talents. None of Mozart's contemporaries realized his full stature.

[6]*Honour* is good!

jections. Gracious Lord and Master! The elders go to great
pains to enable the children to earn their own bread: and for
that are they responsible to themselves, to the State. The
more talent the children have received from God, the more
are they bound to make use of it in order to improve the conditions of themselves and their parents, to succour their
parents and to provide for their own development and for the
future. This we are taught in the Gospel.

"I am therefore before God responsible in my conscience
to my father for all the exhausting hours spent on my upbringing, to be grateful, to lighten his burdens, and to take care of
myself and also of my sister, for it would be a sad thing to me
if she should have spent so many hours at the piano without
being able to make practical use of her labour.

"I beg your gracious Excellency therefore graciously to
allow me to request my discharge as I am compelled to make
use of the forthcoming autumn month in order not to have to
travel during the following cold months in bad weather. Your
gracious Excellency will not take this most humble request
ungraciously since more than three years ago when I asked for
permission to go to Vienna you graciously informed me that
I had nothing to hope for and would do better to seek fortune
elsewhere. I thank your gracious Excellency most humbly for
all gracious favours received and with the flattering hope that
I shall be able to serve you in my mature years with more
success I am,

> "Your gracious Excellency's,
> "my gracious Prince and Master's
> "most humble and obedient servant
> "*Wolfgang Amadé Mozart*"

The Archbishop, enraged at having the tables turned upon
him in this way, accepted Wolfgang's resignation most ungraciously. It was feared that Leopold would suffer, but the
Archbishop expressed his displeasure only verbally and Leopold was allowed to keep his position. Indeed, anything else
would have been too outrageous and, as it was, in the general
opinion Wolfgang had been badly treated. Wolfgang's friend
Count Firmian, on his return to Salzburg from a journey in
October 1777, was met by the Archbishop with the remark:
"We have one musician less since you left." Firmian replied:

"Your Grace has lost a great performer." "How so?" "He is the greatest clavier-player that I ever heard in my life; he has done Your Grace good service on the violin and he is a first-rate composer." Whereupon the Archbishop was silent.[7]

After his departure Wolfgang writes to his father:

"I hope that you are less annoyed than when I was in Salzburg, for I must acknowledge that I was the cause of it. I was badly treated; I did not deserve it. You naturally took my part but too strongly; I assure you that was the chief reason that I hurried out of Salzburg."

To this his father replied on November 17, 1777:

"You are quite right as to my extreme annoyance at the tyrannical treatment you received; it gnawed at my heart and prevented my sleeping; it was always in my thoughts and would in the end have destroyed me. My dear son, when you are happy, I am happy; and your mother and sister—we are all happy; and this happiness I hope for by the grace of God and my confidence in your own good sense."[8]

It was doubtless with considerable anxiety that Leopold reconciled himself to Wolfgang's departure for the first time without him on a long tour. The presence of his mother would not make up for Leopold's absence and the nature of Wolfgang, in its frankness, excitability, and careless good nature, was such as to make him an easy victim to ill nature and unscrupulous enmity. One of the most interesting passages in all Leopold's letters, part of which I have already quoted,[9] must be given fully here. It is dated Salzburg, February 16, 1778, and addressed to Wolfgang and his mother in Mannheim:

". . . My son! you are too hasty and hot in all your affairs. Your character has entirely changed since your childhood and boyhood. As a child and a boy you were more serious than childish and when occupied with music at the piano or otherwise nobody might venture the least jesting with you. Even your countenance was so grave that many people in different countries feared that your precocious talent and constantly serious and reflecting expression betokened an early death. Now, however, it seems to me that you are far too ready to

[7]Letter from Leopold Mozart dated October 4, 1777.

[8]This remarkable letter shows the real nature of Leopold Mozart under his iron exterior.

[9]See pages 28–9.

answer jestingly on every occasion—and that is already the
first step to familiarity which one must avoid in this world if
one wishes to preserve its respect. . . . It is your good heart
which causes you to see no fault in a man, to give him your
full confidence if he praises you to the skies; whereas as a boy
your excessive modesty made you weep when you were praised
too much. The greatest art is to learn to know oneself and
then, my son, do as I do and study other people so as to understand them well. You know that has always been my study
and it is truly a good, useful, indeed invaluable study. . . ."

The tour was arranged so that Wolfgang should visit the
principal German towns and Paris. Leopold carefully impressed upon Wolfgang that his sole aim must be to extend
his fame, make money, and obtain a sound position. It was
indeed putting a strain on a young man of twenty-one to be
instructed so categorically that personal gratification and
mere amusement were to be kept altogether in the back-
ground, but Leopold, with his knowledge of the world, was
emphatic. He writes in a letter dated Salzburg, October 15,
1777:

". . . To earn money and to be economical must be your
constant care; otherwise one cannot travel honourably; indeed,
one comes to a standstill and gets into debt—"

Leopold's long letters are full of the minutest instructions
as to how to take the fullest advantage of every possible opportunity. He thinks of everything, of the music to be taken,
of the difficulties with copyists, of the necessary introductions,
of the routes, the expenses, and so on. He foresees that Wolfgang and his mother will probably need more money than
Wolfgang can earn, and as he has no private means and has
long ago spent the profits of the first and most successful tour,
he is compelled to borrow from his friends Hagenauer and
Bullinger, which, as Jahn remarks, must have been "abhorrent
to so conscientious a man." He cut down his own household
expenses to the barest minimum, took up again the drudgery
of giving lessons, he and Nannerl sacrificing together all they
could to make the tour possible. An outfit for Wolfgang and
his mother had to be provided and also a carriage in which the
two should travel with their luggage, clothes, music, and instruments in a respectable style; for Leopold knew well the
importance of cutting a good figure in the world, especially

when one is on the brink of beggary. Nevertheless, in spite of all the circumspection, common sense, foresight, and hard labour of Leopold the tour failed, as we shall see, to achieve its object.

x. *The Last Grand Tour Begins*

September 23, 1777–October 30, 1777 AGE 21

Munich, Augsburg, Wallerstein

On September 23, 1777, early in the morning Wolfgang and his mother left Salzburg. I intend to allow this extraordinary journey with all its adventures to speak mainly for itself; it is so vividly narrated in the letters exchanged between Wolfgang and his father that no description from a third pen could ever have the freshness and vitality of that first-hand account. But these letters are frequently so long and so full of detail that I shall have to select and cut them pretty drastically. Also, I shall interpolate a commentary where I think it necessary.

[FROM WOLFGANG] *Wasserburg, September 23, 1777*
11 o'clock at night

Mon très cher Père,

God be praised and thanked, we have passed safely Wagin, Stain, Ferbertsheim, and arrived at Wasserburg; now for a brief description: . . . before Schinn we met with a number of cows, among which was a remarkable one—for it was one-sided, which we had never seen before. . . .

At Schinn . . . we had to change . . . Mamma and I were talking when a stout man came up whose "symphony" was immediately known to me—he was a merchant from Memmingen, he looked at me a long while and said at last: "Are you Herr Mozart? . . . I have seen you at the musical performances in the Mirabell."[1] Thereupon he disclosed his name, which I have forgotten, thank God. . . . From Stain we had a postilion who was a man of marvellous phlegm, we

---

[1] The grounds of this palace, once belonging to the Archbishop, are now laid out as a beautiful public park in the centre of Salzburg. The palace possesses an exceptionally fine rococo marble staircase which is little known.

thought we should never arrive. From Ferbertsheim to Wasserburg all went well. We live like princes and lack nothing
but Papa, but God will have it so, all will yet be well. . . . I
am the other Papa, I look after everything. . . . At the Star at
Wasserburg one is looked after marvellously. I sat there like
a prince. Half an hour ago the servant knocked and asked for
instructions and I answered him with my most grave demeanour, such as I have in my portrait;[2] I must finish, Mamma
is ready dressed. We both beg Papa to take care of his health;
not to go out too early; not to let himself be vexed; to laugh
heartily; be merry and always joyful, remember, as we do, that
the Archbishop[3] is a rat but that God is compassionate, charitable, and loving. I kiss Papa's hand a thousand times and embrace my sister Canaglie as many times as I today already
have—taken snuff. I believe I have left at home my *Dekreter*[4]
—I beg you to send them soon. In the early morning at half
past six.

Your obedient son,

Wolfgang Amadé Mozart

[FROM LEOPOLD]   *Salzburg, September 25, 1777*
My two Loved Ones,

I received dear Wolfgang's letter this morning with the
greatest pleasure; Bullinger has just now read it; he laughed
heartily and sends his compliments. Am delighted that you are
well; I am now, thank God, much better. After your departure
I climbed the stairs wearily and threw myself in an armchair.[5]
I had taken the greatest care . . . not to make our parting
painful and in so doing I forgot to give my son a father's
blessing. I ran to the window and sent it after you both, but I
could not see you pass out of the gate[6] and no doubt you had
already gone by for I had been sitting there for some time incapable of thought. Nannerl wept bitterly and I had great difficulty in consoling her. She complained of headache and pains

[2] I think this must refer to the portrait recently made for Martini,
reproduced as frontispiece.

[3] In cipher.

[4] Diplomas of the musical academies of Bologna and Verona and
the testimonial from Padre Martini.

[5] Leopold might well have felt sad. Wolfgang was to be absent
nearly two years and he was never to see his wife again.

[6] The town gate.

in the stomach, finally she was sick . . . went to bed . . . the sorrowful Pimps[7] lay beside her.

I went to my room, said my morning prayers, lay on my bed until eight-thirty, read in a book, composed myself, and dozed. The dog came, I was awake, he made signs that I should go with him and I understood from this that it was nearly twelve o'clock. I got up, took my fur coat, found Nannerl sound asleep, and saw by the clock that it was twelve-thirty. When I came back with the dog I woke Nannerl and had the meal brought in. Nannerl had no appetite; she ate nothing and afterwards went to bed and I spent the time after Bullinger had gone in praying and reading and lay on my bed.

In the evening Nannerl was quite well and hungry, we played piquet, then we had our meal in my room and afterwards had a couple more games, then we went in God's name to sleep. Thus passed a sadder day than I ever expected to live through in my whole life. . . .

Wolfgang and his mother arrived in Munich at four-thirty on the evening of September 24. They went to the inn of Herr Albert, an old friend, who was known as the "learned landlord," in the Kaufingerstrasse. Wolfgang immediately set about paying the necessary visits and called upon Count Seau, the superintendent of the Playhouse, who advised him to approach the Elector at once as there was no doubt that a good composer was needed in Munich. In his letter to his father dated September 26, 1777, he gives full details of his visits, tells him he has seen a comedy: *Henriette, or She is Married Already?* and relates a story of Johannes von Grönner, who had just been appointed Concertmeister "through an impudent speech." He had produced two symphonies.

"The Elector asked him: 'Did you really compose this?' 'Yes, Your Excellency.' 'From whom did you learn it?' 'From a schoolmaster in Switzerland . . . this schoolmaster has taught me more than all our composers here were capable of.'

"Today Count Schönborn and his wife, sister of the Archbishop, arrived. I was at the Playhouse. Herr Albert told them I was here and that I had left the service. They were astonished. They would hardly believe him when he said I received twelve florins and thirty kreutzer of blessed memory! Mamma and I hope you are both well. I am in a continuous

[7] Their dog.

good humour. My heart is as light as a feather since I have left all this chicanery—I am also fatter. . . ."

Wolfgang also visited the Prince Bishop of Chiemsee, Count Zeil, who was in Munich on a diplomatic mission and promised to help him; but a few days later he said to Wolfgang:

"I do not think you will do much here. I spoke privately to the Elector at Nymphenburg and he said to me: 'It is too soon. Let him travel in Italy and make a name. I do not refuse anything, but it is too soon yet.' "

"There it is," writes Wolfgang to his father on September 29-30, 1777:

"Most of these great lords have a frightful foreign obsession. Nevertheless he advised me to see the Elector. . . . I have spoken today privately with Herr Wotschicka[8] and he . . . will obtain me an audience without fail. . . .

"I like it here and am of the opinion, as are many good friends of mine, that if I stayed here a year or two I could earn respect through my work and would likelier be sought after by the court than have to apply to it. Herr Albert has an idea which seems to be not impossible: namely, he will collect ten good friends each of whom need only spare one ducat for me to have monthly ten ducats, fifty gulden, or annually six hundred florins; if in addition I had two hundred yearly from Count Seau, that would be eight hundred florins—what does Papa think of this idea?—Is it not most friendly—would it not be nice if it were really serious?—I am perfectly satisfied with it; I should be near Salzburg and if the desire came to you, my dearest Papa (as I from my heart should wish), to leave Salzburg and to make your life in Munich it would be quite easy and jolly to do. For if we have to live in Salzburg on five hundred and four florins we could manage well in Munich on six hundred to eight hundred florins."

Wolfgang had his interview with the Elector, which he describes to his father in his letter of September 30:

"Today after a talk with Mr. Wotschicka at nine o'clock I went to the court. Baron Kern was the gentleman-in-attendance. All were in hunting uniform. . . .

"At ten o'clock I was taken to the small room through

[8]Franz Xavier Woschitka, violoncellist in the Munich Court Chapel.

which His Highness would pass to hear Mass before the hunt. Count Seau passed through and greeted me most friendly: 'My best wishes, dearest Mozart!' When the Elector approached me I said: 'I trust Your Highness will allow me to lay myself and my services at Your Highness's Feet.' 'Indeed, have you left Salzburg altogether?' 'Altogether, Your Highness.' 'Indeed—why? Have you had a row?' 'May it please Your Highness, I asked only permission to travel, which was refused, whereupon I was compelled to take this step although I long had realized Salzburg was no place for me, that is certain.' 'My God, young man! But your father is still at Salzburg?' 'Yes, Your Highness, he humbly commends himself, etc. I have been in Italy three times, have written three operas, am a Member of the Academy of Bologna after a trial accomplished in one hour which has taken many *maestri* four or five hours of hard labour; this may serve as witness that I am qualified to serve any court. My only wish is to serve Your Highness, who himself is a great—' 'Yes, my dear young fellow, but there is no vacancy! I am sorry, if only there were a vacancy—' 'I assure Your Highness I should be an honour to Munich.' 'No doubt, no doubt, but there is no vacancy. . . .'[9]

PS.—My dear sister, I shall write you next time a letter all for you . . . remember me to A.B.C., M.R. and other similar letters. *Addio.* I beg you to take great care of your health, I kiss Papa's hand a hundred thousand times and am and remain

"his most obedient son

"Someone here built a house and wrote on it:

"To build is truly a great pleasure

"But its great cost I did not measure.

"During the night another added:

"And that it cost so much to do,

"You ought to have known, you idiot, you!"

[9]Few people in authority today realize the social importance of a plentiful supply of "vacancies." Since Mozart's days artists have exchanged the patronage and official employment of heads of States, Churches and people in authority for the "freedom" of selling their work competitively in the market. For a time this worked tolerably well, but with the twentieth century and universal education the artist found that he was now at the mercy of the lowest common taste of the multitude. Mozart's situation today would be even worse than in 1777.

[FROM LEOPOLD]

Salzburg, September 27, 1777

. . . I beg of you, my dear son, do not write again to me such things about the Archbishop; remember that I am here and that such a letter might be lost or get into other hands. . . . It does the Prince (Archbishop) no honour that he gave you such a wretched salary and does you no honour that you served him so long for such a trifle. If anyone asks you what your salary was you had better reply straightway that you only remained there out of love for your father until you were a little older, since the salary in Salzburg was only three to four hundred florins apart from the foreigners to whom the Prince pays more. . . . Mitzerl, Trefel, and all Salzburg greet you. Nannerl has put everything straight, she sends her greeting and kisses Mamma and you a million times and I—you know well that my whole heart is with you, God keep you well! On your life depends mine.

I am

the forlorn father and husband

[FROM LEOPOLD]   *Salzburg, September 28, 1777*

Today I went out for the first time and actually to the Mirabell to the last Mass . . . I am very well today, thank God, and have coughed very little, often scarcely three times in a couple of hours. Now I am going on with the taking of moistening things and will also speak with Dr. Barisani for I have become very thin. I hope it will pass away, for my mind is quieter now and I shall take great care of myself.

Only I beg of you, my dear Wolfgang, to indulge in no excess. You have been accustomed to good discipline from your youth and to avoid heating liquor, for you know that you get quickly overheated and you prefer cold to warmth: a clear proof that your blood is inclined to a high temperature and is easily excited. Strong wines and much drinking are thus harmful to you. . . .

[FROM LEOPOLD]   *Salzburg, October 4, 1777*
Mon très cher fils,

I had no great expectations of Munich. The Elector is bound to take nobody unless there is a vacancy and one has always secret enemies to hinder one. The Albert project shows indeed the greatest friendliness but, likely as it seems to you to find ten persons who will pay you a ducat monthly, it seems unlikely to me. And who could these friends of man or of music be?—And what sort of security *is* there or what service in return? That Count Seau should give something seems more promising but that without the other is useless. . . . In short I cannot see where these ten charming friends are to come from . . . you can continue your journey and await letters from Albert.

The craze for Italians does not prevail everywhere, but is almost confined to Munich. I mean the excessive craze! In Mannheim all are German except a pair of *castrati*. In Trier with . . . Prince Clemens of Saxony there is only Maestro Sales, the rest are German. In Mainz all are Germans; in Wurzburg only Sgr. Fracassini,[10] a violinist . . . At all small Protestant courts there are no foreigners. . . .

[FROM WOLFGANG]   *Munich, October 3, 1777*

. . . At Count Salern's for three days I played many things out of my head, including the two *Cassationen* for the Countess[11] and the final music with the Rondeau,[12] these latter by heart. You cannot imagine what pleasure they gave Count Salern;[13] he understands music for he cries: "Bravo!" when other gentlemen take a pinch of snuff, cough, or begin a conversation. I said to him I wished the Elector were there to hear what I could do, of which he knows nothing. . . . All these great people believe whatever is told them and refuse to judge for themselves. That is always the way.

I offered him a trial; he was to get all the composers in Munich and any he chose from Italy, France, Germany, England, and Spain; I dare compete with them all.[14] I told him what had happened in Italy and begged him if there were any talk of me to mention all this. He said: "I have very little influence but will do what I can with all my heart."

[10]A pupil of Tartini's.

[11]Probably the Divertimenti in F and B (K. 247–8) composed in Salzburg for Countess Lodron in 1776.

[12]Perhaps the Serenade in D (K.250) or one of the two Divertimenti in D and B (K.251 and K.254).

[13]Count Joseph von Salern, chief director of music and the opera.

[14]Wonderful, charming, and incomparable Mozart, aged twenty-one!

He is firmly of the opinion that if I could remain here the thing would come of itself. For me alone this would not be impossible for I should get at least three hundred florins from Count Seau; for food I should not have to trouble for I should be invited everywhere and, if not, Albert would be delighted to have me at meals. I eat very little, drink water, and at the end with fruit a small glass of wine.[15]

I would make a contract with Count Seau (only with the advice of my good friends) thus: I deliver yearly four German operas, some seria and some buffa, with one evening's takings of each for myself, which is the usual custom. That alone would bring me at least five hundred florins, which with my salary would make eight hundred florins; but certainly more, for the Reiner player and singer gets two hundred in an evening; and I am very popular here and how popular I should become if I should help to raise the national German opera high in the musical world! And that certainly would be done by me; for I was at once full of desire to compose as soon as I heard the German singspiel.

The prima donna is named Keiserin, she is the daughter of a cook by a nobleman here, a charming girl and pretty on the stage. I have not seen her nearer yet . . . when I heard her it was the third time she played. She has a beautiful voice, neither strong nor weak but very pure and with good intonation. Valesi is her teacher, and her style shows that her master understands singing as well as teaching. When she had to sustain a note for a couple of bars I was surprised at the beauty of her crescendo and decrescendo. She has a slow shake and that delights me for it will be all the more clear and true when she wants to make it quicker. She is a great favourite with the people here and I agree with them. Mamma was in the parterre, she went at four-thirty to secure a seat. I did not go till six-thirty for I am well enough known to have the entry to the boxes. . . . I watched Keiserin through my glasses and she drew more than one tear from me. I cried: "Brava, bravissima!" many times. . . . The piece was called *The Fishermaiden* with a good translation.[16] They want to have a German opera seria soon and would like me to compose it. . . .

[15]What is the food of genius? Air, fire, and water!

[16]*La Pescatrice* by Piccinni, composed 1766.

[FROM LEOPOLD]   *Salzburg, October 6, 1777*

. . . That you would live alone in Munich is true but what honour would it be to you [without an official position]? How the Archbishop would sneer! You can do this much in any place, not only in Munich. You must not make so little of yourself and throw yourself away; there is certainly no need for that. Mamma may console herself, I am much better . . . what troubles me occasionally is that I no longer hear you play the clavier or violin and whenever I return home I feel a little melancholy, for as I near our home I think I shall hear you playing the violin. . . . You must now, with the help of God, continue your journey and go to Augsburg and stay at The Lamb in the Heil. Kreutzergasse.[17]

The composer Mysliweczek, whom Wolfgang had met in Bologna in 1770, turned up in Munich, where his opera *Ezio* was produced, and was kept there by illness. This illness had been brought on by excess and Leopold had forbidden Wolfgang to visit him, but he was so insistent that Wolfgang saw him in the garden of the Ducal Hospital.[18] He suggested that Wolfgang might get a libretto to compose for Naples and wrote on his behalf to the impresario Santorio. To his father on October 10–11 after describing this meeting he writes:

"I have an inexpressible desire to write an opera again . . . composition is my one and only passion and joy. . . . I only have to hear of an opera or go into a theatre and hear tuning up to be almost beside myself. . . ."

Nothing, however, came of this or of an attempt by Leopold to get him a commission to write an opera for the Feast of the Ascension in Venice. On October 11 Wolfgang and his mother left Munich and arrived the same evening in Augsburg. Following the instructions of Leopold, Wolfgang called upon the town councillor von Langenmantel, whom Leopold had been well acquainted with, and gave his father the following ironical account of his visit to this ridiculous dignitary of Leopold's native town:

[17]". . . where you pay thirty kreutzers for dinner, get nice rooms and good society, English, French, etc."

[18]His illness seems to have been syphilis, which explains Leopold's attitude. Nevertheless Leopold writes on October 12, after receipt of Wolfgang's description of his meeting: "Your horror, your anguish when you saw him is more than understandable to me. I should have felt the same. You know my heart. He is indeed to be pitied."

Augsburg, October 14, 1777

. . . My first visit was to Herr Town-councillor Longotabaro;[19] my cousin, a dear good man and an honest citizen, accompanied me and had the honour of waiting in the anteroom
like a lackey until I came out from the arch-town-councillor.
I did not fail to begin by presenting my father's humblest respects. He was pleased to remember all about it and asked me:
"How has the gentleman been all this time?" To which I
replied: "God be praised, quite well and I hope that your
health has also been good?" He then became still more polite
and said: "Sir," and I said: "Your Grace," as I had done from
the first. Nothing would satisfy him but I must mount to his
son-in-law on the second floor, and with my cousin waiting on
the steps all the while! It was with difficulty that I refrained
from saying something, with all my politeness. Upstairs I had
the honour of playing for three-quarters of an hour upon a
good clavichord by Stein[20] in the presence of the stiff and
starched son, his long-necked, gracious lady-wife, and her silly
old mother. I played fantasies and then everything he had
prima vista; among others some very pretty pieces by a certain
Edelmann.[21] They were all exceedingly polite and I was exceedingly polite, for it is my custom to be to people as I find
them; it is the best way.

Wolfgang next visited Stein, incognito at the suggestion
of Leopold, and he was accompanied by the young Langenmantel, who nearly let the cat out of the bag by blurting
out: "I have the honour to introduce to you a virtuoso on
the clavier." "I protested," Wolfgang tells his father in the
letter from which I have already quoted:

"and said I was an unworthy pupil of Herr Sigl in Munich.
. . . He shook his head and said at last: 'Have I the honour of
seeing Herr Mozart?' 'Oh, no!' said I, 'my name is Trazom
and I have a letter to you.' He took the letter and was going to
open it. I did not give him time and said: 'Why read the letter
now? Let us go into the hall, I am most curious to see your

[19]This is Wolfgang's cipher for von Langenmantel.

[20]J. A. Stein (1728–82), famous organ- and clavier-maker.

[21]Probably the composer Johann Friedrich Edelmann (b., Strassburg, 1749); he was beheaded in Paris on July 17, 1794, with his
pupil, Baron Dietrich.

pianofortes.' 'With all my heart; but I do not think I am deceived.'

"He opened the door. I ran to one of the three claviers and played. He could scarcely take time to open the letter, his curiosity was so excited, he only read the signature. 'Oh!' he cried, and embraced me. He crossed himself, made grimaces, and was absolutely delighted. . . . He took me to a coffeehouse where, as I entered, I thought I should succumb to the thick air and smell of tobacco. I had to endure it for a whole hour."

The main object in going to Augsburg, Leopold's native town, where there was no court, was to give a concert and earn some money. The son of the town councillor promised to arrange this with the local "aristocrats," but later told Wolfgang that the "aristocrats" had no money; this was after a supper to which he had invited Wolfgang when he had played "as long as the company pleased."[22] In addition they thought fit to make fun of him. On his father's advice Wolfgang had worn the cross of the order given him by the Pope.[23] Although he had explained exactly what it was and how he had received it to young Langenmantel, this petty bourgeois and his friends thought it a great joke in the true style of the bourgeoisie all the world over, who always believe that the hereditary nobility are born out of sealed test-tubes sent down from heaven by God while they themselves and all others are merely the descendants of monkeys. It was impossible for Town-councillor Langenmantel and his entourage to conceive of Mozart as the equal of a baron and it is this servile ignorance of the middle class which really has justified in the past the attitude to it of the aristocracy so tersely expressed in the famous remark of a German nobleman that below the rank of a baron nobody exists. The infuriated Wolfgang lost his temper with them and wrote to his father a full account:

Augsburg, October 17, 1777

I shall be truly delighted when I am again in a place where

---

[22]He played two concertos, something out of his head and a trio by Hafeneder on the violin. "I would have gladly played the violin more but I was so badly accompanied that I got colic."

[23]After this Augsburg experience Mozart seems never to have worn his Papal order again.

there is a court . . .[24] I must say that if I had not found such
good cousins[25] and such a dear little cousin (Bäsle)[26] there,
I should regret as many times as I have hairs on my head that
I ever came to Augsburg. Now I must tell you something
about my dear young Bäsle, but I shall wait until tomorrow for
one must be in thorough good spirits to praise her as she deserves. . . .

Early on the 17th I write and assure you that our little
cousin is beautiful, sensible, charming, clever, gay, and knows
something of the world. She was also for some time in
Munich. We suit each other well for she also is a little bit
wicked. We hoax people and have great fun. . . .

I beg you to write soon to the poor Mysliweczek as I know
it would give him great pleasure. In my next I shall tell you
all about the pianofortes and organs of Stein and about
the chamber concert. A crowd of the nobility were there
—Duchess Arsefountain, Countess Firejoy, and Princess
Stinkdirt with her two daughters, who are, however, already
married to the two Princes Papbelly of Swinetail. . . . I
kiss Papa's hands a hundred thousand times, embrace my
sister Canaglie with a bear's tenderness, and am your most
obedient son. . . .

Mamma, I, and our little cousin went after lunch to Herr
Stein's. At four o'clock came the Herr Kapellmeister and Herr
Schmittbauer, organist at St. Ulrich's, a splendid old man. I
played at sight a sonata of Beeché which was rather difficult.
How the Kapellmeister and the organist crossed themselves in
astonishment is indescribable. Here as in Munich I have
played by heart and all my six sonatas. . . .

Now I must begin about the Stein pianos. Before I had
seen something of Stein's work I liked Späth's[27] best but now
the preference must be given to Stein; they mute much better. If I strike hard whether I raise my finger or not the sound
passes the instant I have heard it. I may come upon the keys as

[24]Mozart found (as many others have found) that responsibility
and dignity, culture, amiability, simplicity of manners, and respect for
individuals are occasionally prevalent among those who are at the top
and at the bottom but hardly ever among those who are in between.

[25]Really, his uncle and aunt.

[26]More will be heard of this young woman.

[27]Späth, famous organ- and pianoforte-maker of Regensburg.

I like, the tone is always the same; it does not waver, it neither becomes stronger nor weaker, nor does it cease altogether; in a word it is all equal. It is true such a piano is not to be had under three hundred florins but the trouble and labour bestowed upon it is inestimable . . . his hammers fall back the instant they strike the strings whether the keys are held down or not. . . . He often says: "If I were not such a passionate music-lover myself and were not able to play a little on the clavier I should have long ago lost patience, but I am a lover of instruments which do not tax the player and which wear well." His pianos truly are durable . . . the pedal which is pressed by the knee is also better contrived by him than by others. I need only touch it and it works and when the knee is removed one does not hear the least vibration. . . .

When I told Herr Stein I should like to play upon his organ (in the Barfüsserkirche), for I had a passion for the organ, he was greatly astonished and said: "What, such a man as you, so great a clavier-player, wish to play on an instrument in which there is no place for *douceur*, expression, and has no piano, and no forte, but goes on always the same?"[28] "That means nothing at all. The organ is to my eyes and ears the King of Instruments." So we went together. I could see from his remarks that he did not expect much; he thought I would play clavier-fashion. He told me how he had taken Schobert, also at his request, to his organ and: "I feared for him, for Schobert had told everybody and the church was rather full. I thought that the fellow would be full of spirit, fire, and pace and that would tell on the organ, but when he began I changed my opinion."

I only said: "What do you think, Herr Stein? Do you imagine I shall come to grief on the organ?" "Ah, you! That is another matter." We went into the choir. I began the prelude, he laughed with delight, then followed a fugue. "I can well believe you like playing the organ when you play like that."—

At first I did not quite understand the pedal because it is

---

[28]Very strange of Stein! This was the great beauty and artistic merit of the old organs; of course it has now gone altogether. The modern organ has no *douceur* and is nothing but "expression"—the trumpetings of elephants, the howls of cats, the squeak of rats, and the *vox humana*, all tremolo!

not divided. It begins C then D E in a row. With us D and E are above, as E flat and F sharp are here, but I soon got accustomed to it. . . .

[FROM LEOPOLD]   *Salzburg, October 15, 1777*

You must know that one must call the Lutherans "Evangelicals" for they do not wish to be called Lutherans; one also says the Evangelical, not the Lutheran, Church, in the same way as the Calvinists wish to be known as "Protestants," not Calvinists . . . one may often put a fussy person into a temper with one inappropriate word. . . .

You stayed too long in Munich and must give one or two concerts in Augsburg to make something, however little. Fine words, flattering speeches, and *bravissimos* will not pay the postmaster or the innkeeper and as soon as one can get nothing more one must move on. . . .

I ought to have told you that as soon as you got to Munich you should seek out a good copyist and do the same everywhere where you are staying for some time. For you must also endeavour to make something by composing and that can happen when one has symphonies and *divertimenti* copied in readiness to present them to a prince or music-lover. The copying must be arranged so that at least the first violin or another principal part is written in your presence; the rest can be taken away. Now you must absolutely have something ready for Prince Taxis. You can quickly give the oboe, horn, and viola parts of six good symphonies to one or more (so as to get it done quicker) copyists . . . the *divertimenti* are quickly copied, though in truth yours have many parts and are long. *Basta!* In every place you must immediately seek out a copyist, otherwise you will lose much. . . .

There are all kinds of copyists. You must get a sample of the work first and also see to the paper that is used. . . . In short, you must look after everything so that no mistakes are made, which can only be done by having one's head in the right place. . . .

In my opinion you need not bother about the opera in Mannheim which you can see during the Carnival, but you must not neglect to visit Prince Taxis on his estate. . . .

We are well and I should be better still if I were one of those careless fathers who in three weeks can forget wife and

child. That I could not do in a hundred years. . . . Nannerl
and I kiss you both a million times. . . .

[FROM LEOPOLD]   *Salzburg, October 18, 1777*
. . . I am not surprised that they made eyes at your playing of your last Cassation. You yourself do not know how well
you play the violin and if you did yourself the honour and
wished to play with distinction, courage, and spirit you would
be the first violinist in Europe. . . .

What you have written about your visit to Town-councillor Longotabaro . . . made us all, including Herr Bullinger,
laugh immoderately. . . . This gentleman does not readily
know how to talk to others as he is accustomed only to the
servants of the magistracy or to speak down to the burghers
from the height of his dirty throne. . . . As for young Longotabaro . . . you have made yourself too cheap with this boob
. . . you were not reserved enough and too trusting. In short,
you were too natural for such a nitwit and so he thought he
could make fun of you. . . .

When you get to Mannheim the principal person you can
trust must be Sgr. Raaff,[29] who is a God-fearing, honourable
man who loves Germans and can help to bring about your
being retained by the Elector during the winter. . . .

[FROM WOLFGANG]   *Augsburg, October 24, 1777*
. . . Badly as they fiddle, yet the music at the monastery is
preferable to that of the Augsburg orchestra. I gave a symphony and played the Violin Concerto in B by Wanhal with
universal applause. The Dean is a good, jolly fellow, a cousin
of Eberlin's named Zerchinger, and remembers Papa very well.
In the evening at supper I played the Strasbourg Concerto. It
went as smooth as oil. Everyone praised the beautiful pure
tone. Afterwards they brought a clavier. I preluded and played
a sonata and the Fischer variations. Then someone whispered
to the Dean that he should hear me play organ-fashion. I said
he might give me a theme; he would not, but one of the
monks did. I began andante and in the middle (the fugue was
in G minor) I began in the major quite playfully but in the
same tempo and then returned to the theme but backwards;
at last it occurred to me that I might try the playful style for
the theme of the fugue. Without more ado I tried it and it

[29]Anton Raaff (1714–97), a famous tenor at the Mannheim court.

went as accurately as if it had been measured for by Daser [the Salzburg tailor]. The Dean was beside himself. . . . "I could never have believed what I have heard," he said; "you are a wonderful man. My Abbot told me that never in his life had he heard such solemn and convincing organ-playing." The Abbot had heard me some days before when the Dean was not there.

Finally someone brought me a sonata, which was fugued, to play. I said: "Gentlemen, this is too much; I must acknowledge I shall not be able to play the sonata straight away." "I think so, too," said the Dean eagerly, as he was all on my side, "that is too much, it would be impossible for anyone." "Nevertheless," I said, "I shall try." And as I played I heard the Dean calling out behind me: "Oh, you rascal! Oh, you young scamp!" I played until eleven o'clock and was bombarded with themes for fugues. . . .

Apropos of Stein's daughter:[30] whoever sees and hears her play without laughing must be as much of a stone as her father himself. . . . Herr Stein is quite infatuated with his daughter; she is eight and a half years old and learns everything by heart. She may become something, she has genius; but if she goes on as at present, nothing will come of it. . . . She will never learn the most difficult, most necessary, and principal thing in music: namely, *time*, because she has been accustomed since youth to play out of time. Herr Stein and I have certainly talked for two hours on this point. I think I nearly converted him. He now asks my advice on everything. He was quite infatuated with Beeché[31] but now he sees and hears that I play better, that I make no grimaces and yet play so expressively that I show off his pianofortes better than anyone. The correctness of my time astonishes them all. The tempo rubato in an adagio with the left hand keeping strict time was quite beyond their comprehension. They always follow with the left hand.[32]

[30]Maria Anna Stein (1769–1833). She grew up a good pianist and married J. Andreas Streicher, the famous pianoforte-maker. In after-life she was a friend of Beethoven.

[31]Beecke. See page 190.

[32]This is the hall-mark of true musicianship. The ordinary amateur has no idea of how rare it is. One hears it only from a few of the greatest instrumentalists. In the performance of Mozart's works, whether operatic or instrumental, accurate and steady time is of the

Count Wollfeck [Wolfegg] and others who were very enthusiastic for Beeché, said lately openly at the concert that I had thrown Beeché quite in the shade. Count Wollfeck kept running about the hall saying: "have never heard such playing in my life. . . ."

In the Concerto for three claviers[33] Herr Demmler[34] played the first, I the second, and Herr Stein the third. Then I played alone the last Sonata in D for Dürnitz,[35] then my Concerto in B,[36] then again alone organ-fashion a fugue in C minor, and suddenly a brilliant Sonata in C major[37] out of my head with a Rondeau. . . . There was a fine din and uproar. Herr Stein could do nothing but make faces in astonishment and Herr Demmler laughed incessantly. He is a strange man, if anything pleases him exceedingly he bursts into laughter, with me he began to swear also. *Addio*, I kiss Papa's hands and embrace my sister with all my heart.

[FROM LEOPOLD TO HIS WIFE] *Salzburg, October 23, 1777*

. . . Tell Wolfgang that the big-eyed royal baker's daughter who danced with him at the Stern and so often made him friendly compliments and then finally went into the Loretto convent has returned to her father's house. She had heard that he was leaving Salzburg and thought to see him and prevent him; he will therefore be so kind as to compensate the father for all the expense, the ceremony, etc., which her entering the convent cost. . . .

PS.

Mon très cher fils!

I must wish you happiness on your saint-day's anniversary! But what can I wish that I do not always wish for you? I wish you the grace of God that will everywhere accompany you and never leave you if you sedulously carry out the obligations of a true Christian and Catholic.

---

first importance; in the case of inferior composers it matters less—except that such playing makes their music sound better than it is, as is the case when Toscanini conducts Wagner and Strauss.

[33](K.242) composed in February 1776.

[34]Johann Michael Demmler, organist at Augsburg.

[35](K.284), one of set of Six Sonatas (K.279–284).

[36]Perhaps the Concerto in B flat (K.238).

[37]Perhaps (K.309), but see page 197.

You know me. I am no pedant, no *Bettbruder*, still less a hypocrite; you will not refuse your father's request, which is that you will take heed of your soul, that you will occasion your father no anxiety in his last hour so that in that dark moment he may not reproach himself that he had been neglectful in his care for your soul. Farewell! Be happy! Live reasonably. Honour and protect your mother, who now in her age has many cares. Love me as I do you and as your true and anxious father.

[FROM WOLFGANG]   *Augsburg, October 25, 1777*

The concert brought in ninety florins without deduction of the expenses. So we have, with the two ducats from the chamber concert, made one hundred florins. The expenses were not more than sixteen florins thirty kreutzers. . . .

As for the Royal baker's daughter I have nothing to object to. I foresaw it long ago. That was actually the reason why I delayed so long in starting and why I found it so difficult. I hope that this story will not be known throughout all Salzburg! I beg Papa urgently to keep it quiet as long as possible and in God's name to repay on my account the expenses which the entry into the convent caused her father until I return and make the poor young girl . . . who naturally is ill . . . well again.

I kiss Papa's hands and thank him for his anniversary wishes. Do not be worried. I have God always before my eyes. I recognize His power, I fear His anger; but I also know His love, His compassion, and His charity towards His creation. He will never abandon His servant—what happens according to His will happens also according to mine. . . .

Papa writes in his first letter that I had made myself cheap with the boy von Langenmantel—not in the least! I was quite natural, that is all. . . . I must stop, Mamma insists on eating and then packing. Tomorrow we go to Wallerstein direct. . . . My dear little cousin . . . to please me yesterday dressed in the French style and looked five per cent prettier. . . .

Wolfgang gave his cousin his portrait in medallion and asked his father to send her something out of the souvenirs accumulated from their tours. They parted very sadly and Leopold tells Wolfgang in a letter dated November 1, when describing their last Salzburg shooting-party, at which Nan-

nerl won, that on the following Sunday the parting of Wolfgang and his cousin, both dissolved in tears, will be represented on the target. Bolt-shooting was the favourite pastime
of the Mozart family and their friends in Salzburg. Leopold's
letters frequently contain references to it and during Wolfgang's absence on this tour his sister, Nannerl, would shoot
regularly for him and occasionally win a few kreutzers. In a
letter dated November 17 Leopold describes the promised
Sunday shooting-party:

"Yesterday at the shooting the best was Herr Wolfgang
Mozart. The target was charming. An Augsburg maiden stood
on the right and presented to a young man in top-boots dressed
for travelling *einen Reise-buschen*; in the other hand she held
an immense linen cloth trailing to the ground on which she
had dried her weeping eyes. The gentleman had a similar cloth
which he used likewise and in his other hand he held his hat,
on which was the bull's-eye as it was easier to see there than
on the *Reise-busch*. Above was written:

Adieu, my young cousin—adieu, my cousin dear,
Good fortune on your journey, good health and weather clear.
We both for fourteen days have been right gaily mad
And this it is which on both sides doth make our parting sad.
O, cursèd fate! Alas! to come and then to go!
Now you are far away and sadly my tears flow."

In the earlier letter of November 1 Leopold gives an account of a Mass by Michael Haydn performed at the Salzburg
Cathedral with the composer conducting and Count Lodron
officiating, which is interesting for the musical details it gives:

"It pleased me exceedingly because six oboes, three contrabasses, two bassoons, and the *castrato*[38] who has been engaged
for six months at a hundred florins monthly were present.
Ferlendis and Sandmayr were the solo oboists. The oboist with
Lodron was a student, Durnermeister and Obkircher were the
second oboists. Cassl and the Prebendary Knozenbry were the
contrabasses next the organ and close to the trombones.
Estlinger was with the bassoon, Hofner and Perwein next to
the oboes close to the violins. What pleased me particularly
was that as the oboes and bassoons were near the voices, the
tutti seemed to be a pure, strongly set vocal music while the
soprano and alto voices, strengthened with the six oboes and

[38]Ceccarelli.

the alto trombones, maintained with tenors and basses the right equalizing power, and the first full choir was so majestic that I would gladly have dispensed with the oboe solos. The whole lasted one and a quarter hours and for me it was too short, for it was really excellently composed. . . ."

On October 26 Wolfgang and his mother left Augsburg and proceeded via Donauwörth and Nördlingen to Hohen-altheim, residence of Prince von Öttingen-Wallerstein, who was a lover of music and had a good orchestra, notable for the delicacy of its playing under the conductor, Antonio Rossetti. Ignaz von Beecke, the pianist of whom we have heard so often, was a Captain in the Württemberg dragoons and Kapellmeister at Wallerstein (where he died in 1803) to the Prince. The Prince, a young man who had formerly invited Wolfgang to visit him in Naples, was on this occasion suffering from melancholia and could bear no music. Wolf-gang and his mother, who was suffering from a severe cold, stayed a few days at Wallerstein, dined with Beecke and his fellow-officers and discussed the Emperor Joseph with him, agreeing that he had "a knowledge of counterpoint but was not a true lover of music."[39]

xi. *Mannheim*

October 30, 1777–March 14, 1778   AGE 21–2

On October 30, 1777 Wolfgang and his mother arrived in Mannheim, which was at that time a town of about twenty-five thousand inhabitants, the seat of the Court of the Elec-tor Palatine, Karl Theodor (1724–99), who later, on the death of the Elector of Bavaria, Maximilian, on December 30 of this year, 1777, became Elector of Bavaria.

Mannheim under Karl Theodor, who was a good example of an eighteenth-century German prince with a genuine taste

---

[39]In his letter dated Mannheim, November 13, 1777, Wolfgang gives his father full particulars of his meeting with Beecke. Wolfgang confesses that bad music gives him a headache but Beecke replies that he is never thus affected by bad music but can be by good, whereupon Wolfgang comments to his father: "Such a shallow head might well get a headache when it hears something it can't understand."

for science, art, literature, and music—he was educated by the Jesuits and had been a friend of Voltaire—was a real centre of German artistic activity. It housed the Palatinate Academy of Science, founded in 1763, which encouraged historical and scientific research and possessed the best collection of pictures, engravings, and antiquities of the time in all Germany. A national theatre had been built and the Elector had endeavoured to retain Lessing as dramatist and Eckhoff as actor and in 1775 had founded a German Society which was the fruit of the literary renaissance then taking place in Germany under the lead of Klopstock and others.[1] At his palace of Schwetzingen, which was the Versailles of the Palatinate, Karl Theodor had produced Schweitzer's *Alcestis* on August 13, 1775, and commissioned from Professor Anton Klein a national patriotic libretto, *Günther von Schwarzburg*, composed by Holzbauer and performed on January 5, 1777 in the splendid new opera-house. Between 1749 and 1792 the Elector Karl is reckoned to have spent about thirty-five million gulden on art and science. Karl Theodor has been described as a weak, pleasure-loving man and in a book entitled *Letters of a French Traveller on Germany*, published in Zurich in 1783, we may read:

"Everything that has ever distinguished a reign in the way of priests, mistresses, natural sons of the Prince, parvenus, speculators, *castrati*, bankrupts, and the like are to be found gathered together in the Palatinate."

Well, it all depends upon the point of view; but even if most of Karl Theodor's expenditure on art and music was to provide pleasure and amusements for himself and his mistresses, all that it becomes anybody to say is that his pleasures and amusements were of a more engaging and fruitful character than those of the majority of people who have the power to gratify their tastes freely.

Although its theatre was one of the glories of Mannheim[2] its music was even more so, Mannheim at that time being described as the "paradise of musicians." It was here that German opera made one of its earliest appearances. Schweitzer's

[1] Lessing produced *Laokoon* in 1766, and *Minna von Barnhelm* in 1767. He became director of the National Theatre in Hamburg in 1767.

[2] Schiller's star rose there in 1782 with *Die Räuber*.

above-mentioned *Alcestis,* first produced in Weimar on May 28, 1773 and given in Mannheim in 1775, was considered by the poet Wieland to be superior to Gluck's and to approach the musical dramatic ideal. It was a German opera, written by a German poet, composed by a German musician, and sung by Germans. This was considered a great step forward in German culture, which had been hitherto so dependent on Italy for opera and on France for drama.

The national character of such a movement is apt to be exaggerated for purposes of political propaganda at all times of international struggle and most biographies of Mozart, as also critics writing about his music, have been at pains to emphasize Mozart's interest in trying to found a national German opera. That Mozart expressed the desire to compose German opera is true; but this only meant that he wanted to be allowed to compose operas and to be considered as capable of so doing as any Italian. It was not that he had a new conception of opera, a *German* or *Austrian* or *Salzburgian* conception which he was anxious to introduce into the world as the contribution of the German-speaking race to operatic music. Not at all! No great musician could have such an absurd idea. But he rightly resented, as every man of talent must, the snobbish notion that nationality or birthplace was a deciding factor in the determination of musical values. Actually this is an anti-national attitude. It amounts to the assertion that nationality plays no part whatever in the valuation of music. And this is absolutely true of music on the highest level. Whatever differences nationality may introduce into the character of music are on the lower levels only. The higher an artist goes, the farther does he depart from local, national, and perhaps even personal or individual values.

When we speak of a national renaissance[3] what we really mean is that the peoples of a country are becoming more active and are taking a livelier part in the general cultural life of the civilization to which they belong. In music as in painting and, I would even maintain, also in literature, the whole of Europe has belonged to one culture ever since the rise of Christianity. What was happening in Germany in the middle of the eighteenth century was a livelier participation

[3]Such as that which was taking place in Germany during Mozart's childhood and boyhood.

in the more advanced culture of Italy and of France. It was not at all—as is often misinterpreted, especially by writers of music—a national reaction *against* Italian and French culture but a new, more vigorous national participation in the general European culture to which Italy and France had temporarily been making the greatest contribution.

One among many proofs of this is that though hailed by Wieland in his "Letters on the German Opera of 'Alcestis' "[4] as an important step in the direction of German opera and superior to Gluck's, Schweitzer's *Alcestis* was just like any Italian opera of the time; as for Holzbauer's *Günther von Schwarzburg*, Schubart might refer to its mixture of "German feeling and foreign grace" and to the "glorious revolution in taste"; but even Jahn—who like a true nineteenth-century German frequently indulges in such vague and idiotic phrases as "a German heart" and "a German artist"—admits that Holzbauer "never deviates from the customary Italian form." In Mozart's criticisms of contemporary operas we never meet with any such nationalistic criticism. Music is always music to him; no matter where it comes from, it is criticized from a purely artistic point of view as music. There is a sense in which it is true to say that Mozart is the most eclectic of all the great European composers. Everything was grist which came to his musical mill and he acquired and made use of every sort of material—whether it came from Italy, France, or Germany—consuming it, transforming it, and by the strength of his genius making it his very own completely. All other seventeenth- and eighteenth-century music—whether Italian, French, or German—now sounds to us like inferior Mozart, with the exception of the great personalities of Handel, Bach, and Haydn, who succeeded in the best of their work in reaching as high a plane as Mozart and yet contributing something of their own.[5]

[4] Burlesqued by Goethe, especially on account of Wieland's comparison of himself with Euripides.

[5] This is only partly true of Handel, who, though he occasionally rose to great heights, did not live as a composer on the same level as Mozart and Bach. The difference is analogous to that between the amateur of genius and the professional of genius in billiards. An amateur may make the most brilliant of strokes *occasionally*, but the professional is habitually on that level. Handel had not got the universality of Mozart. Mozart might have composed the *Messiah* (only

Finally, what needs to be remembered in considering Mozart's environment is that the German artistic renaissance and the new Romantic movement were already in full flood at the time when Wolfgang arrived in Mannheim in 1777 at the age of twenty-one. Goethe's *Sorrows of Werther* had already been published (1774), *Götz von Berlichingen* had appeared in 1773, and the first part of *Faust* was written in 1775 (the peak of the *Sturm und Drang* period), although it was not actually published until 1790. Wolfgang was seven years younger than Goethe and the conception of Mozart as belonging to the earlier artificial and imitation French-salon period of German artistic life is historically false and is the source of much of the misunderstanding of Mozart's music throughout the nineteenth century, a misunderstanding which is still largely current today. It is necessary to bear always in mind that Mozart was only twenty-one years old at the height of the great *Sturm und Drang* movement in German history and that, as I have said before, historically he belongs to the age of revolution in Europe, not to the earlier Augustan age.

Even the revolution in orchestral playing made by Stamitz (1717–75), was by this time over. The Mannheim orchestra under his successor, Christian Cannabich,[6] was unanimously considered to be the finest in Europe. It was strong in numbers and in quality—Mozart writes to his father on November 4, 1777:

"The orchestra is very good and strong; on either side ten or eleven violins, four violas, two oboes, two flutes and two clarinets, two horns, four violoncellos, four bassoons, four contrabasses, trumpets, and drums."

Its standard of playing was extremely high, with delicate gradations of tone unknown hitherto. Crescendo and diminuendo are supposed to have been invented at Mannheim, and Reichardt,[7] referring to a Berlin orchestra, writes:

"I must not speak in this place of the masterly effect produced in the Mannheim orchestra by the swelling and diminu-

---

it would have been still better) but Handel could never have composed *Don Giovanni*.

[6] Christian Cannabich (1731–98), pupil of Johann Stamitz. Sent by the Elector to Italy, where he studied under Jomelli. Appointed leader under Stamitz in 1759 and succeeded him as conductor in 1775.

[7] *Briefe eines aufmerksamen Reisenden*, Vol. I, p. 11.

tion of a long note, or of several successive notes, which gives, if I may so speak, to the whole colouring a darker or lighter shade. This would be considered too great an innovation by Hasse and Graun."

He also relates that:

"The first time Jomelli made use of the crescendo the audience gradually rose from their seats and at the diminuendo they began to breathe freely and became conscious of having stopped their breath."

He declares that the same effect was produced upon himself at Mannheim. Schubart[8] gave a celebrated description of the Mannheim orchestra's playing which deserves quoting since it presents a model which all orchestras should strive to follow in the execution of certain effects:

"No orchestra in the world has ever surpassed that of Mannheim in execution. Their *forte* is a thunder, their *crescendo* a cataract, their *diminuendo* a crystal streamlet babbling away into the far distance, their *piano* the soft breath of early spring."

The Mannheim was the first of the succession of outstanding orchestras whose performances have made them famous throughout the world. During the nineteenth century, as even the German patriot Jahn admits, the Paris orchestra under Habeneck (1781–1849)[9] achieved this pre-eminence. Later Hans von Bülow (1830–94) made the Meiningen orchestra the best in Europe. The Meiningen orchestra had retained its pre-eminence even so late as 1913–14 when I heard it in Munich under its then conductor, Max Reger, who had revived its glories. Its playing made a tremendous impression upon me at the time. Since then I suppose Furtwängler and the Berlin Philharmonic and Toscanini with the New York and the Vienna Philharmonic orchestras have provided the outstanding examples of orchestral playing.

In Mannheim Mozart first met with the clarinet as an or-

[8]In his *Ästhetik*, p. 130.

[9]Habeneck was merciless to singers who did not keep strict time. He introduced Beethoven's symphonies to Paris, and Berlioz no doubt learned as much of orchestral possibilities from his orchestra as Mozart did from the Mannheim orchestra. Sibelius has recently declared his opinion that Mozart is one of the greatest masters of orchestration; this is a sign of the new understanding of Mozart.

chestral instrument. He writes to his father after his return
to Mannheim from Paris, on December 3, 1778, about a
newly engaged oboist at Salzburg:

"Can Feiner play the cor anglais? Ah! if we only had clarinets also! You cannot imagine what a wonderful effect a
symphony with flutes, oboes, and clarinets makes."[10]

Wolfgang soon made friends with the Kapellmeister Cannabich and other members of the Mannheim orchestra such
as Wendling (the flautist), Le Brun and Ramm (oboists),
Ritter (bassoonist), and Lang (horn). He writes to his father:

> *Mannheim, October 31, 1777*
> . . . Today I have been with Herr Denner at Cannabich's.
> He is very cordial. I played on his pianoforte (which is very
> good) and we went together to the rehearsal. I thought I
> should burst out laughing when I was introduced to everybody.
> Some who had heard of me were very polite and full of re-
> spect. Others, however, who knew nothing about me, stared
> at me contemptuously. They think just because I am small
> and young there can be nothing important and mature behind
> my appearance. They will soon be undeceived. Tomorrow
> Herr Cannabich will himself take me to Count Savioli, the
> Intendant of Music. . . . The oratorio which they are re-
> hearsing is by Handel[11] but I did not stay, for before that they
> rehearsed a Psalm and Magnificat by the vice-Kapellmeister
> here, Vogler,[12] which lasted quite an hour. Now I must close
> as I must write to my little cousin . . .

[TO LEOPOLD]   *Mannheim, November 4, 1777*
   . . . This is my second letter from Mannheim. I am with

---

[10]The clarinet was described as an innovation by Hiller in Agricola's
opera *L'Amore di Psiche* in 1769; but Rameau had used it in *Acante
et Céphise* in 1751. Its general use as an orchestral instrument, however, dates from Mozart's "Paris" symphony. It is said to have been
invented in 1690 by Johann Deuner of Nuremberg.

[11]Actually the *Messiah*. Mozart does not mention the performance
on November 1 but in the *Mannheim Tonsch.* (I, p. 119) it is observed that the audience yawned during the *Messiah* but were delighted with Vogler's *Magnificat*. The second part of the *Messiah* was
omitted because it was thought too dry.

[12]Georg Joseph Vogler (1749–1814), famous composer, theorist,
and teacher; studied with (but was not approved of by) Martini; also
studied with Vallotti and Mysliweczek. C. M. von Weber and
Meyerbeer were his pupils.

Cannabich every day. Today Mamma also went with me. He is quite different from what he used to be; the whole orchestra says so. He is much prejudiced in my favour. He has a daughter who plays the clavier well and so as to make him a good friend I am working now on a sonata for his daughter, which is already complete up to the Rondo.[13] When I had finished the first allegro and andante I brought it and played it. Papa cannot imagine what a success it was. There were present young Danner, a French-horn player, Lang, the principal oboist whose name I can't remember but who plays very well and has a nice clean tone.

I made him a present of the oboe concerto.[14] It was written out in Cannabich's room. The man is mad with joy; today I played him the concerto on the pianoforte at Cannabich's and although they knew it was mine it pleased greatly. Nobody said it was not well written, because here they don't understand things—they should ask the Archbishop, he would put them right.

Today I played all my six sonatas for Cannabich.[15] The Kapellmeister Holzbauer today took me himself to Count Savioli and told him in Italian that I should like to have the honour to have His Highness the Elector hear me, that I had been here fifteen years ago when I was seven years old but was now older and bigger, also musically. . . .

Wolfgang had not the same high opinion of the church music as of the orchestral music in Mannheim and writes to his father in the same letter that he would not care to have one of his own Masses produced there:

[13]Authorities differ as to the sonata referred to. Wyzewa and Saint-Foix place both (K.309) and (K.311) in the Mannheim period and are for (K.311). Deiters is for (K.309), Scheibler for (K.311), and A. Heuss for (K.309). The question is of interest because Mozart told Danner that he meant to make the andante "exactly like Mlle. Rose herself." His further remark (November 14–16) that "the andante will give us most trouble, for it is full of expression and must be played accurately with forte and piano as it is marked" seems to suggest (K.309). After playing over the two andantes I am left with no doubt whatever in my own mind that the andante of (K.309) can be a conception of a young girl while that of (K.311) certainly is not.

[14]Unfortunately this work, presented to Ramm, is lost, although he played it five times with great success in Mannheim during that winter.

[15](K.279–284.)

"Why?—Because of their brevity? No, here everything must be short.—On account of the style? Not in the least. But because here one must write under present conditions for instruments since one cannot imagine anything worse than the vocal department. Six sopranos, six tenors, and six basses to twenty violins and twelve basses stand in the proportion of 0 : 1. Is that not so, Herr Bullinger? . . . They have only two *castrati*, who are already old. They are letting them die off. The soprano prefers to sing alto because his upper notes are gone. The few boys they have are wretched. The tenors and basses are like our funeral singers.

"The Herr Vice-Kapellmeister Vogler, who is new in office, is a musical clown, a man who has a very good idea of himself but has not much capacity. The whole orchestra dislike him. Today, however . . . I heard a Mass by Holzbauer which is already twenty-six years old, but good. He writes very well, in a good church style, with good passages for voices and instruments.

"They have two organists here for whose sake alone it would be worth a trip to Mannheim. I had a good chance of hearing them for it is the custom to omit the Benedictus and let the organist play instead. The first time I heard the second organist and the next time the first. I have a higher opinion of the second than of the first. When I heard him I asked: 'Who is at the organ?' 'Our second organist.' 'He plays wretchedly.' When I heard the other: 'Who is this?' 'Our first.' 'He plays more wretchedly still.' . . .

"It is enough to make one laugh to death to see these gentlemen. The second sits at the organ like a child at stool; one sees his art already in his face. The first at least wears spectacles. I stood at the organ and watched him with the intention of learning something. He lifts his hands up in the air at every note. His *tour de force* is that he uses the sext stop but mostly the fifth or octave stop![16] He often playfully lets fall the right hand and plays with the left alone—in one word he does as he likes, he is in this sense complete master of the instrument.

"Mamma informs Nannerl that the lining for the dress is in the large chest on the right-hand side and at the bottom. . . .

[16]In the original: "das er 6 stimmig spielt, meistentheils aber quint-stimmig und octav-stimmig!"

"Mamma and I beg Papa earnestly to have the kindness to send our dear little cousin a memento. For we both regretted that we had nothing with us. . . ."

[TO HIS COUSIN IN AUGSBURG][17]
My Dearest Bäsle Häsle!

I have duly truly received your letter and from it get net that the Herr Father Lather, the Madam Mother, Brother, and you are right quite in health. We, thank God, are very merry well. Today I have a tall scrawl from Papa, haha. I hope you also had my scribble dribble from Mannheim.

. . . I beg you, why not, I beg you, dearest idiot, why not, if you write to Mlle. Tavernier in Munich to give my compliments to the Madselles Freysinger, why not? Curious, why not? And from the younger, namely, Fräulein Josepha, I ask for forgiveness, why not—why should I not ask for forgiveness? Curious—I don't know why not?—I ask for her forgiveness that I have not yet sent her the promised sonata but I shall send it as soon as possible. Why not? What? Why not? Why should I not send it? Why should I not forward it? Why not? Curious! I don't know why not? . . .

Now farewell. I kiss you ten thousand times and am as always the old-young

Sowtail Wolfgang

On November 6 at a State concert Wolfgang played a concerto and a sonata and also improvised. He writes to his father:

Mannheim, November 8, 1777

. . . The Elector and the whole court are very pleased with me. Every time I played the Elector came quite near my clavier. After the concert Cannabich intimated that I might speak to the Elector. After kissing hands he said: "I believe it is fifteen years since you were here . . . you play incomparably well." The Princess when I kissed her hand said: *"Monsieur, je vous assure on ne peut pas jouer mieux."* . . .

This morning I wrote the Rondeau at Cannabich's for his daughter and afterwards they would not let me go. Yesterday

[17]It is impossible to translate this letter, but I wished to give English readers who know no German a specimen of Mozart's style of writing to his cousin. It is so extraordinarily individual that a brief attempt must be made to convey the spirit of it.

I went with Cannabich to the place Mamma has already described.[18] I talked to the Elector quite familiarly. He is both gracious and good. He said: "I hear that you wrote an opera at Munich." "Yes, Your Highness. . . . My greatest desire is to write an opera here. I beg Your Highness not to forget me. I can write German, too, thank God!" "Well, that may happen."?[19] He has a son and three daughters. The eldest and the young Count play the clavier. The Elector consulted me quite confidentially about his children. I spoke quite openly but without blaming their master. Cannabich shared my opinion. When the Elector left he thanked me very politely.

Today after lunch at two o'clock I went with Cannabich to the flautist Wendling's. . . . His daughter Auguste, a former mistress of the Elector, played the clavier well and I played afterwards. I was in such wonderful spirits—not to be described! I did nothing but improvise and also played three duets for violin which I had never seen by a composer I had never heard of. Everybody was delighted. . . . I had to kiss the ladies, which was no task as regards the daughter, who is far from ugly. . . .

Now follow the congratulations:[20]

Dear Papa,

I can write nothing poetical; I am no poet. I cannot distribute phrases with light and shadow; I am no painter. I cannot even indicate through signs and pantomime my feelings and thoughts; I am not a dancer. I am a musician. Tomorrow at Cannabich's I shall play all my congratulations for your name- and birth-day on the clavier. Today I can only wish you, my dear father, from my heart what I wish for you every day, morning and evening, good health, a long life, and a joyful heart . . . I wish you as many years' life as are needed in order to have nothing more left to do in music.[21] Now farewell. . . .

[18]The residence of the Elector's mistress. The Elector took Mozart to see his natural children by the actress Seiffert (Countess Haydeck) and to advise about their musical studies.

[19]We shall see that it did happen. The opera was *Idomeneo* and was written for the Elector at Munich—after he had become Elector of Bavaria—in 1780.

[20]On his father's birthday.

[21]A wish that we could have desired for Mozart himself.

Wolfgang was much liked by the musicians in Mannheim. His mother[22] describes his success as a clavier-player in a letter to Leopold dated December 28, 1777:

"Wolfgang is made much of everywhere but he plays quite differently from what he does at Salzburg for there are pianofortes everywhere here and he manages them in a way that has never been heard of. In short everyone says who hears him that his equal is not to be found. Although Beecké and Schubart have been here everyone agrees that he far surpasses them both in beauty, taste, and delicacy; and what they most admire is that he plays whatever is put before him and out of his head."

These "successes" did not bring him in much money. In the letter to his father dated November 13 he tells how he had to go with Cannabich to get a present from Count Savioli, which turned out to be a gold watch "worth twenty carolines":

". . . I would rather have had ten carolines, one needs money travelling. I have now five watches. I have a good mind . . . to have a pocket made . . . and to wear two watches (which is indeed the fashion now) so that it may not occur to anyone to give me another. . . ."

In Mannheim Wolfgang heard in *Günther von Schwarzburg*[23] the celebrated tenor Raaff, then sixty-three years old, for whom he was to write the part of Idomeneo. He was one of the great singers of the age, a friend of Farinelli, under whom he sang in Madrid from 1755 to 1759; he is said to have made such an impression by his singing in Naples in 1759 on the Princess Belmonte-Pignatelli as to cure her of a deep melancholy into which her husband's death had thrown her. Wolfgang's first impression was not at all favourable:

"Whoever hears him begin an aria and does not at the same

---

[22]Wolfgang's mother writes to her husband in a letter dated December 6 complaining of the cost of fires, that a small one which is soon burnt out and leaves the room as cold as before costs twelve kreutzer and that during the day she is so cold that "I can now, as I write, scarcely hold the pen I am so frozen." In the same letter she mentions the salaries of the Elector's musicians and adds: "It makes one's mouth water."

[23]Some authorities find reminiscences of Holzbauer's *Günther von Schwarzburg* in *Die Zauberflöte* (see *Denkmäler deutscher Tonkunst*, Vols. VIII and IX).

moment remind himself that it is Raaff the old and once so famous tenor who is singing could not help laughing."

In Paris the following year Wolfgang heard him again and wrote on June 12, 1778 to his father:

"Now I must write something about our Raaff. You will doubtless remember that I did not write very favourably of him from Mannheim . . . that was because in Mannheim I had not heard him, so to speak. I heard him at the rehearsal of Holzbauer's *Günther*. He was in his own clothes, with his hat on his head and a cane in his hand . . . he began the first recitative quite well but when he made a dramatic exclamation it was not pleasing. He sang the arias lazily and often some notes with too much intensity . . . it is a habit he has always had, which comes perhaps from the Bernachi school, for he is a pupil of Bernachi. . . .[24]

"Here at his début in *Concert Spirituel* he sang the Bach[25] scena *Non so d'onde viene*, which is my favourite song . . . he pleased me . . . but the style of this Bernachi school does not please me. There is too much cantabile. I admit that when he was younger and in his prime the effect would be fine and surprising. I like it too but there is too much of it . . . what most pleases me in him is when he sings certain little things andantino, which he does in a style of his own. Everything in its place. I imagine that his forte was bravura singing . . . a good chest and long breath and then this andantino. His voice is fine and very pleasing. When I shut my eyes as I listen I find much resemblance to Meissner, only Raaff's voice is pleasanter. . . . Meissner, as you know, has the bad habit of trying to make a tremolo . . . and I have never been able to bear that. It is truly horrible. . . . Raaff does not do it . . . he sang four German songs wonderfully. He is very fond of me and we are good friends together. . . ."

Another musical celebrity, already mentioned, whom Wolfgang met in Mannheim was the famous Abbé Vogler. Whether because Wolfgang's friends among the Mannheim musicians belonged to the anti-Vogler party or because the mixture of pious cleverness and learned pretentiousness (Vogler seems almost to have been a sort of earlier Liszt)

[24] Antonio Bernachi (1690–1756), founder of the Bologna school of singing.
[25] Johann Christian Bach.

was antipathetic to Mozart, he certainly gives a very unfavourable portrait of this remarkable man. In his letter to
his father dated November 13, 1777 he writes of Vogler:

". . . he is a fool who imagines that there is nothing better
or more perfect than himself. . . . His book[26] is of more use
for learning to count than to compose. He says he can make a
composer in three weeks and a singer in six months but one
has not seen it yet. He despises the greatest masters. To me he
has spoken contemptuously of Bach. . . ."

On January 17, 1778 he writes to his father that he is
going to pay a brief visit to Kirchheim-Poland to the Princess of Orange, who was musical and had an orchestra, and
that he is taking with him to sing some arias the fifteen-year-
old daughter[27] of a certain Herr Weber[28] who is copying
them out. He then goes on to describe his meeting with
Vogler at a party:

"Herr Vogler has strongly wished to make my acquaintance; he already has often plagued me to come to him and now
he has subdued his pride and paid me the first visit. . . . After
dinner he had two claviers brought which were tuned together
and also his boring printed sonatas. I had to play them and he
accompanied me on the other clavier. At his insistent request
I had to send for my sonatas also. (N.B. Before dinner he had
stumbled through at sight my concerto, the Litzau[29] one
[K.246].) The first movement went prestissimo, the andante
allegro, and the rondo really prestissimo. He played the bass
mostly other than it was written and at times the harmonies
and even the melodies were altered. This is indeed inevitable
at such a speed; the eyes cannot see and the hands cannot
grasp it. But what kind of playing at sight is that? The hearers
(I mean those worthy to be so named) can only say they have
seen music and clavier-playing. They hear, think, and feel just

[26]*Tonwissenschaft und Tonsetzkunst* (Mannheim, 1776).

[27]Aloysia Weber, later Aloysia Lange (1750–1839), a famous
singer. Mozart's first love. He wrote for her the part of Constanze in
Die Entführung, six airs (K.294, 316, 383, 418, 419, 538), and a
rondo (K416). She married the actor Lange in 1780.

[28]Fridolin Weber (1733–79), an uncle of Carl Maria von Weber,
and father of Aloysia and Constanze (later Mozart's wife). He was
singer, prompter, and copyist at the Mannheim theatre.

[29]Composed for Countess von Lutzow, wife of the Commandant of
Hohensalzburg.

as little as the performer. You can imagine that the worst was my not being able to say: '*Much too quick.*' Moreover it is also much easier to play a piece fast than slow; notes can be dropped out of passages without being noticed; but is that right? . . .

"In what does the art of playing at sight consist? In playing the piece in the correct time with all the notes, appoggiaturas, etc., with the appropriate expression and taste so that one believes the player has himself composed it.[30] Vogler's fingering is also wretched: his left thumb is like Adlgasser's and he makes all the runs with the first finger and thumb."

Wolfgang wrote constantly from Mannheim to his "little cousin" in Augsburg. It is almost impossible, as I have already said, adequately to translate these letters but here is a specimen, for those who can read German, with Mozart's spelling and punctuation preserved:

Mannheim, le 13 novembre, 1777

iezt schreib ihr einmahl einen gescheiden brief, Du kannst dessentwegen doch Spass darein schreiben, aber so, dass du alle die briefe richtig erhalten hast; so darf sie sich nicht mehr sorgen, und kümmern.

Ma trés chére Niéce! Cousine! Fille! mére, sœur, et Epouse!

Potz himmel tausend sakristey, Croaten schwere noth, Teufel, hexen, truden, kreuz-Battalion und kein End, Potz Element, Luft, Wasser, erd und feuer, Europa, asia, affrica und America, jesuiter, Augustiner, Benedictiner, Capuziner, minoriten, franziskaner, Dominicaner, Chartheuser, und heil: kreuzer herrn, Canonici Regulares und irregulares, und Bärnhäuter, Spitzbuben, hundsfütter, Cujonen und schwänz übereinander, Eseln, büffeln, ochsen, Narrn, Dalken und fuxen! Was its das für eine Manier, 4 soldaten, und 3 Bandalier? . . . so ein Paquet und kein Portrait? . . . ich war schon voll begierde . . . ich glaube gewis . . . denn sie schrieben mir ja unlängst selbst, dass ich es gar bald, recht gar bald bekommen werde. Zweifeln sie vielleicht ob ich auch mein Wort halten werde? . . . Das will ich doch nicht hoffen, dass sie daran zweifeln! Nu, ich bitte sie, schicken sie mir es, je ehender, je lieber. es wird wohl hoffentlich so seyn, wie ich es mir auzgebeten habe, nemlich im

[30]Here indeed is the true touchstone for all pianoforte-playing! But it also shows what Mozart's sight playing was and it is no wonder that good musicians were astonished at it.

französischen aufzuge. wie mir Mannheim gefällt? . . . so gut immer ein ort ohne bääsle gefallen kann. Verzeihen sie mir meine schlechte schrift, die feder ist, schon alt, ich scheisse . . .

Ich hoffe auch sie werden im Gegentheil, wie es auch so ist, meine briefe richtig erhalten haben, nemlich einen von hohenaltheim und 2 von Mannheim, und dieser, wie es auch so ist, ist der dritte von Mannheim, aber in allen der 4te, wis es auch so ist. Nun muss ich schliessen, wie es auch so ist, denn ich bin noch nicht angezogen, und wir essen iezt gleich, damit wir hernach wieder scheissen wie es auch so ist; haben sie mich noch immer so lieb, wie ich sie, so werden wir niemahlen aufhören uns zu lieben, [wenn auch der Löwe ringsherum in Mauern schwebt] wenn schon des Zweifels harter Sieg nicht wohl bedacht gewefen, und die Tiranney der wütterer in abweg ist geschliechen, so frist doch Codrus der weis Philosophus oft Rotz für habermuss, und die Römer, die stützen meines arsches, sind immer, sind stehts gewesen, und werden immer bleiben . . . kastenfrey. Adieu, j'espére que vous aurés deja pris quelque lection dans la langue française, et je ne doute point, que . . . Ecoutés: que vous saurés bientôt mieux le françois, que moi; car il y a certaine. ment deux ans, que je n'ai pas ecrit un môt dans cette langue-a dieu cependant. je vous baise vos mains, votre visage, vos genoux et votre . . . afin, tout ce que vous me permettés de baiser. je suis de tout mon cœur votre

trés affectionné Neveu et Cousin

Wolf. Amadé Mozart

Two members of the orchestra, the flautist Wendling and the oboist Ramm, contemplated making a visit to Paris during Lent and Wolfgang thought of going with them; but Leopold was against it at first, as he thought it was useless for Wolfgang to stay any longer in Mannheim and suggested his going to Mayence and Coblenz. He was beginning to be not at all pleased at the light-hearted way Wolfgang was enjoying himself in Mannheim. He had urged him to get some appointment to enable him to stay the winter in Mannheim, but as nothing of this sort materialized, Leopold began to get impatient. It is clear that Wolfgang in his letters does all he can to cheer his father, being aware—as his father more than once declares—that the eagerly awaited post-days when letters arrived from Mannheim were his chief entertainment in Salzburg, and not only Leopold's and Nannerl's but probably also Bullinger's. Wolfgang's letters are full of lively touches and comic endings such as his signature to his letter of November 22, 1777:

"Wolfgang Amadé Mozart, Cavalier des Goldenen Sporns and, as soon as I marry, of the Double Horns, Member of the great Academy of Verona, Bologna."

Leopold and Bullinger laughed, as Leopold often says, "immoderately" at Wolfgang's letters except when the material side of things became too pressing. Then Leopold has to remind Wolfgang of the need for him to earn some money. In his letter of November 20, 1777 Leopold writes:

". . . Where do you want to go next? To Paris? Which way will you go? Do you want to go to Paris without any letters of introduction? And what route will you take in order to be able to earn something on the way? Without this supposition you know well what a lot of money will be needed for this tremendous journey? And if it is forthcoming to whom shall you go? Must there not be enough money in your pocket to be able to live until you have made the necessary acquaintances in order to be able to earn something?

"By giving lessons one can make a good deal in Paris. This is certain; but can one get pupils immediately and will people dismiss their teachers immediately in order to get the first newcomer?

"One can earn much by getting compositions engraved, that is true! But all this requires patronage, one or more friends, a subscription, and necessities, does it not, a previous acquaintanceship? . . . It is quite clear that the journey and the first part of your stay will demand a long purse.

"You know that we owe Herr Bullinger three hundred gulden, Herr Weiser over a hundred gulden. I don't know how much we owe Kerschbaumer but it will run to forty gulden.[31] In the new year the men's and women's tailors will send in their accounts and there are other liabilities besides our daily indispensable living. Eating costs little but there are

[31]In every city there should be a statue erected to the unknown men who have lent money to artists. A statue to the UNKNOWN LENDER who was responsible for the country's art!

other extras, now in winter there is wood and lighting, etc. . . ."

Leopold was indefatigable with good advice and must have spent an immense amount of time studying maps and routes and in recollecting acquaintances, notabilities, princely music-lovers throughout the country so as to select a route to Paris which offered most favourable opportunities for earning money. His letter of November 24 covers more than six printed pages and Wolfgang received such letters every few days. In this letter of November 24 Leopold writes:

". . . Such a journey is no joke and you have not yet realized this. You must have something more serious in your head than nonsense; you must take the trouble to think beforehand of a hundred things, otherwise you will find yourself in a mess, without money—and where there is no money there is no friend left even if you give a hundred fruitless lessons, compose sonatas, and instead of doing more sensible things play the fool from ten to twelve nightly. Ask one of these friends of yours for money! All the jokes will come to an end and the most jocular face will suddenly turn grave. . . .

"All this you will, I hope, take reasonably, for on whom will everything fall in the end but on your poor old father? . . ."

Wolfgang, in his letter of November 26, admonishes his father not to lose time in superfluous speculations. "What will happen," he says, "we don't know and yet we do—what God wills,"[32] and on November 29, 1777 he writes:

". . . You reproach us both without our deserving it. We spend nothing that is not necessary. . . . Can you believe that I should remain anywhere without reason? . . . Good! you shall know the reason, yes, the whole course of events. But, by God, I did not want to write a word because I could not do so in detail, and a vague account would, as I know, have perturbed you, which is what I always try to avoid. But if you ascribe my inaction to carelessness and laziness I can do

[32]One cannot avoid the suspicion that occasionally Wolfgang uses his father's devout expressions against him slightly maliciously; but I am convinced that although Wolfgang's enormous sense of humour made this possible the expressions are nevertheless sincere on his part. If there is one thing that Wolfgang was not, it is cynical. He is realistic but not cynical.

nothing but thank you for your good opinion and lament from my heart that you do not know your son better.

"I am not careless. I am only prepared for everything and so can wait with patience and endure all—provided my honour and good name of Mozart do not suffer. Well, if it must be, it must. But I beg you beforehand not to rejoice or to be vexed before it is time; for whatever happens it is all right if only one is healthy; for happiness consists—entirely in the imagination."

To this Leopold replied on December 4, 1777, saying that what is past is past and not to be altered:

". . . But that you, my son, should write to me *that all speculations*[33] *are useless and do not help, that we don't know what may happen,* that is indeed utterly without reflection and certainly senselessly written. That all will and must go according as God wills no reasonable man, I will not say Christian, will deny. But does it follow that we are to act blindly and live without forethought, make no preparations and only wait until something from above falls of its own accord under the roof? . . .

"Is it indeed enough that you have taken the step to remain by the Elector during the winter?

"Your dear good Mamma writes to me that she will make a careful account of your expenditure. Good! I do not ask for an exact account and never thought of such a thing. . . . From Mannheim you should at least in your second letter have written: 'The journey has cost us so much, we have now so much'—then I would have had time to make arrangements . . . was my preparation to provide a letter of credit at Augsburg an unnecessary speculation? . . . Good God! I am not to speculate when I am already in debt on your account four hundred and fifty florins and you think you can put me in a good humour by writing all sorts of absurd nonsense. . . .

"To have something in hand and to form two or three plans and to make the necessary preparations so that if one fails one may pursue the other are not useless speculations. Whoever acts differently is a silly or frivolous person who, especially in the world as it is today, will in spite of the greatest cleverness

[33]Leopold uses the word *Speculationen,* which is not a German word and, of course, does not mean speculating with money but taking into account future possible events.

always remain in the rear and be continually unhappy; especially if, in addition, he is deceived by flatterers, lip-friends, and those envious of him.

"Mark well, my son, that *one man in a thousand* who is not your true friend merely out of self-interest *is one of the greatest wonders of this world.*

"Examine all who call or show themselves as friends and you will find the reason why they are so; if they have no self-interest in it they are concerned for others."

Meanwhile Wolfgang had kept his father informed about his prospects with the Elector. On November 29, 1777 he writes that he discussed with Cannabich his interview with Count Savioli, who said:

" 'I should be very glad if you remained with us the whole winter but I should be still more pleased if you were taken into service here altogether.' I replied: 'I could wish for nothing better . . . but I do not see how that is possible. You already have two kapellmeisters and I do not see what I could be. I could not consent to come after Vogler.' 'Nor need you,' he said; 'no musician here is under the Kapellmeister, not even under the Intendant. The Elector could appoint you his chamber composer. Just wait a while. I shall speak to the Count about it.'

"The following Thursday was the State concert; when the Count saw me he apologized for not having spoken yet . . . he would speak [to the Elector] on Monday. I let three days pass and as I had heard nothing I visited him to inquire. He said: 'My dear Mozart (this was Friday; i.e., yesterday), today the Elector went hunting and it was impossible to speak to him, but tomorrow I shall certainly have an answer.' I begged him not to forget. In truth I was a little annoyed . . . and I determined to take my easiest six variations on the Fischer Minuet [K.179] to the young Count so as to get an opportunity to speak myself with the Elector.

"When I brought them the governess could not contain her delight. I was very politely received and when I produced the variations and said they were for the young Count she said: 'Oh, you are very kind! But have you nothing for the Countess?' 'Not yet,' I said, 'but if I remain here long enough to have time to write I shall—' 'Apropos!' she said, 'I am glad that you are staying here for the winter.' 'Indeed! I did not

know!' 'That surprises me, that is strange, for the Elector told
me so himself.' . . .

"I then told her the whole story. We agreed that I should
come the next day at four o'clock and bring something for the
Countess. She would speak to the Elector before I came, and I
should meet him there. I went today but he was not there. Tomorrow I shall go again. I have written a Rondeau for the
Countess. Now have I not reason enough to remain here and
await the issue? . . . The Elector likes me, thinks much of
me, and knows what I can do. I hope to be able to give you
good news in my next letter. I beg you once more not to rejoice nor to worry about it too soon and to say nothing to anyone but Herr Bullinger and my sister. . . ."

But for some reason the affair hung fire,[34] as his next letter
shows:

Mannheim, December 3, 1777

Monsieur mon très cher Père,

I can still tell you nothing certain. . . . Last Monday I
had the good fortune after having gone for three days, morning
and afternoon, to see his natural children, to meet the Elector.
We all thought our trouble was again in vain . . . when we
saw him coming. The governess at once placed the Countess
at the clavier and I sat near her giving her a lesson; the Elector
saw us so when he entered. We stood up but he told us to
continue. When she had finished playing, the governess remarked that I had written a charming Rondeau. I played it
and he was highly pleased. Then he asked: "But will she be
able to learn it?" "Oh, yes!" I said, "I only wish that I had
the happiness of teaching it to her myself." He took some
snuff and said: "I should also like it but would it not harm her
to have two masters?" "Oh, no, Your Highness! It only matters whether she has a good or a bad master; I hope Your
Highness has confidence in me." "Oh, certainly!" he said.
Then the governess said: "M. Mozart has also written variations on the Fischer Minuet for the young Count." I played
them and he was again very pleased.

Then he began to play with the Countess. Then I thanked
him for the presentation watch. He said: "Well, I shall think

[34]Those who think a Mozart would come off any better today ap-
plying to a Government committee in a Fascist, Communist, Socialist,
Capitalist or any other kind of State are incurable optimists.

it over. How long will you remain here?" "As long as Your Highness commands. I have no engagement elsewhere." And that was all. This morning I was there again and was told that the Elector had said several times last night that Mozart was remaining all the winter. Now it has gone so far I must wait.

Today for the fourth time I dined at Wendling's. Before dinner Count Savioli came with the Kapellmeister Schweitzer, who arrived yesterday evening. Savioli said to me: "I have spoken several times yesterday with the Elector but he has not yet made up his mind." I said I should like to have a word with him and we went to the window. I told him my doubts of the Elector, complained of being kept waiting, that I had spent so much here, and begged him to induce the Elector to engage me. I feared that there would be so little work for me that I should not be able to stay the winter. Let him give me work. I wanted work. He promised to propose it. . . . Now let happen what will. If he does not keep me I shall ask for a parting gift for I do not intend to make the Elector a present of the Rondeau and variations. I assure you that I take the matter quite calmly since I know for certain that only good can come, happen what may. I have resigned myself to the will of God . . . the Kapellmeister Schweitzer is a good, decent, honest man, dry and smooth like our Haydn [Michael], only with a more cultivated speech. In his coming opera there are very good things and I don't doubt it will succeed. His *Alceste* pleased greatly and it is not half so good as this *Rosemunde*. No doubt it has helped it considerably that it is the first German singspiel. . . .

Finally the Elector was compelled to make up his mind and the result was communicated by Wolfgang to his father on December 10, 1777:

"There is nothing to be done here at present with the Elector. The day before yesterday I went to the concert at court to get my answer. Count Savioli avoided me but I went up to him and when he saw me he shrugged his shoulders. 'What!' I said, 'still no answer?' 'A thousand pardons,' said he, 'but unfortunately there is nothing to be done.' '*Eh bien!*' I answered, 'the Elector might have told me that before.' 'Yes,' he said, 'he would not have made up his mind now if I had not driven him and represented to him how long you have been waiting here and spending your money in the hotel.'

" 'That vexes me most of all,' I said, 'it is not at all good behaviour. But I am exceedingly obliged to you, Count (he is not called 'Excellency'), that you have taken such trouble on my account and I shall be obliged if you will thank the Elector for his gracious though somewhat tardy intelligence and assure him that he would never have regretted it if he had engaged me.' 'Oh,' he said, 'I am more sure of that than you believe.'

"I told the outcome to Wendling, who went red and said hotly: 'We must find some means of keeping you here for the two months before we go together to Paris.' . . .''

Wolfgang went to the Cannabichs' and told his wife what had happened, as Cannabich was away hunting:

"When Mlle. Rose, who was busy . . . three rooms away . . . came in and said to me: 'Is it your pleasure that we begin?'—for it was time for a lesson—I said: 'I am at your service.' 'Today we shall have a good lesson,' said she. 'Yes, indeed,' I replied, 'for it will not last much longer.' 'How so? Why is that?' She went to her mother, who told her. 'What!' she said, 'is it really true? I do not believe it.' 'Yes, yes, quite true,' I replied. Then she played my sonata through quite seriously; believe me I could not refrain from weeping. . . .''

Wolfgang then tells his father that when he dined the following day with the flautist Wendling, he made him a proposal. A Dutch nabob of independent means named De Jean, or Dechamp, an admirer of Wolfgang's, offered to give him two hundred florins for three small, easy concertos and two flute quartets; Cannabich would guarantee him at least two pupils who paid well. Wendling also offered him free board and quarters at the house of the Chamberlain Serrarius. Then, he tells his father, he must find quarters for his mother, who will return home when he departs with Wendling for Paris. He continues:

"Mamma is quite content with this plan, it now depends on your consent, of which I am so certain that if it were the right time for travelling I should set off for Paris without waiting for an answer; for from a father who up to now has been so reasonable and considerate for his children one could not expect a refusal. Herr Wendling, who sends his compliments, is a great friend of our great friend Grimm. . . .

"I would also ask you to obtain for me, if possible, as we shall not leave before March 6, through either Herr Messmer

in Vienna or someone else, a letter to the Queen of France—
it is of no great importance but it is better to have it, no
doubt. This has been suggested by Wendling.

"I imagine that what I have written appears strange to you,
for you are in a town where one is used to stupid, hostile, silly,
and faint friends who because the sorrowful bread of Salzburg
is indispensable to you are always flattering. . . . You see the
reason I am always writing jokes and childish stuff to you and
little that is sensible is that, having to await the outcome here,
I wanted to spare you vexation and to exempt my good friends
who guiltlessly would have taken the blame as though they
had secretly worked against me, which is certainly not
true. . . .

"I am obliged by your letter to tell you the whole story. I
beg you, above everything, don't make yourself ill about this.
God has willed it. Only reflect on this too certain truth . . .
one often thinks this would be very good and that would be
very bad and then after the event one finds the contrary is
true. Now I must go to sleep. I shall have plenty to do in the
two months to write three concertos, two quartets, four or six
clavier duets, and I also have in mind a Grand Mass. . . . I
beg you to let me have your answer quickly. I kiss your hand
a hundred thousand times and embrace my sister from my
heart and am your obedient son

"*Wolfgang Amadé Mozart*

"Baron Durnitz was not in Munich when I was there. I shall
write next post to Count Zeil about the Munich business. If
you would write also to him it would be good, but short and
to the point. Only don't crawl, for I can't bear that."[35]

In his letter of December 8 Leopold explains to Wolfgang
that all his anxiety was due to his fear that he was leaving
Mannheim without adequate preparation. If he had told him
he was staying on, then neither he nor Nannerl nor Bullinger
would have been worried. He impresses on him again the
necessity of always having letters of credit properly provided
for travelling in case of misfortune and reminds him how
lucky it was that he had not been without resources when he
himself was dangerously ill in England and the two children
were so ill in Holland. Then he adds:

[35]Little did Wolfgang dream of the humiliations he would have to
endure later in his life!

"You think that I cannot accommodate myself to good or ill fortune. Do you know when I can do so? When I can think without care of all preparations carefully made and cannot reproach myself; then I can rest perfectly happy because there is nothing I can reproach myself for. . . . Enough! nothing can oppress my heart and cause me such deadly anxiety as uncertainty and doubt. . . . Remain the winter in Mannheim, a winter journey was causing me anxiety on account of your Mamma. . . .

"Now I must reply to your saying that happiness is only in the imagination. I agree completely. I only ask you whether this is to be understood so generally that a traveller who sits in an inn or a post-house and has no more money . . . can then convince himself that happiness is in the imagination.

"My dear Wolfgang, this saying is a moral for men who are content with nothing. And as most men, in fact almost all, are discontented and each considers his neighbour more fortunate than himself, so one may learn from this—and rightly—that every man should be content with his position and circumstances in which he is placed according to his capacities and not envy his neighbour, whom it is most probable he would not find enviable if he knew his secrets, for we judge always by outward appearances and everyone keeps the darker side carefully hidden.

"Yesterday Nannerl was the best. I won and for Mamma shot ten kreutzers' worth. . . ."

Leopold adds a note to his wife that he is sufficiently informed about their expenses and tells her to be careful of the cold and buy a man's fur coat. In a letter of December 15 he writes to his wife:

"May I ask whether Wolfgang has not forgotten to go to Confession lately? God before everything! From Him alone must we expect earthly happiness and have care for eternity. Young people don't like to hear such things, I know. I have been young myself. But, God be praised, I never failed to come to myself after youthful follies, to flee from all danger to my soul, and always kept before my eyes God and my honour and the dangerous consequences of my actions."

In the same letter he asks whether Wolfgang's beard is cut, burnt, or shaved off. His wife replies that up till now his beard had been cut by scissors but that in future it would have to be shaved. She also informs Leopold that Wolfgang had confessed at the Feast of the Immaculate Conception and that they went to Mass regularly on Sundays. Wolfgang himself wrote on December 20, after wishing his father happiness for the New Year:

"By your last letter of December 15 I was made very happy since I learned that you were—God be praised—in good health. We are also, thank God, both well. . . . I am writing this at eleven o'clock at night as I have no other time. We cannot get up before eight as it is not light in our room (which is on the ground floor) until eight-thirty. Then I dress quickly. At ten I sit down to compose until twelve or twelve-thirty, then I go to Wendling and write there a little more until one-thirty. Then we eat. At three I have to go to the Mainzischer Hof to give lessons to a Dutch officer in gallantry and thoroughbass, for which if I am not mistaken I get four ducats for twelve lessons. At four I return home to give a lesson to the daughter of the house but we never begin before four-thirty, waiting for lights. At six I go to Cannabich and teach Mlle. Rose. I remain there to dinner and then we talk and play a little or I take a book from my pocket and read—as I used to do at Salzburg.

"I have written that your last letter gave me great pleasure; that is true; but one thing vexed me a little, the question: whether I had forgotten to confess—I have nothing to reply to this except to make one request, which is, not to think so badly of me. I am fond of fun, but be assured that nevertheless I can be serious. Since I left Salzburg (and also in Salzburg itself) I have met people whose speech and behaviour I should be ashamed to copy although they were ten, twenty, and thirty years older. So I beg you earnestly to have a better opinion of me."[36]

On December 18 Leopold replied in full to Wolfgang's letter of December 10, agreeing to the proposal that Wolfgang should remain in Mannheim for the winter and go to Paris in the spring. He tells him to be patient and adds that a young man, "even if he has fallen from heaven and overlooks all masters," will have to wait until he is older before he obtains due recognition. He also tells him that he is not to leave

---

[36]The latter concludes with twenty lines of rhymed couplets addressed by Wolfgang to Nannerl.

his mother and that he will not allow him to let his mother live alone: "So long as Mamma remains there, you must stay with her."

So far all seemed well and both Leopold and Wolfgang were contented; but a situation was developing which was to alter everything. An attempt by Leopold to get Wolfgang a commission from the Emperor to write a German opera for Vienna failed and he was informed by Herr von Heufeld in Vienna that the Emperor already had Gluck and Salieri in his service and would not take on anyone else at present. Adlgasser, the organist at Salzburg, died on December 21, 1777, and the authorities began to hint to Leopold that the post might be given to Wolfgang if he applied, which, however, was the last thing Wolfgang wanted.

In the meantime the friendship between Wolfgang and the young Aloysia Weber had been steadily deepening. Wolfgang had taken her on his visit to the Princess of Orange at Kirchheim-Poland, where she sang the aria he wrote for De Amicis (K.135), as well as the bravura arias *"Parto m'affretto"* and *"Dalla sponda tenebrosa"*[37] "superbly." On January 17, 1778 he had written to his father about Herr Weber:

"He has a daughter who sings superbly, has a beautiful, pure voice, and is fifteen years old. . . ."

On February 4, 1778 he writes about their visit, on which she sang the above-mentioned three arias, and tells his father how well she plays the clavier and that he would rather hear her play his sonatas than Vogler. He adds that his sister would find her a true friend and comrade and that the whole Weber family is truly "Mozartisch." He has the idea of touring Switzerland and Holland with her and her family and then goes on to say:

"Apropos, you must not be surprised that out of seventy-seven florins not more than forty-two remain. That has happened in the pure enjoyment of being once again with honest and sympathetic friends. . . . I have paid half but that won't happen on our other journeys, I have already made it clear that I shall only pay for myself. Afterwards we stayed five days at Worms, where we were very jolly. . . ."

In this same letter he calmly tells his father:

"Now comes something important about which I beg an

[37]Both these arias are out of Mozart's opera *Lucio Silla.*

immediate answer. Mamma and I have discussed the matter and agreed that the Wendling manner of living does not suit us.

"Wendling is a thoroughly honest and good man but unfortunately is totally lacking in religion. It is quite sufficient that his daughter was [the Elector's] mistress. Ramm is a good fellow but a libertine. I know myself. I know that I have so much religion that I certainly could never do anything which I would not do in the face of the whole world; but the mere thought of travelling alone with people whose way of thinking is so remote from mine (and from that of all honest people) shocks me. They can do what they please but I have not the heart to accompany them; I should not have one pleasant hour. I should not know what to say, for in one word I do not trust them. Friends who have no religion do not last long. I have already prepared them. I have said that while I was away three letters arrived of which I can say no more than that it is doubtful whether I can go with them to Paris. Perhaps I shall follow, perhaps I shall go elsewhere. . . ."

The astonishment of Leopold on receiving this letter may easily be imagined. Wolfgang was in love and his extraordinarily impressionable nature is perfectly displayed in this letter, which for flexibility, naïveté, ingenious but transparent humbug is precisely what many men of character would deplore in a young man unless they were unusually clear-sighted and understanding. But I would claim that this letter is another example of the absolutely sincere but protean character of a man whose genius is rooted in his extreme sensibility. His father, however, was shocked. He had already (February 5) given Wolfgang a long list of their Paris acquaintances on whom to call and on February 12 he answers:

"Your letter of the 4th has been read by me with astonishment and alarm."

In this letter Leopold good-humouredly but nevertheless ironically refers to his changeability and recalls how in Munich he was full of enthusiasm for the young soprano Keiserin; then in Augsburg spent his time gaily with his pretty young cousin; played the fool in Wallerstein; then in Mannheim wrote a sonata for Rosa Cannabich; and could not speak highly enough of Wendling, Ramm, etc., until he met the Webers; and now all the others are forgotten. The Webers are the most Christian family and the daughter is the favourite and is to be made at once a prima donna in Italy. He goes on to beg Wolfgang to reflect more, telling him he is responsible to God for the extraordinary talent he has been given:

"It depends now on your good sense and way of living whether you become an ordinary musician, forgotten by the whole world, or a celebrated kapellmeister of whom posterity will read in books—whether you are herded with a woman in a garret full of beggarly children on straw bedding or live a Christian life in honour, pleasure, and renown with your family provided for and respected by the world. . . ."

On February 16 Leopold adds:

"That you should not travel in such company is right enough but you have been familiar with the bad side of these men for a long time, but you had so little trust during this period in your attentive father that you did not write and ask his advice; and (shocking) neither did your mother. . . ."

In his letter dated February 7, 1778 Wolfgang added another reason for not going to Paris—namely, that he does not see what he could do there except give lessons, which is distasteful to him, except in the case of a pupil who has some genius, gaiety, and a desire to learn, but
"to be compelled to go at a fixed hour to a house or wait at home is impossible for me even if profitable. I leave that to those who are incapable of anything more than playing the clavier. I am a composer and am a born kapellmeister, I cannot thus bury my talent for composition which a gracious God has so richly given me (I can say this without arrogance for I feel it now more than ever) and that would be the result of having many pupils, for it is a distracting occupation. I would rather neglect the clavier than composition, for the clavier is secondary for me but, God be praised, a useful second string. . . .

"To write opera is my firm intention; French rather than German; Italian rather than French or German. Wendling and his friends have the opinion that my compositions would please exceptionally in Paris. I certainly have no fear about it for, as you know, I can adapt myself to every kind and style of composition. . . ."

He also criticizes adversely a Salzburg friend, Schidenhofen, for marrying for money and adds:

"I could not make such a marriage. I hope to make my wife happy, not make my fortune through her. Therefore I shall wait and enjoy my golden freedom until I am in a position to provide for a wife and children. . . ."

In the same letter he speaks again of Aloysia Weber (who sings a "superb cantabile"), to whom he has given the De Amicis aria, the scene composed for Duschek ("Ah lo previdi," K. 272, composed in Salzburg in August 1777 for the Prague singer Josepha Duschek), and four arias from Il Rè Pastore. In his letter of February 14, 1778 he describes how charmingly Mlle. Weber sang two of his arias at a Cannabich concert. On February 4 he tells his father how like him Herr Weber is and that travelling with Weber is just like travelling with Leopold: "Mamma would say the same if she were not so averse from letter-writing";[38] he suggests that he and the Webers should go to Italy. He asks his father to make inquiries as to what pay a prima donna gets in Verona and he vouches with his life for Aloysia's singing. On the journey to Italy, he adds, they would all have the pleasure of visiting Leopold for a fortnight. On the 14th he informs his father that Herr de Jean is leaving for Paris and has only paid him ninety-six florins because he had only written two concertos and three quartets:[39]

"That I have not done more is quite simply explained. I have no peace. I can write nothing except at night and so cannot get up early. One is not always in the right mood for working. Of course I can scribble the whole day long, but such pieces go out into the world and I am determined not to be ashamed of them if my name is on them. Besides, as you know, I become bored and dull if I have to write always for one instrument (which I can't bear). . . . Don't forget about Italy. . . ."

But Wolfgang's mother had taken a hand in spite of her

[38]This was all so transparent that it could not have annoyed Leopold to be told that a mere ordinary Herr Weber was almost exactly the same as Leopold Mozart!

[39](?) Quartets for flute, violin, viola, and 'cello in D (K.285) and A (K.298); Flute Concerto in D (K.314); Andante for flute and orchestra in C (K.315); Flute Concerto in G (K.313); Quartet in G for flute, violin, viola, and 'cello, not in original Köchel, but in Peters's edition. See no. 293, Wyzewa and Saint-Foix, Vol. II, p. 404.

aversion from writing, and on February 4 wrote to her husband as follows:

"From this letter you will have seen how when Wolfgang makes a new friendship he will give his blood and substance for such people.

"It is true that she[40] sings incomparably but one must never put one's own interest quite aside; I have never approved of the company of Wendling and Ramm but dared not make any objection and am never listened to.

"As soon as he knew the Webers he altered his mind; in one word, he prefers being with other people to being with me. I tell him what I do not approve of and that displeases him. You must reflect what is to be done. . . . I write this in the greatest secrecy while he is eating. . . ."

On February 23 Leopold replied to Wolfgang:

"As if to convince me that you are distracted and unobservant you say at the beginning of your letter of the 14th that you see from my letter of the 9th that I have not received your last two letters. So I should have answered your visionary letter of the 5th, which almost killed me, on the 9th, although by our long exchange of letters from Mannheim you must know that every letter takes six days. . . .

"I know quite well when you can get my letters and have taken trouble that they should always reach you in time. But what is the use of all my exactitude, care, reflection, and fatherly trouble about such a weighty and vital undertaking if you . . . have no proper trust in your father? . . .

"So you have got only ninety-six instead of two hundred florins—and why?—Because you have only completed for him two concertos and three quartets. How much had you to write for him that he has only paid you the half?—Why do you write me a lie, that you had only to write three easy concertos and a pair of quartets? And why did you not follow my advice when I expressly told you to deliver to this man as quickly as possible? Why? So as to make sure of the two hundred florins, because I know mankind better than you. Did I not guess what would happen? I have to see further ahead . . . than you. . . .

"You will only give lessons as a favour! And you will leave your old father stranded. To give lessons is too much trouble

[40] Aloysia Weber.

for you, a young man, even though well paid. It is more fitting for your fifty-eight-year-old father to run round for a miserable pittance to support himself and his daughter and to send what little is left to support you instead of paying his debts—and merely that you may amuse yourself giving superfluous lessons to a young girl!

"My son, reflect and listen to your reason! Consider whether you are not dealing more hardly with me than our Prince himself. . . . You can be the death of me, he can only make me ill. . . . My dear Wolfgang, you convince me in all your letters that you go by the first wild idea that enters your head or is brought before you, without proper consideration. For example, you write: 'I am a composer and I must not bury my talent for composition.' Who said you should do this?— Is vagabondage a way to exercise your talent? To make yourself known in the world as a composer you must go to Paris, Vienna, or Italy. Paris is nearest. . . . In Naples alone there are three hundred *maestri* and through the whole of Italy these composers have libretti in hand for two years, but in Paris only two or three write for the theatre and one can count on one's fingers other kinds of composers. . . .

"In short, could I bring about in you a more stable frame of mind and induce more reflection into your excitable impressions I would make you the most fortunate man in the world. But I see you are not ripe in this respect. And yet in respect of your talent you are wholly ripe. Also you grasp every kind of knowledge with the greatest ease. Why can't you learn to know men—to guess their intentions—to hide your heart before the world? . . .

"My dear son, God has given you a wonderful understanding . . . try to understand yourself, my dear Wolfgang; you will find a little too much arrogance and self-love and then that you make yourself too quickly familiar and open your heart to everybody. . . . Your pride and self-love are only hurt when one does not immediately show you the appropriate esteem; so that people who do not know you must read on your forehead that you are a man of genius. If, however, they flatter you with the intention of drawing you according to their own plans and laud you to the skies, then you open your heart with the greatest readiness and believe in them as in the Gospel. . . .

"Reflect in cold blood with sound impartial reason and you will realize that I speak not only as your father but as your true friend, since, agreeable and dear as is the name of son, very often the name of father is hated by children. That is not so with you . . . I beg you do not think that I mistrust your filial love; all I say is said only with the object of making a thorough man of you. Millions of men lack the great favour you have received from God. What a responsibility! Would it not be an everlasting pity if such great genius were to go astray! And that can happen in a moment. . . .

"Mamma must go with you to Paris. . . . By the next post I shall give you all particulars."

In his letters of February 19 and February 22 Wolfgang again speaks of Mlle. Weber and expresses his feelings still more clearly when he says there are people who believe it is impossible to love a young girl without "bad intentions" and that he is no Brunetti or Mysliweczek, but
"a Mozart, a young and well-meaning Mozart, and so you will, I hope, forgive me if at times I express myself hastily and heatedly. . . . I had a great deal to say on this matter but I cannot, it is impossible. I have among many faults also this one, that I always believe that my friends who know me do know me! Words then are superfluous; if they don't know me what is the use of words? . . .

"That does not refer to you, dear Papa; no, you understand me well. . . .

"I fully expected that you would disapprove of the journey with the Webers, for I myself was unable to conceive it under our present circumstances. But I had given my word to write to you about it. Herr Weber does not know how we stand. I have told no one and so, as I wanted not to have to think about anyone and for us all to be happy together, I forgot its impossibility at present. . . .

"What you write about Mlle. Weber is all true and, as I have written, I knew as well as you that she is too young and needs acting experience. . . . The good Webers are as tired of being here as others you know of. They think everything is possible. I promised them I would write to my father but even before my letter reached Salzburg I was telling them they must be patient and that she was still a little too young, etc. They take everything well from me for they have a high opinion of me. Now her father has taken my advice and talked to Mme. Toscani (an actress) about giving his daughter lessons in acting.

"All you have written about Mlle. Weber is true except that she sings like Gabrielli,[41] which I should be very sorry for. Those who have heard Gabrielli know that she is nothing but a scales and roulade machine and while she does it in a way to excite astonishment, which, however, does not last longer than the fourth time one hears her . . . in a word she sings with technique but without understanding. Mlle. Weber sings from her heart and by preference cantabile."

Wolfgang resigned himself to the sheer impracticability of his scheme to go to Italy with the Webers and began to make preparations for his departure with this mother to Paris. In his letter of February 28 he tells his father of an aria, "Se el labbro mio non credi" (K.295), which he has written for the singer Raaff which pleased him greatly; also of an aria for Aloysia Weber, "Non so d'onde viene" (K.294), with a second aria, "Ah non lasciarmi,"[42] which he composed for Mlle. Wendling. The words "Non so d'onde viene" come from Metastasio's Olimpiade and their setting by J. C. Bach was described by Wolfgang as his favourite aria. He describes to his father how he has tried to set it quite differently from Bach and that in two days Aloysia Weber knew it and sang it, accompanying herself with perfect accuracy.[43]

Into the aria "Non so d'onde viene" Wolfgang put much of the tenderness with which the fifteen-year-old Aloysia then inspired him. The Italian text is as follows:

Non so d'onde viene
Quel tenero affetto.
Quel moto, che ignoto
Mi nasce nel petto,

[41]In his letter of February 12 from Salzburg Leopold writes: "I will grant that Mlle. Weber sings like a Gabrielli, etc. etc."

[42](K.486a), = (K.294a) in Dr. Einstein's edition of Köchel.

[43]Wolfgang was not blinded by love in his admiration of Aloysia Weber's singing. As Aloysia Lange she became one of the best singers of the time. Schubart in his Ästhetik (p. 135) attributes her portamento, accuracy, delicacy, excellent piena-voce and mezza-voce and wonderful cadenzas to "her great master," Vogler; but Vogler only gave her lessons later and her earlier association with Mozart was not then well known.

Qual gel, che le vene
Scorrendo mi và.
Nel seno a destarmi
Si fieri contrasti
Non parmi
Che basti
La sola pietà,

which may be translated thus:

I do not know whence comes
This tenderness of feeling;
What is this new emotion
That in my breast is stealing,
This ice which so benumbs,
Burning through my veins?
Can pity in me waken
This strife by which I'm shaken?
No, I fear
Pity ne'er
Such dominion gains.

In this same letter of February 28, 1778 Wolfgang tells his father:

"I put my trust in three friends: namely, God, your head, and my head. Our heads are naturally different but each very good of its kind, serviceable and useful, and with time I hope that my head will approach nearer to yours in the things in which yours is best. Now farewell! Be jolly and in high spirits. . . ."

Wolfgang was always chiefly concerned that his father should not worry and his letters are always written with this intention. On the same day as his letter of February 28 to his father from which I have quoted, he writes to his cousin (*das Bäsle*) in Augsburg. As usual it is written with frequent rhyming and play on words and in Wolfgang's own particular and lively vein of foolery. He begins by telling her that she must have thought him dead as it is so long since he has written, but he has had time only to think of her, not to write to her. He asks how she is getting on with her French and asks if he shall write her a letter in French from Paris, where he is going in fourteen days. Then he adds that as he has nothing to do at the moment he will relate to her a short story, which happened recently in the neighbourhood and caused a great stir, "though one doesn't yet know the outcome of the story."

Then he continues (and I shall leave his first sentences in the original, for they are hardly translatable):

"Also kurz zu sagen, es war etwa 4 Stunden von hier, das Ort weis ich nicht mehr, es war halt ein Dorf oder so etwas; Nu das ist endlich ein Ding ob es Tribsterill wo der Drek ins Meer rinnt oder Burmesquik wo man die krummen Arschlöcher dräht war; mit einen Wort, es war halt ein ort.

"There was once a shepherd or herdsman who was already rather old but who still looked strong and robust; he was single and comfortably off and lived happily and—this I must tell you beforehand ere I begin to tell the story—he had a frightful voice when he spoke so that one was always terrified when one heard him speak. Now, to be brief, you must know that he had a dog whom he called Bellot, a very fine and large dog, white with black spots. Now, one day he was going along with his sheep, of which he had eleven thousand; he had a stick with a fine red-coloured ribbon in his hand. For he never went without his stick. That was his custom. Now, to continue: when he had been walking for a good hour he was tired and sat down by a river. There he fell asleep and dreamed that he had lost his sheep and in his fright he awoke and to his great joy saw all his sheep again. At last he got up and went on but not far, since before half an hour had gone by he came to a bridge which was very long but was protected on both sides so that one could not fall off. There he observed his flock, and as they had to cross, he began to drive over his eleven thousand sheep. Now, please have the kindness to wait until the eleven thousand sheep are across, then I will tell you the whole story. I told you at the beginning that the result is not yet known. . . .

"Adieu, Bäsle. I am, I was, I were, I have been, I had been, I might have been, oh, if I were that I were, would God I were; I should be, I will be, if I should be, oh, that I would be, I would have been, I might have been, oh, if I had been, oh, that I had been, would to God I had been, what?—A dried cod. *Adieu, ma chère Cousine. . . .*"

On March 14, 1778 Wolfgang and his mother left Mannheim and they arrived in Paris at four o'clock on March 23. The next day (March 24) Wolfgang wrote to his father describing his departure:

"Mlle. Weber kindly knitted me two purses as a remembrance and a slight acknowledgment of my services. Her father copied for me what I needed and gave me some music-paper and presented me with the comedies of Molière (because he knew that I had never read them) with the inscription: *Ricevi, Amico, le opere del Molière in segno di gratitudine e qualche volta ricordati di me,* and when he was alone with Mamma he said: 'Our best friend and benefactor is leaving us. Yes, it is certain . . . your son has done much for my daughter and has interested himself in her so that she cannot be grateful enough to him.' The day before I left they invited me to supper but I could not go as I had to be at home. Nevertheless I spent two hours beforehand with them. They never ceased thanking me. . . . When I left they all wept. I am sorry but the tears come into my eyes when I think of it. . . .

"We have been nine and a half days on the journey. We thought we should never last out. I have never been so bored in my life. . . ."

There can be no doubt that Wolfgang was in love with Aloysia Weber and he probably consoled himself with the thought of her age and the possibilities that Paris might offer to him.

xii. *Paris*

March 23, 1778–September 26, 1778   AGE 22

When Mozart arrived in Paris in March 1778, there existed a highly developed school of French opera, and to Joseph Frank, who later found him engaged in the study of French scores and asked him if it were not better to study Italian composers, he is reported to have said:[1]

"As far as melody is concerned, yes; but as far as dramatic effect is concerned, no; besides, the scores which you see here are by Gluck, Piccinni, Salieri, as well as Grétry, and have nothing French but the words."

The development of French opera may be best stated diagrammatically, showing the chief operatic composers and their principal works and dates of production in Paris, in historical perspective, thus:

[1]Jahn, from Prutz (*Deutsches Museum*, Vol. II, p. 28).

THE DEVELOPMENT OF FRENCH OPERA

LULLY (1639–87)
*Les Fêtes de l'Amour et de
Bacchus* (1672)

RAMEAU (1683–1764)
Castor et Pollux (1737)

GLUCK (1714–87)
*Iphigenie en Aulide (1774)
*Orphée et Eurydice (1774)
*Alceste (1776)
*Armide (1777)
Iphigenie en Tauride (1779)

PICCINNI (1728–1800)
*Roland (1778)
Alys (1780)
Iphigenie en Tauride (1781)

PHILIDOR (1725–95)
*Ernelinde (1767)

MONSIGNY (1729–1817)
Le Déserteur (1769)
Félix ou l'enfant trouvé (1777)

GRÉTRY (1741–1813)
Le Huron (1768)
Le Tableau parlant (1769)
Zémire et Azor (1771)
*Le Jugement de Midas (1778)
L'Amant jaloux (1778)
*Matroco (1778)
*Les Trois Ages de l'opéra (1778)

GOSSEC (1734–1829)
*La Fête de Village (1778)

The operas in the above schedule marked with an asterisk
are those which are known to have been performed during
Mozart's stay in Paris in 1778;[2] but it is likely that, in addition, he heard excerpts from many others sung and played
in private houses and also that he saw the scores of all the important works of the century. The names of Gluck and
Piccinni are included in this table for the reason that Gluck
revised his earlier works specially for Paris, where they received their first performance, while *Armide* and *Iphigenie
en Tauride* were actually composed for Paris and of course
all of them were written in French. Piccinni, though then a
famous Italian composer, was brought to Paris as a rival to
Gluck and was coached in French by Marmontel, who helped
him with the libretto of Piccinni's first French opera, *Roland*.

What chiefly distinguished French opera, as founded by
Lully and Rameau and developed by Gluck and others, was
its bias towards the poetical and dramatic rather than the
purely melodic and vocal bravura of the Italian school and

[2] Also Rousseau's *Le Devin du village*, Piccinni's *Le Finte Gemelli*,
Paisiello's *Le due Contesse* and *La Franscatana*, Pergolesi's *La Serva
Padrona* and Anfossi's *Il Curioso Indiscreto*.

that is why Gluck's work found more favour in Paris than in Vienna, where Italian opera was paramount. Truthful and forceful dramatic declamation was a feature of French opera, and Gluck's famous preface to *Alceste* setting forth his creed that the music should be subordinate to the words (though it was only the expression of that ever-recurrent need to return to nature in the history of art when an art has become too conventional and is in danger of being lost in mere virtuosity) was attuned to the French taste of the time. The Italian opera buffa is a similar reaction—that is, a break away from the too stiffened conventions of the opera seria in an attempt to get back to nature. One brand of French opera, the comic opera, however, developed a feature of its own in the substitution of spoken dialogue for recitative, which must be considered as a musical loss, though it is certainly suitable for special texts. One other feature must be mentioned, since it was to find its fullest development in Mozart, and that was the mixture of serious and comic together. This was a French contribution to opera and may be described as an example of the French genius for realism.

Gluck had left Paris when Mozart arrived, and Grétry is never mentioned by Wolfgang, nor does the French composer mention Mozart in his *Mémoires*. Grimm, who was the chief hope of Wolfgang and his father in Paris, was a supporter of the Piccinni faction in the fierce rivalry existing at the time between the Gluckists and the Piccinnists, and Wolfgang met Piccinni at one of the *Concerts Spirituels* which were held at the Louvre. He writes to Leopold on July 9, 1778:

"I met Piccinni at the *Concert Spirituel*—he is very polite to me and I to him—when we meet by chance—otherwise I do not make the acquaintance of other composers—I understand my affairs and they theirs and that is enough . . . that my symphony[3] at the *Concert Spirituel* pleased enormously I have already told you. If I get an opera to compose I shall have trouble enough. That does not worry me much, as I am used to it, but if only this cursed French language were not so deadly to music! That is the worst, German is divine by comparison—and then the singers, male and female! One can scarcely call them such, for they do not sing, they shriek and howl and all from the nose and throat. . . ."

[3]"Paris" Symphony in D (K. 297).

Wolfgang had arrived in Paris with his mother in no good mood, and their circumstances were not pleasant, since they found everything very dear and had a dark lodging in the Hôtel des Quatres Fils Amyon in the rue du Gros-Chenet. Leopold had not been able to obtain a letter to the Queen, Marie Antoinette,[4] so that their chief hope lay in Grimm, whom Wolfgang at once visited. Grimm gave him a letter to the Duchesse de Chabot recommending him to the Duchesse de Bourbon. "There," he tells his father in a letter dated May 1, 1778,

"I waited half an hour in an unheated, ice-cold, large room without a stove. At last the Duchess came and very politely begged me to excuse the clavier since she had none in proper condition; would I try it? I said I would willingly play something but it was impossible as I could not feel my fingers for the cold and requested that she might at least let me be taken to a room in which there was a stove. '*Oh, oui, monsieur, vous avez raison*,' was her only answer. Then she sat down and began to draw for a whole hour in company with other gentlemen who all sat in a circle round a large table. Then I had the honour of waiting for a whole hour. Doors and windows were open. Not only my hands but my feet and my whole body were cold and my head began to ache. Nobody spoke and I did not know what to do for cold, headache, and weariness. If it had not been for Herr Grimm I should have left.

"At last to cut it short I played on the wretched pianoforte. What was most irritating was that Madam and the gentlemen never for a moment stopped drawing, so that I played to the walls, table, and chairs. In these circumstances I lost patience. I began the Fischer variations, played half, and then stopped. Then followed no end of praise but I said what had to be said—namely, that I could not do myself justice with this clavier and should like to play another time on a better one. But she did not comment and I had to wait another half-hour until her husband came. He, however, sat down beside me and listened attentively and I—I forgot then my headache and the cold and played, disregarding the

[4] Her husband, Louis XVI, had become King in 1774 in succession to his grandfather, Louis XV. She was the daughter of Queen Maria Theresa of Austria. It was through her influence that Gluck obtained the first performance of *Iphigénie en Aulide* in Paris in 1774.

wretched clavier, as I can play when in a good mood. Give
me the best clavier in Europe but with an audience who do
not or will not understand and have no sympathy, I lose all
pleasure in it. I told the whole affair to Mr. Grimm.

"You write to me that I must pay visits, make acquaintances, and renew old ones. But that is not possible. The dis-
tances are too far to go on foot or it is too filthy, for the dirt
in Paris is indescribable. To drive is to waste four to five livres
in vain, for people pay you compliments and then it is finished. They ask me for such and such a day; I play and then:
'Oh, c'est un prodige, c'est inconcevable, c'est étonnant,' and
then: 'Adieu.' . . ."

Nevertheless he was offered through Rudolph, a French
horn-player in the royal service, a post as organist at Versailles for two thousand livres a year, but refused it as this
pay was small and Grimm and other friends were against it.
A renewed acquaintance with Noverre[5] led to his being commissioned by him to compose a ballet, Les Petits Riens,[6]
which was produced on June 11, 1778. A suggested commission for an opera on the subject Alexandre et Roxane
came to nothing. It was very hard to find a good poem: "The
old, which are the best," he tells his father, "are not suited
to modern style, and the new are worthless." "Nevertheless,"
he writes in a very long and interesting letter dated Paris,
July 31, 1778,

"I must write a great opera, not a little one; if I write a little
one I get little (for here everything is taxed), and if it has the
bad luck not to please the stupid French, all is lost—I get no
more to write, have little profit, and my reputation suffers.
. . . I assure you that I shall be only too pleased if I get an
opera to compose. The language is the invention of the devil,
it is true, and I see all the difficulties . . . but nevertheless feel
as well able to overcome them as any other composer—when
I imagine all goes well I feel a fire in my body and my hands

[5] Jean Georges Noverre (1727–1810), famous ballet-master, director
at Vienna 1770–5; appointed maître des ballets en chef at the Paris
Opéra in 1775.
[6] (K. anh 10 = K–Einstein 299[b]). The score was discovered in
1872 in the library of the Paris Opéra by Victor Wilder. Vestris
danced in the original production of this ballet.

and feet tingle with the desire to make the French learn to know, honour, and fear the Germans more. . . ."

In the meantime Wolfgang's mother, who had been ill for three weeks in May, fell ill again in June and wrote to Leopold on June 12 that she was still weak, but better. She then became worse again, a physician was sent in by Grimm, but after a fortnight's anxiety she died on July 3. Wolfgang, in order to soften the blow, wrote a letter to his father informing him that his mother was very ill, but to Bullinger he wrote the truth and asked him to break the news personally to his father. Some extracts from these letters must be given, as they show the sensitiveness to other people's feelings typical of imaginative minds and especially characteristic of Mozart. On July 3 he wrote to Bullinger as follows:

Best of friends, for you absolutely alone,

Grieve with me, my friend! This has been the saddest day of my life—I write this at two o'clock in the morning—I have to tell you that my mother, my dear mother, is no more! God has called her. He wished to have her, I saw that clearly, and I have accepted the will of God. He gave her to me and He could take her away. Imagine the unquiet, the anxiety and care which I have endured during the past fourteen days. She died unconscious, went out like a light. She had confessed three days before, taken Communion and received the Blessing. The last three days, however, she was constantly delirious, but today at twenty-one minutes past five o'clock her death-agony began, she lost all sensibility—I pressed her hand, talked to her, but she did not see me or hear me and understood nothing—so she lay until she died five hours later, at 10.21 in the evening. Nobody was present except myself and a good friend of ours, Herr Haina, and the nurse—I cannot tell all about her illness today. I am of the opinion that she had to die. God would have it so.

I beg you out of pure friendship to prepare my poor father for this sad news. I have written to him by the same post but only that she is very ill. . . . God give him strength and courage. My friend, I am not only now but have been for a long time consoled. I have been able by the special grace of God to bear all with firmness and resignation. When her condition became dangerous I prayed God only for two things: namely,

a happy last hour for my mother and then strength and
courage for myself, and the good God heard me and has
granted me my desires completely.

I beg you, best of friends, to support my father, lend him
courage so that he does not take it too hardly when he first
hears the worst. I commend my sister to you with all my heart.
Go straightway to them, I beg you; do not say that she is dead
yet, but prepare them for it. Do what you think best . . . act
so that I may be reassured and have not to suffer a further
misfortune. Sustain my dear father and my dear sister and
write to me at once, I beg you.

                                    Wolfgang Amadé Mozart

> *Rue de gros chenet*
> *vis a vis celle du croissant*
> *a l'hôtel des quatres fils aimont.*

To his father he wrote first of all a letter on the same day
informing him of his mother's illness, from which I take the
following:

". . . I believe (and this I am not to be dissuaded from)
that no doctor, no man, no misfortune, no accident can give
or take away a man's life but only God—those others are only
the instruments which He for the most part uses . . . we see
how people collapse and die—when once their time is come,
then nothing avails. . . ."

In this same letter he goes on to speak of other things and
then continues:

"Now I give you a piece of news which perhaps you know
already—namely, that the godless, arch-scoundrel Voltaire is
dead, like a dog, like a beast—that is his reward."[7]

We need not be surprised at the tone of Wolfgang's reference to Voltaire. He probably had not read a word of Voltaire's works; he was also writing to his father, to whom—
except on personal matters about which he felt strongly—he
always adapted his language, and he only later in life freed
himself from the conventional form of his strong and genuine
religious feeling. It is, however, fitting to refer here to the
fact that Wolfgang himself was, also, thirteen years later, to
die unconfessed, "like a dog," unblessed by the Church to
which he nominally belonged. I shall deal with the general
intellectual development of Mozart when I come to give the

[7] Voltaire died at Ferney at the age of eighty-four on May 30, 1778.

account of his later association with Freemasonry in Vienna. It is enough to say here that although at twenty-one Wolfgang may not have been ripe for the appreciation of a mind such as Voltaire's—even if he had come in contact with it— we can only take this reference to him as the mere instinctive ignorant attitude of a deeply religious nature to someone whom he only knew by hearsay as an "atheist."

On July 9, 1778 Wolfgang writes again to his father, this time saying that he will know by now of the death of his wife:

"You can only imagine what I have suffered, what need I had for courage and steadfastness so as to endure patiently everything becoming harder and worse and yet God lent me this grace—I have had grief enough, have wept enough—but what is the use of this? I had to console myself. Do you likewise, my dear father and dear sister—weep, weep your hearts out—but at last be consoled—consider that Almighty God would have it so and what can we do against Him? . . .

"Dearest Father, take care of yourself—and you, dearest sister—you have as yet had no enjoyment of your brother's good heart for there was not yet occasion for it—both my dearest, take care of your health—remember that you have a son and a brother who directs all his powers towards making you happy. . . .

"Oh, then we shall live so peacefully, so honourably, so happily (as far as is possible in this world—and finally, when God wills, we shall come together again—for the purpose for which we have been destined and created. . . ."[8]

On hearing that his father and sister were now aware of the death of Wolfgang's mother he wrote on July 31:

". . . I have received your letters of the 13th and 20th. The first forced painful tears from me because it reminded me of the sad dying of my dear, blessed mother and it all came before me vividly again. I will not forget it all my life—you know that never (although I had wished to) had I seen anyone die—and the first time it must be my mother. . . .

"Sad as your letters made me I was nevertheless quite beside myself with joy when I realized that you had taken it all as it had to be taken and that I need not be worried about my best of fathers and my dearest sister. As soon as I had fin-

[8]This sentence of Mozart's is worth noting.

ished your letter I fell on my knees and thanked my dear[9]
God from a full heart for His mercy. . . . Now I am quite at
rest for I know that I have nothing to fear for the two persons
dearest to me in this world. . . ."

In the same letter he informs his father that Herr Grimm
had told him he did not push his affairs enough, to which he
replied that the long illness of his mother had not allowed
him much time for going about. Two of his pupils, he adds,
are in the country and the third, the daughter of the Duc de
Guines, is not going on with her lessons, "which is certainly
on my honour no great loss, for the Duke does not pay more
than anybody else."[10] Even this he got with difficulty and by
dint of constant asking. "Monsieur le Duc," he says, "has no
particle of honour in his body . . . he has had already for
four months a Concerto for flute and harp[11] from me, for
which he has not yet paid."

Grimm, although he took Wolfgang into his house after
the death of his mother and lent him small sums of money
from time to time, was an experienced and adroit man of the
world and began to doubt of the possibility of Mozart becoming successful in Paris. He recognized his talents up to a point
but we must remember that he could not see Wolfgang with
our eyes. He wrote to Leopold the following letter on August
13, 1778 about Wolfgang:

"He is too sincere (*treu-herzig*), too little concerned with
the means by which one may become successful. Here, to
make your way, you must be shrewd, enterprising, bold.[12] I
should prefer, from the point of view of making his fortune,

[9]I have taken care to translate Wolfgang's letters faithfully. This is
an interesting example of what I consider a chief element in his
genius, his extreme sensibility, that in his affectionate nature he includes God among his loved ones.

[10]I am surprised at this. I should have thought that he would have
paid less. It is notorious that the richer and more powerful you are,
the less you pay; some of the French nobility, however, may still have
had a sufficient sense of dignity and responsibility to pay *as much* as
less important people; and a few in every age have always put their
honour before their convenience.

[11]Concerto for flute and harp in C major (K. 299).

[12]He really means "impudent." Impudence is the key that unlocks
the golden gates of fortune in the everyday world.

that he had half his talent and twice as much tact; then I should not be troubled about him.

"For the rest, there are only two ways of getting on here. The first is to give clavier-lessons; but apart from the fact that one does not get pupils without much effort and even charlatanry I doubt if he is strong enough for this occupation, since it is extremely fatiguing to run about Paris and wear oneself out talking for effect. And then this occupation does not please him as it prevents him composing, which he prefers to everything else.[13] He could give himself up to that altogether but the public in this country is not a judge of music. Consequently names are everything and the merit of a work can only be judged by a few. At the present moment the public is so ridiculously divided between Piccinni and Gluck that all the arguments one hears about music are ludicrous. It is thus very difficult for your son to succeed in the midst of this rivalry. You see, *mon cher maître*, that in a country where so many mediocre and inferior musicians have made fortunes I much fear that your son will not come off very well."

It ought to be remarked here that just as Wolfgang was little fitted for getting on in the world, having none of the arts of the careerist,[14] he was also little suited to the life and ways of the Bohemian artist and did not therefore get the support of that world either. He was too sober, self-disciplined, and, above all, too fastidious, especially as a young man, for Bohemia. His remarks to his father about the sons of Stamitz in reply to a question by his father are significant on this point. Leopold in a letter dated Salzburg, June 29, 1778, writes:

"Not a word whether Wendling is still in Paris? Whether Wolfgang has seen the Baron Bach?[15] Whether Piccinni is

[13]On July 31 Wolfgang wrote to his father: "To give lessons here is no joke. . . . You must not think it is laziness. No! But it is quite contrary to my genius, to my way of life. You know that I am, so to speak, immersed in music, that I am haunted by it all day long, that I speculate, study, reflect. Now I am hindered from this by giving lessons."

[14]The reader will have understood by now that this is quite a different matter from being unable to see through people. At the latter Wolfgang was very good indeed—for example, he writes to his father on July 9 to be careful when he is talking with the sister of the Archbishop: "she has sugar and honey on her lips but pepper in her head and heart."

[15]Bach = Bagge, Baron Karl Ernst Bagge.

still in Paris? Whether he knows the two Stamitzs?[16] Whether he has seen Grétry?"

To which Wolfgang replies on July 9:

"To see Baron Bach I should need very good eyes as he is not here but in London. . . . Kapellmeister Bach is said to be coming here soon. . . . Of the two Stamitzs, only the younger is here, the elder . . . is in London. They are two wretched music-dabblers—gamblers, soakers, and lechers—they are not my sort . . . the one that is here dresses like a ragamuffin."

In addition to the symphony for Le Gros, Wolfgang composed a *Sinfonie Concertante* in E flat (Köchel, supplement 9) for flute (Wendling), oboe (Ramm), horn (Punto), bassoon (Ritter), and orchestra, as well as a number of smaller works; but he obtained no important commissions and, above all, no suggestion of an opera. He would have had to remain years in Paris in order to achieve any real position. His father, after receiving Grimm's letter, must have had very little hope of Paris; but as it happened there was a prospect of getting Wolfgang a position at Salzburg and Leopold set himself warily to work to try to get a definite offer from the court for a position good enough and well-paid enough to induce Wolfgang to return. He knew how Wolfgang hated Salzburg[17] and that he would need no small inducement to return, so he had to play his cards carefully.

In the meantime Wolfgang had quite different ideas in his head. He corresponded from Paris with Aloysia and her father, Fridolin Weber, but of his letters to Aloysia only one has survived. It is written in Italian and dated July 30, 1778. It begins: "*Carissima amica*" and has a warmth and seriousness of tone markedly different from the style in which he writes to his Augsburg cousin; it is the letter of a man in love who is avid of every scrap of news. "You know," he says, "how everything that concerns you interests me"; and to her father he writes on July 29:

"If I had no father and no sister for whom I must live more than for myself, for whose support I must care—I should with the greatest joy neglect my own fate and only be concerned

---

[16]Karl Stamitz (1746–1801) and Anton (1753–1820).

[17]Wolfgang constantly expresses his hatred of Salzburg in his letters. He writes to Bullinger on August 7: "You know, best of friends, how I hate Salzburg."

with hers—for her well-being, her pleasure, her happiness makes up (if I think of myself alone) the whole of mine—farewell."

One of the reasons Wolfgang detested Salzburg was the small respect paid to music there. "If only music were appreciated as it is in Mannheim," he writes to his father on July 9, and continues:

"The discipline that rules in this orchestra! The authority that Cannabich wields . . . and he is respected by the whole town and also his soldiers[18]—they behave themselves quite differently, have good manners, are well dressed and don't soak themselves in pubs. . . ."[19]

After the Mannheim orchestra he was not to be unduly impressed by the Paris orchestra and he still considers Cannabich "the best director I have seen." As for the famous *premier coup d'archet* (first attack of the bow) on which the strings of the Paris orchestra prided themselves, he writes to his father (June 12, 1778):

"What the devil is it? They begin together—as in other places. It is ludicrous. Raaff told me a story of Abaco[20] that is apropos: he was asked by a Frenchman in Munich or somewhere: *'Monsieur, vous avez été à Paris?' 'Oui.' 'Este-ce-que vous étiez au Concert Spirituel?' 'Oui.' 'Que dîtes-vous du Premier Coup d'archet? Avez-vous entendu le premier coup d'archet?' 'Oui, j'ai entendu le premier et le dernier.' 'Comment le dernier? Que veut dire cela?' 'Mais oui, le premier et le dernier et le dernier même m'a donné plus de plaisir.'*"

Meanwhile Leopold with great diplomatic skill had manœuvred matters in Salzburg after the death of Adlgasser so that the suggestion that Wolfgang should return came from the Archbishop's side. On June 29 he writes to Wolfgang:

". . . After the litany Count Starnberg asked me to see him the next day as he wanted to speak to me. I went, there was nobody there but his brother, the Major . . . who is here recovering from the fright Prussian powder and lead has given him. He told me that an organist had been recommended but

[18]Members of the orchestra.

[19]Like every great artist Wolfgang in his youth detested dissipation and squalor—the refuge of the minor artist in every age.

[20]E. F. dall' Abaco (1675-1742), composer.

he would not have him unless he were sure that he was good
. . . his name was Mandl or something like it; he himself did
not know exactly—'Oh, you idiot!' I thought, 'is it likely . . .
that a recommendation from Vienna should not mention the
candidate's name? As if I should not guess this was by way
of inducing me to mention my son!' But I? Not a word! I said
I had not the honour of knowing the name and that I should
never venture to recommend anyone to the Archbishop, as it
would always be difficult to find anyone exactly to suit him.
'Yes,' he replied, 'I also will not recommend anyone, it is too
difficult—your son should be here now!' ('Bravo! the bait has
taken,' thought I. 'What a pity this man is not a great
minister of State or ambassador!') I then said: 'We shall speak
plainly—is it not the case that everything possible was done
to drive him out of Salzburg?' I began at the beginning and
enumerated every circumstance, so that his brother was
astounded. . . .

"He wanted to persuade me to write to my son. I said I
could not do so, that it would be useless, that my son would
laugh unless I could tell him what salary he could expect, for
Adlgasser's salary would be quite unacceptable. . . .

"There's the rub! I do not write, my dear Wolfgang, to persuade you to return to Salzburg for I place no reliance on the
words of the Archbishop and I have not yet spoken with the
Countess.[21] I have rather avoided meeting her as she would
take the least word as consent and petition. . . ."

More manœuvring took place and Bullinger was induced
to write to Wolfgang hinting that the Archbishop would engage a fresh singer, who might be Aloysia Weber, to which
Wolfgang sarcastically replied that the Archbishop was
always talking about engaging people and as for himself
nothing would please him more than to be able to embrace
again his dear father and sister but that his joy would be
doubled if it were to happen anywhere else but in Salzburg,
where there was no opera and where music was not properly
respected.[22]

However, Leopold in the meantime had spoken his mind
to the Countess and the result was that he was asked whether

[21]Countess Franziska von Wallis, sister of the Archbishop.

[22]This letter to Bullinger, dated August 7, goes into great detail on
these points.

Wolfgang would return if Leopold were given Lolli's place[23]
and Wolfgang Adlgasser's,[24] which would bring in about a
thousand florins a year, with permission to Wolfgang to travel
to Italy every second year. "The Countess and old Arco,"
writes Leopold on August 27,
"are afraid that I shall leave. They have nobody to undertake
the teaching of the clavier. I have the reputation of being a
good teacher and the proofs indeed are there. They know of
no one and should a teacher come from Vienna is it likely he
would give twelve lessons for four florins and one ducat when
one pays elsewhere two or three ducats?

". . . If this happens [the offer to Leopold and Wolfgang
of the positions of Lolli and Adlgasser] you could safely reckon
on our having one hundred and fifteen florins a month at least
. . . without reckoning on the sale of my *Violin School* which
brings in annually fifty florins at the lowest and without the
earnings of your sister, which are now ten florins monthly and
with which she dresses herself . . . in this way we shall be
better off than anywhere else where it is twice as dear . . .
only the principal point is that I don't place any reliance on
the matter because I know how hard it will be for our Prince
to come to such a decision. . . .

"You are always writing about the hard circumstances of
the Weber family. But tell me how can it enter your sound
head that you are the one who is in a position to make the fortune of these people? You realize more and more (I hope)
how much money a single person needs to maintain himself
decently. You are now in the position—and have been since
September 23 of last year with your mother of blessed memory
—of calculating for two persons and I have been obliged to
support you for the journey and travelling expenses first with
three hundred florins and then with two hundred florins more.
Now you are alone have you not to be very careful about
your daily expenditure? And have you enough? . . . Sup-
posing—which God forbid—you were ill and had saved no
money? . . .

[23]Joseph Franz Lolli succeeded Eberlin as Kapellmeister in 1763 at
Salzburg and died in August 1778. Leopold had been his vice-Kapellmeister during that period.

[24]Anton Cajetan Adlgasser (1728–77), court composer and organist.

"You write that you have many good friends who, however, are not in a position to help you. Such friends . . . exist in plenty . . . I beg you to have some regard for yourself and for your poor father. . . .

"One can take pains to help Mlle. Weber as much as possible . . . but have we means to aid one out of the six children in this family? Who can do this? I? You? who can scarcely maintain ourselves! How can you help others before you have helped yourself? You write: 'dearest Father, I commend them to you from the bottom of my heart. If only they had a thousand florins a year!' My dearest son! when I read this how can I help fearing that you are not in your right mind? . . ."

In his next letter, dated August 31, Leopold was able to announce that owing to his clever tactics in hiding from people in Salzburg their true position and making them think that Wolfgang was very successful in Paris he had got the definite offer from the Archbishop of the appointments indicated in his previous letter:

"You are to have five hundred florins and he has excused himself for not being able to make you a Kapellmeister straight away. You are, however, to be allowed to act as my deputy . . . further he has given five florins more to Paris[25] so that he can take the heaviest duties. . . . The Archbishop has declared that he will allow you to travel if you want to write an opera. . . . Mlle. Weber has made a great impression on the Prince and everybody . . . she must stay with us . . . her father seems to have no head. I shall manage the affair better for them if they take my advice. You must speak a word for her, for there is another singer required for opera besides the *castrato*. . . .

"But I do not wish you to leave Paris until I have the decree in my hands. . . ."

Wolfgang was ready under these circumstances to please his father and return to Salzburg; meanwhile, however, Aloysia Weber obtained an operatic engagement at Munich at a salary of a thousand florins, her father getting four hundred florins with an additional two hundred as prompter. This made Wolfgang wish to try to get a position with the Elector of Bavaria, which he determined to try to do on his return journey before definitely accepting the Archbishop's offer. His

[25]Anton Paris, assistant organist.

father did not object to this and wrote to him on September 3, 1778:

"As the Elector with his court is expected in Munich on September 15, you can, on your journey through, speak with Count Seau and perhaps the Elector himself. You can say that your father writes you to return to Salzburg, that the Prince has offered you seven to eight hundred florins (add on two or three hundred florins) as Concertmeister, that you, out of filial respect to your father, have accepted although you knew he wished to see you in the Elector's service. But, note well, no more than that! Then you may want to write an opera in Munich and that you can and must manage from here; that cannot fail to happen as there is a lack of German opera-composers. Schweitzer and Holzbauer will not write every year. . . .

". . . My heart laughs when I think of the happy day when I shall again have the pleasure of seeing and embracing you . . . now the day is approaching, I hope, my dear son, God will let me live to see it. You will scarcely know your poor father; the Archbishop, whom I had to see twice, was so startled that he told everybody. When you left I was ill and that is a year ago—and what I have had to endure this year! My nature is of iron, otherwise I should be dead, and if you with your presence do not lift the heavy stone from my heart everything is in vain. . . . Nobody can save me from death except you. . . ."

During the end of Wolfgang's stay in Paris J. C. Bach came over from London and both were delighted to renew this acquaintance. On August 27 Wolfgang writes to his father from Saint-Germain:

"You can imagine our joy—perhaps his is less than mine, yet one must admit that he is an honourable man and does people justice. I love him, as you know, from my heart and esteem him and he, it is certain, praises me to others as well as to myself—not exaggeratedly as some do, but seriously. . . ."

On September 11 Wolfgang writes from Paris to his father that his friends are surprised at his intention to leave Paris; he repeats that it is only his desire to see his father and sister again and the promise that he can make a journey every two years that influence him:

"I assure you that without travelling (at any rate for people belonging to the arts and sciences) one is a paltry creature—and furthermore if the Archbishop did not allow me to make a journey every two years I could not possibly accept the engagement; a man of mediocre talent remains always mediocre, let him travel or not, but a man of superior talent (which I cannot deny myself to be, without blasphemy[26]) deteriorates when he has to remain always in the same place.

"If the Archbishop would trust me I should soon make his music famous, that is certainly true. I assure you my journey has not been useless—for composition, that goes without saying; as for the clavier, I play as well as I can.[27] One thing I must insist on in Salzburg and that is that I do not play the violin as formerly—I am not going to be a violinist again . . . it would be well if I had a written assurance about the position of Kapellmeister, for otherwise I shall have the honour to render double services for the pay of one and then find a stranger put in front of me.

"Dearest Father, I must say that truly if it were not for the pleasure of seeing you both again I could not decide to leave Paris just as my affairs are beginning to improve, and I don't doubt that if I could resolve to hold out here a few years my affairs would go well. . . .

"*Chi va piano va sano*; with my good nature I have gained friendship and protection; my fingers would ache were I to write you everything—this I shall tell you by word of mouth and make you see clearly that Herr Grimm is in a position to help children but not grown-up people and—but no, I shall write nothing—yet I must; don't imagine that he is as he once was; if Mme. d'Epinay were not here I should not stay in his house; he need not plume himself on his hospitality for there were four other houses offering me the same. . . ."

This was Wolfgang's last letter from Paris, which he left on September 26, 1778, in an ordinary conveyance which took seven days to get to Nancy, where he arrived on October 3. From there he wrote to his father for the first time since September 11, complaining how Grimm had deceived

[26]Every great man knows exactly what he is. This fact is to be recognized in the famous remark: "He spoke as one having authority."

[27]He means: "I could not play better."

him, saving himself money by sending Wolfgang by a slow conveyance, which, however, cost Wolfgang more in food and lodging. In this letter he mentions that Le Gros thinks he has the only copy of the *Sinfonie Concertante* (K. An.9) but

"it is not so; I have it fresh in my memory and as soon as I am home will write it out again."

In Strassburg, where he arrived about the middle of October, he gave a small concert on October 17 and made three louis d'or, the principal takings consisting of *"Bravo!"* and *"Bravissimo!"* and another on October 31, which brought in one louis d'or. On November 6 he arrived at Mannheim, which he had left in company with his mother on March 14 of the same year.

XIII. Munich and Salzburg

December 1778–June 1781 AGE 22–25

In Mannheim Wolfgang stayed from November 6 to December 9, enjoying the society of his old friends, especially that of Mme. Cannabich, who seems to have been an understanding admirer of his genius. His dislike of Salzburg kept him in Mannheim in spite of his father's reproaches. The Webers were in Munich, where the Elector had moved with his court. The Mannheim National Theatre, soon to become associated with Schiller, had, however, started on its renowned career under Dalberg, who wanted Mozart to compose a duodrama,[1] a sort of composition which he describes to his father after seeing several examples—"a *Medea* and *Ariadne auf Naxos* by Benda, my favourite among Lutheran kapellmeisters"—performed by the Seyler troupe. He writes on November 12:

"I have always wished to write a drama of this kind . . . you know that it is not sung but declaimed and the music is like an obbligato recitative. Speaking is sometimes introduced with striking effect. . . . Imagine my joy at having just what I have so wanted to do. Do you know what my idea is? One

[1] This was *Semiramis*, text by von Gemmingen.

should have mostly recitatives of this kind in opera and only occasionally when the words are suitable for musical expression have the recitatives sung. . . ."

In this same letter he expresses his pleasure at the good fortune of the Webers in Munich:

"The daughter [Aloysia] gets a thousand florins herself and the father four hundred and another two hundred as prompter."

To Baron Dalberg, who suggested he should compose music to a libretto *Cora*, having already applied to Gluck and Schweitzer, he writes on November 24 asking for twenty-five louis d'or as a remuneration, in return for which he undertakes

"to write a monodrama, to remain here two months and attend rehearsals. . . . As for your opera . . . I could not undertake such a work for twenty-five louis d'or since, reckoned at the smallest, it means twice as much work as a monodrama and what would make me hesitate most is that, as you yourself told me, Gluck and Schweitzer are working at it. Even if you were willing to give me fifty louis d'or nevertheless as an honest man I would advise you against it . . . an opera without male or female singers! What can one make of that? . . ."

In the meantime his father was pouring cold water on Wolfgang's idea of getting a position at Mannheim. On November 19 Leopold writes:

"Indeed I do not know what to write. I shall go out of my senses or just waste away. It is quite impossible to recollect all the projects which you have had in your mind and written to me about since you left Salzburg without going off one's head. . . ."

He reminds Wolfgang of the time he has wasted getting to Mannheim from Paris and the money he has spent and tells him finally that the Mannheimers are crazy to think that the Elector will leave Munich and return to live in Mannheim. On November 23 he writes again that he is tired of hearing of Wolfgang's projects and tells him that he, Wolfgang, is incapable of thinking about anything in cold blood and without prejudice and knows nothing of the world:

"Two things fill your head and prevent all reasonable judgment. The first and principal is your love for Mlle. Weber. I am not at all against it. I was not when her father was poor so why should I be now when she might make your fortune instead of you hers? I suppose her father is aware of your love since all Mannheim knows it, since Herr Fiala has heard of it, since Herr Bullinger, who is instructor at Count Lodron's, tells how travelling with Mannheim musicians . . . they spoke of nothing but your ability, compositions, and love for Mlle. Weber."

Leopold then goes on to say that by accepting the Salzburg position Wolfgang will be nearer Munich (eighteen hours), where he can see the Webers, and that he will be able to invite the Cannabichs and other Mannheim friends to Salzburg and have the chance of visiting Italy:

"The acceptance is absolutely indispensable unless you have the most abominable and damnable idea to bring your considerate father into scorn and derision . . . I am not in a position to repay the thousand florins I owe unless my burden is lightened by you. . . ."

The desperate Leopold then describes the preparations he has made for Wolfgang's comfort: "I have had a comfortable coffer made in your room where you can put your clothes . . . the little clavichord is by the writing-table," and ends, finally:

"I should like, God willing, to live a few years longer, pay my debts—and then you can if you like run your head against the wall—but no, you have too good a heart! You have no wickedness, you are only thoughtless—it will all come right!"

Wolfgang was not at all pleased with these letters. He writes on December 3, 1778, asking his father's pardon for not having written before and for the shortness of his present letter. He says:

"That I have not replied sooner is your fault alone through your first letter [dated November 19]; I had truly never imagined that—but silence! I will say no more for it is now past! Next Wednesday, the 9th, I am leaving. . . . I must be short because . . . I am writing now, to please Herr von Gemmingen and myself, the first act of the declamatory opera gratis; I am taking it with me to finish at home, so great is my desire for this kind of composition . . . this duodrama is called *Semiramis*. . . ."

Nevertheless Wolfgang did not go direct to Munich but

accepted an invitation from the Bishop of Kaisersheim to make a visit there on the way to Munich, which he reached on December 25. On the 23rd he wrote to his Augsburg cousin asking her to come to Munich, where she might "have to play an important role"—thus referring to his anticipated suit for Aloysia Weber.

In Munich came a terrible disillusionment.[2] He went to stay with the Webers, who invited him. What exactly happened is clear in effect although lacking in detail; every biographer has to rely on Nissen's bald statement that Aloysia —now further developed as a singer, with an excellent engagement at the Munich opera—was not prepared to return Wolfgang's love. Wolfgang, wearing a red suit, with black buttons in mourning for his mother, found Aloysia altered.

"It seemed as if she no longer recognized him for whom she had wept. So Mozart sat down at the clavier and sang aloud: 'I leave that maiden gladly who does not want me.' From now on, her sister Constanze, who had perhaps more feeling for his talent than his person and was sorry for the deceived one, sought to entertain him. He taught her—a pupil eager for learning—the pianoforte with pleasure. Later they met again in Vienna and it happened that Constanze made more impression on Mozart than Aloysia once had done."

I have translated Nissen's statement literally from the edition published in Leipzig in 1828, as it was sponsored by Mozart's widow, Constanze, after the death of her second husband, Georg Nikolaus von Nissen. Nissen may have written the sentence about Constanze's feeling for Mozart out of mere male vanity but this book was edited by Constanze *after Nissen's death* in 1826. One cannot believe that Constanze, if she had really ever loved Mozart, would have allowed that sentence to stand. I think, therefore, we may take it that it accurately represents her true attitude, which was one of admiration for his talent rather than of love for the man. This accords with her general nature, which was clearly not profound.

---

[2]Wolfgang must have been to some degree prepared for it through correspondence, or lack of correspondence, with Aloysia. This might explain his delay in Mannheim, for one would have expected him to rush as fast as possible from Paris to Munich, where Aloysia was.

On December 29 Wolfgang wrote to his father:

". . . I arrived here, God be praised and thanked, safely on December 25 but it was impossible to write until now. I keep all until I shall have the pleasure to talk with you again, for today I can do nothing but weep—my heart is much too sensitive. . . . I have naturally a bad writing I know, for I have never learned to write, yet I have never written so badly as now; for I cannot write—my heart is too disposed to weep!"

The profound realism of Wolfgang and the depth of his nature could not be better indicated than in a few sentences of his letter of December 31 to his father:

". . . What does this mean, 'rosy dreams'? As for dreaming I shall not stop, for there is nobody living on this earth who does not often dream! But 'rosy dreams'!—serene dreams, refreshing, sweet dreams—that is the thing—dreams which, were they true, would make my more sorrowful than happy life bearable. . . ."

On January 8, 1779 Wolfgang completed for Aloysia the fine recitative and aria "*Popoli di Tessaglia*" (K.316), on the words of Alceste used by Gluck in his opera.[3] About two years later, May 16, 1781, Wolfgang wrote to his father:

"I was a fool about Lange's wife,[4] that is true, but who is not when he is in love? But I did indeed love her and feel that I am not yet indifferent to her[5] and it is well for me that her husband is a jealous fool who never lets her out of his sight so that I seldom see her. . . ."

In 1788 Aloysia Lange added to the voice part of the aria "*Ah se in ciel*" (K.538), written out in Mozart's hand, the following words of her own: "*Nei giorni tuoi felici pensa qualche volta al Popoli di Tessaglia.*" That is all we know about Aloysia and Wolfgang.

On January 8 Wolfgang also wrote to his father expressing his pleasure at their approaching meeting but adding:

"I swear on my honour that I cannot bear Salzburg and its

[3]Schweitzer's *Alceste* was performed in Munich on January 11, 1779 and was heard by Mozart before his departure for Salzburg.

[4]Aloysia Weber married the actor Joseph Lange on October 31, 1780.

[5]This has appeared in some translations into English as: "She is not yet indifferent to me."

inhabitants . . . to me their speech and their manner of living
are quite unendurable. . . ."

However, it had to be borne and he arrived in Salzburg
on the 15th or 16th of January accompanied by his Augsburg cousin, who had come to Munich as he had asked. One
very natural result of his youthful disillusionment with Aloysia
must be remarked upon, and that is the freedom and sensu-
ality of his letters to his cousin, which now breaks out afresh.
These letters are almost impossible to translate, not so much
owing to their outspokenness but owing to Mozart's use of
dialect, of idiom, and of puns, rhymes, and allusions. It is
sufficient to say that they would shock all ignorant people
who are unaware that an extreme degree of vitality is bound
to take such forms when it is thwarted or disturbed in its full
development into a profound and harmonious love-union such
as Wolfgang had hoped for with Aloysia but was doomed
never to experience.[6]

It is not necessary to go into much detail about the year
1779, spent in Salzburg. It is sufficient to say that he felt
miserable there and unappreciated at his true value. In spite
of this he composed many instrumental works and several
Masses and other church music. One work should be mentioned here, *Thamos, König in Ägypten* (Thamos, King of
Egypt) (K.345), a music-drama with text by Baron Tobias
Philipp von Gebler, which had been produced at the Vienna
Burgtheater in 1774. Wolfgang had met Gebler in Vienna
during his visit there between July and October 1773 and
had then composed part of the music for *Thamos*: namely,
the choruses "*Schon weichet Dir Sonne*" and "*Gottheit über
all mächtig*"; he now added instrumentation, also composed
a third chorus (words by Schachtner) and incidental music
in the hope of performance in the Salzburg theatre, which
was visited by theatrical and operatic troupes. One troupe
under Böhm was playing there in 1779 and another under
Schikaneder[7] in 1780. On this occasion Schikaneder made
the acquaintance of the Mozart family and used to join

[6]On July 25, 1781 Wolfgang writes to his father: "If I had been
compelled to marry all with whom I have trifled I should have had
easily two hundred wives."

[7]Johann Emanuel Schikaneder, (b., Regensburg, 1751), actor,
singer, and impresario.

their bolt-shooting parties, but Wolfgang's revised *Thamos* was not performed.[8] It is of interest to students as a precursor to *Die Zauberflöte*. It is also worth noting for the confusion of those academic minds who love strict categories that Mozart, who is commonly considered the most abstract of composers (whatever that means!), actually wrote above the themes denoting the characters in this play such expressions as "Pheron's Hypocrisy," "Thamos' Noble Nature," "Pheron's despair, blasphemy, and death" in purely instrumental movements where there were no words but where the dramatic situation was to be musically depicted. The revised choruses of *Thamos* are superb and are worth reviving by choral societies. Latin words were later, in Vienna, fitted to the first and third choruses.[9]

Another unperformed work of this Salzburg period must be mentioned, *Zaide* (K.344), a German singspiel in two acts, words by Schachtner.[10] The full score was found complete, all but overture and conclusion, after Mozart's death and was first published by André. It is a delightful work and has many resemblances to and foreshadows the later *Die Entführung aus dem Serail*. An opportunity for a production that did materialize was, however, soon to present itself. Wolfgang received a commission to compose an opera for the Munich Carnival of 1781. This was the chief fruit of his stay in Mannheim and Munich and of his and his friends' attempts to interest the Elector Karl Theodor in him and to obtain for him a post in his service. The libretto chosen, *Idomeneo, Rè di Creta* (K.366), was written by the Salzburg court chaplain Varesco and was based on a French opera by Danchet composed by Campra and produced in Paris in 1712 and revived in 1731. Varesco turned the old five-act tragedy into an Italian opera seria, but with choruses in the French manner. Mozart began the music about Octo-

[8]Wolfgang wrote from Vienna to his father on February 15, 1783: "I am extremely sorry that I cannot make use of the music of *Thamos*. The piece has failed here and won't be revived. It would have to be done solely for the music and that's not likely. It is a pity."

[9]The whole work was performed in Frankfurt in 1865.

[10]It was performed in Frankfurt on January 27, 1866, in Vienna in an arrangement by R. Hirschfeld in 1902, and in Mannheim in an arrangement by A. Rudolph in 1915.

ber 1780 and went to Munich to continue it, arriving there about November 8.

At the end of November the first act was rehearsed and there were many difficulties with the singers. On December 16 the first and second acts were rehearsed with orchestra. At the end of December these acts were again rehearsed in a large room in the palace instead of as previously in Count Seau's small room. In January Mozart was writing the third act and the dances for the divertissement, and the end was reached on January 18, 1781. The last rehearsal was on Wolfgang's twenty-fifth birthday, January 27, 1781, and the first performance took place on January 29, 1781. It now remains to say something of this opera, which was highly thought of by Mozart himself and is one of the greatest and most ambitious of his works.

IDOMENEO

The full score in Breitkopf and Härtel's edition of *Idomeneo* (K.366) runs to three hundred and thirty-three pages without the appendix of twenty-seven pages—which, however, contains among other things a marvellous recitative of Elettra (No. 10). This compares with other scores in the same edition thus: *Don Giovanni* three hundred and fifty-three pages, *Così fan Tutte* three hundred and fifty-eight pages. *Idomeneo* is thus one of Mozart's largest as well as one of his best works. The original cast was as follows:

IDOMENEO, rè di Creta . . .	Il Sign. Raaff, virtuoso di camera
IDAMANTE, suo figlio . . .	Il Sign. Dal Prato
ILIA, principessa Trojana, figlia di Priamo	La Sigr. Dorothea Wendling, virtuosa di camera
ELETTRA, principessa, figlia d'Agamemnon	La Sign. Elizabeth Wendling, virtuosa di camera
ARBACE, confidente del rè . .	Il Sign. Domenico de' Panzacchi, virtuoso di camera
GRAN SACERDOTE di Nettuno .	Il Sign. Giovanni Valesi, virtuoso di camera

This is the plot:

ACT I: Idamante, son of Idomeneo, King of Crete, awaits his father's return from the Trojan War. Elettra, daughter of Agamemnon, has taken refuge and is in love with Idamante. But Ilia, daughter of Priamo, sent as a captive with their women to Crete by

Idomeneo also loves Idamante and is loved by him. A storm threatens the returning fleet of Idomeneo but is calmed by Neptune, to whom in gratitude Idomeneo vows to sacrifice the first person he meets on shore. Idamante, his son, enters and offers shelter to Idomeneo, whom he does not recognize, but in course of conversation makes known that he is mourning for his father, Idomeneo. Idomeneo then reveals who he is, but overcome with horror of his situation departs, forbidding Idamante to follow him. The returned soldiers of Idomeneo disembark and join their wives and children amid scenes of rejoicing.

ACT II: Idomeneo informs Arbace of his vow and decides to send Idamante to Argos with Elettra. Ilia comes to express her delight at Idomeneo's safe arrival and in extolling Idamante reveals her love. Elettra and her followers prepare to depart with Idamante, who does not understand the reason of his father's displeasure. As they prepare to sail, a storm arises and a sea-monster appears. This convinces Idomeneo of Neptune's anger at his broken vow and he decides to die himself.

ACT III: The High Priest, with the multitude, demands deliverance from the monster and to know the name of Idomeneo's promised victim. Idomeneo names his son and in their horror the people offer prayers to the god. Arbace enters announcing that Idamante has slain the monster. Idamante arrives and is prepared to be sacrificed, but Ilia demands to take his place. As Ilia kneels before the altar there is a subterranean disturbance, the statue of Neptune totters, the High Priest stands spellbound, and a voice announces the will of the gods: Idomeneo shall renounce the throne and Idamante is to ascend in his place and marry Ilia. Idamante is crowned amid rejoicings with ballet and chorus.

In *Idomeneo* we may see the influences of Gluck and of his *Alceste*; in particular both in the use of the chorus and in the recitatives; but Mozart remained what he was always, not so much an innovator or inventor of new forms but rather a master who used and filled every traditional form that came his way. If ever there were an artist who poured new wine into old bottles (but wine of an incomparable and never to be repeated vintage!), it was Mozart. So in *Idomeneo* we find the tradition of the Italian opera seria in full force and this must be accepted just as we accept the conventions of Giotto's painting and see in his works masterpieces that have never been surpassed, if ever equalled. The musical public of today is totally ignorant of *Idomeneo*. There is a version by Richard Strauss which has been produced in Germany but should not be used; there is another version—better, I am informed, because more conservative than Strauss's—by Wolf-Ferrari. One can

only say that the first essential in the stage production of
Idomeneo is fidelity to Mozart's own text.[11] When *Idomeneo* is produced correctly with adequate singers, chorus,
orchestra, and a first-rate conductor who understands and
believes in the work, then all music-lovers will be able to
recognize it for what it is—namely, one of Mozart's grandest and most ambitious works and unique among his operas
for brilliance of instrumentation, virtuosity, and dramatic
intensity and in the splendid use of the chorus. It may be
mentioned here that Mozart had a large share in the planning
of the libretto—making many suggestions and requiring numerous alterations by Varesco—and displayed far more
dramatic sense than the librettist. *Idomeneo* is a work written in a white heat of artistic passion and belongs to the
class of works which a great genius can only create in the
first flowering of his maturity before too much and too long
endured bitter experience has cast a shadow upon the bloom
of his imagination.

After the successful production of *Idomeneo* in Munich
the Archbishop of Salzburg summoned Wolfgang to accompany him to Vienna in the spring of 1781. It was here
that the final rupture between Mozart and the Archbishop
took place. Much more has been written about this event
than its importance deserves. Given the character of the
two men, the fact that Mozart was a great genius and that
the Archbishop was not even dimly aware of it—as, for
example, in Beethoven's case his patrons, the Archduke Ru-
dolf and Prince Lichnowsky, on the contrary, seem to have
been—the result was inevitable. It is not true, however, to
say, as some biographers have done, that the Archbishop
was not to blame. One might admit that he was not to blame
for not being naturally more perceptive than he was; but
nevertheless he did not behave like a gentleman, and his un-
derling, Count Arco, went even further in the same direction, as all underlings do. I am not proposing to recount here
all the grievances Mozart and the Archbishop had against
one another, I shall merely quote from Wolfgang's letters to
his father, acquainting him of the breach:

[11]Some of Mozart's alterations, made in 1786, may be adopted—
but not the curtailment of the part of Elettra, which was due to an
incompetent singer in the part.

Vienna, April 28, 1781

. . . How and when I am leaving I cannot tell you at present. It is lamentable how one never knows with this gentleman—suddenly it will be *allons, weg!* First we are told a carriage is being made in which the Comptroller, Ceccarelli, and I shall travel, then it is going to be by the diligence, then that everyone will be given the money for the diligence and can go as he pleases—which would please me best. First it is to be in eight days, then fourteen, then three weeks, then sooner again —God! one doesn't know where one is. . . .

Vienna, May 9, 1781

I am still full of gall—and you as my best and dearest father will certainly sympathize. My patience has been taxed so long—finally it has given out. I am no longer so unfortunate as to be in the Salzburg service—today was the most fortunate of my life; listen:

Twice already this—I don't know what to call him—has used the grossest and most impertinent language to my face, which I have not wished to mention, out of consideration for you, and for which—were it not that I have you always before my eyes—I should have revenged myself on the spot. He called me a knave and a slovenly fellow, said he would send me packing, and I—bore it all—allowed not only my honour but also yours to be attacked and—you would have it so—was silent. Well, listen:

Eight days ago the courier came unexpectedly and told me I was to leave at once. All the others were advised beforehand but I was not. I packed up and old Frau Weber was so kind as to offer me her house—there I have a nice room, am with obliging people who get me everything I want at once, which I should not be able to get living alone.

I fixed my journey for Wednesday (that is today, the 9th) with the stagecoach, but as I could not get in the money that was owing to me I deferred my departure until Saturday. Being seen about today, one of the valets said the Archbishop had a parcel for me. I asked if it were urgent; he said: Yes, it was of the greatest importance; whereupon I replied: "I am sorry that I cannot have the honour of obliging His Grace but I cannot leave before Saturday for the above reasons: I am out of the house, living on my own means, and it is clear that I cannot leave until I am ready, for nobody will collect my debts." Kleinmayr, Moll, Benecke, and the two valets thought I was right.

When I went in to him (I must tell you that Schlancher had advised me to excuse myself by saying I had already taken my seat in the coach as that would have more weight with him), as I entered he began:

"Well, fellow, when are you going?" *Mozart:* "I wanted to go tonight but there was no seat." Then he broke out—that I was the most careless fellow he knew, that nobody served him so badly; he advised me to be off today, otherwise he would write home to stop my pay. It was impossible to get a word in; he blazed like a fire. I listened quite composed. He lied to my face, saying I had five hundred florins salary, called me objectionable names—oh, I really could not write it all! At last as my blood was boiling I said: "Is Your Highness not contented with me?" "What, you threaten me, you villain? There is the door; I will have nothing more to do with such a wretched fellow." At last I said: "And I also will have no more to do with you." "Then go!" And as I went I said: "Let it be so—tomorrow you will hear from me in writing."

Tell me, my dear father, whether I did not say that rather too late than too soon. Now listen: my honour is dearer to me than anything and I know it is to you also. Don't worry about me. I am so certain of my affairs here that I might have resigned without any cause. As I now have had one, and that three times, I am not to blame. On the contrary, twice I was a coward; the third time I could not be one any longer.

So long as the Archbishop is here I shall give no concert; your belief that I may suffer in the estimation of the Emperor and the nobility is groundless. The Archbishop is hated here and most of all by the Emperor. I shall send you by the next post a little money and convince you that I shall not starve. Above all, I beg of you to be in good spirits, for my good fortune is beginning now and I hope that mine will be yours also. Write to me privately that you are contented—and that you can be, indeed!—and publicly scold me so that no blame can attach to you. Should, however, the Archbishop show you the least impertinence, then come with my sister to Vienna at once; we can all three live, I assure you of that, on my honour, though it would be better if you could hold out for a year. Do not write to me any more at the Residence or with the mail— I don't want to have anything more to do with Salzburg. I hate the Archbishop to frenzy. . . .

The worldly side of Leopold's character now showed at its worst. He was far from backing up Wolfgang as he should have done and the many subsequent letters written by Wolfgang to his father justifying his action make melancholy reading. Nothing, however, could alter Wolfgang's determination and from this time onward we see that a certain change has taken place in the relation between father and son. Wolfgang is no longer the son; he is at last completely independent and his father can influence him only as a friend. It was a misfortune for Wolfgang that his father— after having been in many ways the model of what a father should be to a son of genius—when it came to the harder task of relinquishing his special position and taking up that of his son's dearest, wisest, and least selfish of friends, was not equal to that exacting relationship. He failed Wolfgang at this critical period in his life and also—a little later—on the occasion of Wolfgang's marriage; so that from henceforth Leopold sinks back into a relatively unimportant position in his son's life. Before we leave this subject, however, I must give one example of the sensitive and passionate nature of Wolfgang, since this is truly part of his genius.

On May 12, 1781 he writes to his father:

"All the edifying things which the Archbishop said to me in the three audiences, especially the last, and the language used by this truly worthy man of God, had such a physical effect on me that in the evening at the opera in the middle of the first act I had to go home and lie down, for I was feverish, trembled in every limb, and tottered along the street like a drunkard. . . ."

What men of genius suffer is commensurate with the joy they are capable of experiencing and giving to others.

The attitude of Mozart to his father after the breach with the Archbishop is best conveyed by quoting a passage from his letter to Leopold of May 19:

"I also do not know what to write first, my dearest father, for I cannot and never will be able to recover from my astonishment while you continue to think and to write as you do. I must tell you that I don't recognize a single trait of my father in your letter—a father, certainly, but not the best, most loving father, considerate of his own and his children's honour—in a word, not my father. . . ."

It is also significant that in this letter for the first time he abandons the cipher in which all references to the Archbishop had hitherto been made and openly refers to him in plain words as if he wanted to make his new independence clear to all the world.

xiv. *Manhood and Marriage in Vienna*
June 1781–December 1783   AGE 25–27

In Vienna Mozart renewed old friendships with the Messmers, von Aurnhammer, and the Kapellmeister Bono, who performed one of his symphonies,[1] which went very well, he writes to his father on April 11, 1781, "played by forty violins, all the wind instruments doubled, ten violas, ten double-basses, eight violoncellos, and six bassoons."

Among new acquaintances were the Hofrat von Braun, Countess Thun, and Countess Rumbeck (née Cobenzl). Mozart also played at a concert of the famous Vienna Tonkünstlersozietät, in the Kärntnertor Theatre, which had been founded by Florian Gassmann in 1771. His chief immediate hope of supporting himself in Vienna was as a pianist giving subscription concerts, obtaining pupils for the clavier, and then publishing his compositions by subscription. Countess Thun set about securing subscriptions for a set of sonatas and during the summer succeeded in obtaining seventeen subscribers at three ducats each, with the result that Mozart published in November 1781 the six sonatas for pianoforte with violin accompaniment (K.296 and K.376–380).[2] At a concert given during Lent he played his Concerto in D (K. 175) with a new Rondo (K.382) and selections from *Idomeneo*. He also showed the music of *Zaide* to the younger Stephanie, then Inspector of the Opera, and

[1] Possibly (K.338).

[2] No. 2 in C major was composed in Mannheim and No. 4 in B flat major had also been composed earlier, in 1779 at Salzburg.

through Count Rosenberg, director of the theatre, who had heard portions of *Idomeneo* at Countess Thun's house, he received a libretto to compose for the opera. He writes to his father on August 1, 1781:

"The day before yesterday young Stephanie gave me a libretto. . . . It is very good. The subject is Turkish and it is called *Bellmont and Konstanze* or *Die Verführung³ aus dem Serail*—the overture (symphony), the chorus in the first act, and the final chorus I shall compose in Turkish music. . . . I am so delighted to have the book that, already, I have finished the first aria for Cavalieri and for Adamberger and the terzet which closes the first act. The time given is short, certainly, for it must be produced by the middle of September. . . ."

On August 8 he wrote that he had just finished the chorus of the janissaries and on August 22 that he had finished the first act; but he learned that the Grand Duke Paul of Russia, in whose honour the opera was to have been performed, was not coming until November, and on August 29 he writes that this will give him time to write "my opera with more reflection." As an example of the attention Mozart always gave to his libretto I shall quote from his letter of September 26, 1781, to his father:

". . . I had nothing important to write and thought it would give you pleasure to have a short description of my opera.

"It begins with a monologue and then I begged Stephanie to write a short arietta and instead of the two chatting after the little song of Osmin's, to have a duet. The role of Osmin is intended for H. Fischer, who has a fine bass voice . . . and one must use such a man, especially as the public likes him. This Osmin, however, in the original book has only one little song and nothing else except his part in the terzet and finale, but he has now got an aria in the first act and will have another in the second. I gave Stephanie the aria—and most of the music of it was composed before Stephanie had written a word of it. . . .

"The rage of Osmin will be rendered comic in it as the Turkish music is thus brought in. In the execution of the aria

³A mistake of Mozart's; *Verführung* of course means *seduction*, *Entführung* means *abduction*. It would have to be *Die Verführung im Serail*, not *aus dem Serail*.

I have let his fine deep voice . . . display itself. The *drum beym Barte des Propheten* is actually in the same tempo but with quicker notes and as his rage increases then—when one thinks the aria is at its end—the allegro assai in quite another tempo and in another key must make a splendid effect; for a man who is in such a rage oversteps all moderation, measure, and bounds; he does not know himself—so the music must not; although the utmost passion, violent or not, must never be pushed as far as the disgusting, and music even in the most awful places must not offend the ear, but give pleasure; that is, music must always remain music; so I have chosen no foreign key to the F (the key of the aria) but a consonant one, not, however, the nearest D minor but the further A minor.

"Then comes the aria of Belmont in A major, 'O wie ängstlich, o wie feurig' . . . here is indicated the beating, loving heart—two violins in octaves. This is the favourite aria of all that have been heard, mine also, and is written wholly for Adamberger's voice. One sees the trembling, hesitating—one sees the swelling breast heave—which is expressed by a crescendo—one hears the whispering and sighing—which is given by the first violins with mutes and a flute in unison.

"The janissaries' chorus is all that one could ask for a janissaries' chorus—short and lively—and written specially for the Viennese. The aria of Konstanze I have had to sacrifice to some extent to the flexible throat of Mlle. Cavallieri . . .

"Next the terzet, the close, namely, of the first act . . . as the text permits I have written it rather well for three voices. Then begins immediately the major pianissimo, which must go very fast, and this close will make a really good row—and that is everything desirable in the finale of a first act—the more noise the better; the shorter the better, so that the audience does not cool off in its clapping. . . .

"The first act has been ready for three weeks—an aria in the second act and the drinking duet (for the Viennese gentry) . . . are ready. I can't do more because the whole thing is turned round, and at my request. At the beginning of the third act is a charming quintet, or rather finale, but I should prefer to have this at the end of the second act. For this a large alteration, even an entirely new intrigue, must be made and Stephanie is head-over-ears in work. . . .

"Fräulein von Auerhammer and I await eagerly the two double concertos[4]—I hope we shall not wait as fruitlessly as the Jews for the Messiah. . . ."

In the meantime the performance of the opera was delayed considerably, partly owing to the production of Gluck's *Iphigenia in Tauris* and *Alceste*, the latter being presented in honour of the Grand Duke Paul of Russia at Schönbrunn on November 25, 1781. About this time there was a prospect of Mozart's becoming the teacher of the Princess Elizabeth, who was the prospective bride of the Archduke Franz. The Emperor's younger brother, the Archduke Maximilian, was a supporter of Mozart, but unfortunately for him the Emperor Joseph II[5] recommended Salieri,[6] and Salieri, who had succeeded Gassmann, his master, in the Emperor's favour, was chosen. This was the first occasion out of many in which Salieri proved an obstacle to Mozart's success.

In December 1781 the famous clavier-player Clementi[7] arrived in Vienna, and the Emperor Joseph was immediately anxious to have a rival display between Clementi and Mozart and according to Bridi he laid a wager with the Grand Duchess that Mozart would prove the superior, and won it. Clementi's account to his pupil, L. Berger, is as follows:

"I had only been a few days in Vienna when I received an invitation to play before the Emperor on the pianoforte. Entering the music-salon, I saw there someone whose elegant attire made me take him to be an Imperial gentleman-in-waiting, but we had scarcely begun to speak when the conversation turned on music and we recognized each other as fellow-artists —as Mozart and Clementi—with the friendliest greetings."

Clementi described Mozart's playing thus:

"I had until then never heard playing so full of spirit and grace. Especially was I delighted with an Adagio and with several of his extemporized variations, the theme of which was

[4] Two concertos; probably (K.242) for three pianos and (K.365) for two pianos.

[5] Emperor Joseph II (1741–90) succeeded to the Austrian throne in 1780.

[6] Antonio Salieri (1750–1825), composer, succeeded Gassmann as court composer at Vienna in 1774 and Bono as court Kapellmeister in 1788.

[7] Muzio Clementi (1752–1832), pianist and composer.

chosen by the Emperor, each of us varying it, alternately accompanying one another."

The composer Dittersdorf in his autobiography (p. 236) gives an account of the conversation he had with the Emperor:

"*Emperor:* 'Have you heard Mozart play?' *I:* 'Three times already.' *Emperor:* 'How do you like him?' *I:* 'As every connoisseur must.' *Emperor:* 'Have you heard Clementi also?' *I:* 'Yes, I have also heard him.' *Emperor:* 'Some prefer him to Mozart, Greybig[8] chief among them. What do they mean by it?' *I:* 'In Clementi's playing there is only art, in Mozart's art and taste.' *Emperor:* 'That is just what I have said.'"

Characteristically, Mozart's account of Clementi's playing is nothing like so favourable as Clementi's is of his. He writes on January 16 to his father:

". . . Now about Clementi. He is a fine player but that is all. He has great facility with the right hand, his great forte is his thirds—but apart from this he hasn't a particle of taste or feeling—he is a mere machine.

"The Emperor, after sufficient compliments had passed, gave the signal to commence, '*La Santa Chiesa Catholica*,' he said, because Clementi is a Roman. He preluded and played a sonata. Then the Emperor said to me: '*Allons drauf los* (Fire away).' I preluded and played variations. Then the Grand Duchess produced some sonatas by Paesello (miserably written out in her own hand) and I had to play the Allegro and Clementi the Andante and Rondo. Then we took a theme and developed it on two pianofortes. I may say I had borrowed the pianoforte of Countess Thun but only played on it when I played alone, as the Emperor wished it so. The other instrument was out of tune and had three keys sticking—'It doesn't matter,' said the Emperor. I took it that the Emperor knew already my art and knowledge of music and wished to treat the stranger justly. Moreover I know from a reliable source that he was content with me . . . also he has spoken to me about my marriage."

About six months later (June 7, 1783) Mozart wrote to his father as follows:

[8]Greybig, or Kreibich, first violin among the Emperor's chamber musicians.

". . . Now I must say a few words to my sister about the Clementi sonatas. That they are valueless as compositions everyone who plays or hears them will recognize.[9] There are no noteworthy or striking passages apart from sixths and octaves and I beg my sister not to be too much taken with these lest she spoil thereby her quick, firm hand and ruin its natural lightness, suppleness, and rapidity. For what is the object of these passages? They must be executed with the greatest speed (which nobody, not even Clementi, can achieve) and the result is a horrible hash, nothing else in the world!

"Clementi is a charlatan like all Italians. He writes *Presto* and even *prestissimo* and *alla breve* on a sonata and plays it allegro in ¾ time. I know this for I have heard him do it. What he does well are passages in thirds, but he had sweated day and night in London to achieve this; apart from this he has nothing, absolutely nothing, not the slightest enunciation (*Vortrag*)[10] or taste and still less feeling."

I wish to draw special attention to these remarks of Mozart's because they reveal the ruthlessness in his character, which so many biographers and writers on music have completely missed. Nobody who has a genuine musical understanding could ever have conceived that the composer of *Don Giovanni*, *Così fan Tutte* and the great quintets and symphonies was a merely amiable and agreeable man with an enormous talent for music. Of course inferior characters will impute motives of jealousy to Mozart in such harsh judgments and I have no doubt whatever that Mozart must have appeared as arrogant to people who had not the instinct to recognize the colossal differences between him and his gifted contemporaries such as Clementi and Salieri. The fact is that only an exceptional man of genius, like Haydn, among Mozart's contemporaries could have had the slightest inkling of Mozart's superiority, and when one considers Mozart's judgments harsh one has also to remember that time has proved them to be just. A man like Mozart raises the standard in his art to a level so high that for hundreds

[9]An example of the isolation of a man of great genius, Mozart never realized that people without his genius did not hear with his ears.

[10]I take it he means sense of phrasing, intelligent expression.

of years gifted musicians of every generation remain struggling beneath it.[11]

Everywhere Mozart went he made for himself bitter enemies. Every mediocrity who met him immediately hated him; only those who loved music more than themselves admired and loved him; the egoists and careerists immediately recognized him as not one of their kidney and detested his superiority, which they called arrogance. Mozart's outspokenness earned their undying enmity. His father had always reproached him for his lack of tact but this unconscious sincerity was a part of his genius. How could he praise rubbish? How could he enjoy, or pretend to enjoy, inferior music? His reaction was instinctive, immediate, and intense. He spoke out of his intensity and with mortal offence to everybody who did not share it. But how could they share it? They did not feel what he felt. His father writes to him that he was making himself "detested in Vienna by his arrogant manners" and Mozart replies on July 31, 1782:

"The whole world declares that through my boasting and criticizing I have made the professors of music and also other people into enemies! What world? I presume the world of Salzburg. . . ."

Here is another instance of Mozart's inevitable blindness. In his hatred of Salzburg he finds an easy explanation for the criticism his father retails. But what his father told him was true. The professors of music and many others hated the superiority of this man who always spoke on musical matters as if he were a god, "as one having authority."

One concrete example of how Mozart inevitably made enemies on all sides must be given here. One of the most successful pianists and teachers in Vienna at the time of Mozart's settling there was Leopold Kozeluch. Niemetschek, Rochlitz, Griesinger (the biographer of Haydn), and Nissen are the authorities for the following story:

[11]On his return from London Haydn writes (December 20, 1791): "I am childishly glad to be home and welcomed by my old friends. I only regret to miss the greeting of the great Mozart, whose death I deplore. Posterity will not see such a talent for a century to come." It is now nearly a hundred and fifty years and posterity has not yet seen such a talent.

A new quartet of Haydn's was being performed before a large company. Kozeluch, who was standing beside Mozart, began finding fault first with one thing, then with another, and at last he exclaimed with the impudent effrontery of his kind: "I should never have done it in that way!" "Nor should I," replied Mozart, "and do you know why? Because neither you nor I would ever have had such a good idea."

This is how a great man makes implacable enemies. It always has been so and it always will be so. On the other hand sincere and sound natures who truly loved music never failed to recognize Mozart's quality.

Does it surprise the reader that in spite of his extraordinary virtuosity Mozart, as Jahn says, "was never a fashionable and well-paid music-master in Vienna such as Steffan, Kozeluch, or Righini"? There is no doubt, too, that teaching bored him. A celebrated physician, Joseph Frank, known to his contemporaries as a great musical amateur, gives an account[12] of going to Mozart in 1790 for twelve lessons. He writes:

"I found Mozart a little man with a large head and plump hand and was somewhat coldly received by him. 'Now,' he said, 'play me something.' I played a fantasia of his own composition. 'Not bad,' he said, to my great astonishment. 'But now listen to me play it.' It was a miracle! The piano became another instrument under his hands. It was strengthened by a second piano which served him as a pedal."[13]

Teaching must always be an intolerable drudgery to a man of genius except when he has pupils of exceptional talent. Even then Mozart was not often inclined to teach, for a mind like his, constantly working at high pressure, needed relaxation when his serious work was over and for him the only serious work was composition. Actually his serious work was never over. We have to try to realize with our utmost effort of the imagination how a mind like Mozart's never rested from music. Music was going on in his head continuously, probably even in his sleep, and the disinclination to teach was due to the fact that this disturbed

[12]Prutz's *Deutsches Museum*, Vol. II, p. 27.

[13]On March 12, 1785 Leopold writes to his daughter from Vienna: "He has had a great forte piano pedal made which stands under the instrument and is three spans long and tremendously heavy."

his natural musical thinking in a way that dancing, playing billiards, bolt-shooting, and so on, did not. Most of his pupils were women of talent with whom he could have some genuine personal relationship, as, for example:

1. Franzciska von Lagusius (née von Jacquin), for whom he wrote the Trio for pianoforte, clarinet, and viola (K.498) and to whom he sent the Sonata in C major for four hands (K.521) with a message that it was rather difficult.

2. Frau von Trattner, for whom he composed his Fantasia in C minor (K.475).

3. Babette Ployer, for whom he composed the Concerto in E flat (K.449) (February 9, 1784), the Concerto in G major (K.453).[14]

4. Josepha, or Josephine, Aurnhammer, to whom he dedicated the Sonatas for pianoforte and Violin (K.376–380), published in 1781.

Mozart played with Josepha Aurnhammer at one of his own concerts (May 25, 1782); at a concert of hers on November 24, 1781 he played with her the Concerto *a due* (K.365) and a Sonata (K.381) and also played at her concert in the theatre at Vienna on October 26, 1782. She became well known as a teacher. Mozart, in spite of the assistance he gave her, wrote a very unfavourable account of her, which is so characteristic of him as to deserve quoting. To his father he writes on August 22, 1781:

". . . As I have observed from your letter that you have confidence in this family I see myself obliged to let you know the bad as well as the good about them.

"He [Herr von Aurnhammer] is the best of men—too good; as for his wife she is the most stupid and idiotic gossiper in the world—wears the trousers, so that when she speaks he has nothing to say. Whenever we have gone for a walk he begs me not to say in his wife's presence that we have taken a cab or drunk some wine. Now I have no confidence in such a man. . . .

"I am not in their house for my convenience but for theirs

---

[14]Mozart writes to his father on June 9, 1784: "Tomorrow Herr Ployer . . . will be at the concert where Fräulein Babette plays her new Concerto in G, I the Quintet in E flat [K.452] and both of us the great Sonata for two claviers. I shall take Pasiello in the carriage so that he may hear my compositions and my pupils."

and have met nobody there whose name is worth putting on paper . . . decent people and that's all. . . .

"Of the mother I shall say nothing beyond that one has enough to do to keep from laughing at her at table. Enough! . . .

"As for the daughter, if a painter wanted to paint the devil from life he could take refuge in such a face. She is thick like a peasant, sweats so as to make one sick . . . to see her is enough to make one blind . . . one is punished enough for the whole day if one's eyes have unluckily fallen upon her, for then one needs cream of tartar—she is so hideous, dirty, and horrible—*pfui teufel!*

"I have already written to you how she plays the clavier and why they begged me to help her. I am most willing to help people but not people who pester me. She is not content that I should pass two hours daily with her, she would have me sit there the whole day. And then she makes herself agreeable and what is more is seriously in love with me. I thought it was a joke but now I am certain of it. . . ."

These extracts are sufficient evidence in themselves of Mozart's natural manner of expressing himself. Like many other passages from his letters they have always been softened down (with the most forcible expressions omitted) by previous translators. This has helped to create the totally false image of the "sweet" Mozart current among schoolboys and schoolgirls and those who have taught schoolgirls and boys at colleges of music for generations past. But it is absolutely essential for our understanding of Mozart and of his failure to obtain in Vienna any of the remunerative posts during his lifetime (which habitually go to those who have a moderate talent in their art but know how to be complaisant, to flatter and make themselves agreeable to everybody) to realize how different his true personality was from this pretty picture.

On December 15, 1781 he wrote to his father that he wanted to marry Constanze Weber:

". . . Nature speaks as loudly in me as in any other, and perhaps louder than in many a great heavy blockhead. I cannot live like most of the young men nowadays. Firstly, I have too much religion; secondly, too much love of my neighbour and too much feeling to be able to lead astray an innocent girl, and, thirdly, too much fear and disgust and horror of illness and too much regard for my health to go running after whores. I can swear that I have as yet had nothing to do with any woman in this way, for if it had happened I should not conceal it from you, for such errors are natural enough in men and to fail once would be mere weakness—although I could not guarantee that I should not repeat it if I had once given way on this point. . . .

"I know that this reason, strong as it is, is not enough for marriage. But my temperament, which is more inclined to a quiet domestic life than to rowdiness . . . makes a wife indispensable. . . . I am quite convinced that I could do better on my income with a wife—and with a wife one lives—in a word—an orderly life. In my opinion a single man only half lives. . . . I have thought and reflected enough. I shall not change my opinion. . . .

"But who is the object of my love? Don't be alarmed, I beg of you—not a Weber? Yes, a Weber, not Josepha, not Sophie, but Constanze, the middle one. In no family have I seen such variety of character. The eldest is a lazy, clumsy, false, person. . . . The Langin [Aloysia, wife of Joseph Lange] is false, unprincipled, and a coquette; the youngest is too young to be anything . . . the middle one, however, my good dear Constanze, is the martyr and just on that account, perhaps, the best-hearted, cleverest, and in a word the best of all. She does everything in the house and yet can do nothing right.

"She is not ugly but is far from being beautiful. Her whole beauty is in her small black eyes and good figure. She is not intellectual but has enough common sense to fulfil her duties as a wife and mother. She is not used to luxury—that is completely false; on the contrary she is accustomed to be poorly dressed, since the little her mother can do is done for the two others, never for her. It is true she likes to be clean and neat but not smart, and most of what a woman needs she can make for herself . . . she understands housekeeping, has the best heart in the world. She loves me and I love her truly—could I wish for a better wife?

"I must tell you that at the time I left,[15] love was not there but was first born through her tender care and attention when I lived in the house.

"I now wish for nothing more than that I have something

[15]He means, left the Archbishop's service.

a little more settled to do (of which, God be praised, I have hopes) and I shall then beg your permission to rescue my unfortunate one and me with her and make, as I dare to think, us all happy—for are you not happy when I am? . . . Now have compassion on your son!"

This was the second crisis in Mozart's adult life and again his father did not approve of what he was doing. Leopold quite genuinely thought very badly of the Weber family and not only looked on Wolfgang's proposed marriage with one of the Webers as foolish from every point of view but considered that his unworldly-wise son had been trapped into this marriage by old Frau Weber. He was not without grounds for so thinking. Frau Weber, by suggesting that Wolfgang was compromising her daughter's honour, obtained his signature to a document drawn up by Johan Thorwarth, who had been left as guardian of his children by Weber, in which he pledged himself to marry Constanze within three years or to pay her three hundred florins a year. Mozart tells his father that as soon as the guardian was gone his dear Constanze tore the agreement up; but the affair had developed too far and all Leopold's remonstrances and criticisms were useless. In spite of the fact that there is not the slightest doubt that Mozart was not in love with Constanze as he certainly had been in love with Aloysia and that there is little evidence that Constanze was in love with him, the relationship "worked." By July 1782 Mozart is writing to his father:

"I must beg of you . . . give me your consent to my marrying my dear Constanze . . . it is essential for my honour, for the honour of my dear girl; and for my health and wellbeing it is unavoidably essential. My heart is disquieted, my head swims—how can one work and think? . . . most people here believe we are married already—the mother is quite upset and the poor girl and myself are tormented to death. . . ."

On August 4, 1782, without waiting further for his father's consent, Wolfgang and Constanze were married, but letters from Wolfgang's father and sister with the father's consent arrived the following day.

I shall not attempt a description of Constanze's character.[16] Mozart's own account of her, which I have quoted, must in

[16]Perhaps her worst failing was her bad health. She played the clavier and was a good singer.

any case be nearer the truth than any I could possibly give.
The marriage turned out a moderate success. That Constanze
was not an ideal wife for Mozart is undoubted; that she suited
him in many ways is also not to be doubted; but the fact that
the relationship lasted, that it "worked," until Mozart's death
is proof that there was some solid substance in it. This is the
place to mention that there were six children[17] born of this
marriage, of whom two survived to manhood—namely:

1. Karl Thomas, born in Vienna, September 21, 1784, died
in Milan, October 31, 1858, a gifted pianist who became an
official in the Austrian Government service and was unmar-
ried.

2. Franz Xaver Wolfgang, born in Vienna, July 26, 1791,
died in Carlsbad, July 29, 1844. He became a well-known
professional musician; his compositions have never been studied thoroughly.

In the meantime the first performance of *Die Entführung
aus dem Serail* had taken place on July 13, 1782 at the theatre
in Vienna, and had a considerable success. It received sixteen
performances in the course of the year. Gluck at his own request heard it on August 6 and complimented Mozart on it
and asked him to dinner on August 8.[18] But it must not be
assumed that its success was unquestioned. Niemetschek relates that the Emperor Joseph declared of it:

"Too fine for our ears and a tremendous number of notes,
my dear Mozart."

To which Mozart replied:

"Exactly as many, Your Majesty, as are necessary."

The composer Dittersdorf in his autobiography was also
critical and found that the orchestration overpowered the
voices. Nevertheless, the success of the opera greatly strengthened Mozart's position as a new arrival in Vienna, enabled
him to take the decisive step of marrying Constanze—he
described his marriage jokingly as *Die Entführung aus dem
Auge des Gottes*, the Auge des Gottes being the name of the

[17]The four children who did not survive their father were:
    (a) Raimund Leopold (b. June 17 and d. August 21, 1783),
    (b) Karl Johann Thomas Leopold (b. October 18 and d.
        November 15, 1786),
    (c) Theresia (b. December 27, 1787 and d. June 29, 1788),
    (d) Anna (b. and d. November 16, 1789).
[18]Letter to Leopold dated Vienna, August 7, 1782.

street where the Webers lived—and gave him and his friends confidence in his future.

Of this opera, *Die Entführung aus dem Serail* (K.384), I intend to say little. Many authorities have affected to see in it a great achievement in the history of music: namely, the development of an essentially German opera on the grand scale.[19] This seems to me mere academic categorism. What is German opera? In my opinion there is no such thing; or if there is, it is utterly unimportant musically, though it may be of sociological or historical interest for those who lecture or attend lectures or write or read books on sociology and history. All these things belong to the realm of information, and information as such is of no æsthetic importance.

Die Entführung is well known to musical audiences today. It is one of the most popular of Mozart's operas and is a work of genius. Nevertheless it is not in the highest class of his productions. This is not because it is a beginning of German opera with the faults of a primitive work. We know now that the primitive are usually the best works. Giotto is a primitive Italian painter who painted his pictures before artists properly understood the "laws of perspective"; but Giotto is nevertheless one of the greatest of all painters and the knowledge of the laws of perspective is not worth a damn to a painter and has nothing to do with the creative art of painting. It is a subject for lectures on painting, not for painters. The chief defect of *Die Entführung* is the dullness of Constanze, who is not a woman but a mere singer in the opera; but given a singer of great virtuosity and with a beautiful voice we should not even worry so much about this. The fact that we never hear a really good Constanze is the explanation for most adverse criticism of this opera on the part of music-lovers. As for experts, they are so apt to be misled by irrelevant sociological and historical theories that they rarely have any genuinely direct experiences of works of art to discuss.

Mozart was very busy arranging *Die Entführung* for wind instruments when he received a commission from the Haffner family in Salzburg to compose a new serenade. In a letter dated July 20, 1782 he writes about the score of *Die Entführung*:

[19]Professor Edward J. Dent: "The development of an essentially German dramatic style out of the old German chamber style."

"Before I gave it to be copied I first made here and there alterations and cuts . . . here and there parts for the trumpets, kettle-drums, flutes, clarinets, and Turkish music are missing because I could get no paper with enough lines . . . they are written on a separate paper. . . .

"Now I have no light task. Sunday week my opera must be arranged for wind, otherwise someone else will forestall me and get my profit and now you ask me for a new symphony! How is that possible? You cannot think how difficult it is to arrange anything for wind, so that it suits the wind instruments and yet loses nothing . . . well, I must give my nights to it, otherwise it can't be done and to you, my dearest father, they shall be sacrificed. You shall get something by every post and I shall write as quickly as possible and as well as the time allows. . . ."

On July 27 he writes that he has only been able to send an allegro, as he was called upon to compose a serenade, but only for wind instruments, otherwise it might have served for the Haffner work. He promises the two minuets, the andante, and the last movement; also a march, if possible:

". . . otherwise you must just use the Haffner music [K.249], which is very little known.

I have written it in D because you prefer it."

On July 31 he writes:

"You see that my will is good, but if one cannot, one cannot! I cannot slur over anything, so I cannot send you the whole symphony before the next post.

"I have received today your letter of the 26th, but such an indifferent, cold letter as I could not suppose you to be capable of on receiving the news of the good reception of my opera. . . .

"You will in the meantime have received my last letter and I do not doubt that in your next I shall receive your consent to my marriage. . . .

"All that you have written or could write can be no more than mere idle advice which, good as it may be, no longer meets the case of a man who has gone as far with a girl as I have. . . ."

Under such conditions was the celebrated Haffner music (K.385) and the superb Serenade for Wind Instruments in C minor (K.388)[20] composed.

It was about this time that Mozart came into contact with a prominent official, President of the Education Commission in 1781, Baron van Swieten, who had been for many years in Berlin, where he had acquired a taste for Handel and Bach. He was a passionate music-lover and had musical parties every Sunday morning in his house, at which Mozart soon became a constant visitor. One of the first results of Mozart's closer acquaintance with the music of Handel and Bach was that he asked his father to send him six fugues by Handel and toccatas and fugues by Eberlin, telling him[21] that he is making a collection of Bach fugues: "of Sebastian's as well as Emanuel and Friedemann Bach's." Ten days later he writes to his sister sending her a Prelude and a three-part Fugue (K.394), on which he makes the very interesting remark that it was badly written out because he wrote out the fugue, which he had composed first, while he was thinking out the Prelude.[22]

"If Papa has not yet had the Eberlin works transcribed do not bother about them. I have found them here and unfortunately see that they are of little importance and do not deserve a place between Handel and Bach. . . ."

The fugue for two pianofortes in C minor (K.426),[23] composed on December 29, 1783, and the great but incomplete Mass in C minor (K.427)[24] were fruits of this study of Bach. Also Mozart wrote an adaptation for string quartet of five four-part fugues from J. S. Bach's *Wohltemperirte Klavier*

[20]He later arranged this Serenade for string quintet (K.406).

[21]April 10, 1782.

[22]In this same letter he tells his sister that his wife Constanze has a passion for fugues.

[23]Beethoven wrote out this fugue in score. The autograph was in the possession of Artaria.

[24]Parts of this Mass were used by Mozart in 1785 for his cantata *Davidde Penitente* (K.469). Completed by the addition of the finale from the C major Mass (K.V.262) by Mozart and edited by Bernhard Paumgartner and now frequently performed. It ranks with the *Missa Solemnis* and the Bach B minor Mass as one of the greatest works in music of its kind.

(K.405).[25] What is less known is that Mozart composed four Adagios for String Trio (in F minor, G minor, D minor, and F major) as introductions to his adaptations of the fugues of Sebastian and Friedemann Bach (K.404a).

Since it has become known, this Mass has been criticized adversely in some quarters for being "operatic" rather than "religious." As this criticism is likely to be foolishly repeated and levelled also against his other church compositions when they are performed, owing to the flower-like richness of Mozart's style and the high standard of virtuosity he expected from his singers, let me say that it is entirely mistaken. Mozart's church music is intensely serious but the Anglo-Saxon mind, with its puritan cast, invariably associates seriousness with plainness. The extraordinary efforts modern singers have to make to sing this music ought, in the course of time, to dispel this illusion, for only when such a high degree of virtuosity has been achieved that its difficulties are no longer apparent is it possible to give its intense seriousness proper expression.

Mozart was one of the supreme masters of counterpoint. His early studies under Martini, his later study of Bach, corresponded to something innate in his musical genius. Every great composer must be a polyphonic writer, but Mozart and Bach shall be considered to be in a class by themselves above all others in their power to combine creatively freedom with form in their polyphonic writing. Much of Mozart's finest polyphony is in his great ecclesiastical works, such as the Litaniæ (K.243), the Kyrie in D minor (K.341) the Kyrie in C (K.323), the Mass in C major (K.337), the Vesperæ de Dominica (K.321), the Vesperæ Solennes (K.339), the Graduale (K.273) and the Missa Brevis (K.258).

xv. Brief and Incomplete Success

1783–1787   AGE 27–31

The success of *Die Entführung* was chiefly useful in increasing Mozart's prestige, but it won him no permanent appointment

[25]No. 2 in C minor; No. 5 in D; No. 7 in E flat; No. 9 in E; No. 8 transposed from D sharp to D.

such as he needed. The available musical positions were all occupied. Gluck, Salieri, and Bono were in possession and the Emperor would have had to create a new post—which, of course, he could easily have done—in order to give Mozart the liberty he so much needed. Even as early as August 1782 he writes to his father complaining of the indifference shown by the Emperor to men of talent, and adds:

"Where did they make their fortune and their fame? Certainly not in Germany! Even Gluck—was it Germany that made him the great man he is? Unfortunately not—Countess Thun, Count Zitschy, Baron von Suiten, even Prince Kaunitz are very discontented with the Emperor that he no longer prizes men of talent and keeps them in his service. Recently the latter said to the Archduke Maximilian when the conversation turned on me that *such people only come into the world once in a hundred years* and that one must not drive such people out of Germany, especially if one is so lucky as to have them in the capital. . . ."

Characteristically, Mozart began to think of leaving Vienna and trying his fortune in Paris or in England and actually took lessons in English for this purpose. It was also characteristic of him to inform his father of these notions, but they only drew from Leopold the habitual animadversions on his son's character; as, for example, the following written on August 23, 1782 to Baronness Waldstädten:—

"I should be quite reconciled [to the marriage of Wolfgang with Constanze] if I did not see a great fault in my son; he is too indolent and easy-going; at times too proud even, and all these qualities make a man inactive; or else he grows impatient and cannot wait. He is ruled absolutely by opposite extremes —too much or too little, never any medium. . . ."

Leopold goes on to say very sensibly that the Kapellmeister Bono was an old man and that at his death Salieri would be promoted and leave a place vacant, and that Gluck also is old. This was all very sensible but it did not help Mozart to earn money at the actual moment when he needed it so badly or obtain for him the commissions to write operas with the certainty of their production for which he was burning.

There was nothing for him to do but to go on giving lessons and concerts—at which the great attraction was his own playing. He played at a concert given by Aloysia Lange on

March 11, 1783, and gave a very successful concert of his own, which the Emperor attended, on March 22, 1783, the program of which he copied out for his father. It was as follows:—

1. Haffner Symphony (K.385).
2. Air from *Idomeneo*, "*Se il padre perdei*," sung by Aloysia Lange.
3. C major Pianoforte Concerto (K.415).
4. Scena "*Misera dove son*" (K.369), sung by Adamberger.
5. Sinfonia Concertante in G major from Serenade in D (K.320).
6. Concerto in D for pianoforte and orchestra (K.175). This was composed in Salzburg in December 1773, but Mozart wrote a new final Rondo (K.382) for this concert.
7 Scena "*Parto m'affretto*" from *Lucio Silla* (K.135), sung by Mlle. Teyber.
8. Impromptu Fantasia beginning with a fugue, followed by variations on an air by Paisiello, "*Salve tu Domine*," and as an encore he chose the air "*Unser dummer Pöbel meint*" by Gluck as a theme for variations.
9. Scena and Aria in B flat for Mme. Lange, "*Mia speranza adorata*" (K.416).

For a number of years Mozart gave regular subscription concerts, for which he wrote many of his pianoforte concertos, and these concerts were patronized by the Austrian nobility and were in every way successful. This was his main source of income, but for some reason—perhaps through growing loss of interest due to familiarity—these concerts seem to have gradually fallen off. After 1788 there is no record of them and he ceased composing symphonies or concertos until January 1791, when he composed the last pianoforte concerto in B flat major (K.595). As there was no copyright law in those days he made very little by the publication of his music, which was frequently pirated. He sold his famous set of six string quartets dedicated to J. Haydn to Artaria for a hundred ducats;[1] but, according to Rochlitz, the publisher Hofmeister is said to have found that he could not sell Mozart's works owing

---

[1]These are the quartets which, on being sent by the publisher Artaria to Italy, were returned with the complaint: "the engraving is full of mistakes." On first hearing them, according to Nissen, the Hungarian Prince Grassalkowitsch declared that his musicians were playing incorrectly and on being handed the parts to convince him that they were playing what was written he tore them up in a rage. There is still occasional controversy over the introduction to the C major quartet, of which Haydn declared that if Mozart wrote it thus he must have had his own reasons for doing so.

to their difficulty; a Berlin publisher, whose name does not deserve to be recorded here, boasted that he had refused many works by Mozart, of whom he declared he had a poor opinion. Nevertheless it is clear that Mozart earned a considerable amount of money in Vienna during the period from 1783 to 1786, when he was most in demand. In spite of this he began very soon after his marriage to get into debt and Leopold in his statement in a letter to his daughter, dated March 29, 1785, says:

"I believe that my son if he had no debts to pay could now deposit two thousand florins in the bank; the money is certainly there and the household expenses, as far as food and drink are concerned, are extremely economical."

Leopold overlooked the fact that these earnings were irregular and that there were long periods when Mozart earned comparatively little. It is possible that Leopold could have saved a large sum out of Mozart's earnings but we do not need to ask where this money went. One can say with perfect truth that it went in composing. What most people fail to understand is that creative work takes a great deal of time and during that time the artist is earning nothing; nor does he feel in the mood to earn anything and so Mozart, when busy with a big work, used to put off pupils regardless of money. If one looks at the list of Mozart's compositions written between 1783 and his death in 1791, one is astounded that any man could have done so much and such work within eight years. To expect him to earn large sums of money in addition by other means is absurd; but this is actually what he had to try to do because the total sum brought in by all these works during eight years would hardly have kept him and his family for a single year.

Mozart and Constanze paid a visit to Leopold in Salzburg at the end of July 1783. Wolfgang took with him the Kyrie, Gloria, Sanctus, and Benedictus of his great Mass in C minor (K.427), which was performed at St. Peter's Church on August 25, with Constanze singing the difficult soprano part. While in Salzburg he composed two duets for violin and viola (K.423 and 424) for Michael Haydn, who was ill and had been ordered to write them by the Archbishop. In Salzburg he induced Varesco to supply him with another libretto for an opera. This was *L'Oca del Cairo* (K.422), for which Mozart wrote considerable portions of the music, but he eventually abandoned it owing to his dissatisfaction with the libretto. The same fate befell another libretto, *Lo Sposo Deluso* (K.430). In 1936 a two-act opera containing nothing but Mozart's own music was made out of these two fragments by Giovanni Cavicchioli and Virgilio Mortari and produced under Alberto Erede at the Salzburg town theatre. It foreshadows *Figaro*; there is a fine quartet for two tenors and two sopranos, but some of the music has been left in a rather sketchy state and it does not make a really successful whole.[2]

On his return from Salzburg to Vienna he went to Linz, where he wrote a symphony in a few days for a concert on November 4, 1783; this is the Symphony in C major (K.425). Jahn relates that at Linz Mozart was so much impressed by a painting *Ecce Homo*, that he made a drawing of it for his wife with the inscription *"dessiné par W. A. Mozart Linz ce 13 novembre 1783; dédié à Madame Mozart son épouse."* After his death Constanze wrote to Breitkopf and Härtel that this drawing, which she had preserved, showed that Mozart had "some talent for drawing"—which is also shown by the occasional sketches in his letters.

Throughout 1784 he was giving concerts and playing at the private homes of Esterhazy and Gallizin. For these concerts he wrote the pianoforte concertos in E flat (K.449), composed in February 1784, in B flat (K.450) and in D (K.451), both composed in March, as well as the Quintet in E flat for pianoforte, oboe, clarinet, horn, and bassoon (K.452), of which he writes to his father on April 10 that these works were much appreciated and that the quintet "is the best which I have as yet written in my life. I wish you could have heard it."

Another concerto for the pianoforte (K.453), in G, written for Babette von Ployer, as well as a Sonata in B flat for pianoforte and violin (K.454), was written in the following April. The period between 1784 and 1786 is that of Mozart's greatest popularity in Vienna and his works rather reflect this fact, which is why Wyzewa and Saint-Foix call it *"la grande période de virtuosité."* Mozart himself, in a letter to his father dated

[2]In a letter to his father, dated December 6, 1783, Mozart writes of *L'Oca del Cairo:* "Only three arias are now lacking for the first act. I can say that I am perfectly satisfied with the buffa aria, the quartet, and the finale."

May 26, 1784, refers to these three concertos (K.450, 451 and 453) as "concertos to make one sweat."

Early in 1785 Leopold paid a visit to Vienna, staying from February to April. A few extracts from his letters to his daughter, which were not all accessible to Jahn, may be given here:

> *Vienna, February 16, 1785*
> *[dated February 14 by Schiedermair]*

On Friday at one o'clock we were in the Schulerstrasse, No. 846, on the first floor. You may see what a fine apartment your brother has from the fact that he pays four hundred and sixty florins' rent.

The same day we went in the evening to his first subscription concert, where there was a large assemblage of persons of rank. Everyone paid for these six Lenten concerts a gold sovereign or three ducats. . . .

The concert was incomparable, the orchestra splendid . . . there was a superb new concerto by Wolfgang,[3] which was still being copied out when we arrived, and your brother had not had time to play through the Rondo because he had to supervise the copying. . . . On Saturday evening Herr Joseph Haydn and the two Barons Tindi came to us and the new quartets[4] were played, but only the three new ones which he has added to the other three we have—they are actually a little easier but marvellously composed. Herr Haydn said to me:

> "*I tell you before God and as an honest man that your son is the greatest composer of whom I have ever heard; he has taste and in addition the most complete knowledge of composition.*" . . .

> *Salzburg,*[5] *May 27, 1785*

I cannot deny that I find time hangs heavily on my hands. . . .

Have I anyone with whom I can exchange a sensible word? I don't know whether I am too clever or others are too stupid. Briefly, I find too great a drop from the acquaintances I had in Vienna, Linz, and Munich.

[3](K.456), Concerto in B minor?

[4]B flat (K.458), A major (K.464), and C major (K.465).

[5]Written on his return to Salzburg to his daughter Nannerl, who lived at St. Gilgen with her husband, Baron von Berchtold zu Sonnenberg, whom she married in 1784.

November 3, 1785

. . . I have not had a single line from your brother, his last letter was dated September 14 and since then the quartets should have come by any post; were he ill Herr Artaria would have informed me in his letter of October 28. . . .

November 11, 1785

. . . At last I have had a letter, dated November 2, from your brother but only twelve lines. He excuses himself because he has been up to the neck in work getting the opera *Le Nozze di Figaro*[6] finished. He thanks me and you for our congratulations and asks me to make you especially his excuses and to tell you that he has not had time to answer your letter immediately; that in order to have the mornings free to work he has put all his pupils off until the afternoons, etc., etc.

I know the piece [*Figaro*], it is a tiresome work and the translation from the French must certainly have been revised to make a possible opera. God grant that it may please in performance; about the music I have no doubts. But it will cost him much running about and discussion before he gets the libretto arranged to his liking. . . .

Mozart had made the acquaintance of Lorenzo da Ponte (1749–1838) at the house of Baron Wezlar, a musical amateur of Vienna, and Mozart asked da Ponte to adapt as a libretto Beaumarchais's comedy *Le Mariage de Figaro*, which had been first produced in Vienna on April 27, 1784. Lorenzo da Ponte had come from Venice, where he was a schoolmaster, with a letter of recommendation from the Italian poet Mazzola to Salieri, and through Salieri's influence he was appointed a court theatrical poet by the Emperor Joseph II. Fortunately the first libretto written by da Ponte for Salieri and composed by him, *Il Ricco d'un Giorno*, was a failure, whereas Paisiello made a great success with an opera *Il Rè Teodoro*, the libretto of which was written by a rival poet, Casti. Salieri now abandoned da Ponte for Casti and so da Ponte turned to Mozart, after having also arranged to write

[6]It is worth remarking that Beaumarchais's famous play *The Barber of Seville* (1775) was known to Wolfgang in 1782, for on October 19 of that year he writes to his father: "The Barber of Salzburg (and not of Seville) came to see me. . . ."

a libretto for the composer Martin. According to da Ponte,[7] the music was composed by Mozart as the words were written, and the whole was finished in six weeks. Like most theatrical writers da Ponte scorns dates; there is scarcely a date to be found in the whole of his *Mémoires*. There is no doubt that, once committed to Mozart, he helped to get the opera produced and was of assistance to Mozart in the midst of the intrigues against him on the part of Count Rosenberg and such musical rivals as Salieri. The composition of *Figaro* was begun in the autumn of 1785. It was finished before April 29, 1786, the overture being written just before the first performance on May 1, 1786.

In spite of the fact of his being busy with the composition of *Figaro* we know that Mozart found time to write during the winter of 1785-6 a number of other works, which were entered by him in the Thematic Catalogue which he had begun to keep in February 1784;[8] these are as follows:

1785. Nov. 5—Quartet   {to Villanella Rapita
      Nov. 21—Terzet   {(K.479 and 480)
      Dec. 12—Sonata for pianoforte and violin in E flat (K.481).
      Dec. 16—Pianoforte Concerto in E flat (K.482).
1786. Jan. 10—Pianoforte Rondo in D (K.485).
      Jan. 18—Terzet for *Der Schauspieldirektor*.
      Feb. 3—*Der Schauspieldirektor* (K.486).
      March 2—Pianoforte Concerto in A (K.488).
      March 10—Duet and Aria for the private performance of
         Idomeneo (K.489 and 490).
      March 24—Pianoforte Concerto in C minor (K.491).
      April 29—*Le Nozze di Figaro* (K.492).

The dates entered are the dates on which the works were completed and one may sometimes reckon the time they took from the finished date of the preceding composition.

A few words are needed here on the short opera *Der Schauspieldirektor*, which was the musical part of a dramatic gallimaufry by Stephanie performed in the Orangery at Schönbrunn for the entertainment of the Governor-General of the

[7]*Mémoires* (Paris: Pagnerre; 1860).

[8]Mozart also for a short period from March 1784 to February 1785 kept an account of his receipts and expenses. On May 1 he enters "flowers 1 kreutzer" and on May 27 "a starling 34 kreutzers." Mozart was extremely fond of birds and animals and when the starling died he buried it in his garden and raised a monument to it.

Netherlands on February 7, 1786. The opera consists of an overture, two arias for two rival sopranos, a terzet for the two sopranos and the manager (or impresario), and a final quartet. The music is superb in the brilliant virtuoso style of Mozart at this period.[9]

On May 1, 1786 Le Nozze di Figaro was first performed at the National Theatre in Vienna. It was a success, but no extraordinary success; certainly nothing to compare with the success, a few months later, of Martin's Cosa Rara, which quite overshadowed Figaro both in popular estimation and in that of "connoisseurs" such as the Emperor Joseph II and the composer Dittersdorf. For example, during the whole of the two following years of 1787 and 1788 Figaro was not once performed in Vienna. It was first performed in Berlin in 1790; but although praised by the criticis, the public preferred the operas of Martin and Dittersdorf. It was a complete failure in Italy, where it was first produced, only after Mozart's death, in 1792, and Mozart has remained incomprehensible to the Italian opera public practically ever since.[10] On the other hand it was performed in Prague in the winter of 1786-7 with tremendous success, of which I shall have more to say presently.

Something must be said here about Figaro, which is the best-known and most popular of Mozart's operas.

LE NOZZE DI FIGARO

The original cast, according to Mozart's own thematic catalogue, was as follows:

IL CONTE ALMAVIVA	Signor Mandini
LA CONTESSA	Signora Laschi
SUSANNA	Signora Storace
FIGARO	Signor Benucci
CHERUBINO	Signor Bussani
MARCELLINA	Signora Mandini

[9] In the excellent English adaptation of the text by Eric Blom this opera, under the title of The Impresario, was performed at the Arts Theatre, Cambridge, England, with great success, where I heard it in July 1937.

[10] This is no "Latin" inferiority. Mozart is even misunderstood by numbers of eminent German and Anglo-Saxon musicians; but I venture to think that a lack of something I shall risk calling "vulgarity" in Mozart's music has been responsible for its lack of popularity in modern Italy.

BASILIO DON CURZIO	Signor Kelly
BARTOLO ANTONIO	Signor Bussani
BARBERINA	Signora Nannina Gottlieb

Beaumarchais's original French play *Le Mariage de Figaro*, first publicly performed in Paris in April 1784, was a social and political satire, but in constructing the Italian libretto the political sections were entirely omitted by da Ponte, and although this may have been partly out of regard for the Austrian Emperor and the court, it was certainly done at the express wish of Mozart, who had no interest in politics. This is a point on which all his biographers have to agree. Unlike his father, Leopold, he never mentions political affairs in his letters and Abert has rightly pointed out that for him the State "came even less into consideration as primary experience than society." He was indifferent to political principles and had only an interest in the men who represented them. This indifference to mere abstractions extended naturally to moral as well as political principles, and if many people advocating certain moral principles have found *Figaro* an immoral work it is because Mozart is never concerned with expounding theories of right and wrong or with mere tendentious caricature but only with life in all the manifestations of its individual reality. It is significant that although he lived in the midst of the French Revolution he never once mentions it. Napoleon, according to Sainte-Beuve, in his *Causeries de Lundi*, declared of Beaumarchais's *Figaro*: "*c'était la révolution déjà en action*"; but there is nothing of this in Mozart's *Figaro* and the famous "frondeur-monologue" in the fifth act is replaced in Mozart's work by an outburst of rage and jealousy. This remarkable piece, however, is of the most fiery character but it is entirely personal. Mozart understood and had every sympathy with a hatred of injustice, but he was too realistic to express a revolutionary detestation of the strong as such and a glorification of the weak as such with the object of changing their places so that the oppressed might become the oppressors. He was also far too personally humane to be carried away by mechanical theories and in this his resemblance to Shakespeare is most marked.

But little as Mozart's *Figaro* is a political work, it is equally
far from being a social document aiming either at glorifying
or at decrying the aristocratic society of the age he lived in.
To look upon his *Figaro* merely as a sort of rococo memorial
to the fashionable brilliance of the great age of Vienna is to
misunderstand it completely. That it is also a mirror of its age,
as one might almost say all great works of art—including
Dante's *Commedia* and Milton's *Paradise Lost*—are, is true;
but it is far more than that. It is the expression of a great
individual personality with a unique experience of and attitude
to life; just as I would say Proust's *A la recherche du temps
perdu* is. The characters in *Figaro* are not the characters of
Beaumarchais's play at all; they are entirely the creation of
Mozart and the expression of his own personality in every
single respect. How utterly Mozart has transformed the Countess and Susanna! And what are we to say of that miraculous
creation Cherubino, a figure absolutely unique in the world's
dramatic literature? Never has the dewy freshness, sensitiveness, sensuousness, and ecstasy of the human heart in the first
bloom of its youth had such adequate, let me say perfect, expression! Cherubino's first aria: "*Non so più cosa son, cosa
faccio* (I no longer know what I am, what I do)," must always
remain one of the loveliest things the genius of an artist has
ever conceived in the history of the world. That the artist who
could conceive such exquisite things as this and the Countess's
"*Dove sono*" and the "*Zephyr*" duet, was also capable of the
intellectual constructive power of the finale of Act II is in
itself sufficient to rank him with Shakespeare as the complete
artist, the musician of all musicians who was truly universal.

A final word must be said. It has been suggested that Mozart's apparent unconcern with the world-events about him
and even, after he was mature, with the work of musicians
who were his contemporaries is a sign of limitation. Surely this
is not so, but quite the opposite is true. Mozart took so very
much for granted which lesser minds argue about. He was too
understanding and too profound (though active) a fatalist to
be a partisan. He never turned his works of art into judgments.
He merely—like the Creator of nature—gave them individual
life, and in his works his music, like the rain and the sunshine,
falls alike on the just and the unjust.

I now continue with a few more extracts from Leopold's letters to his daughter:

January 13, 1786

. . . At last I have had an answer, dated December 28, from your brother, to my two letters. He writes that he has given three subscription concerts with a hundred and twenty subscribers[11] and that he has written a new Piano Concerto in E flat for them, of which the Andante was encored, which is rather unusual. . . .

March 31, 1786

I am sorry the letter has been lost. . . . I wrote that . . . seven of the riddles[12] had been correctly solved that none of us could solve the eighth and that I have written to your brother about it as he is the philosopher and author of the riddles and the fragment.[13] The riddles are only fun but the fragment is of serious use for the cultivation of morality in every reflecting person. . . .

end of April 1786

On the 28th *Le Nozze di Figaro* had its first performance. It will be a great thing if it succeeds, for I know that he has a tremendously strong clique against him. Salieri and all his followers will again set heaven and earth in motion. Duschek told me recently that your brother has so many cabals against

[11]In a letter to his father, dated Vienna, March 20, 1784, Mozart gives a list of his subscribers, numbering one hundred and seventy-four. He also gives a list of his engagements, which is worth quoting:

"Thurs.	Feb. 26, Count Gallizin.	Sun.	Mar. 21, 1st Concert in theatre.
Mon.	Mar. 1, Joh. Esterhazy.	Mon.	Mar. 22, Esterhazy.
Thurs.	Mar. 4, Gallizin.	Wed.	Mar. 24, 2nd S. Concert (private).
Fri.	Mar. 5, Estherhazy.	Thurs.	Mar. 25, Gallizin.
Mon.	Mar. 8, Esterhazy.	Fri.	Mar. 26, Esterhazy.
Thurs.	Mar. 11, Gallizin.	Sat.	Mar. 27, Richter.
Fri.	Mar. 12, Esterhazy.	Mon.	Mar. 29, Esterhazy.
Mon.	Mar. 15, Esterhazy.	Wed.	Mar. 31, 3 S.C. (private).
Wed.	Mar. 17, 1st S. Concert.		
Thurs.	Mar. 18, Gallizin.	Thurs.	Apr. 1, 2 S.C. (theatre).
Fri.	Mar. 19, Esterhazy.		
Sat.	Mar. 20, Richter.	Sat.	Apr. 3, Richter

[12]Sent by Mozart to amuse his father.

[13]What this was I do not know.

him just because he is so greatly esteemed for his exceptional
talent and ability.

November 17, 1786

. . . Today I have had to reply to a letter from your brother
which has cost me so much writing that after it I can write
very little to you. . . .

That I have had to write a very emphatic letter you can
easily imagine since he made me no less a proposal than that I
should take his children into my care while he during Lent
might make a trip through Germany to England. . . .

But I have spoken my mind . . . it would be a nice thing
indeed—they could travel in peace, might die—might remain
in England and leave me with his children on my hands. . . .
Enough! my answer is strong and full of good advice if he will
make use of it.

December 8, 1786

. . . You will see from the enclosed very illegible letter
from your brother that my reply has calmed him and that he
is giving four Advent concerts at the Casino.

May 10, 1787

. . . Your brother now lives at 224 Landstrasse. He does
not explain why. Not at all! But unfortunately one can
guess.

Some time before March 1785 Mozart had entered one of
the eight lodges of Freemasonry in Vienna, for we have it on
the authority of Nissen that his father, Leopold, was introduced as a member by him in the spring of that year, when
Wolfgang was already a member. Freemasonry was very much
in vogue in intellectual circles in Vienna about this time
under the leadership of Ignaz von Born (1742–91) and was
favourably regarded by the Emperor. All institutions lend
themselves readily to abuses and necessarily sink to the common level of the majority of their members, but there was a
serious and highly intellectual section in the Vienna Freemasonry of this period and it was to this that Mozart and his
father belonged. Mozart's lodge was the *Zur gekrönten Hoff-
nung im Orient in Wien,* of which Count Franz von Esterhazy became Grand Master in December 1785.

We may find in their common membership in Freemasonry
the explanation of certain phrases written in the following
letter by Mozart to his father:

Vienna, April 4, 1787

Mon très cher Père,

. . . Just now I have had news which quite overwhelms
me—all the more since your last letter led me to suppose that
you were, God be praised, well. Now I hear that you are really
ill! How earnestly I look forward to reassuring news from
yourself I need hardly tell you. And I certainly hope for it although I have accustomed myself to expect the worse in all
things.

Since death (properly understood) is the true ultimate purpose of our life I have for several[14] years past made myself
acquainted with this truest and best friend of mankind so that
he has for me not only nothing terrifying any more but much
that is tranquillizing and consoling!

And I thank my God that He has bestowed on me the good
fortune to provide the opportunity (you understand me) of
recognizing death as the *key* to our true blessedness.

I never lie down in my bed without reflecting that perhaps
I (young as I am)[15] shall never see another day; yet none of all
who know me can say that I am socially melancholy or morose.
For this blessing I daily thank my Creator and wish it from
my heart for all my fellow-men.

I wrote to you on this point in the letter which Mlle.
Storace mislaid on the occasion of the sad death of my dearest,
best friend, Count von Hatzfeld—he was thirty-one years old,
as I am. I do not mourn for him but for myself and all those
who knew him as well as I did.

I hope and pray that even as I am writing this you may be
better; but should you, contrary to expectation, not be better
I beg you . . . not to conceal it from me but to write, or have
written for me, the exact truth, so that I may be as quickly as
possible in your arms. Nevertheless I hope to receive soon a
reassuring letter from you and with this hope my wife, Karl,[16]
and I kiss your hands a thousand times and am ever,

Your most dutiful son.

Leopold made a slight recovery but died suddenly on May
28, 1787. On May 29 Mozart wrote to his friend Gottfried
Freiherr von Jacquin in Vienna:

[14] *"ein paar."*

[15] Mozart was thirty-one years old when he wrote this letter.

[16] His son Karl, born in 1784.

"I must let you know that today when I returned home I reecived the sad news of the death of my dear father.[17] You can imagine the state I am in.

And on June 16 he wrote to his sister:

My dearest and best of Sisters,

That you yourself did not advise me of the sad and unexpected death of our dearest father did not offend me as I could easily guess the reason. . . .

Be assured, my dear, that when you have need of a good, loving, and protecting brother you will certainly find one in me.

My dearest and best of sisters, if you were still unprovided for[18] all this would be unnecessary.[19] I should, as I have a thousand times said and thought, give up everything to you wholeheartedly; since, however, it is in a way not needed but is of great assistance to me, I hold it my duty to think of my wife and child.

From a letter dated August 1, 1787, written to his sister, we learn that Mozart received a thousand florins from his father's estate.

With the death of his father and the production of *Figaro* a definite phase of Mozart's life was concluded. The failure of *Figaro* to make any material difference to his life in Vienna marked the beginning of Mozart's realization that worldly success was not to be his. He was destined for other and higher things. The success of *Figaro* in Prague was a success due to the purer musical taste of the Bohemians at that time. Among the musicians of Prague (where the conductor, Strobach, and the orchestra used to get so excited in playing *Figaro* that they declared they would willingly have played it all over again) Mozart must have come to the conclusion that henceforth he had to write mainly for himself and for a handful of musicians capable of understanding his music.

Chief among these must be remembered Joseph Haydn, who wrote a justly famous letter which was first published in 1798 by Niemetschek. He obtained it from Chief Administrator Roth, to whom it was addressed, and in printing it stated

[17]I am at a loss to understand how Mozart could have received the news of his father's death so quickly.

[18]She had married Freiherr von Berchtold zu Sonnenberg in 1784.

[19]Reference to the inheritance.

that it was: "one of the finest flowers that can be strewn upon the grave of the artist so prematurely taken away." Haydn's letter, written in December 1787, is as follows:

"You desire an opera buffa from me; right gladly, if you wish to possess for yourself one of my compositions. But not for presentation in your theatre at Prague because all my operas are intended too particularly for our own company (at Count Esterhazy's in Hungary) and would never have the intended effect outside the prescribed setting. It would be quite different if I were to have the good fortune to get a new libretto to compose for that theatre. Even then, however, it would be a risk since one can hardly compete with the great Mozart.

"Could I only impress in the soul of every music-lover, and especially the great, the inimitable works of Mozart as deeply and with such musical understanding as I myself feel and comprehend them, then the nations would compete to possess such a precious jewel within their walls. Prague must stick to this precious man but also reward him; for otherwise the history of a great genius is a sad one and gives to future times little encouragement for similar striving; on the contrary, unfortunately! How many hopeful spirits have gone under! I am indignant that this unique Mozart has not yet found employment at any imperial or royal court. Pardon me that I digress but I honour the man so dearly.

"*Joseph Haydn*

"My compliments to the Prague orchestra and virtuosos."

At the end of a visit in January 1787, Mozart left Prague with a contract to compose a new opera for the following season at a fee of one hundred ducats.

xvi. *Last Years*

1787–1791 AGE 31–35

The history of Mozart during the last four years of his life is the history of a great man of genius who is so completely superior in every respect that he is practically left alone to be consumed in his genius (which in his case is the refining fire

of which great religious teachers speak!) and die—unregarded
by the world at large.

In the *Magazine für Musik*, 1788, Vol. II, Cramer, a musical connoisseur visiting Vienna, writes:

"Kozeluch's works hold their own and are everywhere acceptable, but Mozart's are not by any means so popular. It is
certainly true—and it receives additional support from the
quartets he has dedicated to Haydn—that he has a decided
leaning to what is difficult and unusual. But on the other hand
how great and noble are his ideas, how daring a spirit is displayed in them!"

During the greater part of the year 1787, in which occurred
his father's death, Mozart was at work on the composition of
Don Giovanni, for which Lorenzo da Ponte again furnished
the libretto. Nevertheless he found time for other compositions, the following being entered by him in his own Thematic
Catalogue:

1787. March 11—Rondo for pianoforte, A minor (K.511).

March 18—Scena for Fischer, *"Non sò"* (K.512).

March 23—Aria for Gottfried von Jacquin, *"Mentre ti lascio"*
(K.513).

April   6—Rondo for horn for Leutgeb (K.514).

April   19—Quintet for two violins, two violas, and 'cello, in
C major (K.515).

May   16—Quintet in G minor (K.516).

May   18⎫
20⎪
23⎬Four Songs (K.517–520).
26⎭

May   30—Pianoforte Sonata, four hands, in C (K.521).

June   11—*Musikalischer Spass* (K.522).

June   24—Two Songs (K.523 and 524).

Aug.   10—Serenade (K.525). *"Eine kleine Nachtmusik."*

Aug.   24—Sonata for pianoforte and violin, in A (K.526).

Mozart is supposed to have brought his opera *Don Giovanni* (K.527) to Prague in an unfinished state in September
1787 and to have completed it in the summer-house in the
vineyard of his friend Duschek. He is said to have written
"La ci darem le mano" five times before being able to satisfy
his singers, and this duet is written on smaller paper in the

autograph score, as is Masetto's aria. On October 14, 1787 *Figaro* was performed in his presence and on October 29 the first performance of *Don Giovanni* took place, the overture, it is said, being only written out on the previous night.[1] The opera was received with enthusiasm in Prague and the following account appeared in the *Wiener Zeitung*, No. 91, 1787:

"On Monday, October 29, Kapellmeister Mozart's long-expected opera *Don Giovanni* . . . was performed by the Italian opera company of Prague. Musicians and connoisseurs are agreed in declaring that such a performance has never before been witnessed in Prague. Herr Mozart himself conducted and his appearance in the orchestra was the signal for cheers, which were renewed at his exit. The opera is exceedingly difficult of execution and the excellence of the representation, in spite of the short time allowed for studying the work, was the subject of general remark. The whole powers of both actors and orchestra were put forward to do honour to Mozart. Considerable expense was incurred for additional chorus and scenery. The enormous audience was a sufficient guarantee of the public favour."

The success of *Don Giovanni* in Prague had one minor result, which was that after the death of Gluck, on November 15, 1787, Mozart was appointed by the Emperor Joseph II his successor as Kammermusikus on December 7, 1787; but not, unfortunately, with Gluck's salary, for he received only eight hundred florins a year instead of several thousands. It is recorded that he attached to one of the receipts of his pay a note stating:

"Too much for what I do—too little for what I could do."

Don Giovanni was nevertheless not given in Vienna until May 7, 1788, and then it was only by the command of the Emperor Joseph II. It was a failure, although it was not withdrawn but was given fifteen performances during that year. Then it fell out of the repertory and was not revived until after Mozart's death and then in a wretched German adaptation. The Vienna production, however, was responsible for

[1] But in Mozart's Catalogue the whole opera, including the overture, is entered as finished on October 28. Probably it was written on the night of October 27, before the second rehearsal.

Mozart's making two additions: namely, the famous aria for Elvira, "*Mi tradi*," and the duet between Leporello and Zerlina, "*Per queste due manine*." The aria "*Mi tradi*" is generally retained but the duet seems to have been an attempt by da Ponte and Mozart to make the opera more acceptable to the Viennese and is generally omitted in present-day performances. The aria for tenor, "*Della sua pace*," was also added for this production as the tenor found the big aria of Octavio's beyond his powers.

Don Giovanni in both Prague and Vienna had a *succès d'estime*—that is, a success with the few discriminating musiclovers and musicians, just as *Figaro* had; for even *Figaro* did not have a popular success, being quite eclipsed by Martin's *Una Cosa Rara*; just as Salieri's *Axur* and Dittersdorf's *Der Doktor und Apotheker* were everywhere preferred to *Don Giovanni*. A contemporary writer named Schink in the *Dramaturgische Monate* of 1790 (Vol. II, p. 320) put the matter very well:

"How can this music, so full of force, majesty, and grandeur, be expected to please the lovers of ordinary opera . . . ? The grand and noble qualities of the music in *Don Giovanni* will appeal only to the small minority of the elect. It is not such as to tickle the ear of the crowd and leave the heart unsatisfied. Mozart is no ordinary composer. . . ."

Another contemporary, Schneider, in the *Geschichte der Berliner Oper*, after the first performance of *Don Giovanni* in Berlin wrote:

". . . Vanity, eccentricity, fancy have created *Don Giovanni*, not the heart. . . ."

A writer in the *Chronik von Berlin* (Vol. IX, p. 132) praises the music but adds:

"Oh, that he had not so wasted the energies of his mighty mind! that his judgment had been brought to the aid of his imagination and had shown him a less miry path to fame! . . ."

Goethe, however, seems to have had a sense of the greatness of *Don Giovanni* for he writes to Schiller on December 30, 1797, after the performance in Weimar:

"Your hopes for opera are richly fulfilled in *Don Giovanni* but the work stands absolutely alone and Mozart's death prevents any prospect of its example being followed."

Mozart himself may have had qualms whether he was not giving the musicians and music-lovers of Prague rather more than they were able to digest in *Don Giovanni*; for Niemetchek, after referring to the fact that Mozart, in spite of having had a natural genius like Shakespeare's, had also studied his art profoundly, relates the following story:

"Once—it was after the first rehearsal of *Don Juan*— Mozart went for a walk with the then director of the orchestra and Kapellmeister, Herr Kucharz. Among other things they spoke of *Don Juan*. Mozart said: 'What is your opinion of the music of *Don Juan*? Will it please as much as *Figaro*? It is of a different character!'

KUCHARZ: How can you doubt it? The music is beautiful, original, profound. What comes from Mozart will certainly please the Bohemians.

MOZART: Your conviction reassures me, it comes from a connoisseur. But I have not spared trouble and labour to accomplish something exceptional for Prague. People err who think that my art has come easily to me. I assure you, dear friend, nobody has devoted so much time and thought to composition as I. There is not a famous master whose music I have not industriously studied through many times."

Here it is worth mentioning some remarks of Niemetschek on Mozart's methods of composing, since Niemetschek's evidence is contemporary evidence. Niemetschek says:

"Mozart wrote everything with such ease and speed as might at first be taken for carelessness or haste; also he never went to the pianoforte while composing. His imagination held before him the whole work clear and lively once it was conceived. His great knowledge of composition made easy for him the general harmonic panorama. One seldom finds in his scores improved or erased passages. But it does not follow that he merely sketched out his works hastily. The composition had long been finished in his head before he sat himself at his writing-desk. When he received the text for a vocal work he went about with it for some time, thought himself thoroughly into it, and gave it all the power of his fantasy. Then he worked out his ideas fully on the pianoforte and then for the first time sat down to write. Consequently the writing was for him an easy task during which he often joked and chattered . . . often he spent half the night at the pianoforte, for these actually were the creative hours of his heavenly ideas. In the quiet peacefulness of night, when no object fettered his thought, his imagination flamed to its liveliest and embraced the whole wealth of tones with which nature had endowed his spirit. . . . Whoever heard Mozart in such hours alone knew the depth, the vast extent of his musical genius: free and independent from all other considerations his spirit could then venture on the boldest flights through the highest regions of art. In such hours of poetic inspiration Mozart created his inexhaustible store; out of this he ordered and constructed with an easy hand his immortal works."

Mozart was always in his thoughts occupied with music and he had a habit when eating alone or with his family of taking his napkin and folding it very exactly at the corners and drawing it through his mouth, grimacing in his concentration on some musical idea or problem. Niemetschek's remark that Mozart rarely improved or erased passages is generally true, but there are quite a number of important exceptions where Mozart has had striking and significant second thoughts. Also, like Beethoven, he was occasionally critical of his own works when he heard them. There is a story of his playing an aria from *Die Entführung* in a private house and remarking afterwards: "It may do well enough in this form for the salon but on the stage it is too long. At the time I wrote it I was never tired of hearing myself and did not know how to bring my work to a conclusion!"

Don Giovanni only slowly made its way into the European opera-houses and even up to today this masterpiece remains an unpopular work which is constantly revived owing to the passionate admiration of the best musicians and most discriminating music-lovers from generation to generation who cannot rest until they have heard it. Never, however, in the whole hundred years and more since it was written has it achieved the popularity of a *Bohème* or a *Cosa Rara* or a *Pagliacci* or any other of the great successes of a day and an hour. As a contemporary of Mozart wrote: "Mozart's operas . . . have met with the fate which would befall a sober man introduced to a company of drunkards; the rioters would be sure to treat the sober man as a fool."[2] E. T. A. Hoffmann, in his *Don Juan, eine fabelhafte Begebenheit*, written in Sep-

[2]*Berlinische Musikalische Zeitung*, 1793, p. 77.

tember 1812, which appeared in his *Phantasiestücke in Callot's Manier* in 1813, was one of the first to appreciate the great qualities of *Don Giovanni*. The famous Danish philosopher Kierkegaard's celebrated essay on the opera, written in 1842, has also had a certain influence on the Continent, although it is still unknown in England and America.[3]

The production of great works such as *Figaro* and *Don Giovanni* did nothing to provide for Mozart's future financially. He was compelled to continue to try to earn his living by teaching and by obtaining commissions for dance and other music. In 1788, the year of the production of *Don Giovanni* in Vienna, he composed a considerable quantity of miscellaneous music, including the three last symphonies, in E flat (June 26), G minor (July 25) and C major (August 10), and numerous country dances and waltzes. Having arranged at Baron van Swieten's request Handel's *Acis und Galatea* in November 1788, Mozart did the same for Handel's *Messiah* in March 1789, and in July 1790 for the *Ode for St. Cecilia's Day* and *Alexander's Feast*. A great deal has been written about these additions and alterations to Handel's scores by Mozart and it is a matter of taste whether one prefers the originals or Mozart's versions. In my opinion good schools of music would make their students perform both versions and request critical comments from them, regarding such work as an essential part of their studies.

On April 8, 1789 Mozart set out with a pupil-friend, Prince Karl Lichnowsky, on a visit to Berlin. He played at the court in Dresden in competition with a famous virtuoso named Hässler (1747–1822). Visiting Leipzig, he played the organ at the St. Thomas Church and the Cantor Doles, a pupil and the successor of Sebastian Bach, was so pleased that he made the choir sing for Mozart the Bach eight-part motet *Singet dem Herrn ein neues Lied*. According to Rochlitz he was so delighted that he exclaimed: "That is indeed something one can learn from!" and he asked to see other motets by Bach, of which the St. Thomas school possessed manuscripts; as there was no full score available he spread the parts out around him and was soon deep in study.

In Berlin he was presented to the King, Frederick William II, by Prince Lichnowsky. The Prussian King was an ama-

[3] See Chapter XIX.

teur 'cellist and very fond of music, his taste, according to his Kapellmeister Reichardt, being more catholic than that of his predecessor, Frederick the Great. According to tradition the King made Mozart an offer of a kapellmeistership at a good salary, which he refused out of loyalty to the Austrian Emperor; a number of letters written by Mozart to his wife during this journey went astray and there is no precise mention of this offer in any we possess. On May 21, 1789 he wrote:

". . . my dearest little wife, you must rejoice more at my return than at any money I am bringing. . . ."

On June 4 he was back in Vienna, having had little pecuniary profit from his tour, but having made acquaintance with unknown works of J. S. Bach and having left behind him the famous *Gigue* (K.574), written in the album of the Leipzig court organist Engel on May 17, which is a little masterpiece of Mozart's contrapuntal art.

On July 12, 1789 he wrote a long letter to a friend and fellow-Mason, Michael Puchberg, who was a Viennese business man and music-lover. From this letter I take the following extract:

"My God! I am in a position such as I should not wish my worst enemy to be in and if you, my best friend and brother, forsake me, then I, together with my poor sick wife and child, am blamelessly and lucklessly lost. Even when I saw you last I wanted to pour out my heart—but I had not the heart and still would not have it but only dare do it tremblingly in writing and could not do it even so if I were not sure that you know me and my circumstances and are convinced of my innocence and my most unfortunate and sad position. Oh, God! instead of coming with gratitude I come to you with fresh requests, instead of settlement I bring fresh demands. If you know my heart, then you must know what pain this gives me; how through this unlucky illness[4] I am deprived of my earnings I need not repeat to you; only I must tell you that in spite of my unfortunate situation I decided to give subscription concerts so as to be able at least to provide for my great and increasing expenses—for I was convinced of your friendly willingness to wait—but I did not succeed. My fate is sad but only in Vienna is it so adverse that I can earn nothing even when I

[4]Of Constanze, his wife.

want to. I have to run around for fourteen days with my list[5] and so far there stands the single name of Swieten.[6]

"Now since it appears that my dear wife is improving from day to day I should be able to work once more were it not for this blow, this heavy blow—we have the consolation that at least she is going to improve, although yesterday evening she upset me and made me doubtful again; she suffered so much and I with her; but this night she has slept so well and is so much easier this morning that I am more hopeful; now I can again begin to think of work but I am unlucky in another respect—truly only for the moment—dearest and best friend and brother, you know my present circumstances but you also know my prospects; these remain as mentioned so and so . . . you understand me. Meanwhile I am writing six easy pianoforte sonatas for the Princess Frederika [of Prussia] and six quartets for the King,[7] all of which I am having printed by Kozeluch at my expense; the two dedications will bring in something; in a couple of months my fate in the little affair[8] will be decided, consequently you, my best friend, stand to risk nothing; now it depends on you, my only friend, whether you can and will lend me a further five hundred florins.

"I undertake to pay back until my affair is settled ten florins monthly and then (which must be in a few months) to repay the whole sum with proper interest and also to declare myself for life your debtor, which I indeed must yet remain since I shall never be in a position to be able to thank you enough for your friendship and love. Thank God it is finished! Now you know all, only don't take amiss my trust in you and reflect that without your support the honour, the repose, and perhaps the very life of your friend and brother would be sacrificed. . . .

"PS.

"July 14, 1789

"God knows I can hardly bring myself to send off this letter—yet it must go—If only this illness had not happened I should not have been compelled to seem so shameless to my

---

[5]To obtain subscribers.　　　　[6]Baron van Swieten.

[7]Only three were ever written, namely (K.595, 589 and 590).

[8]This is supposed to be a reference to Mozart's application to the Vienna court for a position in view of the offer made to him by the King of Prussia.

one friend and yet I hope for forgiveness since you know the good and evil of my situation. The evil certainly is only for the moment but the good certainly will last, once the momentary evil is removed. Adieu! Forgive me, in God's name, just forgive me—and—adieu!"

Only a sensitive and imaginative person can understand what it must have cost Mozart, the proud and—as his father even used to declare—"arrogant" Mozart to write this letter. But who was to blame that Mozart during the last years of his life had to endure an ever-increasing pressure of poverty and neglect? Every ardent young spirit reading this book will feel that there is something wrong with a society in which such things can happen. There is. But a society in which such a thing could not happen is not as easy to achieve as most reformers pretend to believe. Of course, one thing may be curable—namely, the mere lack of adequate means of existence which forces men like Mozart into such humiliating positions and exhausts their nervous energy. No society can be considered either satisfactory or stable—that is to say, no society has a proper and firm foundation—which has not secured for every one of its members the means of civilized substance quite independent of merit or what used to be called "desert." It may be true that no man "deserves" to live; but certainly nobody's livelihood should depend upon popular support. No doubt economic security will in time be established because without it no permanency of civilization is possible; but even then the Mozarts of the future may suffer from the neglect and indifference of the majority of their contemporaries and successors. But that is precisely the index of their value and will not interfere with their work; rather, it will often help it.

When Hofmeister, the publisher, advised Mozart that he should write in a more popular style Mozart replied with a bitterness which, as his first and excellent English biographer, Edward Holmes, comments, was "unusual" for him:

"Then I can make no more by my pen, and I had better starve and go to destruction at once!"

There are in existence no less than thirteen letters to Michael Puchberg written during this one year from July 1789 to August 1890, every one of which contains an urgent request for a loan of money. We know that Puchberg sent him, in answer to these letters, the following sums:

July 17, 1789	150 florins
December 1789	300 florins
January 1790	100 florins
February 1790	25 florins
March, April 1790	150 florins
April 8, 1790	25 florins
May 17, 1790	150 florins
June 12, 1790	25 florins
August 14, 1790	10 florins

None of Mozart's many biographers has given sufficient attention to the harassed situation of their hero during the last years of his life. Most people imagine—no, not "imagine," assume—that great artists produce great works out of the air. It is perfectly true. They do, since they are produced in the teeth of the indifference or even hostility of the world around them by sheer dint of courage, tenacity, and genius. Even so, their creators need food and drink and a few other necessities, and the few generous and understanding persons who provide these in times of necessity are indispensable. If one considers the word *indispensable* one will soon realize that I am not giving too much attention to that otherwise unknown business man, Michael Puchberg, to whom the world is so much indebted; for without Puchberg the opera *Così fan Tutte* might never have been written and Mozart might have died a year earlier than he did and before the composition of *Die Zauberflöte*.

Così fan Tutte (K.588) was commissioned by the Emperor Joseph II some time in the middle of 1789, the Emperor possibly being reminded of Mozart's existence by the successful revival of *Figaro* in Vienna in August 1789. Mozart entered it in his Catalogue as finished in January 1790—no doubt by the aid of Puchberg's florins—and it was produced on January 26, 1790 and had, like most of Mozart's works, a *succès d'estime* but no popular success. It was performed ten times during 1790 and was then dropped. It could not possibly have had any other fate since even today—nearly a hundred and fifty years later—it is far beyond the comprehension of the average musician and music-lover.

As the reader will probably think this an exaggeration I shall give him an example of what a well-known musical critic has said about this opera in a book on Mozart written as recently as 1935. Mr. Eric Blom, who is certainly a genuine admirer and appreciator of Mozart's music, writes:

"The supreme joke is that one cannot possibly help seeing the utter harmlessness of this mildly amusing piece which contains nothing so seriously unpleasant as the Count's pursuit of Susanne in *Figaro*. Nor is it possible to see how anyone could fail to be captivated by its deliberately and delectably artificial music."

Mr. Blom—and I once more repeat that I only select Mr. Blom because of his superiority in learning and taste to the majority of Mozart idolaters—has in the same book declared that Mozart

"cannot, in fact, be called one of the world's most distinctive melodists, for the plain truth is that he is often, even in his greatest works, content to use tunes that are part of the common stock of the composers of his time . . . others have been much more individual in their inventions including minor masters like Borodin or Grieg or Chabrier and composers of far less taste like Tchaikovsky and Puccini, who have written far more personal and more immediately striking music and found compensation for the lack of the most judicious artistry in a much more easily gained and general popularity."

Now, I quote this because Mr. Blom has here perfectly expressed what is the considered opinion of a great body of musicians past, present, and possibly to come; but which opinion is, I maintain, utterly wrong. Mozart is not superior to the composers named by Mr. Blom (and to most others!) because he is "incapable of the slightest offence against good taste." Mozart was, on the contrary, a constant offender against what was considered good taste in his day and against what is still considered good taste today. Mr. Blom's own contradictory reference to the "seriously unpleasant" in *Figaro* is in itself a witness to this fact. The truth is that we mediocre men cannot even imagine what it is to be a great man like Mozart or Shakespeare and to be thus free from the domination of the contemporary prejudices, beliefs, morals, artistic rules, scruples (call them what you will!) with which even the most enlightened of us are—often unconsciously—obsessed.

The truth about Mozart is quite the contrary to what Mr. Blom and nearly all other critics and musicians maintain. The truth, as I see it and as I have written this book to demonstrate, is that Mozart was a wholly superior man, intensely serious, deeply compassionate, almost all-comprehending, with a profound understanding of life and a universal sympathy with human beings that reminds one of Shakespeare and is in distinct contrast to Beethoven and Tolstoy. This superiority is an essential part of his nature and therefore of his musical genius. The greater includes the less. Mozart as a melodist is the greatest there has ever been; his melodies are purer and more beautiful than any others because they come from a purer source. While Beethoven could be described for the greater part as a flame (to borrow Artur Schnabel's description of Toscanini), Mozart was a spring, a fountain of the creative spirit, which ran more purely, less muddied and yet more variedly because it came from a deeper source than any other in the history of music. To say that the originator of such melodies as *"Dove sono," "Voi che sapete"*—to say nothing of hundreds of exquisitely lovely themes throughout his instrumental and ecclesiastical music—was not one of the world's "most distinctive melodists" can only mean that Mozart's melodies are too beautiful for ordinary ears—which is undoubtedly true.

The death of the Emperor Joseph II and the accession of Leopold II to the Austrian throne on March 13, 1790 did no good to Mozart. Salieri retired from the conductorship of the opera and was succeeded by his pupil Joseph Weigl. Mozart's candidature for the second kapellmeistership was unsuccessful. The coronation of Leopold II took place in Frankfurt am Main on October 9, 1790. Salieri as Court Kapellmeister, his assistant Umlauf, and fifteen musicians were taken to Frankfurt in the retinue of the Emperor but not Mozart, who, however, in view of his desperate financial plight and the possibility of having a large audience among the visitors to the coronation, pawned his silver plate and ornaments to pay his expenses and took along with him his even poorer brother-in-law, the violinist Hofer. They set off

on September 23. He writes from Frankfurt am Main to his
wife as follows:

September 28, 1790

. . . The journey was very pleasant; we had fine weather
except for one day. . . . In Regensburg we had a splendid
midday meal and had capital music, angelic cooking, and a
first-rate Moselle wine. We had breakfast in Nuremberg—a
hideous town. At Würzburg we strengthened our poor
stomachs with coffee—a fine, beautiful town—the expenses
everywhere were moderate. . . .

I await with longing news from you, of your health, of our
circumstances, etc.,[9] and am quite determined to do the best
I can here and return happily to you. What a splendid life we
shall lead! I shall work—work so hard—in order that I shall
not again through unforeseen circumstances get into such a
desperate position. . . .

September 30, 1790

. . . My love, I shall certainly make something here—but
not as much as you and various friends have imagined. . . .

As I do not know whether you are in Vienna or Baden[10]
I address this letter again to Hofer. I am as gay as a child at
the thought of seeing you again. If people could look into my
heart I should be almost ashamed it is so cold—ice-cold. If you
were with me perhaps I should find more pleasure in people's
kind behaviour to me—but my heart is so empty—adieu. . . .

October 3, 1790

. . . I had so determined to write immediately the Adagio
for the clockmaker[11] so that my dear wife may have a few
ducats in her hand, and I did it but was unluckily—as it is a
most hateful work—unable to complete it. . . . I write every
day . . . if it were for a great clock and the thing sounded like
an organ, then I should enjoy it, but the work is for mere tiny
piping, which sounds shrill and childish.

I live quite retired here and don't go out the whole morning but stick in my hole of a room and write. . . .

[9]A reference to an attempt to raise a loan of a thousand florins
through Hofmeister.

[10]This Baden is not Baden-Baden but a small place in delightful
country outside Vienna.

[11](K.594).

October 8, 1790

. . . I beg you to fix up the business with Hofmeister if
you want me to return. If you could only see into my heart!
There the wish to return and embrace you fights with the
desire to bring home plenty of money. I have often the idea
of travelling farther but when I made myself consider this
decision it always occurs to me how I should regret it if I had
separated myself from my dear wife for so long on a very uncertain and perhaps fruitless quest . . . and then it is mere idle
talk what they say one can make in the German cities—
celebrated, admired, and loved I certainly am here, but beyond
that the people here are even more parsimonious than in
Vienna. . . .

It is somewhere about this time that we may date the following postscript which I quote for its characteristic outburst of Mozart's lively and affectionate nature in gloomy
circumstances. It is not certain to which of Mozart's letters
of this period it belongs, as the original is only a fragment:—

"P.S. As I wrote the foregoing page many tears fell on the
paper. But now let me be merry. Prepare yourself, kisses begin
to fly around amazingly . . . what the devil! I see a crowd of
them. Ha! ha! I've just caught three—they were delicious!
You cannot answer this letter but you can address me poste re-
stante Linz, that is the safest for I do not know whether I go
to Regensburg or not . . . adieu dearest and best of little wives,
take care of your health and don't go on foot in the town—
write to me how you like our new lodging—adieu, I kiss thee
a million times."

"October 15, 1790

"I am still without any news in reply to my Frankfurter
letters, which disquiets me not a little. Today at eleven my
concert took place, which as far as reputation is concerned was
superb but the result as regards money is meagre. . . ."

At this concert Mozart played his own Concertos in F
major (K.459) and D (K.537). On his way back to Vienna
he heard a performance of *Figaro* at Mannheim; he played
at the Elector's court in Munich at the beginning of November and arrived soon after in Vienna, no better off than he
had left it. His sore lack of money would not have been such
a burden had it not been for his wife, Constanze, who clearly
seems to have had no inkling of the real stature of Mozart

but saw in him only a musician of talent, but one who had
never won popular success and who indeed very likely, in her
opinion, was inferior as a composer to such great figures
as Dittersdorf,[12] Salieri, and others, who in contemporary
opinion and in court favour were much more important than
Mozart. In December 1790 the English impresario Salomon
came to Vienna and induced Joseph Haydn to accompany him
back and produce a number of compositions for the Philharmonic Society in London. Haydn left Vienna on December 12 and Mozart probably saw him off. Salomon
apparently suggested a similar trip to Mozart to be made after
Haydn's return; in the meantime Mozart received a letter,
dated October 26, 1790, from the director of the Italian opera
in London inviting him to stay in London from December
1790 to June 1791 and compose two operas for three hundred
pounds sterling.

It may seem strange that Mozart did not accept this offer,
but he probably did not want to leave his home again so
soon. It is clear that he was crippled with debt at the end of
1790 and he probably could not raise the money for the
journey; also, he may have been sceptical about the results.
During that winter, however, he was busy composing, as the
following entries in his Catalogue show:—

1790. December	.	.	Quintet for two violins, two violas, 'cello, in D major (K.593).
1791. January	5	.	Pianoforte Concerto in B flat (K.595).
January	14	.	Three Songs (K.596, 597, 598).
January	23 }	.	Dances (K.599, 607, 609, 611).
March	6 }		
March	3	.	Piece for Clock in F minor (K.608).
March	8	.	Aria for bass with obbligato contra-bass, "Per questa bella mano" (K.612).
			Variations for pianoforte on "Ein Weib ist das herrlichste Ding" (K.613).
April	12	.	Quintet for two violins, two violas, one 'cello, in E flat (K.614).

[12]Dittersdorf, for example, was given a patent of nobility and a
Government post.

1791. April	20 . .	Chorus for Sarti's opera *Le Geloise Villane*, "*Viviamo felici*" (K.615).
May	4 . .	Andante for cylinder on a small barrel-organ in F (K.616).
May	23 . .	Adagio and Rondo for harmonica, flute, oboe, viola, and 'cello, in C minor (K.617).
June (in Baden)	18 . .	Motet, *Ave, Verum Corpus* (K.618).
July	. .	German Cantata for solo voice and pianoforte *Die ihr des unermesslichen Weltalls Schöpfer ehrt* (K.119).

Again, through the spring of 1791, Mozart was compelled to borrow money from Puchberg to keep himself going. In May he wrote a letter to the magistrates asking to be nominated as successor to the Kapellmeister Hofmann at the Cathedral of St. Stephen's as Hofmann was ill and advanced in years.[18]

In the summer of 1791 his wife again went to Baden for her health—she was expecting another child—while Mozart stayed in Vienna working at the opera *Die Zauberflöte*, which the actor-manager and writer Schikaneder had asked him to compose, supplying him with a libretto which he himself had made up out of elements taken from Wieland's Oriental story *Lulu*, which were combined by Mozart and Schikaneder into a rhapsody on the virtues of Freemasonry. Schikaneder and Mozart were fellow-Masons and it is fair to assume that Mozart had as great a hand in the fashioning of the libretto as his friend, Schikaneder; also, from their respective characters, we may be sure that Mozart was chiefly responsible for giving the fairy-tale a serious symbolical expression. Mozart writes to his wife as follows:

June 11, 1791

. . . I cannot tell you what I would give to be with you in Baden instead of sitting here. Out of sheer weariness I have composed today an aria of my opera. . . .

[18]His request was granted; he was nominated as assistant without salary and as successor, but it was too late. Mozart never lived to succeed.

June 12, 1791

Why have I had no letter yesterday? . . . It is not good for me to be alone when I have something on my mind. . . .

In order to raise my spirits I went to the new opera *Kaspar der Fagottist*,[14] which has made such a stir, but there is nothing in it. . . .

[TO MICHAEL PUCHBERG]   *June 25, 1791*

. . . I have a request to make. My wife writes that she notices that they would like to see some money on account of the lodging and also to cover expenses for food and she desires me to send her some. As I expected to settle everything on her departure I am now in a fix. I don't want to disturb my poor wife with these unpleasant explanations but I can't leave myself quite destitute. If you, my best friend, can help me so that I can send something, you will do me a great favour—it is only a matter of a few days before you will receive in my name two thousand florins with which you can immediately settle my debt to you.[15]

[TO CONSTANZE]   *July 2, 1791*

. . . I beg you to tell that lad Sussmayer he is to send me my copy of the first act from the introduction to the finale so that I can instrument it. . . .[16]

July 6, 1791

. . . You cannot give me greater pleasure than by being happy and gay, for if only I am certain that you are all right, then my troubles are light and easy, for the fatal and strained position I am in becomes a mere trifle if I only know that you are well and happy. . . .

July 7, 1791

. . . Now I wish for nothing but that my business were finished so that I could be with you again. You cannot imagine how the time here has gone without you. I can't explain my feeling, it is a certain emptiness which makes me sad, a certain longing which is never satisfied and thus never ceases but is always present, even increases from day to day; when I think how merry and youthful we were together in Baden and what sad, tedious hours I pass here—my work also does not make me happy, accustomed as I am till now to pause and

---

[14]An opera by Wenzel Müller.

[15]Puchberg sent him twenty-five florins.   [16]*Die Zauberflöte.*

exchange a few words with you, which is now unfortunately impossible. If I go to the pianoforte and begin something out of the opera[17] I have to stop immediately as it affects me too much. . . . *Basta!* . . .

It is quite clear from these letters that Mozart was in an abnormal state of sensibility. The persistent ill luck, hard work, and scarcity of money which had now gone on for years with no prospect of improvement were sapping his vitality. There is another cause of strain, too, which is generally overlooked, and that is the inevitable intellectual and spiritual isolation in which a man of such genius is necessarily condemned to live. It is this that was responsible for Mozart's craving for the affectionate companionship of his wife. On July 26 Mozart's youngest son, Wolfgang, was born in Baden, and somewhere about this time Lorenzo da Ponte, according to his account in his *Mémoires*,[18] tried to induce him to go to London with him; but he says that Mozart "was occupied with composing his German opera *Die Zauberflöte* and asked for six months' delay," to which da Ponte could not agree.

Another invitation was received about the same time from a Count Franz von Walsegg, who commissioned Mozart to write a *Requiem* in memory of the Count's wife. The Count was a good amateur musician and used to order compositions anonymously and pretend to be the author.[19] He sent his steward—who was "the mysterious stranger" so often referred to in biographies of Mozart—on this errand and Mozart agreed to compose the *Requiem*. He had hardly started on this when he received an order to compose a new opera for the approaching coronation of Leopold II as King of Bohemia at Prague. This order came to Mozart through the Bohemians and not through the Emperor; so once again we owe an opera of Mozart's to the people of Prague, who were his truest and most consistent admirers during his lifetime.

The subject selected was Metastasio's *Clemenza di Tito*, remodelled by the court poet of Saxony, Mazzola. About the

[17]*Die Zauberflöte.*

[18]Page 168 of the French edition (Paris: Pagnerre; 1860).

[19]He rewrote Mozart's score and had the work performed from his duplicate on December 14, 1793.

middle of August Mozart set out for Prague, accompanied by
his wife and his pupil Süssmayr. He had to work at the opera
during the journey, making sketches in the carriage and con-
tinuing his work at night in the inns they stayed at. The opera
was due for performance on September 6 in Prague and was
completed in eighteen days. Süssmayr is supposed to have
written the *secco* recitatives but nothing else. According to
Niemetschek, Mozart was very unwell when he arrived in
Prague, and was continually taking medicine during his stay.
It is not surprising under the circumstances that *La Clemenza
di Tito* (K.621) is not one of Mozart's greatest operatic works,
and those who think genius cannot be frustrated or hampered
by circumstances may be confronted with the fact that given
other circumstances *Le Clemenza di Tito* might have been
another masterpiece.[20] Nevertheless this work achieved later
a certain measure of popularity. It was the first of Mozart's
operas to be performed in London[21] and it remained in the
German operatic repertory throughout most of the nineteenth
century. There is a good deal of fine music in this opera. Professor Dent has remarked on the beauty of the two duets,
"Deh prendi" and *"Ah perdona,"* the melody of the latter
being that, he says, which apparently inspired Shelley's "I arise
from dreams of thee." Other gems are Vitellia's second aria
(22, 23) and the fine choral finale to the first act, already
mentioned.

The new opera was not an immediate success even in
Prague, and Mozart returned to Vienna in the middle of September, unsolaced and in ill health, to complete *Die Zauberflöte* and the *Requiem*. The chorus "O Isis and Osiris" was
written after September 12 and the overture and march of
the priests was completed on September 28. It is about this
time that we must date an extraordinary letter written by
Mozart in September to an unknown friend. This letter is
written in Italian and is presumed to have been addressed to
Lorenzo da Ponte, who, we know, was seeking to induce
Mozart to accompany him to London. It is as follows:

[20]Mozart took this opera seriously and thought highly of Mazzola's
adaptation of Metastasio's text. It is questionable whether this opera
has received the estimation it deserves. It contains a choral scene
which is one of the finest achievements of Mozart.

[21]In 1806.

My dear Sir,

I should like to follow your advice, but how can I do so? My head is confused, I reason with difficulty and cannot rid my eyes of the image of this stranger.[22] I see him continually begging me, soliciting me, and impatiently demanding my work. I go on because composition wearies me less than resting. Besides, I have nothing more to fear.[23] I know from what I feel that the hour sounds; I am on the point of expiring; I have finished before having enjoyed my talent. Life was so beautiful, my career began under such favourable auspices, but none can change his destiny. Nobody can count his days, one must resign oneself, it will all be as Providence pleases and so I finish my funeral song, I must not leave it incomplete.

Mozart

His wife went again to Baden while Mozart stayed in Vienna. A brief happiness was granted him by the unexpected success of *Die Zauberflöte*, which was produced in Vienna on September 30. Even so, this was not unalloyed, because the success was due more to Schikaneder's tomfooleries than to Mozart's music, and the profundity of Mozart's conception in handling the raw material of this opera completely escaped nine out of ten operagoers then as it does to this day.[24] That this is not mere fancy on my part can be proved from Mozart's own correspondence. For example, in a letter to his wife in Baden dated Vienna, October 8 and 9, he writes about an acquaintance who went to hear *Die Zauberflöte*:

". . . showed himself such a Philistine that I could not remain or I should have had to call him an ass. . . . Unluckily I was in the theatre when the second act began; in the ceremonial [*feierlichen*] scene he laughed at everything; at first I

[22]The then unknown visitor who commissioned the *Requiem*.

[23]In the original Italian the word is *tremere*, which is obviously a slip for *temere*. Mozart was not very accurate in his spelling. There have been other suggested emendations but, personally, I have no doubt the word is *temere*.

[24]If this is thought an exaggeration I refer the reader to the excellent performances at Glyndebourne since 1935 under Fritz Busch. Even these are spoiled by occasional facetiousness and the introduction of asides in English to tickle the dull ears of the public.

was patient enough to want to draw his attention to some things but he was always laughing; that was too much for me. I called him Papageno and went out. I do not believe, however, that he understood. . . ."

The significance of Mozart calling this dolt Papageno will not be lost on those who understand Mozart and *Die Zauberflöte*.

When, towards the end of October, Constanze returned from Baden, Mozart did not conceal his state of mind. One fine autumn day when they were sitting in the beautiful Prater, Mozart spoke of his approaching death and told Constanze that he was composing the *Requiem* for himself. He also said that he must have taken poison.[25] In November Mozart had a slight recovery and composed a cantata (K.623) for a Masonic festival, and then continued working at the *Requiem*. The landlord of the Silberner Schlange, Joseph Deiner, has related how in the winter of 1790 he called on Mozart one day and found him and Constanze dancing up and down his workroom; on his asking him whether he was teaching his wife dancing, Mozart replied: "We are making ourselves warm because we are very cold and have no money for fuel." One day in November 1791 Mozart came to Deiner's inn and ordered a drink, but sat there with his hand on his head and did not touch it and on the next day Deiner called and was informed that Mozart was very ill in bed. He was taken into his room and when Mozart saw him he could be just heard to say: "Nothing today, Joseph; we have to do with doctors and apothecaries today."

A Dr. Closset attended him and on November 28th he called in Dr. Sallaba, the chief physician at the hospital. During the fortnight he was confined to his bed Mozart never lost consciousness. His canary, of which he was very fond and to which he often referred in his letters home when he was travelling, was removed, to his distress, to another room. He used to follow in imagination the performance

[25]The idea that Mozart was poisoned by Salieri is, of course, ridiculous. Mediocre men do not need to poison geniuses; they have nothing to fear from them. But the idea was very prevalent in Vienna long after Mozart's death and his own statement is only a sign of the obscure nature of his death. See Appendix I.

of *Die Zauberflöte* every evening with his watch laid beside him. The day before his death he said to his wife: "I should like to have heard my *Zauberflöte* once more," and began to hum the bird-catcher's song. Kapellmeister Roser, who was at his bedside, went to the pianoforte and played it, to his great pleasure. The *Requiem* was also constantly in his mind. The afternoon before his death, according to Schack, who was present, he had the score brought to his bed and sang the alto part, while Schack took the soprano, Hofer the tenor, and Gerl the bass. When they got to the first bars of the Lacrimosa, Mozart burst into a fit of weeping and laid the score aside.

Towards evening when his sister-in-law came Mozart said to her: "I am glad you are here; stay with me tonight and see me die." She tried to reason him out of this conviction but he replied: "I have the flavour of death on my tongue— I taste death and who will support my dearest Constanze if you do not stay with her?" She left him at the wish of her sister to induce a priest from St. Peter's "to come as if by chance"; but it was only with difficulty that one could be found to come. This, no doubt, was due to Mozart's connection with Freemasonry. On her return she found Mozart talking to Süssmayr about the *Requiem*. Later in the evening the physician arrived and ordered cold compresses. Mozart lost consciousness and became delirious and in his delirium was evidently still occupied with the *Requiem*, or, at any rate, with music, for in his unconsciousness he kept blowing out his cheeks as if imitating trumpets. About midnight he raised himself from his bed, opened his eyes, lay down with his face to the wall, and at 12.55 on the morning of December 5, 1791, he died, aged thirty-five.

Constanze became completely prostrate and the wealthy Baron van Swieten made all the funeral arrangements. As if inspired directly by God he arranged for the cheapest burial possible (third class) at the cost of eight florins thirty-six kreutzer, with three florins for a hearse. A service was held at St. Stefan's and the bier was carried through a storm to the churchyard of St. Mark's. Van Swieten, Salieri, Süssmayr, Roser, and the 'cellist Orsler were present at the service but found the weather too bad to accompany the body to the cemetery. No grave had been bought and nobody was pres-

ent—not a single one of his friends or acquaintances—
when the corpse of Mozart was flung into a common pau-
per's vault containing fifteen to twenty coffins. When his
wife recovered and visited the churchyard there was a new
gravedigger, who could not tell her where Mozart had been
buried. All subsequent attempts to discover the spot have
been in vain. A more fitting end for this great genius could
not be conceived. Shakespeare's "Cursed be he that moves
my bones" was thus made superfluous.

Mozart left books and music to the value of twenty-three
florins forty-one kreutzers and some furniture and household effects of the simplest character. Jahn, who saw the list
which was printed in the *Deutsche Musikzeitung* in 1861
(page 284), says: "It is affecting to see how simple, even
poverty-striken, was the whole ménage." Various people,
including Stadler, who had borrowed five hundred florins,
owed Mozart money, and his debts amounted to about three
thousand florins. It must not be thought by the reader that
the neglect and misunderstanding from which Mozart suffered during his lifetime when he was no longer a child-
prodigy and a novelty ceased with his death. On the contrary, Mozart is as much misunderstood and as inadequately
appreciated now as ever. The music-shops of the world are
full of fake pictures of him which are false in every respect;
he is the victim of innumerable essays and biographies which
reduce him to the size of the writer, while the majority of
the performances of his works are painfully inadequate in
conception and execution. But:

The world knows nothing of its greatest men:
Alive neglected and dishonoured dead,
Renown on them its hydra-dark shall spread,
Digging ten thousand graves for every ten;
Fame on false headstones writes with ironic pen
The glorious name, in the procrustean bed
Of each man's mind a Dummy sleeps instead,
Fitted to match exactly to his ken.

The priests themselves, who think the god resides
Within the temple, kneel to dead Desire
In painted image—Enter! If you would know
Where that Immortal Spirit now abides,
Where springs again the ever-mysterious Fire,
Look in your heart whether its cinders glow.

XVII. The Genius of Mozart

It is my belief that the essential nature of genius is always the same whatever its sphere of manifestation. Therefore we can truly speak of the nature of genius apart from whether, in its objective materialization, it takes the form of music, poetry, mathematics, painting, or any other non-realistic abstraction invented by the human mind. This "essence" of genius is vividly suggested in the well-known saying of Goethe's:

"That glorious hymn *Veni, Creator Spiritus*, is really an appeal to genius. That is why it speaks so powerfully to men of intellect and power."

But we must be careful to discriminate between the emotion—however deep—expressed in the prayer: *Veni, Creator!* which voices the desire for the coming of the creative spirit, and the actual non-emotional functioning of the creative spirit when it has indeed come and *is* actually present.

Within historical times, at all epochs when there has been a pure apprehension of things rather than a mere Philistine interest in things, men and women have naturally regarded all exceptional powers as divine and coming from a spiritual source. Mozart's highly gifted musical sister, referring to her brother, speaks of "the talent given to him by God." This may be accepted as voicing the instinctive popular recognition that genius is not only born and not made by industry applied to a talent; but also that it rather possesses the person than is possessed by him. A man "possessed" necessarily acts otherwise than always sensibly and in his own interests; he can never achieve that purely reasonable goal of all self-education because he is controlled by, rather than in control of, a natural force. But this natural force which possesses him is not without its laws, it is not irresponsible; if it were, then genius would be the same thing as madness, to which it is admittedly akin. Is there a fundamental law of genius, and if so what is it? Goethe has perhaps formulated it in his saying:

"The first and last thing required of genius is the love of truth."

This love of truth is quite a different thing from the love of truths and must be clearly distinguished from it. The love of truths is the necessary and useful passion of all unoriginating minds for rules, formulas, prescriptions, and methods which are of proved utility and can be passed on to others. The "truth" of "truths" is purely pragmatic; it is therefore limited to time, place, and occasion, which it must fit, and it is this fittingness that constitutes its truth. What, then, is this other "truth" about which Pilate asked his famous question? Now, I would answer very simply that it can be nothing else but the love of God.

A light on the meaning of this comes from what may be considered as a very odd quarter—namely, Schopenhauer. Schopenhauer has said in *The World as Will and Idea* that the fundamental condition of genius is an abnormal predominance of sensibility over the will and reproductive power. I believe that here we have a clue to that opposition between self-assertion, the will of the individual ego— which is an uncreative thing reproducing only itself—and the selflessness of creative genius, which is in itself a pure love of God. In the case of Mozart his most striking characteristic is his abnormal or supernormal sensibility. Mozart as a boy burst into tears when he was overpraised. Can one imagine the type which Keats has so well distinguished from men of genius, but which, I think, he not too happily describes as "men of power"—can one think of such a one, an Edison ("Genius is one per cent inspiration and ninety-nine per cent perspiration"), a Napoleon, or a Stalin, bursting into tears at lavish praise?

The modesty of men of genius is not ignorance. This has been well noted by the observation of Miguel de Unamuno that there is "a certain characteristic common to all those whom we call geniuses. Each of them has a consciousness of being a man apart." The modest Mozart calmly informs his father in a letter from Vienna how the Archduke Maximilian had remarked that such a man as he (Mozart) does not come into the world more than once in a hundred years. I am convinced that this remark made about himself did not in the least surprise Mozart because he knew it already and here we have the key to what might seem—and actually did seem to Mozart's father, Leopold—a baffling change in his nature.

"As a boy you were excessively modest and serious," complains Leopold in a letter to his son, "but now you turn everything to joking; your character seems to have entirely changed." Actually what had happened was that, after puberty and his contact as an adult with the rest of the world and the prolonged practice of his art among other musicians, Mozart had come to a fuller realization of himself and his powers and now knew himself for what he was. Nothing could depress him, nothing seemed serious to him compared with this overwhelming secret of which he had become conscious that he was born to the happiness of praising God in music. A rose-bush bursting into blossom does not need advice and Mozart, in whom this hidden joyous creativeness now was fully functioning, could not take anything else seriously at all.

But, even so, this love of God is only the energy, the main-spring of genius. We have more to discover when we examine its functioning. It is here pertinent to recall what Samuel Johnson had to say of genius because of the Doctor's colossal common sense and uncommon penetration. Johnson said: "The true genius is a mind of large general powers, acci-dentally determined to some particular direction." This, as far as it goes, is certainly true. The word *genius* ought not to be applied to gifted men of a minor category in whom their particular talent seems to derive from an absence of other possibly inhibiting qualities—that is, from a minus rather than a plus endowment as human beings. Indeed, this is the deciding factor between talent and genius. The true genius is always a great man in the fullest meaning of the word *great*. He is a superior man, a man in every respect above the average, a man who includes, comprehends, and surpasses the majority. And as he surpasses them in good-ness he can surpass them in badness—"Genius," said Emer-son, "even as it is the greatest good is the greatest harm." And why is the man of genius capable of the greatest evil as of the greatest good? Because of the predominance of his sensibility: "A person of genius should marry a person of character," once wrote that curious American writer Oliver

Wendell Holmes, and this remark, though its biological inferences are probably not sound, is useful as a perhaps unconscious testimony to the fundamental principle of genius —which Schopenhauer has enunciated and which Keats discovered for himself—that there is a certain antithesis or repulsion or incompatibility between genius and what we call "character," in that genius is of its very nature unstable and chameleon-like by virtue of its supersensitive universality. Here we may recall the unconscious testimony of Schachtner on Mozart: "I believe . . . he might have become a profligate—he was so ready to yield to every attraction which offered."

Actually, the man of genius is kept from subsiding into evil by force of that mysterious attraction which we may find symbolized in the myth of the good and the evil angels —on the one side Michael and his fellows, who were faithful, and on the other Satan and his fellows, who instead of loving God turned to hating Him because they loved themselves more. It is significant that no poet has succeeded in portraying the antithesis of Satan so vividly as Milton has portrayed Satan; but to do so it would be necessary to indicate clearly that Michael (taking Michael as the antithesis) contained all the potentialities of Satan. In other words, if a poet is to create a convincing symbol of goodness he must succeed in making it include evil—comprehending, assimilating, and consuming it.

The man of genius is a man of good and evil and that is the explanation why Mozart, who wrote the Isis and Osiris chorus of *Die Zauberflöte*, the *Ave Verum*, and numerous other pieces of the purest single-minded ecstasy, also wrote the Queen of Night music, *Don Giovanni*, *Così fan Tutte*, *Figaro*, and other, wholly instrumental, works in which the elements of darkness and light are both present.

But beyond all this the man of genius not only possesses a mind of larger general powers, but has as its foundation a physical vitality much above the normal. We do not know exactly what is meant by "vitality," but we can feel it, and we feel it in the work of all men of genius. This extra vitality, it may be, is connected with their double intellect— which Schopenhauer considered to be a chief characteristic. There is the normal consciousness functioning in life purposively for the usual practical ends of the individual in his environment and as a social animal and there is the extra consciousness which is dominant and is always dealing with generalities and creating a synthesis which has no practical bearing whatever and is of no use to the genius as a man, but rather a hindrance. And as a man of genius grows older he comes to realize that his genius is nothing but a hindrance and a handicap to his success as an individual man, struggling for the usual aims of the individual—his livelihood and security in the society of his fellows, to say nothing of personal happiness and repose in human relationship.

There is one aspect of genius to which I shall only make the briefest reference and it is that I believe that *intellectually* all men of genius are hermaphroditic. How this comes about and what the particular nature of this synthesis of masculine and feminine elements is I do not wish to discuss here. Mozart (and, as far as we know, also Shakespeare) was passionately fond of women and had not got either the physical or the psychological traits of either of the two main classes of homosexuals who are unattracted by women. Nevertheless, there is a duality of intellect in Mozart which is very striking indeed, just as there is in Shakespeare, and it is this which gives his work its extraordinary comprehensiveness.

It remains to draw attention to a certain characteristic of Mozart's music which does not obviously apply to all his works but is nevertheless a general quality which pervades all and of which he himself was certainly aware and to which he was referring when he said that music, whatever the intensity of the passions and thoughts it was expressing, must always remain music. I cannot do better than extract something of what I have said before on this point, with certain emendations that increased experience has suggested to me.

Mr. Bernard Shaw once remarked that nothing could be more uncharacteristic of Mozart than the portraits of the beautiful young man exhibited above his name in all the music-shops of the world today. These portraits show Mozart as the most handsome, the most regular-featured of all great composers. Such "classic" proportions seem at first sight to be peculiarly appropriate to a composer who is universally admired as the classic of classics. Where else in music shall we find those qualities of serenity, limpidity, simplicity, lucidity, which we concentrate in one adjective, *Mozartian?* It is impossible in music to find a parallel to that flawless perfection. Whether we take a whole opera—such as *Le Nozze de Figaro*—or a mere scrap scribbled impromptu on the page of a visitor's book—such as the Gigue written in 1789 for the Leipzig organist Engel—we are confronted with a completely finished musical composition in which there is not a superfluous bar, not a redundant or meaningless note. There is no "waste" in Mozart—no overlapping, no exaggeration, no strain, no vagueness, no distortion, no suggestion. He is so pure that he seems often meaningless. His music *disappears*, like the air we breathe on a transparent day. All those who have really appreciated Mozart will admit that at one time or another they have felt certain Mozart masterpieces as one would feel a still, bright, perfect, cloudless day. Such a day has no meaning, none of the suggestiveness, the "atmosphere," the character of a day of cloud or storm, or of any day in which there is a mixture of warring elements whose significance has yet to appear. Such a day does not provoke or in the faintest degree suggest one mood rather than another. It is infinitely protean. It means just what you mean. It is intangible, immaterial—fitting your spirit like a glove. Thus, as Sir Charles Stanford has said, when you are a child, Mozart speaks to you as a child—no music could be more simple, more childlike—but when you are a man, you find to your astonishment that this music which seemed childlike is completely adult and mature. At every age this pure, pellucid day, this intangible transparency, awaits you and envelops you in its unruffled light. Then suddenly there will pass through you a tremor of terror. A moment comes when that tranquillity, that perfection, will take on a ghastly ambiguity. That music still suggests nothing, nothing at all; it is just infinitely ambiguous. Then you may remember the phrase of a German critic who wrote of the "demoniacal clang" of Mozart. Then you look at a genuine portrait of Mozart, and instead of that smooth, regular young beauty you see a straight jutting profile with a too prominent nose and an extraordinary salience of the upper lip, and for an instant you feel as if you have had a revelation. But that revelation escapes you as suddenly as it came, and you are left face to face with a mask whose directness and clarity are completely baffling.

One may speak often of a movement of Mozart just as a mathematician might speak of a beautiful proposition. Whereas in the music of most composers it is a case of content *and* structure, it is with Mozart a case of structure only, for there is no perceptible content—*ubi materia ibi geometria.* This is strikingly shown in the overture to *Le Nozze de Figaro.* I would suggest to the reader that he should buy the phonograph records of this overture and of Rossini's overture to *Il Barbiere di Siviglia* and compare them. The difference is astonishing. Rossini was born the year after Mozart's death; he also had the advantage of following instead of preceding Beethoven and he was a composer of striking natural genius. But, after *Figaro,* listen to his *Il Barbiere di Siviglia* overture, with its alluring tunefulness over its easy *tum-ti, tum-ti, tum-ti* bass, and you will be struck with its straggling formlessness. Its tunes are very engaging, but you can carry them away with you and hear them mentally on a penny whistle, a cornet, or any instrument you like. They are like bright threads in a commonplace piece of stuff which you can pull out without compunction as there is no design to spoil. But you can do nothing of the sort with the *Figaro* overture. There are no bright threads to pull out. There is no melodic content as such. You cannot even hear the music in your memory apart from the rush of the strings and the accents of the woodwind. It cannot be played upon the piano. Take away a note of it and the whole is completely disintegrated. Nor can anyone put his hand upon his heart and say what feeling that music arouses in his breast. It is completely without expression, as expression is vulgarly understood; but the oftener you hear it, the more excited you become, the more passionate grow your asseverations that there was never music like this before or since. Its effect upon the mind is out of all proportion to its impingement on the senses. To hear it is as though one had been present at a miracle and had seen a mountain of matter blown into a transparent bubble and float vanishing into the sky. Your desire to hear that overture again and again and again is the simple but intense desire to see the miracle repeated. It is an astonishing experience, and it is an experience which Mozart is constantly giving us.

It would be useless to attempt to explain this peculiar intellectual gift which was Mozart's to a degree that separates him from all other composers. It must just be stated and left. But there are certain facts known about Mozart which are so relevant to this point that they should be mentioned now. He was exceptionally good at dancing and playing billiards, which were his two chief pleasures. He was small, but his limbs, feet, and hands were beautifully proportioned. He composed away from any musical instrument entirely in his head and could complete the whole of a work, from the first note to the last, and then write it down—often weeks or more later—from memory. Thus the overture to *Don Giovanni*, which was written on the night of October 28, 1787 for the first performance of the opera in Prague on the next day, while his wife kept him awake by telling him fairy-stories, was not composed on that night but merely copied out from memory. He would often compose at meals, and while composing would take his napkin by two corners and continually fold and refold it very neatly and exactly. To me this is all extraordinarily illuminating. Conciseness—even conciseness so unparalleled and amazing as Mozart's—is not surprising in a composer who could work in this way. One also cannot but think that his invariable serenity and good temper—upon which all who knew him have left comment—was yet another sign of perfect physical and mental poise. It is on record that Mozart never used glasses and that his eyesight was perfect at his death in spite of the strain which manuscript music imposes. This, also, is not without significance. Mozart's mental grip never loosens; he never abandons himself to any one sense; even at his most ecstatic moments his mind is vigorous, alert, and on the wing. It is from this astounding elasticity that his conciseness largely derives. Most artists are unable to tear themselves away from their most delightful discoveries; they linger on them and handle them fondly, but not Mozart. He dives unerringly on to his finest ideas like a bird of prey, and once an idea is seized he soars off again with undiminished power.

It is not astonishing that a mind so well balanced as Mozart's should show so great a sense of humour. In this he surpasses all other composers and, as the sense of humour is essentially intellectual, it is natural that Mozart, the most intellectual of composers, should be the greatest master of comic opera. But what might be altogether unexpected is his power to make one's flesh creep. Nothing has ever been written of such truly diabolical verve as the aria for the Queen of the Night in *Die Zauberflöte*. It is the rarest event to find a light soprano who can sing this at all; it is certain that we shall never have it sung so as to do full justice to its startling cold-blooded ferocity. And yet that aria has the smooth, glassy surface of a mere bit of coloratura virtuosity; but it is the surface of ice beneath which is a fathomless black water. This sinister ambiguity is a quality quite apart from the more familiar power of striking the imagination which he shows in the music which announces and accompanies the entrance of the statue at the supper-party in the last act of *Don Giovanni*.[1] Yet I would like to insist that there is another and even more troubling quality in Mozart's music. Linked with the "demoniacal clang," which is probably the result of that bareness which makes Mozart's music appear a mere rhythmical skeleton beside the work of more sensuous composers such as Brahms and Wagner (but a skeleton of electric vitality!), there is a profoundly disturbing melancholy. It is never active in Mozart's work as it is frequently in the work of Tchaikovsky, in Brahms, in Chopin, and even in Beethoven. It is a still, unplumbed melancholy underlying even his brightest and most vivacious movements. It is this that gives his music that ambiguity to which I have drawn attention, an ambiguity which makes one sometimes find a peculiar, all-pervading, transparent gloom in Mozart's music. I am not even sure that

---

[1] This is an example of Gluck's precept of using music to enforce the dramatic situation such as was, possibly, within the power of Gluck himself to achieve. But that complex and subtle musical propriety which consists in writing ensemble music in which a number of characters are differentiated psychologically and yet have their separate musical expression coherently combined in a convincing and harmonious form, absolutely beautiful in its proportions and meaning, was not so highly developed by Gluck as by Mozart, for whom music was not a means of enforcing the expression of the poetry but was the very expression and poetry itself.

gloom and *melancholy* are the right words to use. Mozart is very mysterious—far more mysterious than Beethoven, because his music *seems* to express much less of his human character. But the mystery lies also in Mozart himself and there for the present we will let it remain.

XVIII. The Comic and Tragic in Mozart's Operas

Don Giovanni

Musical historians write at length about the genesis of opera and go into great detail on this subject. I prefer to be as brief as possible. The origin of opera is threefold; or we may say that it has a threefold root in Poetry, Dancing, and Music. No matter how opera develops in the future, its seeming changes of form will depend upon the balance and adjustment of these three primary factors. In every good opera, in every opera that is a work of art by a truly creative composer, these three elements are differently combined. We approve of and enjoy all these different combinations according as we are in the mood for this or that proportion of the primary ingredients. The human need for change in order that each element may be freshly experienced is what promotes the so-called new developments; but these new developments are new only in the sense that each opera composed by a musician of genius is a fresh solution of the problem of combining the three primary elements and of making at the same time a creation which is absolutely his. The creative genius not only solves a problem, but his solution is an individual offspring with a life and character of its own.

Instead, therefore, of giving the reader a lengthy description of the development of opera in Italy during the sixteenth and seventeenth centuries, illustrated by the names of Peri (1561–1633), Caccini (1558–c.1616), Cavalieri (c.1550–1600), Monteverde (1567–1643), Legrenzi (1625–90), Stradella (c.1645–82), Carissimi (1604–74), Cesti (1620–69), Cavalli (1602–76), Alessandro Scarlatti (1659–1725), and so on, I shall just present this history, up to Mozart, abbreviated into the following diagram:

THE GENEALOGY OF OPERA

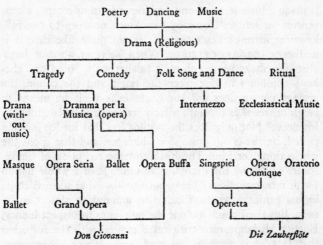

If we take the six best-known operas of Mozart's we shall find that *Idomeneo* is an example of opera seria—that is, an opera in which there is no comedy—springing as it does in my diagrammatic scheme from the "Tragedy" division; that *Die Entführung* is an example of Singspiel—that is, a derivation from Comedy and the more popular sort of Italian variety show known as Intermezzo; that *Figaro* is an example of opera buffa; and that in *Die Zauberflöte* we have a unique example of the combination of Singspiel and Oratorio or Cantata. This leaves us with the two other masterpieces, *Don Giovanni* and *Così fan Tutte*. In these two great works the two forms: (1) Opera Seria and (2) Opera Buffa—that is, of Tragedy and Comedy—are for the first time in the history of opera perfectly united into one, and we may take as a sign that Mozart was aware of this new unity the fact that he described each of them as a *dramma giocoso* instead of *opera buffa*. It is also significant that these two works are precisely those which have most puzzled musicians, musicologists, and music-lovers during the past hundred years.

What puzzles the average person is just this strange blend of the tragic and the comic. Most people like to have these elements carefully separated into different works of art so that they may feel safe. They are prepared to look upon life as either a comedy or a tragedy, since in such a presentation life is made a little less real and provides a form of escape, a convention or refuge. One may thus laugh or weep to the full, knowing in one's heart that life is not quite like this; it is neither so comic nor so tragic. When, however, a major dramatist like Shakespeare (or, on a smaller scale, Ibsen or Tchekov) combines in one piece the tragic and the comic, the average person does not know where he is. Is he meant to laugh or weep? Is the author truly serious or is he laughing up his sleeve? Not only does the auditor feel that his leg is being pulled, but he is not quite sure which leg, and that spoils the whole thing for him. The history of the reception of Shakespeare's plays by the French is an example of a whole nation (with rare exceptions) being outraged by what seemed to its logical genius a frantic illogicality, amounting almost to lunacy. But the French are not the only ones to suspect lunacy. English Shakespearean criticism is tainted with the suspicion that Hamlet is more or less mad, and perhaps Shakespeare, too.

Now, in Mozart we have an exact musical parallel to Shakespeare. Critics have been perplexed to exhaustion by the question whether *Don Giovanni* is or is not a comic opera. Can an opera be comic when its chief character ends by being dragged down to hell in flames, to music of awe-inspiring solemnity and terror? Or is this a great joke of Mozart's—his supreme and final joke? Some have actually thought so and have pointed to the concluding sestet, the tempo of which is marked *Presto*—that is, very fast—in which the three women and the three men sing with the utmost liveliness the words:

"Questo è il fin di chi fa mal (This is the end of one who lived ill)."

This lively sestet has so bothered musicians that in five out of six representations of *Don Giovanni* during the nineteenth century it was cut out as introducing a disturbing levity, or even, perhaps, mockery, at the end of an intensely moral tragedy in which Mozart uses trombones for the first time in the score with terrific effect. "But how can a comic opera have trombones?" groan the musical pedants, enslaved by their knowledge of musical history! In those days, as these scholars are aware, trombones were only used for solemn or religious music; a trombone in a comic opera was unthinkable! Mozart, however, thought of it, for Mozart was not writing a conventional comedy or tragedy. His *Don Giovanni* is not to be put into either class, for in this work Mozart transcends not only the academic formal classifications but also the conventional categories of good and evil, and blends the tragic and the comic into a unity which is not to be dissolved.

Even Professor Dent in his admirable book on Mozart's operas seems to me to have a distorted conception of *Don Giovanni*, owing perhaps to a certain moral conventionality of judgment and a temperamental dislike to intensity of expression. He actually states that Mozart "has intended to depict Donna Anna as not quite in her right mind" and refers to "violence of expression" and "Anna's ravings," commenting that Mozart "had a tendency to lay his colours on more thickly than was always appropriate to the style." Elsewhere he says that there is nothing tragic about Donna Anna; as if what he calls her "ravings" were not completely accounted for by seeing her father murdered by Don Giovanni before her eyes. In fact, he is quite inconsistent in his attempt to make out that *Don Giovanni* is only an opera buffa after all, and actually says: "a really serious treatment of the whole story would have been too utterly repulsive for stage-presentation." This totally disregards the intense realism of Mozart.

But we have the librettist's (da Ponte's) own statement, which Professor Dent even quotes, that Mozart wished to treat the subject seriously, and this he has certainly done. But to treat human experience seriously requires a comprehensive vision that includes both the comic and the tragic. Critics who try to turn *Don Giovanni* into an opera buffa have a conventionally moral attitude to, rather than a tragic view of, life; while critics who, like Beethoven, cannot understand how Mozart could write an opera on what they consider to be so immoral a subject as *Don Giovanni* are deficient in the detachment and universality which enable geniuses such as Shakespeare and Mozart to be serious without being earnest and to preserve that sense of proportion in which the essence of comedy lies. *Don Giovanni*, I maintain, is an intensely serious opera in which the tragic and the comic are inextricably blended with such mastery and truth that the effect is unutterably grand.

Così fan Tutte (Thus do All Women)

The second great opera to be described by Mozart as a *dramma giocoso*, is *Così fan Tutte*. It was commissioned by the Emperor Joseph II of Austria for the Vienna opera in 1789, and the libretto was written by the Italian poet Lorenzo da Ponte, who also wrote the books for Mozart's *Figaro* and *Don Giovanni*. The subject is supposed to have been taken from an actual occurrence in Vienna some time previous to the writing of the opera; nevertheless this groundwork of possible actuality has not been sufficient to put literary and musical critics on their guard against dismissing the plot as absurd, ridiculous, etc., etc., because it did not square with their preconceptions about men and women, love and sex. The libretto of *Così fan Tutte* has been a constant object of attack, and this attack has been prolonged throughout the nineteenth century until the present day by the seemingly irreconcilable fact that Mozart—in the opinion of all the best musicians from generation to generation—had put into this opera some of the finest music he ever wrote and that from a musical point of view it might even be considered to be the most perfect and flawless of all his operas. Consequently there have been numerous attempts during the past hundred years to rewrite the text with the notion of fitting to this flawless music an equally flawless and satisfying libretto. Needless to say, all these attempts have failed, thus showing that fate sets a limit even to the stupidity of men.

The controversy about the text is far from having ceased, even today; for example, Professor Edward J. Dent in his dissertation on Mozart's operas calls the foundation of the libretto an idea "in itself absurd enough." For Professor Dent the libretto of *Così fan Tutte* is an artificial comedy. It may be true that Lorenzo da Ponte wrote it less seriously than Mozart composed it, but none the less I think he wrote it as a serious comedy; by which I mean that it had the ironic truthfulness of deliberately conceived satire, which is essential to true comedy. To call it an "artificial" comedy is to mislead the reader, unless one is very careful to point out that one is using the word "artificial" in a very special sense—namely, in the sense that every work of art must be an artifice—that is, something made within a convention and not something that has happened in nature.

This artifice or convention of the theatre which requires that a drama representing the experience of many years has to be exhibited within the space of three hours consecutively on the stage is all that is artificial about the libretto of *Così fan Tutte*. We are given a dramatic fiction by means of which we are to be shown two pairs of lovers, a maid-servant, and an onlooker who is the mainspring of the action, in a complete and psychologically convincing plot. The action of this plot—which in real life would be spread over at least many months—is telescoped for the theatre into the space of a few hours. This is quite ingeniously and artfully done and shows the exceptional skill of Lorenzo da Ponte as a writer for the theatre. We may also assume that Mozart himself had a hand in the devising of the plot, for although we know no details of the collaboration between poet and composer during the writing of *Così fan Tutte*, as we do in some other cases, yet we know that Mozart was very particular about the text of his operas and that in the earlier operas he made many suggestions to his librettist and secured various alterations to meet his requirements. We may presume, therefore, that in the case of a collaborator such as Lorenzo da Ponte, with whom he had twice before worked successfully, Mozart may be given a fair share of responsibility for the libretto of *Così fan Tutte* as it exists.

Now let us see exactly what the plot of *Così fan Tutte* is. First of all I shall set down the list of characters:

Fiordiligi	sisters from Ferara living in Naples
Dorabella	
Guglielmo	lovers of the two sisters,
Ferrando	officers in the Neapolitan Army
Despina,	maid to the sisters
Don Alfonso,	an old philosopher

It will be noticed that this is an ideal cast for a comedy as it consists of only six characters, not one of whom is superfluous to the action, which is managed with extreme economy. The play opens with the young officers sitting in a café drinking with Don Alfonso and bragging about the merits of their

respective young women. Don Alfonso maintains that they
are like any other two young women and no more or less constant. An absolutely constant woman, he says, is like the
phœnix, a bird often talked about but never seen. Each of
the lovers, however, declares his prospective bride to be this
phœnix. In the end they agree to a wager. The two young men
promise on their word of honour to do exactly what Don
Alfonso tells them to do for the next twenty-four hours and
he in return promises to prove to them the inconstancy of
their two mistresses.

In the next scene the two girls are awaiting the lovers, each
of whom they declare to be the best and bravest of men.
Alfonso enters with the news that the two young men have
been ordered to join their regiment on active service. The
lovers enter, there is a sad farewell, and the two young men
go off to the strains of a military march of the regimental
band. In the next scene the maid, Despina, brings the two
disconsolate young women their chocolate and tries to console
them, but their grief seems inconsolable. Then Alfonso, who
has bribed Despina and let her into the secret as an accom-
plice, arrives bringing in the two young men now disguised as
foreigners. They pay court to the two sisters but are indignantly repulsed, to their own great delight. Don Alfonso,
however, tells them that all is not over yet and reminds them
of their promise to obey his commands. He now instructs
them to persist in their suit and finally to pretend to take
poison in the ladies' presence as a sign of their desperate love.
All this they do. The terrified sisters send Despina for the
doctor and Despina returns disguised as a physician, who re-
stores them to life by waving over their dead bodies a large
magnet. This, incidentally, is a skit on a prevailing medical
fashion of the time, a fashionable cure no more and no less
silly than any of the fashionable medical panaceas before or
since.

The young men restored to life now return to their ardent
wooing of the sisters, each paying his addresses to his friend's
betrothed. But their feigned death has awakened sympathy in
the young women and presently Dorabella responds to Guglielmo's endearments, much to the consternation of Ferrando,
who, when he hears of it, wants to break the pact. Don Alfonso reminds him of his bond and Ferrando again pursues

Fiordiligi, who, being made of sterner stuff than her sister, only succumbs when Ferrando is about to kill himself at her feet. A double marriage is now arranged, with Despina, as the pretended notary bringing the marriage contracts. A feast is prepared and as they are about to sign the contracts the military band of the returning regiment is heard. The young men rush out in their disguises and return as their original selves, to the consternation of the sisters. Reconciliation is made by Don Alfonso, who says philosophically: "This is how all women behave," and the drama ends happily with the marriage festivities of the proper lovers.

Now, it is a sign of the extraordinary imbecility and sentimentality of the average critic that this play, which is not only profoundly true in its portraiture of human nature but reveals four young men and women in a most favourable light, has everywhere been attacked for its unreality and cynicism. There is nothing cynical or disagreeable in it from beginning to end. As a woman once declared to me, it "only shows the charming and essentially responsive nature of women," and those who are so dull-witted as not to be able to accept the necessary stage convention of the young women not seeing through the disguises of their lovers and of the telescoping of the action within the space of a few hours are not yet equipped for the understanding and appreciation of dramatic art.

Now, how has Mozart treated this plot? That is the vital question. Has he written for it charming and superficial music such as would justify the interpretation of those who declare it frivolous and artificial—in the sense of being unreal—the sort of music which a Johann or even a Richard Strauss would write? Far from it! He has written for this opera the most tender, poignant, intensely dramatic and powerful music of which he was capable. He has made every character real, pulsing with life, and has given to each one all the emotions proper to such experiences as young love, the anguish of separation, the horror of infidelity, the ruthlessness of nature, the unexpectedness of one's own natural behavior, the tortures of jealousy, and the differences in human characters even when fundamentally they are subject to the same iron laws of nature. In short, *Così fan Tutte* is a tragicomedy and the most profound and terrifying work of its kind that has ever been written; for it neither idealizes nor sentimentalizes nor falsifies the reality and the depth of human feelings—especially in the sex-relationship between normal young men and women. *Così fan Tutte*, far from being the silly, artificial comedy which it has so often been described as being, is, on the contrary, a work of an iron realism in which Mozart pours out in marvellous music, always just, proper, and adequate to every occasion, the delight, anguish, and desperation of human hearts who, finding themselves behaving exactly contrary to their own preconceived notions of what they are and of what they want to be, are bewildered and tortured.

The music given to Guglielmo when he discovers that Fiordiligi is also untrue; the sublime aria given to Fiordiligi when, in despair, she realizes that she too is weak and is about to give way to newly awakened feelings and sings to her absent lover: "Forgive the error of this loving heart; the knowledge of it shall at least never be revealed except to the flowers of this garden"—these things alone are sufficient to prove how passionately and seriously Mozart conceived this opera, which I personally am inclined to think is his most perfect achievement in opera and a masterpiece of a kind which stands absolutely alone and unequalled in the history of art, even if we think that in some respects *Don Giovanni* is greater and *Die Zauberflöte* more sublime.

We now come to the third of the great operas of Mozart, that in which he has succeeded in attaining to the highest dramatic expression in the comic and in the super-tragic or religious, both united, however, into one work of art so that the two elements of the comic and the serious are inseparable, are indeed made into one great synthesis:

Die Zauberflöte

Grand Opera in Two Acts, words by Schikaneder and Gieseke, based on the story of *Lulu or The Magic Flute* from Wieland's *Dschinnistan*; the plot was modified after the production on June 8, 1791 of an opera based on the same story, *Kasper der Fagottist oder Die Zauberzither*, words from *Lulu* by Perinet and music composed by Wenzel Müller.

Mozart was at work on *Die Zauberflöte* as early as June 11, for on that date he writes to his wife in Baden that "out of sheer tedium I have composed an aria for the opera" and also quotes a line from the text: *"Tod und Verzweiflung war sein*

Lohn,"[1] and on the following day (June 12) he writes that he went to hear the new opera *Kasper der Fagottist*, "which has made such a noise, but there is nothing in it."

The characters and plot of *Die Zauberflöte* are as follow:

Zarastro, a magician who reigns in the Temple of Wisdom
Tamino, a Prince
Orator
First, second, and third Priests
Queen of Night
Pamina, daughter of the Queen of Night
First, second, and third Ladies
Papageno, a bird-catcher
An old woman (Papagena)
Monostatos, a Moor
First, second, and third Genii

It consists of an Overture, an Introduction, 9 Arias, 1 Aria with chorus, 2 Duets, 3 Terzets, 2 Quintets, 1 Chorus of Priests, 1 March of Priests, and 2 Finales.

The plot is, roughly, an account of the trials undergone by Tamino before he is received by Zarastro into the Temple of Wisdom and given Pamina as bride. He is accompanied on his trials by his Sancho Panza, Papageno, who does not have to undergo any of them but lives altogether in a lower world, ignorant of all that happens in the spirit of Tamino but experiencing certain trials and vexations on his own plane and being in his place awarded his proper mate, Papagena.

I now refer the reader back to the diagram at the beginning of this chapter, from which he will see that I have shown *Die Zauberflöte* as a special combination of the whole gamut of opera, comprising the threefold root of poetry, dancing, and music in its entirety; no longer as a primitive beginning but, on the contrary, as a culmination in which the widest divergences—due to the specialized development extending from, though not including, secular dramatic tragedy to religious ritual—are once again recombined. From my diagram, "The Genealogy of Opera," it may be seen how *Die Zauberflöte* descends via singspiel through intermezzo from comedy, folksong and dance and via oratorio and ritual from serious religious drama. From this diagram we may see that *Don Gio-*

[1] Death and Despair were his reward.

vanni and *Die Zauberflöte* are two works which may be
described as two poles opposite to each other, since the tragic
element which is the counterbalance to the comic in *Don
Giovanni* is replaced by the super-tragic or religious element
as a counterbalance to the comic in *Die Zauberflöte*. The
dualism which is inescapable from all human thought thus
returns into *Die Zauberflöte*, which at first sight may seem
one-sided through its lack of the tragic element.

Don Giovanni, in including the tragic, excludes the religious element, while in *Die Zauberflöte* the religious necessarily excludes the tragic. The comic and the serious are nevertheless combined in both works; but, just as the failure of
Papageno to rise to the level of Tamino in *Die Zauberflöte*
is accepted not only as no personal tragedy for him but as a
delightful comic way of life with its own validity, so the
career of *Don Giovanni* in the other opera has no religious
significance but is a purely personal experience in which his
so-called "damnation" (the dragging down into hell) is merely
symbolical of his exclusion from certain other and, if you like,
higher experiences due to his nature—just as Papageno owing
to *his* nature is excluded from certain of the experiences of
Tamino.

There is, however, in Mozart's presentation in both operas
no confusion of the higher and the lower. What Don Giovanni is excluded from is not the mixed good and evil of a
Don Ottavio or a Tamino on a superior plane, or of a Leporello or a Papageno on an inferior plane; he exists on an altogether different plane and his opposite is Zarastro. The extraordinarily universal quality of Mozart's genius enables him to
represent all these human characters and the superhuman
characters with complete sympathy without any conventional
moral judgment. The dualism of the universe as manifested in
human life is accepted by Mozart. Tamino and Papageno are
Don Quixote and Sancho Panza over again. They may be said
to represent the spiritual and the material in their mixed
human manifestations. Mozart shows no desire whatever (any
more than Cervantes) to turn Papageno into Tamino. His
extraordinary dramatic instinct is shown by the fact that the
real counter-figure to Don Giovanni is not put into the opera
Don Giovanni at all. It is Zarastro from *Die Zauberflöte*, not
Don Ottavio in *Don Giovanni*, who is the polar force oppo-

site to Don Giovanni. Mozart has thus heightened the significance of Don Giovanni by giving him full swing—that is, by giving him his full rights and thus not being afraid to let it be seen plainly what a poor figure the Don Ottavios of the world cut beside a Don Giovanni as conceived by a Mozart. The terrific power of Don Giovanni is a witness to the greatness of Mozart, as the figure of Satan in *Paradise Lost* is to the greatness of Milton; but it is an ironic commentary on the moralizers of the world that the good men, the Ottavios and the Taminos, do not attain to the same grandeur and force as Don Giovanni. This is because they are drawn to a smaller scale, since real goodness is not a quality attainable by normal human beings. Mozart's conception of men was the opposite of Rousseau's, who thought all men were born good but became corrupted. For Mozart the good and bad in men was (so it seems, singular as it may appear) necessarily and inevitably mixed; he evidently considers Papageno just as worthwhile as Tamino, and Leporello just as valuable as Ottavio. Neither Don Giovanni nor Zarastro is conceived as a real human being by Mozart but rather as a supernatural force. It is also significant that the women in all his great operas are all neither great nor small but thoroughly real. The one exception to this is the Queen of the Night in *Die Zauberflöte*. In my opinion she is a sheer incidental ebullience of Mozart's genius; he has created her by virtue of his music but she plays no real role in the drama since it would have required a poet of Shakespearean genius to have given her complete significance as a figure on the same superhuman scale as Zarastro and opposed to him in a convincing action. It is sufficient that Mozart made her *appear*. She is a witness to the same instinctive creative power in him which went to the making of a Don Giovanni and a Zarastro, but he was not given a dramatic action which enabled her to display herself completely and as he was a musician and not a poet he could not by himself have invented such a dramatic action. Having made her appear, he had therefore to make her disappear, because such a being could not have existed in the plot of *Die Zauberflöte* as it stands. There would have to have been a real conflict between the Queen of the Night and Zarastro, which in itself would be an all-sufficient theme for another drama. We are not given that drama, but a totally different one, and one from which she must vanish or decline to a mere lay figure in absolute contradiction to her appearance in Mozart's music. That Mozart dropped the Queen of the Night as a serious protagonist to Zarastro is in obedience to the same law which excluded any intrusion of the religious element into the opera *Don Giovanni*, since the inclusion of the Queen of the Night as a real and equal protagonist opposed to Zarastro in a real conflict to be fought out in *Die Zauberflöte* would have introduced into that opera the element of tragedy. By excluding religion from *Don Giovanni* and tragedy from *Die Zauberflöte* Mozart has created two great polar works in each of which the destiny of a group of human beings is worked out under the influence of a dominating supernatural or supernormal power—the power of Don Giovanni and the power of Zarastro respectively. Thus each of these great works is an expression of human life conceived under one of the two poles of Good and Evil and is a sublime demonstration of the fact that human morality is only relative and that above and beyond it are great mysterious forces of the universe working out their own destiny, to whose existence the very music of Mozart is a sufficient testimony.

XIX. *Kierkegaard on Mozart and Music*

The Danish philosopher Sören Kierkegaard[1] in his famous book *Entweder—Oder, ein Lebensfragment,* published in Copenhagen in 1843, wrote a remarkable essay entitled *"Die Stadien des unmittelbar Erotischen oder das Musikalische-Erotische* (The Stages of the Directly Erotic or the Musical-Erotic)." This essay covers eighty-two closely printed pages in the German edition of Eugen Diederichs (Jena, 1922) and ninety-four pages in the German edition of C. Ludwig Un-

---

[1]In justice to Kierkegaard I have to emphasize that his disquisition on *Don Giovanni* is only a part of a book called by him *"ein Lebensfragment"* and that it is rather a declaration of love than a philosophic essay. If I have appeared to treat it unsympathetically here it is because I have confined myself to the examination of some of the very interesting ideas he throws out in the course of his declaration of love for Mozart. With the declaration itself I am in complete sympathy.

gelenk (Dresden and Leipzig, 1927) and has ostensibly as its subject Mozart's opera *Don Giovanni*.

Not being acquainted with the Danish language, I have used these two German editions and I have translated literally in my own hand the whole of this essay solely with the purpose of discovering for myself exactly what Kierkegaard has to say on *Don Giovanni*. He is a difficult writer, owing partly to his extreme elaboration, not to say diffuseness, and neither of the two German translations I have used is particularly lucid. There are famous living Continental musicians who think Kierkegaard's long essay to be the finest thing ever written about Mozart, and in view of Kierkegaard's immense reputation it was obviously necessary to study this essay.

It is easy to sneer at philosophers. What they have to say is generally obvious when it is true, and unsound when it appears original. Kierkegaard is hardly an exception. He abounds in platitudes—in which he resembles German rather than Greek, French, or even Italian thinkers. Also he is long-winded to a degree that almost drives the reader frantic. What he has to say he says over and over again. Worse than this is a sort of latent sentimentality, that sentimentality which seems to spring from pent-up feelings that have been corrupted by repression; so that he is most frequently indirect and rarely direct. His indirectness is not always the ironic approach of a highly subtle and keen mind but frequently the ingratiating, almost apologetic round-aboutness of a man who is nursing his emotion as if it were his illegitimate baby and his respect for legitimacy were greater than his natural love.

Philosophers, without any exception known to me, are never at their best when writing about any of the arts. I think it is impossible for a thinker who is not primarily an artist to discuss art in a way that will satisfy artists that he really understands what he is talking about. This is particularly true of music, which is an art that a great many people can enjoy—and even enjoy deeply—without much understanding of its nature. Since the average educated European is taught as a child the reading and writing of the notation of letters, but not that of music, he is familiar with literature in a way in which he never becomes familiar with music. There seems to him no mystery in literature, but music seems to him a great mystery.

Actually the mystery—I mean by "mystery" that creative use of literature or music which makes it an art—is equally great in both cases and exactly the same essentially.

What is the function of art? I would say that at bottom it is nothing more or less than the expression of the relationship between an individual and the universe. We do not know what an individual is nor do we know what the universe is. Neither art nor science can answer these questions; but it is the foundation of human life that the individual exists separated in some finite way from a surrounding universe and yet in communication with it. The individual is, as it were, isolated but not cut off—and his communication is art. Therefore the nature of all the arts is essentially the same—the communication or relationship of the individual with the universe.

In men of genius this communication is more than commonly intense and profound. That is why their works, in which this relationship is expressed, are so stimulating to other men and women, who find their own living enriched by contact with them just as a piece of steel is magnetized when an electric current passes through it. This "electric current" is the artist's own life, his experiencing power with which he has magnetized his work. Works of art are therefore, as it were, bodies magnetized by the artist. And this living essence of the artist—which is, as I have said, actually a relationship, an experience between him as an individual and the universe —is what used to be called in religious writings the soul.

The value of a work of art is nothing more or less than the value of the soul of the artist—that is, the value of the active relationship between him and the universe. It is this that makes great works of art profoundly refreshing and regenerating. In experiencing a great work of art it is as if we were bathing in the ocean of the universe and all its virtue and richness were passing into us and becoming a part of us. In other words, when we truly experience a great work of art we are, as it were, flooded with new life.

Now, this being so, it is clear that all the arts—poetry, drama, literature, painting, sculpture, music—have essentially the same function; it is only their means which seem different. At this point I can quote the first thing Kierkegaard has to say about Mozart's music in his essay on *Don Giovanni*:

"Since the hour when my soul was most deeply seized by

Mozart's music and inclined before it in humble admiration it has often been both a delightful and quickening occupation to reflect upon it as that joyful Hellenic contemplation of the world (according to which it is named *cosmos* because it appears as a well-ordered whole, as a tasteful and transparent veil of the spirit which forms and transforms it), as that gay and serene way of contemplation repeated in a higher order of things, in the world of the ideal; since here also an ordering wisdom prevails which in a marvellous way brings together in due course all that is related to one another . . . Homer with the Trojan War, Raphael with Catholicism, Mozart with Don Juan.

"There is a miserable incredulity which presents itself with a learned air. It says: such mutual approaches are accidental and it finds in them nothing but a fortunate collision of different powers in the game of life. It takes it as accidental that two lovers meet, as accidental that they love each other; there might be a hundred other maidens with whom he could have been just as happy, whom he might have loved just as tenderly. Such incredulity supposes that many a poet has lived who might have become as immortal as Homer if the latter had not first already used up this splendid material, and many a composer just as undying as Mozart if only the opportunity had offered itself. Now, for all mediocrities this is a marvellously consoling and soothing idea by means of which they and all like them imagine that it is a pure mistake of Fate, a world-wide error that they have not become as excellent as certain others. Thus there spreads a cheapening optimism.

"But to every high-minded person, to every aristocrat to whom it is less important to make something of oneself in this miserable fashion than to forget oneself in the contemplation of true greatness, this is naturally a horror, whereas it is a holy bliss and delight to see united what belongs together. Such marriages are fortunate but not by chance; for they require two factors whereas chance belongs to the unarticulated interruptions of Fate. This divine collaboration of forces is the good fortune of history, making the feast and gala days in the course of the years. The accidental has only one factor: it is an accident that Homer found in the Trojan War the most pregnant epic material conceivable. Fortune has two factors: it is a special luck that the most pregnant epic material was given to a Homer. Here the emphasis is as much on Homer as on the material, whence comes the deep harmony which informs every product we call classical. So it is with Mozart. It is a piece of good fortune that this, in the deepest sense, perhaps unique musical subject was given to no other than Mozart.

"With his *Don Juan* Mozart enters the small immortal band of men whose names and works time will not forget since eternity remembers them and although it may be unimportant to each one among this band whether he stands high or low—since, in a certain sense, all stand equally high, being infinitely high—although, here, struggle for the highest or lowest place is just as childish as a struggle for the first place at Confirmation before the altar, yet I am childish enough or, rather, like a young girl I am so in love with Mozart that, cost what it may, I must place him first. . . . And I shall ask Mozart to forgive me if his music instead of inspiring me to great deeds has turned me into a fool who has lost the little sense he had, so that I now spend my time in melancholy, humming softly what I don't understand, what hovers round me like spirits day and night. Immortal Mozart, you to whom I owe everything, to whom I owe it that once again my soul has lost itself in wonder, yes, is thrilled to its depths, to whom I owe it that I have not gone through this life without being deeply shaken, that I have not died without having loved even though my love has been unfortunate! What wonder then that I am more jealous of his glory than of the happiest moments of my life, more jealous of his immortality than of my own existence! Yes, should he be taken away, his name erased, then the one pillar would fall which till now has prevented everything collapsing for me into a frightful chaos, a terrible nothingness."

Philosophers have an unfortunate habit of letting an idea run away with them and, instead of checking their idea or theory by a scrupulous observation of the facts, they distort the facts to fit their beloved idea. So Kierkegaard starts with several ideas at the beginning of his essay on *Don Giovanni* and all his observations are made to illustrate these ideas. One of these ideas is that speech, or language, is the most concrete medium and music the most abstract medium. He does not define what he means by a concrete medium, he merely states that the "most concrete of all mediums is speech." He further says: "the medium required by architecture is the most abstract one can think of," and also that music is an abstract medium. I think that Kierkegaard has made a mistake in trying to divide the artist's medium into two classes of concrete and abstract and I am supported by the fact that he nowhere attempts a definition of concrete. We cannot accept his dogmatic statement that speech is the most concrete of mediums and that the medium furthest removed from speech is the most abstract as a satisfactory definition.

Actually Kierkegaard is here making a division between the medium and the content which he elsewhere wisely repudiates. For there is no such thing in art as a material or a medium in itself, separated from the idea of which it is the form. The material and the idea are one and inseparable. Kierkegaard himself points this out in an interesting passage:

"Should one emphasize Homer's poetical capacity—shown in the working of the material—one might easily forget that the poem would never have become what it is if the Idea which Homer has expressed, the Idea immanent in the poem, had not already been the innermost form of the material itself. The poet desires his matter. To desire is no art, one may say, and this is quite true of a mass of weak poetic ideas. Rightly to desire is, on the contrary, a great art, or rather it is a gift. This is the inexplicable mystery of genius like the divining rod which never has the idea of desiring unless what it desires is there.

"There has existed a school of æstheticians who, because they suggested the significance of form, were not guiltless of spreading a misunderstanding to the contrary. I have often wondered how those æstheticians could without further explanation adhere to the Hegelian philosophy when even a general acquaintance with Hegel, especially with his *Æsthetic*, convinces us that he actually emphasizes the importance of the material in respect of æsthetics. Naturally, material and form belong together fundamentally and a single reflection will suffice to prove this, since otherwise such a phenomenon would be inexplicable."

If, however, it is impossible to separate the medium from the idea, what becomes of Kierkegaard's analysis of ideas as such? He never faces this fundamental objection, but it is an objection which goes to the root of philosophy, and once we have stated this objection, we see that it is destructive of all absolutes and explains why all that philosophy which deals in absolutes is so lifeless and barren. The more real philosophy is that which is itself a work of art and belongs to the art of writing. Nevertheless, absolutes, though they must never be taken for realities, have their use; so the classification of ideas can be used in a way similar to the use of such unrealities as numbers in mathematics and the use of such non-existent things as points and straight lines in the artificial three-dimensional geometry of Euclid.

Therefore let us consider another of Kierkegaard's ideas:

"The more abstract the idea, the smaller the probability of a repetition. How does the idea become concrete? By being penetrated historically. The more concrete the idea, the greater the probability of repetition. . . . So the idea appearing in sculpture is thoroughly abstract and stands scarcely in any relation to a historical event. . . ."

Whereas, he says, "history incessantly deposits new epic stuff," and so, although Homer is a classic, we can "imagine a number of classic works in the class which includes epic poetry." So he considers *The Trojan War* a concrete idea and *Don Giovanni* an abstract idea and says:

"Because the idea is so limitlessly abstract and the medium likewise abstract there is no probability that Mozart should ever have a competitor. It was most lucky for Mozart to find a material which was absolutely musical in itself, and should at any time a composer want to rival Mozart, there is nothing else for him but to recompose *Don Giovanni*.

"Homer also found a perfect epic material, but one can think of a whole row of epic poems, since history is ever providing epic material. What I mean can be best seen by contrasting with *Don Giovanni* a similar idea. Goethe's *Faust* is certainly a classic work but the idea is historical and therefore every significant epoch will have its *Faust*. *Faust* has speech as its medium, and since this is a much more concrete medium, so on this account many works can be imagined having the same tendency. *Don Giovanni*, on the contrary, remains the only work of its kind, in the same way as the classic works of Greek sculpture.

"But as the idea of *Don Giovanni* is still much more abstract than any in sculpture, so one can easily see that in sculpture one has a number of works, but in music only one.

"Truly, it is possible to imagine many classical works in music; but there remains always only one work of which one can say that its idea is absolutely musical, that music does not enter it as an accompaniment but displays its own innermost being while revealing the idea. Therefore Mozart stands with his *Don Giovanni* first among the immortals."

Nonsense as all this may appear and, as it appears, *is*, yet there is some useful meaning to be extracted from it. The idea of *Faust* is surely not any more or less historical than the idea of *Don Juan?* Kierkegaard is led into confusion by his dogmatic statements; but some of these dogmatic statements have virtue in spite of the contradictions into which they lead Kierkegaard and those who can only follow him literally. But let me take this statement by Kierkegaard:

"The most abstract imaginable Idea is the sensuous quality of Genius."

Here is something valuable. It cannot even be spoiled by Kierkegaard's immediately following sentences:

"But through what medium may it be represented? Only and solely through music. In sculpture it cannot be represented because it is as such something inward. Just as little may it be painted, for it does not allow itself to be put in a definite outline, since it is utterly lyrical, a gusto, a power, a storm, a passion. . . . It cannot be represented in poetry either."

I am afraid it is not only a characteristic of philosophers to avoid difficulties; but they are as tender with their ideas as mothers with their children and as reluctant as are some mothers to let them face hard facts. Surely it is not true that what is inward cannot be expressed by what is outward? The whole problem of every art lies precisely in the necessity of expressing the inner by the outer—that is, of giving form to idea—which otherwise has no sensuous existence. Kierkegaard's "sensuous quality of genius" is precisely what is given line and colour in great painting and sculpture—therein is the whole mystery of all creative art, and to think that music is more inward than painting and sculpture is to have a false conception of it. As for poetry, Kierkegaard does not even attempt to produce an argument; he merely states dogmatically that poetry cannot do it, which is again untrue.

The whole of Kierkegaard's attempt to make out that music is more inward and more abstract than any other art falls to the ground. It involves him in an immense amount of vague or contradictory rigmarole. Let me add, also, that "a gusto, a power, a storm, a passion" are not limited to music but can even be expressed in architecture. And with this collapse of his theory about music collapses also his attempt to make out that *Don Giovanni* is Mozart's one classical work; because it is based on the assumption that the idea of *Don Juan* is the most abstract of all possible ideas and that music is the most abstract of all possible arts, and that since these two super-abstracts are united together in the one work, and only in that work, therefore it follows that *Don Giovanni* is the unique classical work of art in existence. A philosopher might accept this idea, but no musician would.

I myself have something to say on the meaning of "classical," but before dealing with this subject I wish to refer to another notion of Kierkegaard's. I shall not deal here with his acute and interesting remarks about the Greek and Christian attitudes to the erotic because it is much too big a subject and would take us too far afield; but one of his ideas is that Christianity introduced into the world the idea of the Sensual-Erotic as a principle or power that could be represented and that if this is to be expressed directly it can only be done in its directness in music; for if it is expressed in language it must of necessity be given indirect or reflective expression and ranged under ethical rules. Here again we see the philosopher with his limited conception of the nature and power of literature and equally limited—though in the opposite direction—conception of music. It is possible to be as indirect in music as in literature. Poetry and drama can be direct or indirect; so can music. Music can also be as descriptive and imitative as literature. It is an inadequate knowledge of music that has led Kierkegaard to make this unreal division, just as it is a too great acquaintance with the rationalizing and categorizing branch of literature that makes him overlook its tremendous power to express feelings.

Actually, but quite unconsciously, he has been compelled to make his highly elaborate argument and demonstration of the special character of the art of music by his sufferings due to the one-sided development of literature. Even today, when literature is at last escaping from its enslavement to the propaganda of moral, though not yet of ethical, political, and formal criticism, so that its creative function may begin to be enjoyed, the very fact that it lies ready at hand for every man to use and that even educated men do not yet perceive that so-called moral laws, ethical principles, and political, sociological, and economic theories have no more importance than the rules of counterpoint and harmony, and that the true values lie wholly and solely in the realm of the æsthetic is an obstacle which prevents us from realizing that the creative function of literature as an art is the same as that of music or any of the other arts—namely, the expression of the relationship between the individual and the universe. What real differences there may be between the arts are not touched upon by Kierkegaard and I shall not deal with them here.

It is amusing to find Kierkegaard saying:

1. "I think, among other things, that Mozart is the greatest of all classics and that *Don Giovanni* deserves the first place among all classical productions,"
and then:

2. "There is no doubt that music considered as a medium presents in all circumstances a very interesting problem. On the other hand it is doubtful if I am in a position to say anything satisfactory about it. I know quite well that I understand nothing about music. I admit freely that I am a layman. I shall not hide that I do not belong to the chosen class of musical connoisseurs . . . and though I feel that music is an art about which one cannot have a right idea without a high degree of experience, I console myself with the thought . . . that Diana, who had not herself given birth, could come to the help of those giving birth; yes, that she had this gift from childhood . . . so that she was able to help her mother at her own birth."

I shall now leave Kierkegaard's general ideas and confine myself to some of his interesting remarks on the character of Don Juan in Mozart's opera. He says:

"Don Juan is actually neither Idea—that is, Power, Life— nor Individual; he hovers between both. This hovering is, however, the life of music. When the sea is in motion the foaming waves form all kinds of shapes like living beings and it seems then as if these beings wriggled into the waves whereas, on the contrary, the motion of the waves produces them. So Don Juan is an apparition that indeed comes into appearance but never condenses into firm shape, an Individual that constantly arises but never is finished, of whose history we learn no more than what the roaring of the waves tells us.

"If one conceives of Don Juan thus, everything becomes full of meaning and significance. If I think of him as a single individual . . . it seems funny that he has seduced one thousand and three maidens; for while he becomes an individual the accent falls on the wrong place: it matters, it is essential whom and how he has seduced. . . . If I conceive Don Juan musically, I then have before me the power of nature, the dæmonic, which never wearies of seducing, which never stops —as little as the wind stops blowing, the sea rolling, and the cataract tires of falling from a height. . . .

"The number one thousand and three is, namely, odd and accidental and that is by no means unimportant, for it gives the impression that the list is not closed, that Don Juan is still in swing. . . ."

All this is true and is perfectly said. Kierkegaard goes on from this to point out a difference between spiritual and sensual love which I do not think sound—since he bases it on an incorrect *a priori* notion of individuality being in the one and not in the other. I shall therefore not discuss it here but pass on to another idea of his, which is that music does not express the singular but the general because music is too abstract to express differences. The reason Kierkegaard gives here is certainly unsound, because music can express many differences and extremely subtle ones. Surely the distinction is that music can express differences in mood, feeling, character, but not in intellectual concepts as such; that is, music is not argument though it may be persuasion. His representation of Don Juan as not an individual but as the incarnation of Desire is excellent:

"The power of desire never grows weak and only when he desires is he in his right element. There he sits spreading joy like a god and drains the goblet, jumps up, napkin in hand, and is ready for the onslaught . . . his life foams and bubbles like the wine with which he refreshes himself."

If it be true that this Desire can be expressed more directly in music than in any other art, it is because it is pure feeling without reflection. But I think also painting and sculpture and lyric poetry cannot be denied this power.

I shall now pass on to consider Kierkegaard's conception of the idea of the classical in art.

In every definition or description of the word *classical* sooner or later the word or some such word as *proportion* must appear. Everybody recognizes that works of art which we name classical are distinguished by a balance, a harmony of qualities, which is what we mean by saying they have a just proportion. No one element or quality is apparently sacrificed to another in them, and this is the source of their harmony and the satisfaction they give.

I am inclined to believe that, on the other hand, all life—and thus, in works of art, all vitality—is due to disproportion, to a lack of balance, and that life itself is the effort to achieve this balance. This idea is in itself suggested by the very word *static*, which so readily associates itself with the word *classical*. The idea of *cold* is also very near the word *classical*—a cold and classic beauty means essentially a beauty that one admires without passion.

The word *romantic*, on the other hand, is intimately connected with passion. Romantic love is in itself a description of this antithesis to classical admiration and suggests an element of extravagance, also one of temporariness, as if it were a state that could only exist until one had recovered one's balance. Works of art, when they are described as "romantic," again suggest the presence of some element in excess or perhaps merely the neglect of certain qualities for the sake of others, and we love these works of art passionately when these particular qualities they display are what we long for or are in sympathy with at the moment. Should our mood change, we find we like them less and perhaps then not at all, or our intense liking may even become intense dislike.

These are common experiences with regard both to persons and to works of art. Now, what has Kierkegaard to say on this matter? He says that "classical" implies a divine collaboration of forces. It is, he says, "a special luck that the most pregnant epic material was given to a Homer" and that "the emphasis is as much on Homer as on the material, whence the deep harmony which informs every product we call classical." He is writing actually about Mozart and he finds the same explanation in the fact that in *Don Juan* Mozart met the perfect musical subject and that this "perhaps unique musical subject was given to no other than Mozart." He reinforces the importance and singularity of this union between the maker and the subject by reminding us very aptly that if one were to think it were a mere lucky accident that Homer found such excellent epic material as the Trojan War and that Mozart found *Don Juan* we have to remember that what appears to us as the perfect epic material is only known to us through Homer. Similarly one might add that, essentially, we know only of *Don Juan* through Mozart and of *Faust* through Goethe.

It is significant from my present point of view that he regards this coming together of the poet and his subject or the musician and his subject as a marriage, and this marriage he regards as predestined. To repeat his words:

"It is for all mediocrities a marvellous consoling and soothing idea by which . . . they imagine that it is a pure mistake of Fate, a world-wide error that they have not become as excellent as certain others. Thus a universal optimism spreads. But to every high-minded person . . . this is naturally a horror, whereas it is a holy bliss and delight to see united what belongs together."

It is a similar idealism that makes him repudiate the interpretation of those who "take it as accidental that two lovers met, as accidental that they loved each other; there might be a hundred other maidens with whom he could have been just as happy, whom he might have loved just as tenderly."

His comment on this is that, if one thinks this, then one "supposes that many a poet has lived who might have become as immortal as Homer if the latter had not first already used up this splendid material, and many a composer just as undying as Mozart if only the opportunity had offered itself."

The idea of a perfect marriage is not to be got rid of in the conception "classical." And I would go so far as to say that so intimately are works of art a part of life that the analogy is complete, and we shall find what applies to works of art applies also to the creations of love.

But two important points have now to be considered. Let

us first take the element of desire in love. Here again I recall something pertinent said by Kierkegaard:

"The poet desires his matter. To desire, one may say, is no art and this is quite true of a mass of weak poetic ideas. Rightly to desire is, on the contrary, a great art, or rather it is a gift (latent). This is the inexplicable mystery of genius like the divining rod which never has the idea of desiring unless what it desires is there."

This is, in my opinion, profoundly true. But how are we to distinguish classical from romantic love in practice? How are we to tell the perfect from the imperfect marriage? Is there not a simple answer at hand? By its durability. Romantic passions may be extremely strong but they do not last. All experience is at one on this point. Nevertheless, it is necessary to add a reservation here which I have never seen made but which is all-important. Romantic passions do not last only when there is a discrepancy between the two factors. The attraction has been great but it has not been complete because some elements wanted by one are missing in the other. Hence dissatisfaction. But if the one did not require more of the other because it itself lacked what the other lacked and was not aware of the lack, then an imperfect marriage might be enduring. In that case how are we to distinguish between the romantic and the classical, since durability is our test?

My answer to this is that the majority do not distinguish and are incapable of so distinguishing—which is the reason why so many people confuse in one lot artists and works of art, as well as human beings, who really do not belong together. Wagner and Beethoven, Mozart and Cimarosa, are musical examples. If a classical work of art requires the perfect marriage of subject and master, so also the relationship between the work of art and the observer requires the same degree of matching, for one can only see in a work of art what one has to some degree within oneself. The reason why so many amateurs of music do not perceive the superiority of Beethoven and Mozart to, let us say, Wagner and Brahms is that they themselves are lacking in the qualities which Wagner and Brahms lack and therefore do not miss, are not aware of their absence. Now one can understand how a romantic passion may be durable. Also one can see that a true marriage is a marriage of sympathies and not at all complementary in its biological sense—that is, a combination of opposites. The cheap idea of evolution, of progress by a biological combination of opposites, is seen to be not only superficial but contrary to the very nature of things. On the other hand, all nature and every artist strives for the perfect marriage, in which there is complete unity. This unity in works of art is what we call the classical harmony. This classical harmony is actually neither cold nor static; it is only perceived as such by those who lack perception of much that is in the work. On the other hand, there is always a sort of unity where there is satisfaction, and satisfaction may come—as we have seen—by the mere unity of two sympathies. This is the explanation why so many inferior, lifeless, mediocre works have for a time been considered classics—all academic art belongs to this category. Its classicism is negative or exclusive, not inclusive.

Therefore when we get a great artist, like William Blake, saying that all beauty lies in excess, we must understand that this is said, first of all, as a protest against the academic, the mere petty unity of small things. In great art there must be a degree of comprehensive vitality which will appear to the academics as diabolic. Actually we find this is the case and Mozart is a very good example of it. But Mozart is so comprehensive that this diabolic quality is not noticed by many people, just as in a well-proportioned face we are not particularly aware that there is a nose. The nose is there but it is not noticed unless it is out of proportion to the other features. Thus, in the same way, a well-proportioned object always looks smaller than it is. Therefore when the academics consider there is a certain too-muchness or excess, it will be either because they are unaware of or are blind to the other features which would give it due proportion or because it exists in disproportion in themselves.

The word *classical* can only justly be applied to a work of art according to the definition Kierkegaard gives to it—which is, on the whole, the generally accepted definition—when a comprehensive unity has been achieved. We may well ask how are we to judge of the comprehensiveness of any unity or marriage? To which I can only reply that to make such judgments two things are necessary in him who judges: first, gift or talent; secondly, experience. Now, these two factors, gift and experience, are in themselves also complex and not simple, and it is here that we are brought up against that unity in the observer of a work of art or in the partner to a marriage which is an essential to complete understanding of the other party. It may be seen by this that the very appreciation of works of art is in its way a marriage, and that is why complete appreciation is relatively rare and why there are so many false judgments made by critics and why, furthermore, so many popular artists are of inferior quality.

xx. Music and Dialectic

It may be said that every watertight philosophical system conceived so far has foundered on the rock of æsthetics. There may be other rocks in the sea of thought upon which man's intellectual systems go to pieces, but this rock is the most dangerous and destructive of them all.

The sufferings of sensitive and subtle minds owing to the general shoddy use of literature, which in the past has made writers like Kierkegaard and Walter Pater imagine that the art of music was ideally free from this taint and a purely abstract medium for pure expression, become more and more acute with the increasing vulgarization, for utilitarian purposes, of words. Today there are even writers who are so blind to the function of literature as an art that they maintain that its sole and whole duty is that of directly propagandizing changes in the government of states; although they would repudiate indignantly the notion that the immediate duty of literature was to make men drink or abstain from drinking alcoholic liquors, or from committing or not committing adultery.

Within the present century there has arisen as an expression and need of the age a perversion of the Hegelian dialectic which is known as dialectical materialism. The conception of art as a charmed and self-contained world was never one that commanded any general assent, and although the cry of "Art for art's sake" had a certain validity as opposed to the narrow conception of art as the expression of a local and temporal morality or ethical passion, yet even this restricted validity is overlooked in the new puritanism which manifests itself in the political activity of the present age.

Everywhere in Europe and America today there is to be found a group of critics who pretend to be revolutionary and to have a new and infallible criterion by which to determine the value of every artistic work. This criterion is political and, philosophically, it owes its origin to Hegel, who propounded that the will-process and the thought-process are essentially one, the former being only the latter on its objective side. Now, we may think that Hegel's conception was true with the reservation—which I personally would make—that Hegel did not fully perceive how true it was and therefore that some of his conclusions and many of the details of his thought in general are incorrect. For example, Hegel did not give its proper importance to nature (which he considered inferior to thinking) or to art, which he also considered inferior and subordinate to philosophy and religion. But this was to deny the central truth of his own system, because nature and art (works of art) are both part and the largest and most important part of the phenomenal world—*not* politics or social systems, which are never actually objectified but always remain conceptual—that is, an interpretation of an activity rather than an act or thing made. Hegel rightly says that when form and idea are so interfused as to become one, the object is a work of art. I would prefer to put it in another way and say that then—when form and idea have become one—there is creation—that is, something created. Romanticism, Hegel defined, is what happens when the idea is in excess of the form. But what happens when the form is in excess of the idea? Classicism. Well, instead of these two words we can use *Revolutionary* and *Conservative* in connection with the State. Now here we have to apply the Hegelian logic of thesis, antithesis, and synthesis. But is there ever a perfect synthesis of thesis (say the revolutionary idea) and antithesis (the anti-revolutionary or reactionary idea) into a fixed social system? I should say: Never! And there never could be, for that would be Utopia.

Now, nature needs no Utopia or final perfection, neither does art; every creation has its own validity, and the notion of progress in works of art or in nature is an illusion due to misconception. It may be that there is also no progress in society; indeed, if society, or the Hegelian State, is to be thought of as belonging also to the phenomenal category of nature and art, then this must be so. In which case if ever a State deserves to rank as a creation of the order of art and nature it can only be so by a complete synthesis of idea and form, which thus precludes any revolutionary (or reactionary) activity within it.

There has never been such a State. Every society known to history has been either romantic (like the present) or classical (like the eighteenth century); but always with the other element more or less active.

But the very notion of thesis and antithesis in the Hegelian and post-Marxian dialectic is based on the assumption that thought is at the bottom of the Universe or that the fundamental substance of the Universe is thought. And it seems Hegel and his followers have thus started from an incorrect premise, which is the source of all their difficulties. Nothing ever was created and nothing ever can be created by thought. Who by taking thought can add a cubit to his stature? It is love, not thought, that is the creative power and fundamental substance of the Universe. Consequently it is in art, not in philosophy or science, that we may find an objective creation analogous to nature. Creation does not appear by the resolving of thesis and antithesis into synthesis; for the simple reason that this operation is not to be achieved logically—that is, by thought. The very process of thinking is in thesis and antithesis. The synthesis is given, not arrived at by the mind but presented through the senses, and is primary, not derivative. That is why society can only fluctuate from thesis to antithesis, since society or the State is an intellectual conception, not an organism, and all biological analogies on this point are deceptive and invalid.

Hence we may see clearly that all attempts to criticize or judge works of art by sociological criteria are erroneous. The intellectual conception of the Christian religion may be logically destroyed without invalidating the frescoes of Giotto; whereas our dialectical materialists would have us believe that the frescoes of Giotto not only were the product of dogmatic Christianity (which as works of art they are not) but also were dependent for their virtue on the truth of Christianity. And by truth they must mean absolute truth, for they can-

not contend that Christianity only needed to be true for its
time; if they do, how do they explain that then and now artists
have thought Giotto's frescoes better than those of other
equally Christian painters and also have thought this quite
irrespective of whether the judges themselves have been
Christians or not? Is a Jew *ipso facto* to be held incapable of
understanding or experiencing fully the painting of Giotto?
Well, then, a Christian is incapable of appreciating a Jewish
Rembrandt and a dialectical materialist or a Communist is
incapable of appreciating the works of art by non-Com-
munists. If art is but the reflection of society or the expression
of social needs, then when that society changes, all previous
works of art become valueless. Since the theory of dialectical
materialism involves constant change, the oscillation from
thesis to antithesis and back again, there can be—on this assumption—no works of art of permanent value to man. Or
shall we invent a new logical connection? Shall we say that
when the society is classical the works of art that will be considered valuable will be romantic, and vice versa?

This alternation and correspondence is no doubt true of
all man's intellectual contrivances and we may thus explain
the vogue of fashion and the necessity of change; but it is
exactly in their freedom from any connection with these social
phenomena that works of art are what they are—namely, like
nature, *creations*; not intellectual contrivances, but creations
whose value is timeless because they do not belong to any
stage of the world conceived as a process of dialectical materialism.

This distinction becomes exceedingly clear when we consider the art of music. It is the hall-mark of the dilettante
and the intellectual man of fashion to desire novelty in music
or to find modern music fundamentally different from music
of any other age. The historians of music are not perceptive
musicians. It is the unfailing sign of a bad or imperfect
musician to be interested in national or temporal characteristics in music. All the best music has this in common: that
it has neither date nor character, personal or national. On the
contrary, like nature it is super-personal, international, and
timeless. And this proceeds from the fact that it is a primary
synthesis, a creation which we can only apprehend but cannot
obtain by analysis. If by thinking, we could analyse it, then

also by thinking we could put it together; but this is just what we cannot do and it is because we cannot do this that we are entitled to call it a creation and its maker a creator and not merely an intellectual.

Applied to art or to nature the idea of thesis and antithesis is a mere logical conception and as such necessarily a falsification of its reality. Hegel's philosophy, like its offspring, dialectical materialism, is negative. It suffers from the same weakness as Darwin's theory of natural selection, it does not supply any motivating power. As was pointed out long ago, Darwin's theory would not have led to such confusion if it had been more accurately named as a theory, not of natural selection, but of natural rejection. Hegel's thesis and antithesis would long ago have come not to a synthesis but to a standstill if that were all there was in world- or thought-process. It is precisely when music is not a creation that it may be described as a mere process of thesis and antithesis, but in the case of music it is clear that this process is purely logical and has no relation with any world-process or objective reality. Music only achieves reality when, like nature, it is an organism with an inner life of its own which we can apprehend because it is connected with ours, or, in other words, has a meaning for us.

But this "meaning" is not a syllogism, for it can only be apprehended through our senses; otherwise it would be a mere abstraction, a figment of dialectical materialism.

Of What Disease Did Mozart Die?

To a French journal, *La Chronique médicale*, Paris, under the date of November 15, 1905, a French doctor, J. Barraut, contributed an article entitled "*A quelle maladie a succombé Mozart?*" I succeeded in obtaining a copy of this article, in which Dr. Barraut goes into the matter very thoroughly. After consideration of all the evidence available, including the account of his death and the particulars of the various illnesses from which Mozart suffered as a child, he comes to the conclusion that Mozart naturally must have had an exceedingly robust constitution, "the constitution of a centenarian." He adds that there was not the slightest trace of tuberculosis in Mozart or his family and points out that Mozart's sister lived to be an octogenarian.

His final diagnosis is as follows:

"Two factors hastened Mozart's death. The first was a chronic cause, dating from his earliest years and increasing every day. This was simply excessive work, continual fatigue, and profound misery. One should be able to say of a man as of a machine: 'this machine is used up, it has been worked too much.' The word *used* applies perfectly to Mozart. Mozart arrived at the age of 35 worn out, having expended all his vital power.

"It was at that moment that the disease which carried him off laid hold of him. If we consider his rapid emaciation, his difficulty in breathing, his faintings, the swelling of his legs and hands, paresis, and if we remember that when young he had scarlatina, we are indeed led to the conclusion: nephritis. Mozart, in our opinion, died of Bright's disease. And if one considers his extreme weakness when he felt the first attacks of this malady one can readily understand that the disease only took six months, from July to December, to exterminate a man who throughout his life had been obliged to fight . . . in order to have bread to eat."

Catalogue of Works

The numbers without brackets are the original Köchel catalogue numbers; those within brackets are the new numbers assigned by Dr. Einstein in the third edition of Köchel's catalogue published by Breitkopf and Härtel (Leipzig, 1937).

The works in each section are roughly in chronological order but the exact chronological order, according to the latest investigators, is given by the numbers in brackets and dates.

VOCAL MUSIC

Arias for Solo Voice and Orchestra

K.	21	(19ᵉ)	tenor	"*Va dal furor portata*"	1765
	23		soprano	and strings "*Conservati fedde*"	"
	36	(33ⁱ)	tenor	"*Or che il dover*"	1766
	70	(61ᶜ)	soprano	"*A Berenice*"	1769
	71		tenor	"*Ah, più tremar*"	"
	74ᵇ		soprano	"*Non curo l'affetto*"	1771
	77	(73ᵉ)	soprano	Recit. "*Misero me*"; Aria "*Misero pargoletto*"	1770
	78	(73ᵇ)	"	"*Per pietà*"	"
	79	(73ᵈ)	"	"*O temerario*"	"
	82	(73ᵇ)	"	"*Se ardire*"	"
	83	(73ᵏ)	"	"*Se tulli i mali*"	"
	88	(73ᶜ)	"	"*Fra cento affanni*"	"
	119	(382ʰ)	"	"*Der Liebe*"	1772
	143	(73ᵃ)	"	Recit. "*Ergo interest*"; Aria "*Quære superna*"	1770
	146	(317ᵇ)	soprano	"*Kommet her*"	1779
	209		tenor	"*Si mostra*"	1775
	210		"	"*Con ossequio*"	"
	217		soprano	"*Voi avete*"	"
	255		alto	"*Ombra felice*"	1776
	256		tenor	"*Clarice cara*"	"
	272		soprano	"*Ah, lo previdi*"	1777
	294		"	"*Alcandro lo confesso*"	1778

Canons

Kyrie, Te Deum, Veni, Regina cœli, Motets, Offertories, etc.

K.	33		*Kyrie,* F major, 4 voices and strings	1766
	34		*Offertorium in Festo Sti Benedicti,* 4 voices, orchestra, and organ	1766–7
	44	(73ⁿ)	*Introitus* "*Cibavit eos,*" 4 voices and organ	1770
	47		"*Veni, sancte spiritus,*" 4 voices, orchestra, and organ	1768
	72	(74ᶠ)	*Offertorium pro Festo Sti Joannis Baptistæ,* 4 voices, strings, and organ	1771
	85	(73ˢ)	*Miserere,* A minor, alto, tenor, bass, and organ	1770
	86	(73ᵛ)	Antiphon "*Quærite primum regnum Dei,*" 4 voices unaccompanied	"
	89	(73ᵏ)	*Kyrie,* G major, 5 sopranos in canon	"
	90		*Kyrie,* D minor, 4 voices and organ	1771
	91	(186ⁱ)	*Kyrie,* D major, 4 voices, strings, and organ	1774
	92	(Anh. 186ᶜ)	*Salve Regina,* F major, 4 voices, chorus, orchestra, and organ (doubtful authenticity)	
	93		Psalm, "*De profundis,*" 4 voices, strings, and organ	1771
	108	(74ᵈ)	*Regina Cœli,* C major, 4 voices, orchestra, and organ	"
	117	(66ª)	*Offertorium pro omni tempore,* 4 voices, orchestra, and organ	1769
	127		*Regina Cœli,* B flat major, 4 voices, orchestra, and organ	1772
	141	(66ᵇ)	*Te Deum,* C major, 4 voices, strings, and organ	1769
	142	(Anh. 186ᵈ)	*Tantum ergo,* B flat major, 4 voices, orchestra, and organ (doubtful authenticity)	1772
K.	165	(158ª)	Motet "*Exsultate, jubilate,*" soprano, orchestra, and organ	1773

Litanies, Vespers

K. 109	(74ᵉ)	*Litaniæ de B.M.V.* (*Lauretanæ*) for 4 voices, orchestra, and organ	1771
125		*Litaniæ de venerabili altaris sacramento*, 4 voices, orchestra, and organ	1772
193	(186ᵍ)	*Dixit et Magnificat*, C major, 4 voices, orchestra, and organ	1774
195	(186ᵈ)	*Litaniæ Lauretanæ*, D major, 4 voices, orchestra, and organ	"
243		*Litaniæ de venerabili altaris sacramento*, E flat major, 4 voices, orchestra, and organ	1776
321		*Vesperæ de Dominica*, C major, 4 voices, orchestra, and organ	1779
339		*Vesperæ solennes de confessore*, 4 voices, orchestra, and organ	1780

Masses

K. 49	(47ᵈ)	*Missa Brevis*, G major, 4 voices, strings, and organ	1768
65	(61ᵃ)	*Missa Brevis*, D minor, 4 voices, strings, and organ	1769
66		Mass, C major (*Dominicus-Messe*), 4 voices, orchestra, and organ	"
115	(166ᵈ)	*Missa Brevis*, C major, 4 voices, and organ	1773
116	(90ᵃ)	*Missa Brevis*, F major, 4 voices, strings, and organ	1771
139	(114ᵃ)	*Missa Solemnis*, 4 voices, orchestra, and organ	1772
167		*Missa in honorem SSmæ Trinitatis*, 4 voices, orchestra, and organ	1773
192	(186ᶠ)	*Missa Brevis*, F major, 4 voices, strings, and organ	1774
194	(186ʰ)	*Missa Brevis*, D major, 4 voices, strings, and organ	"

220	(196^b)	Missa Brevis, C major, 4 voices, orchestra, and organ	1775

196	La Finta Giardiniera, opera buffa, 3 acts (Calzabigi)	1774
208	Il Rè Pastore, dramma per musica, 2 acts (Metastasio)	1775
K.Anh. 10 (299ᵇ)	Les Petits Riens, ballet music	1778
344 (336ᵇ)	Zaide, singspiel, 2 acts (Schachtner)	1779
345 (336ᵃ)	König Thamos, chorus and incidental music (Gebler)	"
366	Idomeneo, opera seria, 3 acts (Varesco)	1781
367	Idomeneo, ballet music	"
384	Die Entführung aus dem Serail, singspiel, 3 acts (Stephanie)	1782
422	L'Oca del Cairo, opera buffa (Varesco), unfinished	1783
430 (424ᵃ)	Lo Sposo Deluso, opera buffa, unfinished	"
486	Der Schauspieldirektor, comedy with music, 1 act (Stephanie)	1786
492	Le Nozze di Figaro, opera buffa, 4 acts (Lorenzo da Ponte after Beaumarchais)	"
527	Don Giovanni, dramma giocoso, 2 acts (da Ponte)	1787
588	Così fan Tutte, opera buffa, 2 acts (da Ponte)	1790
620	Die Zauberflöte, grosse opera, 2 acts (Schikaneder)	1791
621	La Clemenza di Tito, opera seria, 2 acts (Mazzola after Metastasio)	"

Oratorios (arrangements)

K. 566	Acis and Galatea by Handel (newly instrumented)	1788
572	Messiah, by Handel (newly instrumented)	1789
591	Alexander's Feast by Handel (newly instrumented)	1790
592	Ode for St. Cecilia's Day by Handel (newly instrumented)	"

Songs with Pianoforte

K.	52	(46ᶜ)	"Daphne, deine Rosenwangen"	1768
	53		An die Freude	1767
	147	(125ᵍ)	"Wie unglücklich"	1772
	148	(125ʰ)	"O heiliges Band"	"
	149	(125ᵈ)	Die grossmutige Gelassenheit	"
	150	(125ᵉ)	"Was ich in Gedanken"	"
	151	(125ᶠ)	"Ich trachte nicht"	"
	152	(210ᵃ)	Canzonetta "Ridente la calma" (?)	1775
	178	(125ᶜ)	Air for soprano "Ah, spiegarti"	1772
	307	(284ᵈ)	Ariette "Oiseaux, si tous les ans"	1777
	308	(295ᵇ)	Ariette "Dans un bois solitaire" (de la Motte)	1778
	349	(367ᵃ)	Die Zufriedenheit (Miller) pianoforte or mandolin	1776
	351	(367ᵇ)	"Komm, liebe Zither" (with mandolin)	1780–1
	390	(340ᶜ)	An die Hoffnung (J. T. Hermes)	1780
	391	(340ᵇ)	An die Einsamkeit (J. T. Hermes)	"
	392	(340ᵃ)	"Verdankt sei es dem Glanz" (Hermes)	"
	393	(385ᵇ)	Solfeggien (vocal exercises for his wife)	1782
	468		Gesellenreise (J. F. von Ratschky)	1784
	472		Der Zauberer (C. F. Weisse)	1785
	473		Die Zufriedenheit (C. F. Weisse)	"
	474		Die betrogene Welt (C. F. Weisse)	"
K.Ank.26	(475ᵃ)		"Einsam bin ich"	"
	476		Das Veilchen (Goethe)	"
	506		Lied der Freiheit (Blumauer) (?)	1786
	517		Die Alte (F. von Hagedorn)	1787
	518		Die Verschweigung (C. F. Weisse)	"
	519		Das Lied der Trennung (K. E. K. Schmidt)	"
	520		Als Luise die Briefe ihres ungetreuen Liebhabers verbrannte (G. von Baumberg)	"
	523		Abendempfindung (J. H. Campe)	"
	524		An Chloe (J. G. Jacobi)	"
	529		Des kleinen Friedrichs Geburtstag	"

530		*Das Traumbild* (Hölty)	1787
531		*Die kleine Spinnerin*	"
552		*Beim Auszug in das Feld*	1788
596		*Sehnsucht nach dem Frühlinge*	Jan. 1791
597		*Im Frühling's Anfang* (Sturm)	" "
598		*Das Kinderspiel* (Overbeck)	" "

Vocal Duets, Trios, etc.

K. 346	(439ª)	Trio "*Luci care*"	1783
389	(384An)	Duet "*Welch ängstliches Beben*"	1782
393	(385ᵇ)	Solfeggi	
434	(424ᵇ)	Trio "*Del gran regno*"	1783
436		" "*Ecco quel fiero instante*"	"
437		" "*Mi lagnero*"	"
438		" "*Se lontan*"	"
439		" "*Due pupille*"	"
441		" "*Liebes Mandel*"	"
(441ᵉ)		" "*Liebes Mädchen*"	"
479		Quartet "*Dite almeno*"	1785
480		Trio "*Mandina amabile*"	"
483		Song Tenor solo and chorus, "*Zer-fliesset heut*"	"
484		Chorus "*Ihr unsre neuer Leiter*"	"
489		Duet "*Spiegarti, oh Dio*"	1786
532		Trio "*Grazie agl'inganni*"	1787
549		Canzonetta 2 sopranos and bass	1788
625	(592ª)	Comic Duet "*Nun, liebes Weibchen*" (doubtful)	1790
5An.	(571ª)	Comic Quartet "*Caro mio*"	1789

Cadenzas

Mozart wrote numerous vocal cadenzas, also cadenzas for the concertos of other composers: namely, of J. C. Bach, J. S. Shröters, L. Honauer, and Beecké. He also wrote cadenzas for the following concertos of his own: K.175, K.246, K.271, K.365, K.382, K.413, K.414, K.415, K.449, K.450, K.451, K.453, K.456, K.459, K.488, K.595.

As Mozart was in the habit of improvising his cadenzas, many of his finest concertos are without any written cadenzas of his. It is worth remarking that Beethoven wrote two superb cadenzas to Mozart's D minor pianoforte concerto (K.466), to the first and last movements respectively, which should be used by every pianist playing this work.

INSTRUMENTAL MUSIC

Church Sonatas

K.					
67	(41ʰ)	for strings and organ			1767
68	(41ⁱ)	" " " "			"
69	(41ᵏ)	" " " "			"
144	(124ᵃ)	" " " "			1772
145	(124ᵇ)	" " " "			"
212		" " " "			1775
224	(241ᵃ)	" " " "			1776
225	(241ᵇ)	" " " "			"
241		" " " "			"
244		" " " "			"
245					
263		for strings, 2 trumpets, and organ			"
274	(271ᵈ)	for strings and organ			1777
278	(271ᵉ)	for strings, orchestra, and organ			"
328	(317ᶜ)	for strings and organ			1779
329	(317ᵃ)	for strings, orchestra, and organ			"
336	(336ᵈ)	for strings and organ			1780

Compositions for 2 Pianofortes and for Pianoforte 4 hands

K.				
19ᵈ		Sonata, C major (4 hands)		1765
357	(497ᵃ)	" G " "		1786
358	(186ᶜ)	" B flat major "		1774
381	(123ᵃ)	" D major "		1772
401	(375ᵉ)	Fugue, G minor "		1782
426		" C minor (2 pianofortes)		1783
448	(375ᵃ)	Sonata, D major "		1781
497		" F major (4 hands)		1786
501		Andante, with 5 Variations (4 hands)		"
521		Sonata, C major (4 hands)		1787

Minuets, Variations, etc., for Pianoforte

K.			
1		Minuet and Trio, G major	1761–2
2		" F "	1762

500	12 Variations on an Allegretto	1786
573	9 " on a Minuet of Duporte	1789
574	*Eine kleine Gique*	"
613	8 Variations on "*Ein Weib ist das herrlichste Ding*"	1791

Miscellaneous Compositions

K. 356	(617ᵃ)	Adagio, C major, for harmonica		"
443	(385¹)	Three-part Fugue	(?)	1782
594		Adagio and Allegro, F minor, for a mechanical organ		1790
608		Fantasy, F minor, for a mechanical organ		1791
616		Andante, F major, for a mechanical organ		"

Pianoforte Trios, Quartets, and Quintets

K. 254	Trio (Divertimento) B flat major	1776
442	" D minor-major	1783
452	Quintet, E flat major (oboe, clarinet, horn, bassoon, and pianoforte)	1784
478	Quartet, G minor	1785
493	" E flat major	1786
496	Trio, G major	"
498	" E flat major (clarinet, viola, and pianoforte)	"
502	Trio B flat major	"
542	" E major	1788
548	" C "	"
564	" G "	"
617	Adagio and Rondo, C minor-major for harmonica, flute, oboe, viola, and 'cello	1791

Sonatas and Fantasias for Pianoforte

K. 279	(189ᵈ)	C major	1774
280	(189ᵉ)	F "	"
281	(189ᶠ)	B flat major	"
282	(189ᵍ)	E " "	"

Sonatas, etc., for Violin and Pianoforte

Concertos for Pianoforte and Orchestra

Concertos for Violin and Orchestra

271^a (271^i) D major   1777
373   Rondo, C major   1781
470   Andante, A major   1785

Miscellaneous Concertos

K. 191 (186^e) B flat major for bassoon   1774
293   (416^f) F major for oboe   1783
299   (297^c) C "   " flute and harp   1778
313   (285^c) G "   " flute   "
314   (285^d) D "   "   "   (oboe?)   "
315   (285^e) Andante, C major for flute   "
371   Rondo, E flat major for horn   1781
412   (386^b) D major for horn   1782
417   E flat major for horn   1783
447   E "   "   "   "   "
495   E "   "   "   "   1786
622   A major for clarinet   1791
K.Anh. 56 (315^f) D major for pianoforte and violin   1778
(There are unfortunately only 150 bars of this remarkably
fine work)

String Duets and Trios

K. 266 (271^f) Trio, B flat major (2 violas and bass) 1777
K. 404^a   Six three-part Fugues, arranged for vio-
                 lin, viola, and bass, 3 from Bach's
                 Wohltemperirte Klavier (I, No. 8;
                 II, Nos. 13 and 14); 1 from Bach's
                 Organ Sonata II; 1 from Bach's
                 Kunst der Fuge, Contrapunctus 8;
                 and 1 from a fugue of W. Friede-
                 mann Bach. Also, 6 introductory
                 Adagios, of which 4 are by Mozart
                 (in F minor, G minor, D minor, F
                 major)   1782
423   Duet, G major, violin and viola   1783
424   " B flat "   "   "   1783
563   Divertimento, E flat major, for violin,
                 viola, and 'cello   1788

String Quartets

K. 80	(73ᶠ)	G major	1770
155	(134ᵃ)	D "	1772
156	(134ᵇ)	G "	"
157		C "	"
158		F "	"
159		B flat major	"
160		E " "	"
168		F major	1773
169		A "	"
170		C "	"
171		E flat major	"
172		B " "	"
173		D minor	"
387		G major (Haydn set No. 1)	1782
405		Five four-part Fugues from Bach's *Wohltemperirte Klavier*	"
421	(417ᵇ)	D minor (Haydn set No. 2)	1783
428	(421ᵇ)	E flat major (" " No. 3)	"
458		B " " (" " No. 4)	1784
464		A major (" " No. 5)	1785
465		C " (" " No. 6)	1786
499		D "	"
K. 546		Adagio and Fugue, C minor (Fugue same as K.426 for 2 pianos)	1788
575		D major (King of Prussia set No. 1)	1789
589		B flat " (" " " No. 2)	1790
590		F major (" " " No. 3)	"

String Quintets

K. 174		B flat major	1773
406	(516ᵇ)	C minor (originally composed as Serenade for wind instruments, K.388)	1787
515		C major	"
516		G minor	"
593		D major	1790
614		E flat major	1791

Miscellaneous Chamber Music

K. 64		Minuet, D major (2 vlns, 2 horns and bass)	1769
65ᵃ	(61ᵇ)	7 Minuets with trio (2 vlns and bass)	"
103	(61ᵈ)	19 Minuets, with and without trio (2 violins, 2 oboes, 2 horns, and bass)	"
285		Quartet, D major, for flute and strings	1777
292	(196ᶜ)	Sonata, B flat major, for bassoon and 'cello	1775
298		Quartet, A major, for flute and strings	1778
370	(368ᵇ)	Quartet, F major, for oboe and strings	1781
407	(386ᶜ)	Quintet, E flat major, for horn and strings	1783
410	(440ᵈ)	Adagio, F major, for 2 basset horns and bassoon	"
411	(440ᵃ)	Adagio, B flat major, for 2 clarinets and 3 basset horns	"
487	(496ᵃ)	12 Duets for 2 basset horns	1786
581		Quintet, A major, for clarinet and strings	1789
K.Anh.171	(285ᵇ)	Quartet, C major, for flute and strings	1778

Symphonies

K. 16		E flat major	1764
19		D major	"
22		B flat major	1765
43		F major	1767
45		D "	1768
48		D "	"
73	(75ᵃ)	C "	1771
74		G "	1770
75		F "	1771
76	(42ᵃ)	F "	1767
81	(73¹)	D "	1770
84	(73�q)	D "	"
95	(73ⁿ)	D "	"
96	(111ᵇ)	C "	1771

97	(73^m)	D major		1770
102	(213^c)	C "	(Finale only)	1775
110	(75^b)	G "		1770
112		F "		1771
114		A "		"
120	(111^a)	D "	(Finale)	"
121	(207^a)	D "	(Finale)	1775
124		G "		1772
128		C "		"
129		G "		"
130		F "		"
132		E flat major		"
133		D major		"
134		A "		"

161 and 163 Symphony arranged from overture to

　　　　　　　　Il Sogno di Scipione (K.126)　　　　　　"

162		C major		"
181	(162^b)	D "		1773
182	(166^c)	B flat major		"
183		G minor		"
184	(166^a)	E flat major		"
199	(162^a)	G "		"
200	(173^e)	C "		1774
201	(186^a)	A "		"
202	(186^b)	D "		"
297	(300^a)	D "	("Paris")	1778
318		G "		1779
319		B flat major		"
338		C major		1780
385		D "	("Haffner")	1782
425		C "	("Linz")	1783
444	(425^a)	G "	(Introduction by Mozart, the rest by Michael Haydn)	"
504		D major ("Prague")		1786
543		E flat major		1788
550		G minor		"
551		C major ("Jupiter")		"

K.Anh.8(311^a) Overture in B flat major　　　　　　1778

K.Anh.9(297^b) *Sinfonia Concertante* for oboe, clari-
　　　　　　　　net, horn, and bassoon, with or-
　　　　　　　　chestra　　　　　　　　　　　　　　"

K.364   (320ᵈ) *Sinfonia Concertante* for violin and
                 viola with orchestra   1779

Divertimentos, Serenades, Cassations, etc., for Orchestra

K.			
32		*Galimathias musicum*	1766
62		Cassation	1769
63		Divertimento (*Final-Musik*)	"
99	(63ᵃ)	Cassation, B flat major	"
100	(62ᵃ)	Serenade, D major	"
101	(250ᵃ)	" F "	1776
103	(61ᵈ)	19 Minuets with and without trio	1769
104	(61ᵉ)	Minuets	"
105	(61ᶠ)	6 "	"
106	(588ᵃ)	Overture and 3 Kontretänze	1790
113		Divertimento, E flat major	1771
122	(73ᵗ)	Minuet, E flat major	1770
123		Kontretanz, B flat major	"
131		Divertimento, D major	1772
136	(125ᵃ)	" D "	"
137	(125ᵇ)	" B flat major	"
138	(125ᶜ)	" F major	"
164	(130ᵃ)	6 Minuets	"
166	(159ᵈ)	Divertimento, E flat major	1773
176		16 Minuets	"
185	(167ᵃ)	Serenade, D major	"
186	(159ᵇ)	Divertimento, B flat major	"
187	(159ᶜ)	" C flat "	"
188	(240ᵇ)	" C flat "	"
189	(167ᵇ)	March, D flat major	"
203	(189ᵇ)	Serenade, D major	1774
204	(213ᵃ)	" D "	1775
205	(173ᵃ)	Divertimento, D major	1773
206	(366)	March (used in *Idomeneo*)	1775
213		Divertimento, F major	"
214		March, C major	"
215	(213ᵇ)	March, D "	"
239		*Serenata Notturna* for 2 small orchestras	1776
240		Divertimento, B flat major	"
247		" F major	"

Addenda

APPENDIX III

Bibliography

W. A. Mozart, von HERMANN ABERT neuarbeitete und erweiterte Ausgabe von OTTO JAHNS Mozart, 6 Auflage, 2 vols., Breitkopf und Härtel, Leipzig, 1923. (1st edition, 1919; 2nd edition, 1922.)

Mozart, nach den Schilderungen seiner Zeitgenossen von DR. LUDWIG NOHL, Leipzig, 1880.

Mozart und Haydn in London, von C. F. POHL, Wien, 1867, 2 vols.

Urtheile bedeutender Dichter, Philosophen und Musiker über Mozart, gesammelt und herausgegeben von KARL PRIEGER, 2nd enlarged edition, Wiesbaden, 1886.

Mozarts Leben, von LUDWIG NOHL, 3 Auflage, neubearbeitet von DR. PAUL SAKOLOWSKI, Berlin, 1906. (1st edition, 1863; 2nd edition, 1876.)

W. A. Mozarts Leben, nach Originalquellen von FRANZ NIEMETSCHEK Faksimiledruck der ersten Ausgabe mit den Lesarten und Zusätzen der zweiten vom Jahre 1808 und Einleitung von DR. ERNST RYCHNOVSKY, Prague, 1905.

Wolfgang Amadeus Mozart, Bibliographie und Ikonographie zusammengestellt und nach Materien geordnet aus dem Musik- und Theaterarchiv. G. Fr. Hagen und anderen Quellen von OTTO KELLER, Berlin/Leipzig, 1927.

Wolfgang Amadeus Mozart, Sein Leben und sein Werk auf Grund der vornehmlich durch NIKOLAUS VON NISSEN gesammelten biographischen Quellen und der Ergebnisse der neuesten Forschung dargestellt von DR. ARTHUR SCHURIG, 2 vols., Leipzig, 1913.

Leopold Mozarts Briefe an seine Tochter, im Auftrag der Mozartgemeinde in Salzburg, herausgegeben von OTTO ERICH DEUTSCH und BERNHARD PAUMGARTNER, Salzburg/Leipzig, 1936.

Die Briefe W. A. Mozarts, herausgegeben und eingeleitet von LUDWIG SCHIEDERMAIR, 2 vols., München und Leipzig, 1914.

Die Briefe Leopold Mozarts, herausgegeben von LUDWIG SCHIEDERMAIR, 2 vols., München und Leipzig, 1914.

Mozart-Ikonographie, herausgegeben und erläutert von LUDWIG SCHIEDERMAIR, München und Leipzig, 1914.

W. A. Mozart, Sa vie musicale et son œuvre, de l'enfance à la pleine maturité (1756–1777), T. DE WYZEWA et G. DE SAINT-FOIX, 1st et 2nd vols., Perrin et Cie., Paris, 1912; 3rd vol., Desclée de Brouwer et Cie., Paris, 1936.

Biographie W. A. Mozarts, von GEORG NIKOLAUS VON NISSEN nach dem Tode herausgegeben von CONSTANZE WITWE VON NISSEN, FRÜHER WITWE MOZART, Breitkopf und Härtel, Leipzig, 1828.

Life of Mozart, by EDWARD HOLMES, London, 1845.

Nouvelle Biographie de Mozart, par ALEXANDRE OULIBICHEFF, Moscow, 1842.

Mémoires de Lorenzo d'Aponte, traduit de l'Italien par M. C. D. DE LA CHAVANNE, Pagnerre, Paris, 1860.

Account of a Very Remarkable Young Musician, by DAINES BARRINGTON, Philosophical Transactions of the Royal Society, Vol. I, London, 1770.

Mozart's Operas: a Critical Study by EDWARD J. DENT, London, 1913.

Mozartiana, by GUSTAV NOTTEBOHM, Leipzig, 1880.

Mozart: sein Leben, by ANNETTE KOLB, Fischer Verlag, Vienna, 1937.

Chronologisch-thematisches Verzeichnis sämtlicher Tonwerke Wolfgang Amadé Mozarts, von DR. LUDWIG RITTER VON KÖCHEL, 3te Auflage, bearbeitet von ALFRED EINSTEIN, Breitkopf und Härtel, Leipzig, 1937.

Index

Mozart, W. A.—(Cont'd)

ANCHOR BOOKS